Women and
Representa

Women and Mixed Race Representation in Film

Eight Star Profiles

VALERIE C. GILBERT

McFarland & Company, Inc., Publishers
Jefferson, North Carolina

LIBRARY OF CONGRESS CATALOGUING-IN-PUBLICATION DATA

Names: Gilbert, Valerie C., 1961– author.
Title: Women and mixed race representation in film :
eight star profiles / Valerie C. Gilbert.
Description: Jefferson, North Carolina : McFarland & Company, Inc.,
Publishers, 2021. | Includes bibliographical references and index.
Identifiers: LCCN 2021027070 | ISBN 9781476663388 (paperback : acid free paper) ∞
ISBN 9781476644738 (ebook)
Subjects: LCSH: African American actresses—Biography. | African Americans
in motion pictures. | Minority women in motion pictures. | Race in motion pictures. |
Race relations in motion pictures. | Motion pictures—United States—History. | BISAC:
PERFORMING ARTS / Film / History & Criticism | SOCIAL SCIENCE / Discrimination
Classification: LCC PN1998.2 .G543 2021 | DDC 791.4302/80922 [B]—dc23
LC record available at https://lccn.loc.gov/2021027070

BRITISH LIBRARY CATALOGUING DATA ARE AVAILABLE

ISBN (print) 978-1-4766-6338-8
ISBN (ebook) 978-1-4766-4473-8

On the cover: Lonette McKee, *The Cotton Club* (1984); Lena Horne
stars as tragic mulatto Julie in a mini version of *Show Boat* from MGM's
Till the Clouds Roll By (1947); Lonette McKee plays a studio executive passing
for white in Old Hollywood in the Julie Dash short film *Illusions* (1982)

Printed in the United States of America

*McFarland & Company, Inc., Publishers
Box 611, Jefferson, North Carolina 28640
www.mcfarlandpub.com*

For my parents,
Rosina and Peter

Table of Contents

Preface

If you are lucky, you see yourself reflected back to you in your family, in stories, in movies and television.[1]
—Jennifer Beals

The backstory of how I came to write this book is a personal one. I was born in Trinidad on an extended family vacation. I grew up in Canada and have lived all my adult life in the United States. My Trinidadian mother is black. My British father is white. While working on my BFA degree at the University of Washington, I enrolled in a couple of film studies classes. Prior to this, I was not a film lover nor a regular filmgoer. When I did see a movie, if you had asked me about it the next day, I would likely have remembered very little. Film studies changed all that.

Film classes equipped me with a set of basic skills with which to understand film and aroused in me great appreciation for a medium that, up until then, had been of little or no interest to me. They also made me wonder why up to that point I had been so disconnected from the movie experience. Why was going to the movies not a routine and enjoyable part of my life, as it seemed to be for everyone else? I was then reminded of the first time I saw the 1934 film *Imitation of Life*.

Yes, it's a cliché, but it's also true. The first time I saw *Imitation of Life*, which was in the 1990s on television, was also the first time I saw "myself" represented onscreen. Of course, I was raised in an era and a locale vastly different from *Imitation of Life*'s Peola, and I never had the need nor the desire to "pass" for white as she did. As for my mother, a registered nurse, she never worked as a domestic; she hired them. Nevertheless, I identified with Fredi Washington's character because she looked white, she talked white, and she had a mother who was obviously black, a depiction that is just about as rare onscreen today as it was in the 1930s. The other way in which I identified with Peola is that like her, I was raised and socialized among white people, and while it was seldom discussed, I was aware, at some level, that even though I was fully assimilated, and essentially the same skin color as those around me, I was not like them. I was not, and could never be, white.

When I was about eleven years old, following the lead of my older sister, I decided to get my hair cut into an afro. I guess it was then that I decided if I can't be white, I might as well embrace being black—to the extent that one can embrace blackness growing up surrounded by white people in a small Canadian prairie city like Regina. At the beginning of my high school years, my family moved to Canada's west coast. In the cosmopolitan city of Vancouver, which had a population many times more than that from where we had come, I just knew there would be some other black kids to bond with. Alas, there were none. Though I could not have articulated it this way at the time, in retrospect I can

1

say that after I graduated high school, I moved to the United States to nurture my connection to blackness, or, to put it more bluntly, to learn how to be black.

Later, beginning in my 30s, I decided to pursue higher education, which culminated many years later in the completion of a Master of Arts in communication. This experience, including film classes, was the beginning of a more conscious, ongoing interrogation of my racial and ethnic identity. With respect to my disconnection to the movie experience, I came to the conclusion that my disinterest had quite a lot to do with a lack of film characters with whom I could identify. Rarely, if ever, did I relate to cinematic white heroines. Nor could I connect with what I must have intuited as the typically unflattering, two-dimensional depictions of black people in film. Aside from *Imitation of Life*, where, I wondered, could I find representation of people like me? This book is, in part, an answer to that question. The many years I spent researching and writing it have ultimately freed me to become an equal opportunity spectator. I now identify with all kinds of characters in film, regardless of race. Before I could get to this point, though, it was necessary for me to first find "myself."

Introduction

Stars matter because they act out aspects of life that matter to us; and performers get to be stars when what they act out matters to enough people.[1]
—Richard Dyer

Women and Mixed Race Representation in Film is a gendered look at film, stardom, and performance from a mixed race perspective. It takes as its subject the star personae of eight American-born actresses: Josephine Baker, Nina Mae McKinney, Fredi Washington, Lena Horne, Dorothy Dandridge, Lonette McKee, Jennifer Beals, and Halle Berry. With respect to this book's title, the term "mixed race" is relatively modern nomenclature that refers to people with parents, or ancestors, of diverse racial identities. Most of these women, because of the era in which they were born and worked, were not considered mixed race, but rather Negro, colored, mulatto, or black.

Regardless of how these actresses have been identified, some have struggled to conform to a singular, static racial identity. Lena Horne, for example, in her autobiography, written when she was well into her 40s, talked about growing up without established roots in either a white or black community. Horne confessed to a lifelong search for an identity and credited most of her career successes with being exhibited as an "oddity" of her race.[2] Furthermore, in looking at these women's professional work, as well as commentary on their careers, mixed race themes, such as passing, colorism, interracial romance, and identity, all come to the fore.

There are, of course, multiple variations of "mixed race." For the purposes of this book, unless stated otherwise, when used in general, the term chiefly connotes black/white "mixedness." The terms "biracial" and "mixed race" are also used to refer to individuals who have one parent who identifies as black and the other as white. Of the actresses who are the focus of this book, only McKee, Beals, and Berry fit this latter definition with certainty. By including the other women, it is not my intent to reclassify them racially. Rather, what I have attempted to do is examine their personae through a black/white interracial lens, construing "mixedness" not solely as genealogy, but also as the manifestation of recurring themes and cultural signs.

Today, most scholars agree that rather than having a firm basis in biology, race is nothing more than a social means to categorize and delimit people. Nevertheless, racial categories with profound social and material consequences persist. Race and racism are an American institution. The movie industry is also an American institution. For more than a century motion pictures have been a dominant form of entertainment. Films are not just an experience for the public to consume; they also feature stars, characters, and stories that say something about who we are. Films reflect and construct values and identities, including racial identities.

In the chapters that follow I borrow from Richard Dyer's "star image" theory and the notion of reading the star image as a text. The star image is, among other things, a product of capitalism and mass culture, an expression of performance and art, a signifying element in film, a marketing tool, a sign that carries social and ideological meaning, and a site of contest for marginalized groups.[3]

The star image is embodied by a real person, but it is not the "person." The star image is a manufactured appearance. Our ability to relate the manufactured appearance that is the star image back to the real world is what makes stars so fascinating and prompts us to wonder what stars are *really* like. Dyer's theory, however, assumes that all we can know of stars is that which is publicly available about them. There is no way to get to the *real* "person" because, by definition, the star image is a text, not a human being. That being said, even though the "person" is usually considered to be more real than his or her manufactured appearance in culture, appearances are also a type of reality in and of themselves.[4]

According to Dyer's theory for analyzing film stars, the star phenomenon is made up of all the various media texts that relate to the star. Feature films, which generally hold a more privileged place within the star image, are prominent texts within this study. Short films are also considered, as are made-for-television movies, which in the case of Halle Berry, for instance, were paramount in the shaping and the trajectory of her star image. The star image also incorporates a variety of other verbal, visual and auditory media, including film promotion, press kits, advertisements, newspaper articles, and interviews as well as what critics or commentators say or write about the star.[5]

Biographies are another type of text that can contribute to the star image.[6] Because mixed race is inherently concerned with origins, this book places special emphasis on biography and early life history. After a brief introduction, all of the chapters begin on a biographical note. This combined with the chronological structure that organizes each chapter might give the impression of a life story. While the biographical detail in this book has been carefully researched, and will surely be of interest to some readers, my primary aim is not to get at some biographical truth. Rather, it is to discover and reveal what political, ideological, sociological, or historical meaning can be gleaned from the star image, particularly as it relates to the construction of race.

Origins of another type are also relevant to this study. With regard to films, in a number of instances adaptation analysis is incorporated, that is, adapted films are compared to the source material upon which they are based. Usually this is a novel, but adaptation can also apply to other sources, including historical fact. In the process of adapting for the screen, there are always omissions and alterations and sometimes additions. Looking at what has been deleted, changed, or added in the development from source material to film can lend greater insight into filmmakers' intentions or the interpretation of those intentions. It also provides a richer historical and/or political context within which to situate both the film and the star image.

Another aim of this book is to flesh out the tragic mulatto stereotype and expand the discourse on representation of mixed race people in popular culture and in particular the mixed race woman in film. In this regard, my work has been inspired by Donald Bogle, especially his exhaustive history of blacks in film, *Toms, Coons, Mulattoes, Mammies, and Bucks* (*TCMMB*), which was originally published in 1973 and has been updated and expanded into the present century. From Bogle I take his attention to history and racial representation.

TCMMB tells a history of African Americans in film through the identification of five black stereotypes. The "tom," also known as "Uncle Tom," is a "good" black character who endears himself to white audiences by remaining faithful to God and his white master no matter how much abuse might be heaped upon him. The "coon" is a buffoon presented as comic amusement. The "tragic mulatto," according to Bogle, is a woman destined for unhappiness because of her dual racial heritage. The "mammy," a close relative of the coon, is distinguished by her fierce independence, and she is usually "big, fat, and cantankerous." In his purest form, the "buck" is a big, bad, violent, oversexed character who lusts after white women.[7]

Forty years before Bogle, in 1933, Sterling Brown identified seven similar black stereotypes found in literary fiction written by white authors: the Contented Slave, the Wretched Freeman, the Comic Negro, the Brute Negro, the Tragic Mulatto, the Local Color Negro and the Exotic Primitive. With regard to the mixed race stereotype, Brown made a distinction between the tragic mulatto proffered by anti-slavery fiction and what he simply called the stereotyped "mulatto character" of early 20th-century fiction.[8]

The stereotyped "mulatto character," whether male or female, suffered from a divided racial inheritance. Intelligence and the unwillingness to be a slave came from white blood, while impassioned feelings and ignoble urges came from black blood. The "tragic mulatto" of abolitionary fiction, on the other hand, was almost always a woman, nearly white, and was employed by authors as a roundabout way to illustrate interracial sex, which could not, at the time, be referred to directly.[9]

In the 1960s, Jules Zanger elaborated further upon the abolitionary iteration of the near-white tragic mulatto, calling her instead the "tragic octoroon." Zanger argued that the tragic octoroon was one of the most important characters of pre–Civil War abolitionist fiction. In these works, the tragic octoroon represented four generations of enforced and illicit sexual relations between slave and slave master. Charges of sexual looseness, which were serious at the time, were leveled not against the victim but rather against the Southern slaveholder. The tragic octoroon stood as evidence of the slaveholder's guilt.[10]

Typically, the tragic octoroon of abolitionist fiction is raised as a white child in the home of her slaveholding father. She blossoms into a beautiful young lady who speaks with no trace of slave dialect and possesses few or no signs of her African heritage. Her situation changes dramatically when her father dies unexpectedly. Because he has neglected to take the necessary steps to declare her freedom, she discovers she is a slave and suffers a great reversal of fortune. While not representative of the slave population at large, the plight of the near-white octoroon captured the imagination and sympathy of the antebellum Northern public.[11]

In *Women on the Color Line*, a study of three Southern authors during the last three decades of the 19th century, Anna Elfenbein asserts that at the dawn of the 20th century it was Thomas Dixon, Jr., author of *The Clansman*, who turned the popular stereotype of the tragic octoroon in fiction on its head. Beginning with Dixon, the fictional mixed race woman who had heretofore usually remained chaste, and with the exception of her "tainted" blood, was the symbol of white femininity, became a scheming seductress and the antipode of the symbol of Southern purity.[12]

Thomas Dixon, Jr., was born the son of a Baptist minister in North Carolina in 1864. Dixon grew up during the Reconstruction Era and reached maturity during a time when the South was suffering from economic plight, while struggling to establish white supremacy through the policies and practices of disfranchisement of African Americans, segregation, and epidemic lynching of black men.[13] Before the Civil War, free Negroes in a binary free-white/black-slave society frustrated the white man's sense of identity. After the war, so, too, did the very existence of a mixed race population that was neither black nor white. To Southerners, the mixing of black and white was a catastrophe that had to be avoided at all costs.[14]

The irony was, of course, black and white had already long since merged. In the upper South, where Dixon was from, interracial unions had been going on since the 17th century, and while racial mixing continued in the 18th century among all colors and classes, the majority of unions were between upper-class white slaveholding men and their mulatto slave women. Somehow the white race had fallen, leading some whites to draw the conclusion that they had lost the war because they had sinned against God. Their sin, however, was not that of enslaving other human beings. The sin they had committed was miscegenation, or, to put it more bluntly, interracial sex. For Southerners like Dixon, mulattoes were the embodiment of evil and an unpleasant reminder of devastating loss.[15]

Between 1902 and 1939, Dixon wrote twenty-two novels.[16] Among his works is the Ku Klux Klan trilogy, consisting of *The Leopard's Spots: A Romance of the White Man's Burden* (1902), *The Clansman: An Historical Romance of the Ku Klux Klan* (1905) and *The Traitor: A Story of the Fall of the Invisible Empire* (1907). *The Leopard's Spots*, first in the trilogy, is a response to Harriet Beecher Stowe's 1852 abolitionist novel, *Uncle Tom's Cabin*.[17] Arguably the most popular 19th-century novel written by an American, *Uncle Tom's Cabin* features one of popular culture's most celebrated mixed race heroines, Eliza Harris. *Uncle Tom's Cabin* caused much debate among Northerners when it was first published, just a decade before the start of the American Civil War. Southerners, on the other hand, went to extraordinary measures to prevent its distribution.[18]

In *The Leopard's Spots*, which is a fictional portrayal of the Ku Klux Klan's inception, Dixon attempted to correct what he believed were inaccurate representations of the South, asserting that the Klan originated not as a means to repress freed slaves but rather to prevent government corruption and protect white womanhood from sexually deviant black men.[19] An ultimatum raised by a clergyman in *The Leopard's Spots* is whether the country will be "Anglo Saxon or Mulatto." The future of the world depends on America, the reverend says, and there will be no future for America if "racial lines are broken, and its proud citizenship sinks to the level of a mongrel breed of Mulattoes."[20] For Dixon, it seems, interracial sex was a matter of life or death upon which the future of the world hinged.

Dixon, who dedicated *The Clansman*, second in the trilogy, to his uncle, grand titan of the Ku Klux Klan, probably had firsthand knowledge of the Klan from childhood. *The Clansman* further develops Dixon's tale of the Klan and is told through the interlocking stories of two white families. The Camerons hail from the South, while the Stoneman family is from the North. Thaddeus Stevens, former leader and whip of the Republican Party, is thinly disguised as head of the Northern household, Austin Stoneman.[21] As leader of the Republican's Radical wing, Thaddeus Stevens was unyielding in his battles for African American freedom, suffrage, and schooling. After the South's defeat, Stevens was intent upon preventing the Confederate states from rejoining the Union until they had granted newly freed slaves equality under the law and the right to vote.[22] In Dixon's distorted version of history Stoneman (Stevens) is a villain.

The Clansman also advances the notion that mixed race people pose a threat to the security of the United States. Dixon holds a special vehemence for mulattoes, rendered in the characters of Lydia Brown and Silas Lynch, who are decidedly not the tragic octoroons of 19th-century fiction but rather their antithesis. Silas Lynch is a college-educated "Negro Missionary." A protégé and trusted accomplice of Stoneman, Lynch is eager to assist in imposing the punishment of Reconstruction on the South. Dixon describes Lynch as good looking, "for a mulatto." Lynch has "evidently inherited the full physical characteristics of the Aryan race," however his eyes "glowed with the brightness of the African jungle." One could not look at him "without seeing pictures of the primeval forest."[23] White blood is responsible for Lynch's physical attractiveness yet lurking beneath is his innate untamed savage nature.

Lydia Brown, *The Clansman*'s other menacing mulatto, is Austin Stoneman's maid and mistress. Lydia's character is based on Lydia Hamilton Smith, Thaddeus Stevens' longstanding mulatto housekeeper. For many years, rumors circulated that Smith was also Stevens' mistress. In her biography of Stevens, Fawn Brodie devoted an entire chapter to Lydia and offered convincing evidence as to why the rumors might have been true.[24] Like Lynch, Lydia is also described as having a simultaneously charming (white) and savage (black) nature. Lydia, Dixon writes, was a woman of "extraordinary animal beauty and the fiery temper of a leopardess."[25]

Dixon, as narrator, says no one more sinister than Lydia had "ever cast a shadow across the history" of the country. He then wonders if Stoneman plans to make Lydia the mediator of America's social life and "her ethics the limit of its moral laws." Dixon fantasizes that a mulatto maid will soon have untold, corrupt influence over the entire country. Toward the end of the novel, Stoneman confesses that Lydia is partly to blame for his vengeance against the defeated Confederacy. Three forces motivated him, he says: party success, the desire for revenge, and "the yellow vampire" to whom he had fallen victim.[26]

Thomas Dixon, Jr., had no literary talent to speak of, and *The Clansman* might well have fallen into obscurity were it not for the fact that David Wark Griffith decided to make the novel into a movie, *The Birth of a Nation*.[27] Born in Kentucky, the son of a Confederate army colonel, Griffith was raised in an atmosphere of racial intolerance. Dixon's Ku Klux Klan trilogy exemplified Griffith's Southern values. When Griffith began to search for a large-scale project to film, he probably regarded *The Clansman* as the perfect subject matter. In plot, character, motivation, and theme, *The Birth of a Nation* remains true to its original source.[28]

The Birth of a Nation also retains Dixon's sympathetic bias for a defeated South, vilification of any blacks who are not content to be faithful slaves, and special animus toward mulattoes.[29] Near the end of the film, Silas Lynch, played by George Siegmann, a white actor in a light shade of blackface, is proven to be an oversexed brute when he makes advances toward Stoneman's daughter, Elsie. Lydia Brown is played by the white actress Mary Alden, also in a light shade of blackface. Upon her first introduction, a title card reads: "The great leader's weakness that is to blight a nation." In that same scene, feigning to be a victim of a sexual assault at the hands of one of Stoneman's visitors, Lydia is revealed to be both a seductress and a conniving liar.

Prior to the release of *The Birth of a Nation*, American moviegoers were accustomed to film shorts that ran ten or fifteen minutes. This "one-reel" format, however, did not lend itself to complex narratives. Influenced by multiple-reel films from abroad, American filmmakers gradually began to produce lengthier films. In 1915, Griffith released *The Birth of a Nation* in twelve reels.[30] Running over three hours and synthesizing complex

editing, rapid changes of camera positions and angles, a huge cast, and a panoramic nar-
ration, *The Birth of a Nation* had all the elements of modern filmmaking.[31]

The Birth of a Nation was a huge financial success. It was revered and celebrated by
critics and also contributed to a period of unprecedented growth in Klan membership.[32]
It was the first film to be played at the White House, where President Woodrow Wilson,
Dixon's college classmate and friend, is reported to have exclaimed, "It is like writing history with lightening."[33] The celebration of its technical and artistic achievements combined with its white-supremacist message make *The Birth of A Nation* a controversial
film, even today.

While the impact that *The Birth of a Nation* and its message has had on the film
industry and American culture cannot be understated, it should be noted that the portrayal of black people in Griffith's film, which employs all five of Bogle's stereotypes, was
not much different than what the movie industry was turning out in the period preceding
The Birth of a Nation. From the moment of the movie industry's inception in 1890, blacks
were subjected to what historian Daniel J. Leab called "outrageous and shabby treatment."
According to Leab, blacks in this early period were most often represented in nonthreat-
ening comic or faithful servile roles that tended to humiliate or demean the characters.[34]

Mixed race characters were also represented in film before *The Birth of a Nation*.
An analysis of more than thirty predominantly white-cast films with mixed race or purported mixed race characters (presumably played by white actors) released between 1909
and 1919, the period immediately preceding and succeeding *The Birth of a Nation*, reveals
three recurring types. The near-white "tragic octoroon" of early film is much like and
sometimes identical to the tragic octoroon of abolitionary fiction. Usually gendered as a
woman, she is a sympathetic character who possesses the qualities associated with white
femininity: passivity and dependence. She is sometimes unwise about whom she loves,
and not always chaste, but otherwise loyal and decent. The "tragic mulatto," also usually a
woman, is often conflicted. She is less virtuous than her octoroon counterpart and often
duplicitous. At the same time, the tragic mulatto can also be sympathetic and repentant.
The third type, the "depraved mulatto," usually a man, is evil and often violent, with no
apparent redeeming qualities.

In the years prior to *The Birth of a Nation*, the tragic octoroon was an overwhelming favorite. One of the tragic octoroon's earliest appearance was in *The Sealed Envelope*
(1912). In this film, which was set contemporarily, a wealthy couple adopts a beautiful
child, Arline. With the adoption, the couple is handed a sealed envelope that is not to be
opened until Arline becomes of age. Years pass. A party is thrown to celebrate Arline's
coming of age and her engagement to a wealthy young man. At the party, Arline insists
on opening the sealed envelope with all her guests. Inside a letter reveals that Arline is the
daughter of a white man and an octoroon. The guests are horrified. Arline rushes off to
the Negro settlement in her neighborhood, swoons and dies of a broken heart.[35]

The Debt (1912), a two-reel feature, which also took place in a contemporary post-
bellum setting, had mother and daughter tragic octoroons. Jack, a man from a well-to-do
family, has an affair with his parents' octoroon maid, Zelma. Jack offers to provide for
Zelma, but he will not marry her. Instead he marries Beatrice, a white woman. Zelma
and Beatrice give birth to Jack's babies, Minna and Bert, around the same time. Zelma
dies from the tragedy of her situation. Minna, her one-sixteenth black baby, is raised by
Jack's brother, Paul (apparently unbeknownst to Jack). Years later Minna and Bert meet.
Unaware of their blood relation, the half-siblings fall in love and make plans to marry.

On the day of their wedding Jack receives a telegram from Paul telling him to stop the wedding because Minna is his child. Jack kills himself with a gun and Minna departs. A month later Minna, who is "doomed to follow her mother's weary footsteps," reaches her mother's gravesite out in the forest.[36]

The Octoroon (1913), based on Dion Boucicault's 1859 play, featured the archetypical tragic octoroon. In this film, a white man, returning to the South after many years away, falls in love with the octoroon, Zoe. Zoe's freedom papers are stolen by a villainous overseer who then purchases her at an auction. The overseer's crime is eventually brought to light, but not before Zoe, rather than submit to being a slave, commits suicide.[37]

Films preceding *The Birth of a Nation* also portrayed the less virtuous tragic mulatto, though not as often as the tragic octoroon. *In Slavery Days* (1913), for example, has a white character take on the role of tragic octoroon, and the octoroons, therefore, become the tragic mulattoes. Sue, an octoroon slave, switches her (presumably one-sixteenth black) baby for her slave master's baby. Sue's baby, Carlotta, grows up free and white, while the master's baby, Tennessee, grows up a slave. Jealous of a young man's affection for Tennessee, Carlotta violates a rule of her household and sells Tennessee down the river. Guilt-ridden, Sue confesses her baby-switching crime to her owners. While a wedding follows for Tennessee and her suitor, Carlotta and Sue are accidentally burned to death.[38]

In Slavery Days illustrates that one way for the tragic octoroon to avoid death or other negative consequences was if it turned out that she was not black at all. This was also the case in *At the Old Cross Roads* (1914) in which Annabel, the daughter of an octoroon, learns of her black blood only after she is engaged to be married. In the end, it is discovered that Annabel's mother is not an octoroon after all, but the daughter of an Englishman and a Spaniard.[39] "Racial obstacles are cleared away." Annabel can marry and her mother is "raised to a high social standing."[40] Before 1915, similar scenarios are also found in *The Crimson Stain* (1913) and *The Chest of Fortune* (1914). This pattern continued after 1915 in films such as *Sold at Auction* (1917), *The Bride of Hate* (1917), and *The Liar* (1918).

With the exception of *Uncle Tom's Cabin*, perhaps, the mulatto man, when he appeared prior to 1915, was the depraved mulatto, a monster. A fantastic example occurred in *In Humanity's Cause* (1911), which was set during the Civil War. Its main character is a Confederate officer whose life is saved on the battlefield by a blood transfusion from a black man. The transfusion turns him into a brute. The officer hunts down his blood donor and grapples with him on the edge of a cliff. Both men fall to their deaths.[41]

An even more absurd scenario was found in the murder mystery *The Devil's Signature* (1914). The murder of a young woman has occurred in one of the bedrooms of the Vandiver estate. Douglas, the love interest of young Ethel Vandiver, is at first suspected to be the killer when his blood-stained handkerchief is found at the crime scene by Craven, the Vandivers' mulatto gardener and servant. The detective notes, however, that there is a queer, circular shaped track on the rug near the dead girl's bed and decides to investigate further.[42]

The detective hides out with a newspaper reporter in the dead girl's bedroom, hoping that the murderer will return. At one end of the room, a closet door opens slowly, and a gruesome, claw-like hand appears. The detective shoots four times, but when the closet is opened, it is found to be empty and there's no sign of the bullets. A secret passage in the back of the closet, which leads down a flight of stairs to a dark basement, is discovered. At the bottom of the stairs lays Craven's dead body with four bullet holes in it. One of Craven's shoes is missing, and instead of a foot, his limb ends in a cloven hoof, proving that the mulatto is the murderer (and the devil).[43]

With the *Birth of a Nation*, Griffith added a sexually sinister aspect to the mulatto characters. *The Birth of a Nation* was released in February 1915, and its portrayal of Silas Lynch and Lydia Brown seems to coincide with the decline of the tragic octoroon and a marked change in the way in which mixed race women would be portrayed in film.

Based on my sampling of films, it appears that 1915 was the most popular year for mixed characters, with seven films and ten mixed race characters. Among them, there was one sympathetic male tragic octoroon found in *The Nigger* aka *The Governor*. In this film a Southern governor becomes pro-black and gives up his office and his white woman when he discovers his "touch of negro blood."[44] The year 1915 seems to have yielded no female tragic octoroons, however. Additionally, before 1915, only the men had a propensity for violent behavior. After 1915, with few exceptions, including two 1918 remakes of *Uncle Tom's Cabin*, the mulatto woman became increasingly more jealous, vindictive, and violent.

In *I Will Repay* (1916), the mulatto woman, Beulah, is the mistress of Bascomb, a wild young Southerner who owns a speakeasy. When Beulah learns that Bascomb plans to ask the white Virginia to marry him, she becomes jealous and attempts to stab her rival. Virginia's ex-boyfriend intervenes and the white woman is saved.[45] In later years, the mulatto's attempt at violence would be fatal. In *A Woman of Impulse* (1918), for instance, a white woman stabs a man to protect her womanhood but does not kill him. Out of jealousy, it is an octoroon girl who finishes the man off.[46]

One final example, *Kildare of Storm* (1918) features Mahaly, a beautiful mulatto servant. Kildare, owner of an old Southern estate called Storm, has been having an affair with Mahaly. Kildare led Mahaly to believe that she was his wife, but he now wants legitimate marriage to a white woman, Kate. To keep Mahaly quiet he steals his own son from her. Kate soon realizes what a vulgar man she married and begins to enjoy the company of a doctor and his mother. Mahaly spies on Kate and the doctor and reports to Kildare, who goes after the doctor. Kildare winds up dead, and the doctor serves prison time for his murder. Several years later, Mahaly, on her deathbed, confesses that she is the one who killed Kildare. The mulatto dies and Kate and her doctor start a new life together.[47]

Women and Mixed Race Representation in Film picks up not long after this period, at the tail end of the silent film era, beginning with Josephine Baker in the first chapter. Forged primarily in a European, French colonial context, Baker's image is unique among the other star images in this book, which were shaped by the American racial construct. Baker's image went from that of a coon in America to an exotic savage upon her arrival in France, and, ultimately, she was accepted as fully French.

The second chapter takes a look at the mammy-jezebel dichotomy of black womanhood through the image of Nina Mae McKinney. An immediate successor to the silent film era, McKinney is best known for her portrayal of the jezebel Chick in the all-black film *Hallelujah* (1929). Toward the end of her career, McKinney had a minor supporting role as a bad girl in *Pinky* (1949), a film that featured a white actress in the role of a black woman who passes for white. *Pinky* aside, McKinney would end her career playing bit parts as a maid or a mammy.

Chapter 3, Fredi Washington, provides an opportunity to address the "one-drop rule" for defining blackness in the United States and to continue the discussion on passing started in Chapter 2. In her personal life, Washington, who looked white, embraced a black ("Negro") identity. In her work, Washington played characters who passed for white. Most notably, in *Imitation of Life* (1934), Washington played Hollywood's most iconic tragic mulatto, Peola.

One of the more complex and politically charged images is that of Lena Horne. The main focus of the fourth chapter is Horne's Hollywood image during the years that she was most active in the film industry. Horne had already made a name for herself as a singer before she became an MGM contract player in 1942. Horne's contract stipulated that she would not have to take on the stereotypical roles customarily assigned to black performers of the day. MGM held up its end of the contract by walking a tightrope between advancing racial equality and pandering to Jim Crow. Horne and MGM agreed to cancel their contract in 1950.

In Chapter 5, Dorothy Dandridge crosses racial boundaries that Horne could not. Dandridge started her Hollywood career in the 1930s in musical specialty numbers. For her role as the seductive title character in *Carmen Jones* (1954), she became the first black woman to be nominated for a Best Actress in a Leading Role Oscar. After *Carmen Jones*, Dandridge would become the first African American woman, in a Hollywood feature film, to be held in the loving arms of a white man. For Dandridge, crossing over would become synonymous with interracial sexuality. In her personal life, Dandridge, whose life ended most likely by suicide, seemed to epitomize the tragic mulatto.

Lonette McKee, the subject of Chapter 6, arrived in Hollywood shortly after the old studio system had been dismantled. While her image is tethered to the past, it moves beyond stereotype and illustrates forward-looking revisions to portrayals of the mixed race woman. In Chapter 7, the star image of Jennifer Beals also embodies a revision to the mixed race woman. Beals has never passed for white, per se. She has never denied her black father. Nevertheless, based on her looks, and the countless "white" roles she has played in film and television, her image has been strongly associated with whiteness. Nevertheless, the evolution of the Jennifer Beals image has produced some interesting mixed race roles.

Halle Berry, the subject of the final chapter, is the first and, to date, the only African American actress to have been awarded the Best Actress in a Leading Role Oscar. Berry has appeared in more than 35 feature films, plus numerous television series and television movies. This chapter focuses primarily on those roles in which her characters are mixed race or involved in interracial scenarios. It also argues that Berry's historic Academy Award was won through a successful media campaign that conjoined her image to Dorothy Dandridge's.

1

Josephine Baker

From Exotic Savage to Creole Queen

I intend to be a Creole just like the other Josephine, Napoleon's wife.[1]
—Josephine Baker on her performance in *La Créole*

The world's first black superstar, and one of France's most beloved artists, Josephine Baker began her life a world away from the streets of avant-garde Paris. She was born in the slums of East St. Louis, Missouri, and at a very young age began dancing and performing in vaudeville. As a teenager, Baker made her way to Harlem. When she first appeared on Broadway, Josephine Baker was perceived as neither beautiful nor exotic. Nevertheless, from the beginning, she had a knack for pandering to audiences. Among a chorus line of light-skinned dancers, Josephine stood out—not just for her brown skin color—but also for her particular brand of comic talent.[2]

By 1925 Josephine was on her way to France with a troupe of singers and dancers known as *La Revue nègre*. It was there that her image underwent a remarkable metamorphosis. In the eyes of Parisians, already fascinated with African culture, when Josephine Baker performed a "savage dance," wearing nothing but a skimpy skirt made of feathers, she was no longer the homely member of the cast. For the first time in her career, audiences, and especially men, found her appealing. Josephine Baker became their exotic savage.

Baker's image continued to evolve in France, experiencing a *Creolization* that eschewed its St. Louis–Harlem roots and rendered it a hybrid of her newly adopted French urbanity and the "primitive" persona first expressed in her "savage" dancing. During this period of transformation, Baker made three significant French feature films, *La Sirène des Tropiques* (1927), *Zou Zou* (1934), and *Princesse Tam-Tam* (1935). Given the American racial climate, and its white-dominated film industry, these films stand out for several reasons. First, with references to Josephine's personal life—conflating the person with the star—all three films were conceived as star vehicles for a black woman. Second, in each of these films, Baker's characters assimilate, to some degree or other, into the larger cast of white characters. Furthermore, as part of their assimilation, her characters develop a love interest with a white hero.

Back in the United States, in mainstream Hollywood, it would be another thirty years before a black actress, Dorothy Dandridge, would gain notoriety for being courted by a white man in *Island in the Sun* (1957). French cinema's willingness to show black and white actors portraying an interracial relationship does not mean that French representations of blackness are void of racism. Rather, Baker's position in these films, when compared to her American counterparts, points to a difference between images—or lack thereof—derived from the historical context of slavery and those that emerged from French colonialism.

Prior to Baker's arrival in Paris, the French had a long history of visual and literary representation of the sexualized black female. Up until the early 20th century, however, most French people had never encountered a black person. Because there were so few black people in France, fascination with black women could be openly expressed. By comparison, in antebellum America, black women were visible in daily life, oftentimes living in close proximity to whites under a system that depended on their mandated oppression. Openly acknowledging black women as desirable would have posed a threat to the existing social structure. Therefore, that desire had to be inverted or concealed.[3]

Though visibly black and American-born, Baker is not identified as a black American in any of her feature films, but rather an exotic woman of the colonies. Although she is given a chance at romance with a white man, and an opportunity to succeed in his world, in keeping with contemporary racial ideology, in each of her films, interracial romance is ultimately thwarted and her characters remain excluded from full participation in white life. In two of these films, Baker is portrayed as childlike, "primitive," and in need of edification.

This "primitive" persona, which was responsible for launching Baker's international fame, was a perfect match for the mood of France's postwar cinema which, following a disastrous performance in the First World War, reflected the nation's angst and desire for escape. Of particular note during this time is the Empire film, which provided escape vis-à-vis the colonies, and by virtue of its ability to "civilize" its colonies, it also offered a sense of national superiority.[4] In both *La Sirène des Tropiques* and *Princesse Tam-Tam*, Baker plays a native of the colonies who becomes "civilized" under the influence of the French. In *Zouzou*, though a national origin is not specified, her character can still be understood as an assimilated colonial subject.

She was born Freda Josephine McDonald in 1906. Her mother, Carrie McDonald, was an aspiring dancer who earned a living as a washerwoman. Carrie's boyfriend at the time, the African American drummer Eddie Carson, is often cited as Josephine's father. Other evidence, however, suggests that this might not be the case. Josephine Baker wrote five autobiographies and routinely reworked the story of her early life.[5]

In one autobiography, Baker claims that her biological father was an olive-skinned Spaniard. She also refers to herself as a "pinky,"[6] a term once used to describe very light-skinned black people. Josephine's skin color has been described as caramel-colored, bronze-skinned, the color of strong tea, light brown, the color of *café au lait*, and the color of honey.[7] She was not light-skinned nor "high yellow." Thus, in the context used by Baker, "pinky" might be interpreted as synonymous with biracial or mixed race. Indeed, later in that same autobiography, Baker implies that her father must have been a white man.[8] In his posthumous biography, *Josephine: Hungry Heart*, the star's adopted son Jean-Claude Baker posits rather convincingly that Josephine's father probably was a white man. Jean-Claude also maintains that the question of her father's identity was the most painful mystery of Josephine's life.[9]

As an infant Josephine was abandoned to the care of her mother's relatives. By the time Carrie McDonald returned to claim her, Eddie Carson was out of the picture, and Josephine had a stepfather and three half-siblings to contend with. Josephine's stepfather, Arthur Martin, was a day laborer, and like Carrie, he had dark skin. With her caramel complexion, Josephine was acutely aware that her skin was noticeably lighter than that of the rest of her family. From early on she believed that this difference in skin color made her an unwelcome member of the family.[10] Perhaps Josephine was a reminder to Carrie of the dishonor she might have brought upon her family for having a white man's baby.

Whatever the case, Josephine's feelings of being unwanted were justified. After reuniting with her mother, Josephine was cast out of the home twice more. Around the age of seven, she was sent away to work for a white family, chopping wood, emptying chamber pots, and washing clothes. During the day she would attend school—as required by the law—and at night she would sleep in the basement with the family dog. When this arrangement ended, Josephine returned home only to be hired out again to a seemingly more humane couple. Josephine was let go from this job when she confided to the lady of the household that the lady's husband had started appearing in her bedroom at night.[11]

Josephine often skipped school and spent a good deal of her time at the Booker T. Washington Theater, where she observed and learned to mimic the various acts. At the age of thirteen, Josephine married her first husband, Willie Wells. Because of her age, the marriage was not actually legal. Willie soon fled after Josephine cut his head open with a beer bottle during a quarrel.[12] Shortly after her break-up with Willie, Josephine left St. Louis with a troupe of traveling vaudeville performers. A byproduct of the blackface minstrel show, vaudeville theater incorporated a greater variety of acts, including animal shows, skits, music, dancing, and comedy. Eventually Josephine wound up in Philadelphia, where, at around age fifteen, she married Billy Baker and changed her name to Josephine Baker.

While married to Billy, Josephine continued to work as a dancer. When the musical and comedy revue, *Shuffle Along* came to Philadelphia she tried out for a spot but was turned down, most likely because she was too young. Josephine, however, recalled the rejection in terms of skin color and physical appearance. She was incensed that Noble Sissle, the show's lyricist, had told her that she was "too small, too thin, [and] too dark."[13] A few months later, when Josephine heard that a second *Shuffle Along* company was being formed, she left her husband and marriage behind and took a train to New York to audition. This time, Josephine took great pains to apply light-colored powder to her face beforehand. Though she was not hired as a dancer, Josephine did manage to get a job with the *Shuffle Along* company as a dresser.[14]

Though it was the *Dark Town Follies* revue that first brought New York's downtown whites to Harlem in 1913, *Shuffle Along*, the phenomenally popular black vaudeville musical of 1921, is generally credited as the prelude to white interest in Harlem.[15] Only a half-century after emancipation and immediately following the First World War, the 1920s New York community of Harlem symbolized a new beginning for black people. It became the largest urban black community in the world and included an enclave of Negro writers, artists, and activists. While these black intellectuals are credited with giving rise to the Harlem Renaissance, for poet and playwright Langston Hughes, it was *Shuffle Along* that marked the beginning of the historic literary and cultural movement, and it was *Shuffle Along* that led Hughes to Harlem.[16]

The book for *Shuffle Along* was written by the comedy team of Flournoy Miller and Aubrey Lyles. Miller and Lyles, who first collaborated at Fisk University, became popular with routines that included blackface, completing each other's sentences, and mutilating the English language. When the *Amos 'n' Andy* radio program became a hit, many people, Miller and Lyles included, felt that Godsen and Correll, the show's white minstrels in rhetorical blackface, had achieved their success by copying their style.[17] While the shtick of Miller and Lyles amused audiences, it was the lyrics of Noble Sissle, the music of Eubie Blake, and the energy of its superior jazz dancing that made *Shuffle Along* a big hit.[18] With the song "Love Will Find a Way" *Shuffle Along* also introduced the first earnest African American love story in a musical,[19] and over twenty years later, another *Shuffle Along* tune, "I'm Just Wild About Harry," would become the campaign song for President Harry Truman.

Like Miller and Lyles, Sissle and Blake were also influenced by the minstrelsy tradition. However, as early as 1919, in their traveling vaudeville act, the Dixie Duo, Sissle and Blake began to move away from minstrelsy by playing piano instead of traditional minstrel instruments, like banjo or guitar; dressing in tuxedos instead of shabby minstrel attire; and rejecting blackface makeup.[20] Sissle and Blake's chorus line, made up of sixteen mostly light-skinned female dancers, might have also been an attempt to resist minstrelsy. Reportedly, Sissle wanted to model the chorus line after the Tiller Girls, a famous white dance troupe from England whom, just a few years after *Shuffle Along*, would perform with Baker in the Folies-Bergère of Paris.[21]

In the 1920s, the sight of fair-skinned dancing women, who represented advancement and mobility, could undermine blackface, which was used as a means to stereotype and define African Americans. However, showcasing black women who looked like white women in an all-black revue was also problematic. It reinforced white standards of beauty for all women and strengthened the notion that racial categories are essential and absolute. Indeed, after the Great Depression, to the African Americans invested in protecting black folk culture, light skinned chorus girls became a symbol of complicity with the very system that oppressed blacks.[22]

Shuffle Along was not the first production to feature the all-female chorus line. In 1889, Sam T. Jack's Creole Burlesque Company successfully altered the minstrel show format by eliminating blackface altogether and substituting light-skinned women in the chorus that was traditionally made up of sixteen men. As implied by its name, the Creole Burlesque Company employed a number of mixed race and light-skinned black performers. Unlike other black shows of the day, some of which also featured women, *The Creole Show* received top-notch promotion and booking because its producer was a prominent theater owner and a white man. The Burlesque Company toured across the United States for about seven years. It introduced the cakewalk, the first black dance to become popular with whites, and had a tremendous influence on the all-black shows that would later follow.[23]

Despite its nationwide popularity, *The Creole Show* was not always welcomed everywhere it played. When the company arrived in Louisiana in 1893, it caused quite a disturbance. After a performance in Lake Charles to an audience of men only, many of the city's residents took exception to Jack's use of the term "Creole." An indignation meeting was held, and the city subsequently issued a resolution that protested the Creole Company as an affront to the "fair name" of Louisiana's women. The resolution also took offense to the promotion of "negro half-breeds" as "the Creole beauties."[24] When news of the show from Lake Charles reached nearby Lafayette, there were reported threats of violence, and a committee headed by the mayor refused to let Jack's company perform there.[25]

The controversy caused by Jack's Burlesque Company in Louisiana epitomizes the competing definitions of the word "Creole" and the struggle that ensued over its use in the latter half of the 19th century. Derived from the Portuguese *crioulo*, and the Spanish *criollo*, the term was originally used—without regard to race—to describe a person born in the Americas of parents from Europe. In New Orleans slaves and people of mixed race ancestry have long been associated with a Creole identity. After the Civil War, prompted by pressures to conform to a black-white binary racial standard—and incriminations of impurity—Louisiana Creoles heavily invested in their white heritage moved to "purify" the meaning by arguing that Creoles were natives solely of European extraction.[26] Ultimately, proponents of this argument seem to have lost their battle of words. According to the *Harvard Encyclopedia of American Ethnic Groups*, by the 20th century, the term "Creole" in the United States most often referred to Louisiana Creoles of Color.[27]

Louisiana not withstanding, Sam Jack's success motivated others to put on their own Creole shows, including the very fair-skinned African American producer John W. Isham. By virtue of his ability to pass for white, Isham obtained responsible positions in show business and gained valuable management experience. While employed as the advance agent for Sam T. Jack's Burlesque Company, Isham came up with the idea of forming his own company, which he initially called Isham's Creole Opera Company. When Jack threatened legal action, Isham changed the name to The Octoroons. For eight seasons, Isham's Octoroons was one of the most successful touring companies on the road, offering up what was deemed "high-class" entertainment that included skits, comedy sketches, and even opera.[28]

"That Comedy Chorus Girl"

By the time *Shuffle Along* was conceived, the use of an all-female chorus line made up of Creole beauties was an established practice. As for Josephine Baker's ascent to the chorus line, while she helped *Shuffle Along* dancers get in and out of their costumes, she was also busy committing their songs and routines to memory. When a dancer fell ill one night, Josephine seized the opportunity she had been longing for. On stage for the first time with the other chorus girls, instead of sticking to the routine that she knew by heart, Josephine broke from the line and drew attention away from the solo singer by cutting up and making cross-eyed faces. The other chorus girls were not amused, but Josephine's clowning delighted the audience, and it eventually earned her separate billing as "That Comedy Chorus Girl."[29]

After *Shuffle Along* ended, Baker appeared in another Sissle and Blake production, originally known as *In Bamville* and later renamed *The Chocolate Dandies*. Here, too, she was billed as "That Comedy Chorus Girl" and became one of the highest paid principals in the company.[30] While other performers of the day were retreating from blackface, Josephine embraced it. At her behest, Sissle and Blake wrote Josephine a blackface number for the show.[31]

On September 1, 1924, after touring for six months, *Chocolate Dandies* finally opened on Broadway. In a *New York Times* review of the show, Baker was the only female performer singled out for special mention. The reviewer described her as a dancing freak and compared her to the white cross-eyed vaudeville comedian Ben Turpin.[32] To reviewers who complained that *Chocolate Dandies* had too much white influence, Baker's performance was its only saving grace.[33]

Following *Chocolate Dandies*, Josephine went to work at the Plantation Club. As implied by its name, the Plantation Club was a downtown establishment decorated as a

Southern plantation. It was at the Plantation Club that Josephine was introduced to Caroline Dudley Reagan, a wealthy white American socialite who was unduly interested in African American art and entertainment. Reagan, who was planning to take an all-black revue to Paris, offered Josephine a role in the company she was forming. Before long, Josephine was on her way to France as one of the twenty-five dancers, singers, and musicians that made up the troupe known as *La Revue nègre*.

"The Exotic Savage"

In terms of her immediate rise to fame, Josephine Baker's arrival in Paris in 1925 could not have been more fortuitously timed. To begin with, as a consequence of the First World War, the French had recently developed a special fondness for African Americans. When black American troops first arrived, the French welcomed, with open arms, the soldiers who came to fight the enemy that had invaded their soil. The most famed African American combat unit of World War I was the 369th Infantry from Harlem (formerly the 15th New York Colored Regiment). Nicknamed the "Hellfighters," the 369th earned more decorations for bravery than any other American unit during the First World War, including the Croix de Guerre from the French army.

In addition to their acts of valor, members of the 369th were also known for their exceptional musicality. The music that these black GIs brought with them was another factor that endeared them to the French. The Hellfighters' forty-four-piece band was led by James Reese Europe who, before the war, had been one of New York society's most popular dance bandleaders. Noble Sissle was the band's vocalist. In 1917, when the regiment landed in Brest on the coast of Brittany, the first thing Europe's band did was play for the people who were there to greet them. The French have cherished jazz ever since.[34]

Though the French welcomed the African American soldiers, they were not without their own brand of prejudice toward blacks. Up until 1912, for example, when the government began recruiting men from its African colonies for military service, French authorities had long debated whether Africans were disciplined, civilized, or brave enough to make good soldiers. When in 1914 African troops allayed those concerns by performing admirably, the French modified their image of Africans to that of murderous barbarians. Nevertheless, by comparison and for the most part, the racism that African soldiers experienced was nothing like that which black American GIs were subjected to within their own army or at home in the United States.[35]

Most African American soldiers were unaware of any tension, racial or otherwise, between the French and their colonial subjects. As far as they were concerned the harsh racism and segregation that was a way of life in America was nonexistent in France. There were no restrictions on where or with whom they could go, and French people treated them with far more decency than other white people had.[36] Consequently, when the war ended, some African American soldiers returned to Paris to live and other black Americans followed.

By the mid–1920s a vibrant black community was emerging in Paris. By this time, too, the French had developed a keen interest in African artifacts. In the wake of colonial expansion, beginning in the late 19th century, vast numbers of African sculptures had been taken from Africa to Europe. By the turn of the century, these objects, which the French referred to as *l'art nègre*, captured the fantasy of artists, art dealers, and critics. To them, *l'art nègre*, and what became known in the West as "primitivism," represented the work of a "primitive" people. It symbolized exoticism, mysticism, difference, and a kind of authenticity that had been lost to the industrialized, "civilized" West.[37] African masks and sculpture had a powerful influence over avant-garde artists, such as Picasso, Matisse, and Man Ray. As such, *l'art nègre* was a key inspiration in the development of modern art.

For others, like Paul Guillaume, who was both art dealer and critic, *l'art nègre* became a specialty. In 1918, Guillaume created the modern art journal *Les Arts à Paris*, which featured reviews about Paris's modern art scene, including *l'art nègre*, as well as articles about other cultures. Guillaume also promoted African art by hosting black-themed parties. One of the most significant of these occurred in 1919. Held in conjunction with an exhibit of *l'art nègre* at the Théâtre des Champs-Elysées, Guillaume's *Fête nègre* featured modern music and dancing based on African mythology.[38] Six years later, Guillaume would be among the celebrities and journalists invited to attend a preview of *La Revue nègre* at the very same theater where his black-themed party had taken place.

The history of French interest in Africana, however, predates modern interest in *l'art nègre*. The French had been curious about black culture and black bodies since they first ventured to Africa in the 17th century. Epitomizing their longstanding interest in black bodies is the story of Sara Baartman, also known as the Hottentot Venus. A century before Josephine Baker's arrival in Paris, Sara Baartman became the icon of the female sexualized savage. In fact, parallels are often drawn between the two women who have both served as focal points for theorizing about race.

Baartman belonged to a nomadic group of people of South Africa, known as Khoekhoe. For two centuries, Europeans had been fascinated with reports about the Khoekhoe people, whom the Dutch referred to as "Hottentot." Of specific interest to Europeans were the Khoekhoe women and their genital anatomy. Baartman happened to be acquainted with two men who were well aware of this European curiosity and who wished to profit from it. In 1810, in the hopes of a better life, Baartman left her homeland with these two men to be put on display as a freak across Europe. Events that unfolded when Baartman arrived in Paris would ultimately validate for Western culture long-held myths about black inferiority and black women's sexuality, remnants of which endure to this day.

Sara Baartman was born in the 1770s. During her childhood, Khoekhoe people were either being killed off by the Dutch or forced into indentured servitude. Sara became a servant. Her master, Hendrik Cesars, was one of the men who took Baartman to Europe. A descendant of East or South Asian slaves, by Boer law, Cesars was considered a Free Black man. By the time Baartman set sail for Europe she had lost both her parents, as well as three babies who died shortly after birth. Thus, it's no wonder that Sara was willing to cast her lot with two men who promised her beads, clothes, support, and money.[39]

Baartman was first promoted as the Hottentot Venus in London. A main attraction of Baartman's exhibit was her pronounced derriere. Appearing half-naked, she was put on display much like a wild beast and ordered to move in and out of a cage. As the Hottentot Venus, Baartman became a celebrity of sorts. Her persona captivated the British and inspired caricature drawings, as well as songs, such as the "Hottentot Ballad," which, in part, went as follows:

In Piccadilly Street so fair,
A mansion she has got,
In golden letters written there,
The Venus Hottentot.

But you may ask, and well, I ween,
For why she tarries there,
And what in her is to be seen,
Than other folks more rare.
A rump she has though strange it be,
Large as a cauldron pot,
And this is why men go to see
The lovely HOTTENTOT.[40]

As the transatlantic slave trade had only recently been abolished, Baartman's popularity caught the attention of abolitionists who, after seeing her performance, were moved to take up her case in a court of law. The attempt to free Baartman from her exhibitors caused quite a controversy in the British press, but ultimately it was unsuccessful.

When Baartman went to Paris in 1814 she had a new promoter, who was an exhibitor of wild animals. Newspapers trumpeted her arrival, and as it had been in London, Baartman's persona quickly became part of popular culture. In 1815, Georges Cuvier, France's foremost anatomist and naturalist, expressed interest in the Hottentot Venus. Cuvier was eager to examine Baartman to prove his hypothesis that the "Hottentots" were a link between human beings and other animals.[41]

For a period of three days, a team of zoologists, anatomists, and physiologists scrutinized Sara Baartman's body. To establish that more "primitive" mammals possessed more prominent sexual organs and, therefore, a more exaggerated sex drive, Cuvier had wished to include an inspection of Baartman's genitalia in his examination. During her time in Europe, Baartman had acquiesced to countless demeaning scenarios. On this matter, however, Baartman flatly refused.[42]

Within a year after her encounter with the French scientific community, Sara Baartman passed away, and Cuvier ceased the opportunity to complete his examination. After her death, Cuvier obtained Baartman's corpse from the police. Before dissecting her, he made a plaster cast of Sara Baartman's body, which he affixed to a stand and then painted. Next, with scalpel in hand, Cuvier set to work, excising, weighing and measuring her body parts: brain, organs, buttocks. And then came Baartman's genitalia. Cuvier was delighted to find that Sara Baartman did possess elongated labia, which Cuvier referred to as an "apron." In death, Cuvier literally took from Baartman that which she had adamantly denied him while alive. Cuvier cut away at Baartman's genitalia and preserved them in a jar for posterity.

Cuvier's findings, which were published in 1824 and again in 1865, concluded, among other things, that the Hottentot Venus was more closely related to monkeys and orangutans than other humans and that blacks are inferior and therefore in no way responsible for Egyptian civilization.[43] Baartman's plaster cast and some of her remains were on display at the Musee del'Homme in Paris until 1974. In 2002, at the request of Nelson Mandela, they were finally returned to South Africa for a proper burial.

It was against this potent historical backdrop of art, politics, performance, science, and racial ideology that Josephine Baker made her debut in Paris in the fall of 1925. The city's penchant for African art, African Americans, and jazz was in full swing. Parisians layered their life-to-life interactions with African Americans on top of existing colonial perceptions of blacks and black imagery.[44] The *Revue nègre*, with its tap-dancing, jazz, and so-called "authentic" African dance, exemplified this merging of Africa and African Americans in the French imagination. When Josephine Baker appeared on the stage of the Théâtre des Champs-Elysées to perform *La danse sauvage* wearing no more than a skimpy feather skirt, the audience, whether they liked the dance or not, was already primed with expectations and beliefs ingrained over the centuries.

Choreographer Jacques Charles was instrumental to shaping *La Revue nègre*'s final format. Charles was called in at the last minute to save the show. Upon seeing his first rehearsal, Charles was impressed with some of the show's elements but concerned that the routines of the African American performers were not "black" enough. In particular, he thought that the chorus line lacked authenticity because the dancers—who would introduce the Charleston dance to Paris—executed their moves with far too much precision.[45]

Another factor that might well have contributed to Charles's assessment was that, in keeping with black revues of the 1920s, most of the chorines were light-skinned. Indeed, after the show opened, some audience members, having been attracted to the show by the word *nègre*, were disappointed that the women were so fair-skinned. One dancer was so fair she was forced to wear black body makeup.[46]

It was clear to Charles that the *Revue nègre* needed some blacking up. To him this meant making its elements less congruent and inserting material that expressed the sexual, "primitive" and "exotic" qualities that the French associated with blackness and which they would surely expect. With a brown complexion that set her apart from the other fair-skinned chorines, comic antics, and a statuesque physique, Josephine Baker was a natural choice as the focus of Charles's efforts to revamp the show. One of the first orders of business for the esteemed choreographer was to ask Baker to dance nude or almost nude. Accounts differ as to whether Baker balked at the idea in the beginning but, needless to say, in the end she agreed to take her clothes off.

After some coaxing, Baker also agreed to undress for Paul Colin, the illustrator who was assigned to draw Josephine for a poster and a program cover. For a brief time Colin and Baker became lovers. In fact, Baker said that it was Colin who made her feel beautiful for the first time in her life,[47] a claim that is at times difficult to reconcile with a poster and some of the other work he created based on the show. Colin's artwork is certainly alluring, but it is difficult to say that in the *Revue nègre* poster Baker's representation is flattering.

The work of Mexican-born artist and set designer for *La Revue nègre* Miguel Covarrubias is often cited as the inspiration for Colin's poster,[48] which features Josephine Baker drawn in caricature style. Wearing a sleeveless mini-dress, Baker is placed just left of center and flanked by two masculine figures in the foreground. These two figures, dressed in jacket and tie, represent other members of the troupe. The figure on the left is reminiscent of a spiffed-up variation on the golliwog, a popular British fictional, "grotesque" character of children's books that was modeled after a blackface rag doll. The other figure on the right, who sports a top hat, resembles a chimpanzee. Though Baker looks more hominal than her male counterparts, her mouth, with big red lips and a wide-toothed smile, mirrors the grin of the chimpanzee-man.

From Paul Colin's acclaimed *Le Tumulte Noir* portfolio, there are other drawings of Baker that also employ the racist visual shorthand of the day. Released in 1927, *Le Tumulte Noir* is a series of 45 hand-colored lithographs depicting Josephine Baker, the

Paul Colin's poster for *La Revue nègre* (1925), the show that launched Josephine Baker's international stardom. DEA Picture Library/DeAgostini/Getty Images.

La Revue nègre, and Paris's reaction to the two phenomena. *Le Tumulte Noir* is a complex work, ranging in artistic styles. Some drawings are humanizing and complementary to Baker, while others reduce black people to simians or golliwogs.

One image in particular, titled "Josephine Behind Bars," bluntly captures Baker's exotic savage persona. Looking more threatening than she does in the *Revue nègre* poster, a somewhat crudely drawn image of a dark-skinned, bare-breasted Josephine Baker dances for her audience. Baker is seen from a three-quarter frontal view and casts a menacing glance toward the viewer. As in the poster, her lips are bright red and exaggerated in size. In the pit below her, a musician plays the tuba. All of this takes place behind the bars of a cage.

Popular accounts of the *La Revue nègre* include mention of settings such as a Mississippi steamboat dock, a big city street with a skyscraper in the background, and a Harlem nightclub. None, however, make mention of a cage. Baker's *La danse sauvage*, presumably the inspiration for "Josephine Behind Bars," was set in the Harlem nightclub scene, as though she and her partner were on stage there. Perhaps Colin depicted Baker in a cage to capture the spirit and the energy of *La Revue nègre*. Or maybe the mythical notion that blacks are not much more evolved than apes was so prevalent that placing them behind bars was intuitive. Or had Baker's performance evoked the memory of Sara Baartman, whose repertoire did include a cage? Whatever Colin's motivation might have been, the end result of "Josephine Behind Bars" is that Baker and the entire *Revue nègre* troupe are reduced to wild animals.

La Revue nègre, which opened on October 2, 1925, was made up of a number of acts, and in them Josephine played several parts. What made the show a success and Baker a star was *La danse sauvage*. Baker performed the dance with Joe Alex, a dark-skinned, African-born dancer who was hired in France after the American troupe had already arrived.[49] With the support of André Daven, the theater's director, and Jacques Charles, the two had worked out a routine that was slightly comical and highly erotic.[50] Any irony, however, was lost on the French audience, who perceived the dance as something authentically "primitive."[51]

Both dancers were practically nude as the dance began, with Joe Alex carrying an upside-down Baker on his back. Once Alex placed his cargo on the ground, the spotlight was on Josephine, and the result was something frenetic, energetic, and erotic, the likes of which Parisians had never seen before. In all likelihood, as Baker is said to have improvised, the members of her company had not seen anything like it before, either. Backstage, the other chorus girls were amazed and also embarrassed. They couldn't believe that Josephine would put on such a display, especially for a white audience. They were even more surprised to see that the white audience loved it.[52]

To be sure, *La Revue nègre* and *La danse sauvage* also had detractors. Some people in the audience whistled their disapproval; others simply got up and left. Journalist Robert de Flers felt it was a sign of societal degeneration that would lead to the end of civilization altogether.[53] But de Flers and those like him were outnumbered. Even dance critic André Levinson, who was known for his dislike of black dancing, was impressed by Baker, whom he described as "an extraordinary creature of simian suppleness." Her poses, "back arched, haunches protruding, arms entwined and uplifted in a phallic symbol," were "the finest examples of Negro sculpture." For Levinson, Baker was *l'art nègre* in the flesh. Placing Baker in the French lineage of infamous black women, Levinson also commented that in front of his very eyes Baker had transformed from a "grotesque dancing girl" into "the black Venus that haunted Baudelaire."[54]

Invoking the Black Venus in this way, Levinson draws a correlation between Baker and two other women who performed on Paris stages. Sara Baartman, the Hottentot Venus, was sometimes referred to as the Black Venus. The other signifier of deviant black womanhood conjured up by Levinson's writing is Jeanne Duval, the mixed race lover of acclaimed 19th-century French poet Charles Baudelaire. She too earned the moniker Black Venus. Presumed to be from Haiti, Duval arrived in Paris around the age of twenty

Josephine Baker in one of her banana skirts, circa 1930s. Photograph by Walery/Hulton Archive/Getty Images.

and found work as a singer or actress in small cabarets. It was at one of these cabarets where Baudelaire first met Duval, and the two became embroiled in a destructive relationship that would last for twenty years.

Duval achieved notoriety as the inspiration for Baudelaire's Black Venus cycle of poems contained in his most famous work, *Les Fleurs du mal*. Duval is also the subject of an 1862 painting by Edouard Manet. The 2013 fictional work of author James McManus attempts to humanize Jeanne Duval. Historians, however, have mostly tended to characterize her as the vixen responsible for the downfall of the great poet's career.

Baker quit *La Revue nègre* for a better deal at the Folies-Bergère in 1926. She also traded in her feather skirt for her most iconic costume, a skirt made of bananas. The Folies-Bergère, Paris's first music hall, opened in 1869. Along with the Moulin Rouge, its variety show style was the inspiration for the Broadway revue format that became popular just a couple of decades later in the United States. The spectacle of topless women, which became the Folies' main attraction, first appeared in 1894. *La Folie du jour,* Baker's first show with the Folies, included the Tiller Girls as well as Russian dancers with whom Josephine studied.[55]

Baker's role in one sketch of *La Folie du jour*, a mere extension of her savage dance character, made it perfectly clear that the black female body was an object of white men's fantasies. Baker's character was a young African girl, Fatou. While scantily clad black men played drums, a white man, fully clothed, dreamt of an African girl as he slept. Clad in her banana skirt, and not much else, Baker as Fatou entered the man's dream and began to dance. Baker did the Charleston, a belly dance, mimicked lovemaking, and as her body moved, the phallic rubber bananas moved with her. Baker received enthusiastic approval from audiences and critics alike who, this time, it seems, got the joke and perceived the bawdiness inherent in her banana dance. As one critic put it, "This girl has the genius to let the body make fun of itself."[56]

It was around this time that Josephine met Count Giuseppe Pepito Abatino, a Sicilian man who passed himself off as nobility. In actuality, Abatino was a clerical worker in Rome and probably a gigolo. In business and in love, Josephine and Pepito soon became partners. Despite Baker's numerous sexual escapades, the two stayed together for ten years. The couple never married, but in a 1927 publicity stunt, Josephine, who was still legally married to Willie Baker, claimed that she and Abatino had wed.

With experience at creating his own fictitious identity, Abatino set to work on reconstructing Baker's persona. Under Abatino's tutelage, Josephine learned table manners, etiquette, and how to speak French. By virtue of her association with Abatino and her own thriving career, Josephine's social network expanded. She soon began to withdraw from Paris's emerging black community in Montmarte and added a grave accent to her name.[57] By the end of 1926, under Abatino's management, Josephine was fully capitalizing on her image. In addition to marketing Bakerfix, the pomade she used to slick down her hair, there were perfumes, skin-lightening products, and even Josephine Baker dolls.[58]

La Sirène des tropiques (1927)

While the transformation of Baker's persona, including the adoption of a French identity, is sometimes traced back to the mid–1930s,[59] the *Creolization* of Josephine Baker began shortly after she arrived in Paris. In 1926 Baker apparently appeared in a revue at the Theatre des Capucines as Joséphine de Beauharnais,[60] a white Creole woman who was born and raised on Martinique and became the first wife of Napoleon I. One year later, while still at the Folies-Bergère, in her feature film debut, Josephine Baker played another Creole from the Caribbean in the silent picture *La Sirène des tropiques*, also known as *Siren of the Tropics*.

In 1929, *The Pittsburgh Courier* newspaper began publishing Baker's memoirs in installments. One such installment declared that Maurice DeKobra's script for *Siren of the Tropics* was based on Baker's own life story.[61] Certainly the film's rags-to-riches theme relates to the Baker image, as do particular traits of her character, such as a love for animals and success in the French music halls, but it was not a literal translation of the star's life. The film features Baker as Papitou, the mixed race daughter of an old white colonist. Papitou's mother, presumably an island native, is conveniently never seen nor mentioned.

In Greek mythology sirens are beautiful sea creatures that lure sailors to their death. In today's parlance "siren" refers to an alluring and dangerous woman. Papitou is certainly an alluring character in this film, and near the film's end she comes to the hero's rescue by fatally shooting his rival. Most likely, though, the film's title is a reference to the mixed race women of the former French colony Saint-Domingue now known as Haiti. Mixed race daughters of French planters on Saint-Domingue, rumored to be of extraordinary exotic beauty, were known as "*Les Sirènes*." When the slaves revolted and planters fled the colony for Louisiana, *Les Sirènes* went with them. These free women of color posed such a threat to Louisiana society that in 1786 the governor enacted the *tignon* law, which restricted free women of color from dressing too excessively and required them to cover up their enticing locks of hair with a turban or *tignon*.

Early on in *Siren of the Tropics*, Baker is reunited with Joe Alex, her dance partner from the *La Revue nègre*. The two perform a "primitive" dance together, with moves that include the Charleston. Though Papitou is clearly one of the islanders, her most significant interactions are not with black people, but rather with white men, including Alvarez, a lecherous landlord, and her father, Diego. Because they are behind in rent, Papitou's father overlooks Alvarez's aggressive sexual advances toward his daughter.

Papitou's only love interest in the film, André Berval, is also a white man. André is a French engineer who was sent to the island on business. Though enchanted with Papitou, André has a girlfriend waiting for him back in France. When it's time for André to return home, Papitou stows away on his ship, setting the stage for stunts that make use of Baker's comic sexuality.

One scene, suggestive of Papitou's mixed race and Baker's own emerging amorphous racial identity, finds Papitou hiding out in a coalbunker trying to avoid discovery. She emerges all black. Moments later, after taking refuge in the kitchen's flour bin, Papitou is all white. Next, she steals into a passenger's cabin where she completely disrobes and takes a bath. While splashing about in the tub, Papitou is discovered by a crowd of the ship's passengers and authorities. Though Baker is nude, this scene plays for comedy and speaks more to her character's "primitive" nature than any excessive sexuality. After Papitou is found and determined a stowaway, a benevolent passenger offers to pay her fare to France.

Papitou finds work as an *au pair*, is discovered while dancing for her charges on the streets of Paris, and becomes a star of the musical hall. Eventually she and André reunite. André is happy to see her, but he is engaged to marry another woman. Papitou, a "civilized" woman now, no longer belongs among the island natives, nor does she belong in

France where, despite being successfully colonized, she still cannot find true love (with a white man). *Siren of the Tropics* ends with Papitou dancing away, a broken-hearted misfit, whose only solace is on the stage.

    Siren of the Tropics had its world premiere in December 1927 in Stockholm, Sweden, where it was welcomed by audiences eager to see the "world-famous mulatta" on screen. Local critics, who delighted in the star's graceful dancing and comic contortions, agreed that Baker's presence was the only worthwhile part of an otherwise inferior film.[62] Nearly two years later *Siren of the Tropics* was released in the United States. In September 1929, a portion of the film premiered at a midnight benefit at the Lafayette Theatre in Harlem. The event was attended by New York's mayor, as well as a number of black celebrities.[63] The film had a limited release, and critics stateside, it seems, were not nearly as impressed with *La Baker* as were their French or Swedish counterparts.[64]

    Following *La Sirène des tropiques,* at the beginning of 1928, Josephine left France with Pepito to embark on a world tour. In many places, Baker's presence stirred up controversy. In Vienna a police guard was placed around her after the capital had been flooded with pamphlets denouncing her as the "black devil," and one newspaper likened her to a jezebel. At a performance in Zagreb, audience members, angered by the disparity between Baker's earnings and their own country's economic distress, hurled missiles at her. In Berlin, Nazi critics expressed outrage at the fact that Baker performed on the stage with a blond white woman. In Munich, the police forbade her to perform. In 1929, for the second part of her tour, Josephine went to South America. In Argentina, the president, siding with puritans who objected to her visit, denounced her. And during one performance, an audience made up of puritans and their opponents hurled abuses and firecrackers at one another.[65]

Queen of the Colonies

    When Josephine returned to France at the end of 1929, it soon became evident that Abatino's efforts to make a "lady" out of the clown had paid off. Baker had slimmed down, wore elegant gowns; she could sing, dance, act, and even speak French. With this newfound image, between 1930 and 1932, Baker was engaged at the Casino de Paris to star in a series of flamboyant revues.

    The first of Baker's revues at Casino de Paris was *Paris qui remue,* built around the 1931 Universal Colonial Exposition. When Baker was asked to be Queen of the Exhibition, it seemed that she had finally been accepted by dominant French society. However, when her nomination as Queen of the Colonies was publicly announced, a mass protest ensued. Formal complaints were registered with the French president, the minster of colonies, and the general commander of the exhibition. As a result of the protest, the exhibition withdrew its offer to Baker, but when the fair opened, she toured it as a distinguished guest.[66]

    Publicized as the Tour of the World in One Day, Paris's 1931 world fair was designed to celebrate colonialism and convince the public that modern progress, and the future, depended on the continuation of a world order based on Western imperialism.[67] *Paris Qui Remue* mirrored these aims. In skits that lauded the French colonies, and included props such as Algerian drums, Indian bells, tom-toms from Madagascar, and coconuts from the Congo, Josephine appeared as the quintessential colonial subject.

In one number, dressed in a coolie hat, Josephine played a Vietnamese character and sang what would become one of her trademark songs, "La Petite Tonkinoise" ("The Little Tonkinese"), a song about a little girl from Tonkin, the northern region of Vietnam, who is the mistress of a French colonist. In a sketch called "Ounawa," Baker played another young colonial subject—African, this time—also in love with the colonizer.

Ensuring that Josephine's image did not stray too far from that which originally made her famous, the club's owner, Henri Varner, gave Josephine a cheetah to use in the African sketch and for publicity. Varna told Josephine she could take him everywhere, and so she did.[68] The cheetah, named Chiquita, often photographed with Josephine, was one of the many pets that she adopted over the course of her life.

The song "J'ai deux amours" ("I Have Two Loves"), which was written for Josephine and eventually became her theme song, originated in this African sketch. The song is about the young woman's love for her native country and Paris. Though she sang it in the show as an African woman, in the context of her image, over time, audiences understood her native country to mean the United States. The revue also included a sketch in which she played a Creole native of Martinique.

Paris qui remue was a huge success. Audiences and critics alike were pleased with it, as well as Baker's transformation from a "primitive" black girl to a bona fide artiste. Baker's racial identity was also shifting from one that was fixed and black to something more fluid. She was no longer a black American jazz performer. She was a star of the French music hall. After a brief tour, at the end of 1932, Josephine returned to the Casino de Paris for a new show, *La Joie de Paris*, for which she further assimilated her performance by taking lessons from a Russian ballerina and learning to dance on toe.

One of the biggest hits of the *La Joie de Paris* was a song titled "Si j'étais blanche!" ("If I Were White"). For this number Baker performed wearing a blond wig. With lyrics that extol the joys of whiteness, "Si j'étais blanche!" might be understood as self-referential. Josephine didn't like the color of her skin and made attempts to lighten it with makeup, lemon juice, and milk baths. When she found a photographer who could make her look white she was delighted. Josephine was not fond of her hair, either. During her early years in Paris, she straightened and slicked it down. Not everyone appreciated Josephine's performance of whiteness. Some were disappointed by the break from the "primitive," which the song represented.[69]

Sang Mêlé (Mixed Blood)

While at the Casino de Paris, with the help of co-authors Pepito Abatino and Félix de la Camara, Baker published *Mon sang dans tes veines* (*My Blood in Your Veins*). On one level, in this 1931 novella, Baker seems to be working through the humiliation of her own experiences of racial discrimination. The preface, written by Baker alone, makes several references to her personal life, such as her hometown of St. Louis, her acquaintance with many black girls who were like Joan, the heroine of her story, and an acknowledgment of her own mixed race ancestry.[70] On a broader scale, *Mon sang dans tes veines* can also be viewed as a strike against racist blood discourses once used to justify American policies of segregation, miscegenation, and intermarriage.

Set in the United States, the story centers on Fred, the son of a wealthy white man, and Joan, the daughter of his family's black maid. As children, Fred and Joan are close.

As adults, Joan continues to idolize Fred, even though the two grow apart and Fred is engaged to a Southern racist white woman. When Fred is involved in an accident, Joan gives her blood for a transfusion. Joan's gift turns out to be both a blessing and a curse for Fred. The transfusion saved his life, but Fred is horrified when he learns that he has Joan's "black blood" in his veins. Fred believes he has no choice but to call off his wedding. In response, his fiancée strikes an insulting blow, calling him a black white man.[71] Fred has become an ersatz tragic mulatto, victim of his mixed blood, prohibited from marrying his girlfriend, and destined to a life of sadness.

Although *Mon sang dan tes veines* is a simple and melodramatic tale, it highlights the fundamental role blood once played in racial ideology. Just one year before its publication, Karl Landsteiner received the Nobel Prize in Science for discovering the four human blood groups and demonstrating that transfusions between those in the same blood group, regardless of race, would not result in catastrophe. Nevertheless, in 1941, ten years after Landsteiner's award, when the first American Red Cross blood bank was established, black donors were excluded. When the Red Cross did begin accepting blood from black donors, it adopted a policy of segregating the blood of black and white donors, a policy that remained in effect until 1950.

Ironically, Charles R. Drew, the physician responsible for establishing the first American Red Cross blood bank, was a black man.[72] Thus, well into the mid–20th century, the belief that race was somehow carried in the blood was still popular, and Baker's story is not so far-fetched as it first seems. But no one was interested in Baker's opinions on race at the time. *Mon sang dans tes veines*, which has never been officially translated to English, was a financial failure and did nothing to promote Josephine Baker's career.[73]

Zouzou (1934)

A key development in the construction of Baker's Creole image was her mastery of the French language. In *Zouzou*, a talkie, audiences were able to experience Josephine Baker onscreen speaking and singing in French for the first time. Abatino provided the story on which *Zouzou* is based, and Baker plays the title role. The film's male hero, Zouzou's adopted brother, Jean, is played by the popular French actor Jean Gabin.

When compared to *Siren of the Tropics*, *Zouzou* represents a further distancing from Baker's exotic savage image. It also includes scenes that could never have been shown in an American film during this period, such as Baker, elegantly dressed, and singing against a backdrop of countless admiring, tuxedoed white men. Nevertheless, despite its offer of professional success and assimilation, Zouzou is still excluded from full inclusion in the domestic realm, making race and difference a subtext.

The film begins with a child actress playing Zouzou as a little girl. Zouzou and her white "twin" brother, Jean, are the adopted children of Papa Melé, a white circus worker. The father's name Melé, which is a lot like "*mêlé*," the French word for mixed, symbolizes the family's racial confusion. Melé is a loving father who exhibits his young children in the carnival as freak twins. The exhibition of Zouzou and Jean as twins is just a hoax, though (not unlike that of Sara Baartman's exhibition as a wild savage a century earlier). To account for the fact that Jean is white, and Zouzou is black, Melé proclaims that they were born on a Polynesian island to a Chinese woman and an Indian man who rejected them because of their skin color.

When Zouzou and Jean are late for a performance, their father explains, "Freaks sometimes have the right to be delayed," and he asks the audience to be patient. Melé also points out, "They're not like us." Though he is referring to both siblings, it's really only Zouzou who is not like them. Jean makes his appearance on stage looking like a little Frenchman in a sailor suit. Zouzou's costume, on the other hand, a grass skirt and a floral wreath placed carelessly on her head, is suggestive of difference, as well as their father's Polynesian birth story. "She looks strange," remarks one of the little boys who peeps at her through the trailer window before the show. With his white skin and French name, Jean is assumed to be French. For Zouzou, in addition to her skin color and unusual name, there are other clues that point to her identity as colonial subject.

Once the siblings are adults, Jean, as forecasted by his circus attire, becomes a sailor. In some exotic locale Jean writes home to his sister. Nearby as a topless black woman dances in a grass skirt just, a reminder perhaps of Baker's exotic savage image and the outfit that she wore as a child. Perhaps Zouzou is from a foreign land like this one. Later in the film, Jean's friends refer to Zouzou as a "Creole," and in another scene, she sings of returning home to Haiti. Though the film provides no specific answer as to where Zouzou is from, these details are a perfect match for Baker and, by extension, Zouzou as a generic colonial subject.

Zouzou, much like *Siren of the Tropics*, incorporates incidental aspects of the star's life. A scene of Zouzou as a child applying white face powder in front of a mirror is suggestive of the powder, skin-lightening techniques, and beauty products that Baker herself used to negotiate racism and colorism and might also imply that Zouzou wants to be

Josephine Baker and co-star Jean Gabin in *Zouzou* (1934).

white. Very quickly the freakish, multi-ethnic world of the circus fades away and Zou-zou becomes a young lady. Zouzou is a lone person of color who assimilates effortlessly into the white world that completely surrounds her, yet she can never be white. Zouzou, like Baker's mother in real life, finds work as a laundress. Much to the delight and amusement of her coworkers, Zouzou is an expert at impersonating Miss Barbara, the blonde star of the music hall. Through a series of fortuitous events, Zouzou eventually stands in for Miss Barbara and goes on to become a star in her own right.

Zouzou is permitted to supplant a white woman in show business, but when it comes to love and romance, the film draws the line. After Jean and Zouzou have grown up there is still much love in their small family. Zouzou's affection for her brother, however, borders on the incestuous. She is in love with Jean. For his part, Jean dotes on Zouzou in a brotherly way, but his interest in women lies elsewhere. Making the rejection all the more painful, Jean is in love with Zouzou's best friend Claire, a platinum blond from the laundry shop. As before, Baker's character is left distraught and with nothing to turn to but the stage.

Josephine had wanted a different ending this time. She wanted Zouzou to marry Jean. Abatino, who ignored her wishes, implied that it was not color that prevented Zouzou from winning the love of the film's white hero. Rather, Abatino said, Zouzou, like Josephine, was a star who lived for her work.[74]

La Créole (1934)

In the same year that *Zouzou* was released, Baker accepted a role in a revival of the comic operetta *La Créole*. This little-known opera created by Jacques Offenbach bears some similarity to the world-famous opera *Carmen* by French composer Georges Bizet. Aided by the same librettist, Henri Meilhac, the two operas premiered at the height of European imperialism in 1875. Furthermore, both pieces center on European encounters with exotic peoples, a theme that was already familiar to opera. In *Carmen* and *La Créole*, more specifically, the encounters involve a romance between a European soldier and an "exotic" woman.

The exotic woman in Bizet's opera is Carmen, a Gypsy who falls in love with the Spanish soldier Don José. In *La Créole*, it is Dora, a mixed race Caribbean woman, who forms a romantic relationship with the French soldier René. Where the two operas differ is in the resolution of their respective relationships. Though it would later become something of a cliché, *Carmen*'s tragic ending, which warns that love cannot triumph over racial difference, introduced a new racial ideology to opera. *La Créole*, on the other hand, followed the pattern of earlier 19th-century operas in which the love story was constructed to demonstrate that colonizers could form longstanding bonds with their subjects. Thus, in contrast to Baker's films, which reflect a more modern racial ideology, *La Créole*, with its 19th-century imperialistic view, offers a happy ending for its interracial couple.[75]

La Créole was a significant departure for Baker. The role required her to memorize lines, act on stage, and sing light opera. Furthermore, adding an air of respectability to the Baker image, *La Créole* was performed for family audiences in the legitimate theater, as opposed to the music halls, which catered to mature audiences. As a star vehicle for Baker, *La Créole* underwent several updates. To allow more onstage time for Baker to sing

140 Joséphine Baker dans "La Créole"

Josephine Baker in the comic operetta *La Créole* (1934). Author's collection.

and dance, her character had to be introduced from the very beginning. Therefore, a prologue, which incorporated Baker's own interpretation of Dora, was added.

Other changes, whether intentional or not, brought to the fore racial undertones that were barely evident in the original version of the operetta. For example, a second

Joséphine Baker dans "La Creole" 121

Josephine Baker in the comic operetta *La Créole* (1934). Author's collection.

interracial couple was inserted into the action, a soldier, Cartahut, and Créme fouettee, Dora's black nanny. More songs were added, while others were moved around. One comic song, "Les fariniers, les charbonniers" ("The Millers, The Coalmen"), borrowed from another Offenbach operetta, brings to mind the scene from *Siren of the Tropics* in which, trying to avoid discovery, Papitou concealed herself in a flour bin and then a coal bin. "Les fariniers, les charbonniers" tells the story of a woman involved in a love triangle with two men. One is a coalman (charbonnier), and the other is a flour-covered miller (farinier). The two lovers are identical except in one respect: one is all black and the other is all white. To avoid any trouble, the woman constantly has to brush herself off. While in its original context, the song might have hinted at race; in *La Créole*, with Josephine Baker in the leading role, it took on explicit racial meaning.[76]

In the updated version of *La Créole* four people are caught up in love triangles: Dora, Réne, Antoinette, and Frontignac. Dora, the only non-white person in this entanglement, is supposed to marry Frontignac but is in love with René. Antoinette is supposed to marry René but is in love with Frontignac. In Offenbach's original version, the white couple, Antoinette and Frontignac, was the first to proclaim their love. Remarkably, in this revival, the interracial relationship was given top priority; Dora and René are the first to reveal their love. Thus, Baker, as Dora, was presented as a worthy rival to Antoinette, the blondest of blondes. Dora's mixed race position invited comparison, not only to the white woman, but also to the other exotic woman, Crème fouette. Dora was described as "the little Creole," while Créme fouette was described as "la négrillonne" (pickaninny).[77]

Opening night was December 15, 1934. In interviews leading up to the opening Baker told reporters that she intended "to be a Creole, just like the *other* Josephine, Napoleon's wife." When the big night arrived, much to the director's chagrin, Josephine decided to put on pale makeup to get into character. When the director remarked that the makeup made her look like a clown, Josephine retorted, "Creoles are light-skinned." The director shot back saying that, as far as he and the public were concerned, Creoles are black.[78]

Just as Sam T. Jack's Creole Show sparked debate over the meaning of "Creole" in Louisiana, so, too, did Josephine's whiteface performance in Offenbach's operetta. While the French press generally praised Baker's portrayal of Dora,[79] it also took the opportunity to question whether a Creole was a *mulâtresse* or a white person born in the colonies. Some writers thought Baker was just right for the role, especially when compared with the original Dora, Anna Judic, a white actress in blackface. Another observer noted that Baker had lightened her skin to the same degree that Judic had darkened hers. Others remarked that with her evolution toward opera, Baker was becoming more culturally white and that her skin was fading in transition with her art.[80]

Princesse Tam-Tam (1935)

Compared to *Zouzou*, which some consider the star's most worthwhile film, Baker's next feature, *Princesse Tam-Tam*, takes a regressive turn. Whereas Baker's first two films accept her characters' difference, to a degree, *Princesse Tam-Tam* first fetishizes difference and then rejects it altogether. Written by Abatino, *Princesse Tam-Tam* features Baker as a colonial subject with a fluid racial identity. She begins the film as Alwina, a North African shepherd girl, and is transformed into Princess Tam-Tam, an Indian princess.

Like her previous films, *Princesse Tam-Tam* incorporates random biographical references, and it seems quite likely that this tale of a young woman "civilized" by a Frenchman was inspired by Baker's relationship with Abatino. The white Frenchman in *Princesse Tam-Tam* is Max de Mirecort, played by Albert Préjean. Max is a famous author who is suffering from marital problems and writer's block. At his manager's suggestion, Max travels to Africa for a change of scenery. This is not sub-Saharan Africa, however. The African scenes in *Princess Tam-Tam* were shot on location in Tunisia, and the Africans in this film are Arabs, as is Alwina, who hides among the cacti, carries sheep on her shoulders, and steals oranges from the street vendors in town.

When Alwina is caught trespassing on Max's property, Dar, Max's servant, played by French actor Georges Péclet in blackface, is about to whip Alwina for her crime, but Max intervenes. To stimulate his creative juices for a modern "interracial story" Max decides to conduct an experiment with Alwina. He intends to scrub her off, educate her, pretend to be in love with her, and then see how she will react. Max oversees Alwina's instruction in the French ways of movement, manners, and etiquette, and he helps her transform from urchin to royalty.

Meanwhile, back in Paris, Max's wife, Lucie, is dating the Maharaja of Datane—another actor in blackface—who is rumored to have incredible sex appeal. Thus, at the same time that Max is feigning interest in Alwina to further the interracial story he's writing, back home his wife is carrying on with a maharaja from the Orient. When word of his wife's latest affair reaches Max, Alwina's training is accelerated. Having learned how to dress, walk, play piano, and do math, Alwina travels to France with her married lover, who introduces her to French high society as Princess Tam-Tam.

Mimicking Baker's own life, Alwina becomes the subject of the press, photographers, painters, and sculptors. Hinting, perhaps, at the brief affair that Baker is rumored to have had with a maharaja,[81] Alwina's portrait is seen hanging in the maharaja's home. All the attention elicits jealousy from Lucie who comes up with a plan to expose Alwina

Josephine Baker captures the attention of the Maharajah of Datane, played by Jean Galland in dark makeup, in *Princesse Tam-Tam* (1935).

as a "vulgar tart." Lucie asks the maharaja to throw a party for the princess. The event resembles an elaborate nightclub production. When the African drums begin to play, Alwina, who has been plied with champagne by Lucie's friend, cannot resist. Partygoers are thrilled when she strips off her dress, throws away her shoes, and begins a spirited dance. Alwina's "primitive" nature is laid bare. Max and Lucie are reunited, and Alwina realizes that she is really in love with Dar and must return home.

Given Abatino's penchant as film writer for conflating Josephine Baker, the person with her star image, one has to wonder whether the underlying message of the film is a commentary on his relationship with Baker. Without warning, like a cruel joke, the film's conclusion reveals that Alwina's metamorphosis never actually happened. The entire charade was merely a sequence out of Max's novel. Back in Africa, Alwina and Dar have a baby. In the villa left to them by Max they are surrounded by an assortment of animals, roaming freely inside the house.

In the final shot, a donkey can be seen eating the cover of Max's book, which reads "Civilization." In a departure from Baker's first two films, *Princesse Tam-Tam* seems to have second thoughts about whether the colonial savage can be "civilized." Though Alwina gets a man, Baker was displeased that the man was a servant. If Alwina couldn't have the white man, Baker thought that her consolation should have been the wealthy maharaja.[82]

During the 1931 run of *Paris qui remue*, Noble Sissle paid Josephine Baker a visit. Sissle asked Josephine if she was interested in doing a new version of *Shuffle Along*. Josephine declined. She offered no reason to Sissle, but her autobiography explains that she turned him down because she thought she could fight racism more effectively as a black star in a white show versus an all-black show. Admittedly, when Sissle departed her changing room and a dresser rushed in with feathers and a coolie hat, Baker wondered whether her roles in the French shows were any more progressive.[83]

Four years later, when Abatino negotiated a contract with *Ziegfeld Follies*, Josephine would get the opportunity to counter racism in a white show in her native country. Having been absent from America for ten years Josephine Baker was ill-prepared for such a daunting a task. Inspired by the Folies Bergère, *Ziegfeld Follies* were a series of revues that featured well-known talent, such as W.C. Fields, Bert Williams, Eddie Cantor and Fannie Brice in comedy skits and musical numbers.

This American version of the Folies Bergère was the brainchild of theatrical producer Florenz Ziegfeld, who got his start in the theater business in the 1890s, representing the European musical comedy star Anna Held. Ziegfeld cleverly promoted Held as the ideal desirable white female. Publicizing the "fact" that Held bathed in milk was one of the strategies he employed to simultaneously connect her image with both sexuality and whiteness. To maintain this image of the ideal woman, Ziegfeld also had to work hard at concealing Held's Polish-Jewish identity.[84]

The original *Follies* ran on Broadway from 1907 to 1931, and the highlight was its impressive display of "ideal" women, Ziegfeld Girls, parading around in scant costumes. By 1922, the Glorified American Girl was the *Follies* official theme, and Ziegfeld was known as "the Glorifier of the American Girl."[85] Ziegfeld manufactured the image of whiteness in the Glorified American Girl by exerting influence on the Girls behind the scenes, through promotion and publicity, and in the production itself. Offstage, the Ziegfeld Girls were reportedly rewarded for not getting suntans during the summer months. In the press, Ziegfeld made the claim that all his showgirls were "native" Americans, whose ancestors, going back at least two or three generations, were born in the United

States. Thus, in the early 20th century, the Ziegfeld Girl was one of the sites where white-ness was being constructed along gendered lines.[86]

On stage at the *Follies*, African American comedy, including blackface, was used to establish difference. The *Follies* also made use of the white showgirl's counterpart, the Creole Beauty of the all-black revue, by including numbers with Ziegfeld Girls in brownface or café au lait makeup. The light brown makeup signified a daring sexuality that the "inherently pure" Ziegfeld Girls could not display without a mask. Borrowing between the two racial performances went both ways. In 1922, the same year that the Glorified American Girl reached its pinnacle, *Strut Miss Lizzie* touted itself as "Glorifying the Creole Beauty."[87]

Josephine Baker was the only black woman to ever appear in the *Follies*. In 1932, Florenz Ziegfeld passed away, leaving his wife, Billie Burke, as one of the show's producers. With the show's history of glorifying whiteness, and Fannie Brice already established as the show's comic star, there was little space for a black female superstar. Baker's numbers, inspired by her French music hall persona, cast her as colonial subject.

In the first act of the show, Josephine wore a variation of the Folies banana skirt she had worn ten years prior. Over the years, the banana skirt had seen several iterations, but this one, which substituted pointed tusks for fruit, transformed a costume that was naughty and playful into something sinister and dangerous. In another number, dressed as an East Indian woman in a flashy sari, Baker sang and danced with white men who were also dressed to the nines. A final number, for which she wore a shimmering heavy mesh dress, incorporated ballet, and fantasies of her lovers, both white and black. During at least one performance, this number, which ended with Josephine being carried offstage by four handsome young white men, was met with total silence; no one clapped.[88]

While the sight of Josephine Baker as colonial subject made perfect sense to Parisians, in America, it was disturbing. Despite the glamorous costumes, extravagant settings, and expert choreography, audiences did not take kindly to any hint of glorifying a black American girl. For the most part, neither did the mainstream critics. In the press reactions ranged from lukewarm to outright disdain. One critic, who found her performance "too exotic" to even write about, compared her notoriety to Harriet Beecher Stowe's tragic mulatto Eliza in *Uncle Tom's Cabin*.[89] Brooks Atkinson, theater critic for *The New York Times*, said that Baker's contribution was the singular disappointment of the show and also opined that the star had "refined her art to the point that there is nothing left in it."[90] Perhaps the most vitriolic appraisal came from *Time* magazine. In addition to insulting Baker's art, and the French for its appreciation of it, the review referred to the star as a "Negro wench," a term once reserved for slave women.[91]

Aside from the bad reviews, perhaps one of the most humiliating experiences that Baker had with white America during this trip was being turned away from her hotel. While stories differ as to what actually happened after she disembarked the French ocean liner *Normandie*, most agree that Josephine was deeply pained as a result. One source declares that at the Hotel St. Moritz, where they had reservations, both Baker and Abatino were turned away when hotel employees realized that the "Countess" was a black woman.[92] Another biographer says that they checked in, but Baker had to use the service entrance.[93] Baker's son claims that Abatino moved into the hotel leaving Baker, her maid, and two close friends to fend for themselves.[94]

Upon her return to America, Baker also met with resistance from blacks. In an article Baker wrote for a Paris newspaper (with the aid of a ghostwriter), Baker declared that after being denounced by the Harlem press, she was snubbed in public by blacks and became the recipient of hate mail.[95] Though Baker did spend some time in Harlem during her 1930s visit, it seems that she insisted upon speaking French and preferred to spend her time with white theater people and celebrities. This apparently elicited resentment from some blacks and a feeling that perhaps she deserved all the snubbing she had received for trying to disown her blackness.[96]

The unfavorable response to her performance in the *Follies* meant that there would be no future for her in Hollywood, an ambition that she had very much hoped for upon her return to America. Any film offers that might have been discussed were retracted when the reviews came out. Baker blamed Abatino for her failures and disappointments in New York. After a violent fight, Abatino returned to Paris without her. That was the last time they saw each other. Abatino died of cancer shortly after his return to Paris. When Josephine returned to Paris in June 1936, she had a new contract with the Folies-Bergère.

Josephine continued to perform, yet without Abatino her career never had the same straight-ahead momentum. Her stage persona continued to evolve, and eventually she established a legitimate French identity. Unlike her screen characters, Josephine would get a white husband, two of them, in fact. Baker's first white husband, Jean Lion, was a Jewish French businessman. The two wed in 1937, and shortly thereafter Josephine became a French citizen. One year later Josephine filed for divorce from Lion. By 1940 the Nazis had banned blacks and Jews from the French theater. While many people were attempting to flee Europe for America, Josephine became a member of the Free French forces, assisting an officer in the French military intelligence service carry information in and out of the country. In 1961, she was awarded the Légion d'Honneur for her wartime services.

Josephine Baker's final feature film, *Fausse Alerte* (1945), released in the United States as *The French Way*, is a wartime romantic comedy. As before, her character, Zazou, is an entertainer, much like herself. In addition to entertaining, Zazou's primary function is to further the romance of the young white couple at the center of the film. In contrast to her previous films, in *Fausse Alerte* racial difference seems to play no part. In fact, in one scene, a character who comes looking for Zazou in her apartment building mistakes a white Frenchwoman for her mother. Though it was not a star vehicle for her, *Fausse Alerte* does suggest that Josephine Baker had become fully French.

In 1947, Josephine married bandleader Jo Bouillon, and in the mid–1950s, the couple began adopting children. To prove that all races could live together in harmony, their original plan was to adopt four children: one black, one white, one yellow, and one red. Josephine's need to adopt children, however, became an obsession. According to her son, Josephine ordered children as one would order a take-out dinner.[97] Having played the preeminent colonial subject on stage and screen, Baker went on to play the role of colonial mother at her castle home, Les Milandes. All told, Josephine Baker adopted twelve children from places such as Japan, Senegal, Algeria, and Venezuela, and she created her own version of a multi-ethnic colony, which she called her Rainbow Tribe.

On April 8, 1975, at the age of 68, Josephine performed one last time in Paris, in a retrospective review, *Joséphine à Bobino*, which celebrated her fifty years in show business. Four days later, on April 12, 1975, she was pronounced dead. On the day of her funeral, thousands of mourners crowded the streets of Paris to say their farewells. Josephine Baker is the only American-born woman to have received a French state funeral complete with a twenty-one-gun-salute.

2

Nina Mae McKinney

Dichotomy of a Hollywood Black Woman

I will not act in another Hollywood picture until the prejudice is removed against colored actors in dramatic roles. Personally, I will not accept any maid parts. I am not a maid and will not act one.[1]   —Nina Mae McKinney

Not long after Josephine Baker starred in *Siren of the Tropics*, Nina Mae McKinney became one of the first African Americans to sign a long-term contract with a major Hollywood studio. Nina Mae was discovered singing in a Harlem church choir by the African American dancer, choreographer, and producer Leonard Harper. Harper had a reputation for choosing pretty, shapely chorus girls for his revues, and by the age of fifteen, Nina Mae was one of them.[2] At just sixteen years of age, McKinney landed a groundbreaking lead role in MGM's first all-black cast, all-talking picture, *Hallelujah* (1929). Dubbed the black Greta Garbo, a bronze siren, and a jungle Lorelei, Nina Mae McKinney was mainstream Hollywood's first sexy black movie star.

Beginning in the 1970s with the women's movement, a strain of feminist film theory developed, which employed Freud's psychoanalytic Madonna-whore complex as a means for understanding the function of white women and sexuality in film. Simply put, the Madonna-whore dichotomy refers to men's perception of women as either virginal saints or degraded prostitutes. In terms of film, some have argued that the white male-dominated movie industry used this dichotomy to socialize and regulate the behaviors of (white) women. To convey a film's message, an actress might portray a good girl or the bad girl. In some cases, such as Julia Roberts in *Pretty Woman* (1990), for example, the character can start out as a prostitute, be rescued (by a man), and fashioned into a Madonna.[3]

When it comes to black women, the history of representation in Hollywood presents a similar but slightly different dichotomy. Rather than the Madonna and the whore, black women in early mainstream film were constructed through the mammy and the whore or the mammy and the jezebel, a dichotomy that has its roots in antebellum society when slaves lived in close, often intimate, proximity to their white owners and societal order had to be maintained.[4]

The mammy was initially conceived as middle-aged, overweight, dark-skinned, and clothed from head to toe. As such, she was not considered an object of desire; she was asexual. Among other things, mammy functioned as a means to conceal white men's sexual desires for, and liaisons with, black women. Undistracted by romance, the mammy was free to fulfill her true purpose: to serve white people and nurture their children. In her many incarnations, the subservient mammy's devotion to whites has also stood for a sign of loyalty to and nostalgia for the South.[5]

On the one hand, in pre–Civil War America, white men's desire for black women was disavowed and concealed via the mammy. On the other hand, their lust for black women was very real and often acted upon. Enter the jezebel, the stereotype of a morally loose woman, the seductress who justified white men's sexual exploitation of black women.[6] Almost any black woman could be a jezebel. However, after D.W. Griffith's impactful silent film *The Birth of a Nation* (1915) and its portrayal of Lydia Brown, it seems it was the mulatto woman who became the popular face of the scheming, seductive, morally loose black woman in film.

Griffith's film also had an overweight, dark-skinned character known as "Mammy-Faithful Servant," played by an actress in blackface. With the mulatto woman as jezebel, and the dark-skinned, stout woman as mammy, Griffith's film illuminated the issues of skin color that are entangled in the asexual mammy-hypersexual jezebel dichotomy of black womanhood. Underscoring how deeply ingrained black stereotypes were within early Hollywood culture, *Hallelujah*'s director, King Vidor, said in an interview during the 1970s that thinking differently about the ways in which black people in film could be portrayed was a momentous development, second only to "going to the Moon and jet travel."[7]

Very early on, African Americans were well aware of Hollywood's demeaning representational practices. In 1935, by which time talking pictures were the norm, the *Afro-American* newspaper pointed out that blacks in the industry were not considered actors like their white counterparts, but rather types who were classified according to skin color, age, size, and speech pattern.[8] Within the Hollywood studio system all actors, regardless of race, were encouraged in the direction of a certain "type."[9] However, the types available to African Americans were even more limiting and generally more demeaning than those available to white actors.

For black women, there were essentially two types of roles available: mammy/maid or jezebel/whore. Typically, actresses were associated with one type or the other, and prior to the 1950s, that usually meant the mammy. Hattie McDaniel, for example, had a lucrative career playing mammy roles for nearly two decades. In 1940, for her role as a character known only as "Mammy" in *Gone with the Wind* (1939), McDaniel became the first African American to win an Oscar. McDaniel's win in the Best Supporting Actress category ensured her place as the immortalization of the American cinematic mammy.

Nina Mae McKinney's great cinematic achievement, as the character Chick in *Hallelujah*, represents the other available type, the jezebel. Within the narrow constraints of early Hollywood ideology, however, mammy predominated. There was little space for any other image of black womanhood to exist. Consequently, McKinney spent a good deal of her career performing in theaters and nightclubs at home and abroad. Nevertheless, against the odds, after *Hallelujah*, McKinney did manage to find two significant roles in mainstream films that had integrated casts and were outside the bounds of the mammy-jezebel dichotomy.

McKinney's next important role after *Hallelujah* was as a Creole hotelkeeper on a Caribbean island in *Safe in Hell* (1931). The other was in the British film *Sanders of the River* (1935), where she played the wife of an African chief opposite Paul Robeson. In her penultimate film, *Pinky* (1949), McKinney returned to playing a jezebel type, but by this time, she had already been relegated to playing bit parts as a maid. Taken on the whole, Nina Mae McKinney's Hollywood film career embodies both sides of the mammy-jezebel dichotomy.

The details of Nina Mae McKinney's early life are sketchy. She was born in 1912 in Lancaster, South Carolina, where her family had lived for generations. Her mother, Georgie Crawford, left Nina May in the care of Mary Ann McKinney, her paternal grandmother. At that time, Mary Ann, who was born before emancipation, was a servant for the prominent Leroy Springs family. Around the age of 12, Nina moved to New York to live with her mother, Georgie, and stepfather, James E. Maynor.[10]

While singing in a chorus at Harlem's Mother Zion Methodist Episcopal Church, McKinney was discovered by Leonard Harper.[11] A dancer, choreographer, and prolific producer, Harper was well known for his association with stylish revues at nightclubs and theaters. *Tan Town Topics*, one such example staged by Harper, played at the Plantation Club in 1923 and featured Ethel Waters, Josephine Baker, and a chorus line of very light-skinned dancers.[12] By 1925 Harper had his own dance studio in Times Square where he taught white performers black dance styles.[13] Later in his career, Harper went on to stage revues at the Cotton Club and the Apollo Theatre.

In 1927, Harper produced a revue called *Midnight Steppers*, which featured as principals Joe Byrd, the Alabama Four dancers, and the popular comedian Billy Higgins. McKinney also appeared in this revue. Billed simply as "Nina May," she was described as a "petite chorus lady" who sang "Muddy Waters,"[14] a tune penned by white songwriters of Tin Pan Alley in 1926 and made popular by Bessie Smith. That same year, McKinney appeared at Harlem's Lafayette Theatre in another Harper production, *Highflyers of 1927*.[15]

In describing how McKinney was selected for *Hallelujah*, King Vidor recalled in his autobiography that she "was third from the right in the chorus" of *Blackbirds of 1928*.[16] This show featured tap-dancer Bill "Bojangles" Robinson, comic Mantan Moreland, and singer Aida Ward, but its star was Adelaide Hall, who had replaced Florence Mills after her untimely death. Hall performed "Diga Diga Doo," a peppy song about the joys of interracial sex with "native" people, written by the white songwriting duo Jimmy McHugh and Dorothy Fields. Wearing not much more than a scanty feather skirt, Hall elicited an angry reaction from a few white men in the audience one night, causing a near riot.[17] Not long after Hall's performance, "Diga Diga Doo" became associated with Duke Ellington at the Cotton Club. Years later, it was sung by Lena Horne in the film *Stormy Weather* (1943).

As for Nina Mae McKinney, aside from press reports used to publicize Vidor's film, no other information has surfaced regarding her involvement in *Blackbirds of 1928*.[18] Nina Mae McKinney was one of countless young chorus girls of the 1920s. With her role in *Hallelujah* she became the agent by which both the stage preference for light skinned women and the fictional mulatto woman as jezebel was bequeathed to the talking picture era.

Hallelujah (1929)

Director King Vidor was born in Texas in 1894. Memories of growing up in the South and experiences at his father's sawmills were the motivation behind his desire to make a film about African Americans. In particular, Vidor was interested in creating a drama that would bring together his personal interest in the "sincerity and fervor" of black people's religious expression and the "simplicity of their sexual drives."[19]

Vidor had previously directed successful silent pictures for MGM, most notably *The Big Parade* (1925) and *The Crowd* (1928). For several years he had attempted to get the go-ahead from the studio to make a picture about black Americans, using not whites in blackface, but an all-black cast. In his autobiography, he claimed that studio executives repeatedly denied him that opportunity on the grounds that such a film could never be shown in the white theaters of the South.[20] While the concern proved to be a valid one, years later, in an interview with Frank Manchel, Vidor admitted that MGM was really afraid that the picture would attract "a big bunch of blacks" to the theater.[21]

After three years of being turned down, Vidor offered to invest his salary in the picture. To this offer, Nicholas Schenck, chairman of MGM's parent company, responded, "If that's the way you feel about it, I'll let you make a picture about whores."[22] And so Vidor was given the green light to make his film about whores or, more precisely, one whore. Vidor began the talent search for his film just one year after Warner Bros. released *The Jazz Singer* (1927), a film about a Jewish blackface minstrel entertainer. This part-silent, part-talking picture, which featured synchronized sound in its musical numbers, ushered in the era of the talking picture.

The cast for *Hallelujah* was found mostly in Chicago and New York. The role of main character Zeke went to Brown University graduate Daniel Haynes, who was understudying for Jules Bledsoe in the original stage production of *Show Boat*. To find Chick, the woman who would lead Zeke into temptation, Vidor rented a hall in New York where he auditioned hundreds of chorines. The choice was narrowed down to two women, Clara "Honey" Brown and Nina Mae McKinney.[23] Vidor chose Honey Brown, who travelled to Memphis with the rest of the cast when filming began.

During the early stages of filming, a decision was made to replace Honey Brown. Newspapers reported that Brown fell ill. Some even went as far to say that she had died from her illness. The real reason for Brown's departure, as revealed in telegrams between Vidor and MGM's production head Irving Thalberg, was that Thalberg, after seeing the rushes—prints of early camera footage—decided that Brown was not sexy enough. Vidor defended his casting decision, but Thalberg, who objected to Brown's "certain ugliness particularly around her mouth" and "her flat-chestedness," had more clout, and Brown had to go.[24]

In response to the story that was circulating in the press about her demise, Brown was forced to make a public statement to dispel the rumor. *The Chicago Defender* printed one such statement accompanied by a photo of Honey Brown striking a sexy pose on the set with King Vidor and Daniel Haynes.[25] Thalberg's comments concerning Brown's appearance aside, what appears evident from the photo is that Honey Brown did not conform to white beauty standards as nearly as did Nina Mae McKinney.

Although Thalberg was satisfied with the substitution of McKinney for Brown, he was concerned that her hair was too straight. Nevertheless, he was confident it was a "problem" that could be resolved.[26] It seems likely that McKinney's light complexion was perceived as another problem that needed to be fixed. In some of the film's scenes and publicity photos, especially when compared with other images of the star, it is apparent that she was treated with dark makeup. McKinney's approximation to whiteness made her a believable object of desire, but it also confounded Hollywood's construct of race.

The part of the other woman vying for Zeke's attention, the good-natured, plain and pious Missy Rose, went to the dark-skinned blues singer Victoria Spivey. The casting of chorus girl McKinney as Chick, and blues singer Spivey as her rival for Zeke's affections, happens to coincide with the meaning accorded to black women performers of the day by blacks themselves, including such writers as Sterling Brown and Zora Neal Hurston. Sterling Brown's poem "Cabaret (1927, Black & Tan Chicago)" speaks to a schism between newly urban blacks and their Southern rural roots.

Brown's poem critiques popular black jazz entertainers' complicity in their own exploitation by white audiences. Specifically, Brown likens light-skinned chorus girls to slaves on the auction block and belles of the quadroon balls. Brown also rendered the light-skinned chorus girl as dualistic. She signified the liberation and possibilities of the city, but she was also the incarnate reminder of white subjugation and black people's participation in the dilution of their culture. In contrast to the chorus girl stood the dark-skinned blues singer, who represented the rural South and authentic blackness.[27]

Zeke, the man who can't seem to choose between the two women, is from the South, and lives with his parents, Mammy and Parson, as well as numerous siblings, including a brother named Spunk, and Missy Rose, who has been raised alongside Zeke as a foster-sister. The family grows cotton for a living, and Zeke meets Chick for the first time while on a trip with Spunk to sell their family's harvest. When Zeke first spies Chick, she is wearing high-heel black shoes, an abundance of jewelry, and a knee-length black silk dress with two dice embroidered on the bodice. In addition to associating her with the gambling that will soon lead to tragedy, Chick's attire suggests sexual abandon and an urban life that stands in direct opposition to Zeke's rural home and family.

McKinney dances and sings "Swanee Shuffle," a song written specifically for her character by Irving Berlin. One imagines Zeke, whose interest is immediately piqued, has never seen anyone quite like Chick before. Chick feigns interest in Zeke so that she and her boyfriend Hot Shot can cheat Zeke out of his family's crop money. When Zeke realizes he's been conned, a fight breaks out, during which Hot Shot's gun is discharged and Spunk is shot and killed.

After returning home with his brother's corpse and no money, Zeke is called upon by God and becomes an itinerant preacher. During his travels Zeke encounters Chick once again. She shows up at a revival meeting and begins to heckle him. Surrounded by throngs of believers and taken by the power of God, or the sight of a powerful black man, perhaps, Chick suddenly decides that she wants to be saved. The resulting river baptism scene and the evening Jubilee revival afterward culminate precisely into Vidor's stated aim, a compelling enactment of the comingling of repressed sexual desire and religious hysteria.

At her baptism in the river, Chick is completely overtaken by the spirit and collapses in Zeke's arms. While his family members and followers cast suspicious looks, Zeke carries Chick to a tent and lays her on a cot. He then kneels on the ground next to her and envelops her with an embrace. All the while, Chick is sobbing and moaning. The highly charged carnal moment is interrupted when Mammy enters the tent. Mammy sends Zeke away and scolds Chick.

Later that night, at the revival, believers are singing, jumping out of their seats, and waving their hands about. Chick joins in the worship, making her way up to the front to get closer to Zeke. The tension builds. Some people have fallen out on the floor. Chick takes Zeke's hand up to her mouth and bites it, then dances her way out the door. Zeke,

Mammy confronts jezebel in King Vidor's *Hallelujah* (1929). From left, Fanny Belle DeKnight, Daniel Haynes and Nina Mae McKinney. John Springer Collection/Corbis Historical/Getty Images.

unable to resist, goes after her, leaving behind his congregation, his family, and poor Missy Rose, to whom he was betrothed. Months later we learn that the couple are living together "in sin," and Zeke, who has given up preaching, has taken a job as a laborer in a sawmill.

Chick soon becomes bored with domestic life and wants to get back together with Hot Shot. This leads to a chase scene with Zeke on foot, running after Hot Shot and Chick who have fled in a horse and buggy. Chick takes a fatal spill from the buggy. Right before Chick's demise, Zeke holds her in his arms and declares his love for her, the only tender moment of love between the couple that is not overshadowed by feelings of sexual-religious excitement. After Chick dies in his arms, Zeke pursues Hot Shot and strangles him to death. For his crime, Zeke serves a little time on a chain gang but is soon paroled and reunited with his family, where all is forgiven.

A sincere, albeit inherently prejudiced African American theme, the downfall of a preacher, the conflation of religion and sex, all were provocative subject matter, and any one of these ideas alone would have been reason enough for the film not to be made. In 1929, however, Hollywood was still in its fledgling state. The synchronization of sound was just coming into its own, and the black person's voice was believed to be especially adaptable to it. More importantly, the broader language of film had not yet been co-opted by the Motion Picture Producers and Distributors of America ("MPPDA"), which did not formally adopt its Production Code until one year after *Hallelujah* was released and did not enforce it until several years after that.

Written by a Jesuit priest and a prominent Roman Catholic layman, the Production Code was a sophisticated document that sought to turn Hollywood into the sentinel of American morality by listing numerous prohibitions relating to portrayals of illegal activities, obscenity, profanity, race, sex, and miscegenation. Though it was established in 1930, studios mostly ignored the Code until 1934 when the Production Code Administration Office ("PCA")—also known as the Hays Office after MPPDA president William Hays—began to aggressively enforce it.

The PCA got its authority from the MPPDA board of directors, the bankers and financial backers behind the film industry. In 1934, Joseph Breen, a former journalist and influential Catholic layperson, was named chief of the PCA. Breen's strict enforcement of the Code resulted in studio compliance and consequently made him a hugely influential figure in American popular culture. Yet before Breen came along there was a brief window of time, at the dawn of the talking era, during which the content of Hollywood films was somewhat unrestrained.

The new sound technology, interest in black culture sparked by the Harlem Renaissance, and the atmosphere of relatively free expression during the pre–Code era combined to make *Hallelujah* a pioneering film. Until the 1940s, the only other significant black-cast films were *Hearts in Dixie* (1929), which has one white character among its otherwise all-black cast, and *Green Pastures* (1936), which has an all-black cast. Although the MPPDA had yet to harness its full control, it still attempted to exert influence over *Hallelujah*.

Concerned, for example, about Zeke's transgression as a preacher, MPPDA official Colonel Jason Joy advised MGM that the film might be less objectionable if Zeke were not portrayed as a weak character. Joy was also concerned about the sex in Vidor's film. He was afraid that the image of a strong black man exhibiting passion and desire would inevitably lead to the rape of white women. When it came to the hypersexual mulatto Chick, however, Joy seemed to take no issue.[28]

The MPPDA also cautioned Vidor and MGM about use of the "n-word" in the *Hallelujah* script. Just as they ignored the advice regarding Zeke's portrayal, MGM and Vidor also ignored the caution regarding racial slurs. It was left to the cast to amend the language in Vidor's script, which, according to the film's musical director, Eva Jessye, included copious racial epithets. In her published insider's story of the production, Jessye reported that although the cast regularly disagreed and quarreled among themselves, when it came to the script, they were united in their stand against the use of words that would reflect poorly on African Americans.[29]

As the film contains no use of the "n-word" nor of the terms "pickaninny," "darky," or "coon," all of which, she says, were listed in the original script, we can conclude that the cast was successful in their resistance. With regard to Chick, however, epithets that refer to her skin color and mixed race heritage remain. Mammy, in addition to referring to Chick as a "she-devil," berates her as an "ol' yaller hussy." Near the beginning of the film, Chick's on-again, off-again boyfriend, Hot Shot, also refers to her as "high-yaller." A derisive term, "high-yaller" once implied that light-skinned mulattoes were considered illegitimate and trashy if they could not demonstrate respectable family ties.[30] Presumably, the slurs remained because they were not deemed offensive by the cast, or perhaps because of Chick's duplicitous nature they seemed justified.

Addressing the studio's fears about large numbers of blacks showing up at the theater, in August 1929, *Hallelujah* had a simultaneous, segregated premiere in New York: one downtown at the Embassy for whites and one at the Lafayette in Harlem for blacks. *Hallelujah* was not a big box office success, but in the main it received favorable reviews and accolades, including an Academy Award nomination for best director.

In the African American community, the film was also praised, especially by those who believed it had political significance that would translate into future gains for blacks in all arenas. Illinois Congressman Oscar De Priest, the *New York Amsterdam News*, and W.E.B. Du Bois, writing for *The Crisis*, all came out in support of the film.[31] Dissenters denounced the film as a mockery of blacks and their religious practices. "There is a cultured, respectable devout Christian, progressive life [in the South] which Vidor probably never saw," said a critic in the *New York News*. Others said that had *Hallelujah* depicted a different ethnic group it would never have played in theaters.[32]

Black audiences, at least those in Harlem and Baltimore, had a very different reaction from the prominent critics and black leaders. During *Hallelujah's* most serious and tragic scenes, they burst into fits of laughter.[33] Vidor had two possible explanations for this. The first was "the negro's merriment at tragedy," which, he expounded, was only an initial and temporary response. Vidor's other explanation was that "the Harlem negro does not know his Southern brother as he is so far removed, and as the Northerner is so intent in living like a white man."[34] Vidor's statement, like his film, implies that the African American's natural place is in the South. The Northern black man, rather than being true to himself, is merely imitating the white man. As such, according to Vidor, blacks in Harlem laughed at the film because they did not recognize their authentic selves.

Writing for the *Afro-American*, Richard Matthews also related the audience laughter to its identification, or lack thereof, with the film's characters. Matthews compared the black audience to a person viewing himself in a trick mirror. "He realizes that the thing is himself; although it is exaggerated, and he can't help laughing at himself."[35] Matthews did not find the film objectionable and said that aside from the cotton scenes it could have been filmed in Baltimore.

In contrast to Vidor, who believed the Northern Negro was far removed from the South, Matthews, in voicing his suspicion that some members of the audience had "a lot of that same cotton in their hair,"[36] suggests that they are closer to Southern life than they would like to admit or perhaps care to remember. Aided by its absence of white characters, what is not evident in *Hallelujah* is the South as home to segregation and a legally sanctioned system that diminished, humiliated, terrorized, and denied blacks their basic freedoms.

Matthews was also quite sympathetic to Zeke's character. He found Zeke an improvement over the unethical preachers residing in his hometown, who were much more adept than Zeke at keeping their trysts hidden from their congregation. By comparison, Matthews' appraisal of the mulatto dancer Chick is especially harsh. Likening her to a parasite, he found Chick to be typical of the women who "infest" local cabarets and Zeke merely the victim of her sexual guile.[37] Matthews' assessment of McKinney's character illustrates the disfavor to which the chorus girl had fallen and sums up the film's handling of the two characters, Chick and Zeke.

While Chick may have indirectly had a hand in Spunk's death, she is not a violent character. The film's ending reveals that Chick was just a confused young woman who didn't know what she wanted from life. Zeke, on the other hand, brandishes a knife, fires his shotgun at Chick and Hot Shot, and was directly involved in the death of three people, one of whom he murdered with his bare hands. Yet, clearly, Chick, who symbolizes the city and its deleterious effects on blacks, is the preeminent force of evil in this film. For his crime, Zekes serves a short prison term and then goes home to his family. For her sins, Chick, like many of the filmic mulattoes that preceded her, must die. In making Chick its most evil and maligned character, *Hallelujah* builds upon the precedent established in *The Birth of a Nation* and the early silent films that followed. That the mulatto woman in *Hallelujah* is now embodied by a black actress, as opposed to the white women of earlier films, must have also made the portrayal seem more true to life.

Just as Zeke's love triangle illustrates a schism between newly urbanized blacks and their Southern rural counterparts, so, too, does Chick's love triangle with Zeke and Hot Shot. Zeke represents the South and "authentic" blackness. The citified Hot Shot symbolizes blackness that has been corrupted, blackness that, as Vidor stated in his commentary on the Northern Negro, is an imitation of whiteness. This dynamic, as we shall see, will be carried forward to the all-black films of the 1930s and 1940s. In later years, after the Production Code was abandoned, the mixed race woman's lovers would evolve from representing an urban-rural schism to a black/white schism, a biracial love triangle.

After *Hallelujah* was completed, McKinney signed a five-year contract with MGM, and she and her mother took up temporary residence in Hollywood. While staying in Los Angeles, McKinney and her mother, Georgie, who was only thirty-two at the time, were known to frequent the Apex Night Club.[38] Opened by drummer Curtis Mosby in August 1928, the Apex was *the* hot spot on Central Avenue for well-to-do blacks as well as white Hollywood celebrities. Mosby and his house band, the Dixieland Blues Blowers, can be heard on the *Hallelujah* soundtrack and are conspicuous in McKinney's "Swanee Shuffle" scene.

All the musicians who played at the Apex Club were African Americans, and although the clientele was racially mixed, club etiquette prevented interracial dancing.[39] Four days after the stock market crash, on November 1, 1929, police raided the Apex Night Club and shut it down.[40] The local black press declared that racism was behind the police's actions. Mosby was eventually found innocent of the false charges brought against him. A few months before the raid at the Apex Club, Herbert Howe interviewed McKinney there for an article that appeared in the July 1929 issue of *Photoplay* magazine.

Howe's write-up associated the star with racial admixture and a concomitant duality. The title of the article itself, "Jungle Lorelei," implies that McKinney is like a siren of European lore but with an African twist. The piece included a caption in large type that read, "She may be black but she's got a blonde soul," and it also described McKinney as having "a pagan mouth which she paints like a Christian."[41]

Two accompanying photos illustrate this dichotomy of light and dark, good and evil. The first photo is a publicity headshot from *Hallejuah*. In it, McKinney's complexion appears to be relatively dark, what can be seen of her clothing is black, and her facial expression is very solemn. By contrast, in the second photo, a full body shot, the overall exposure is very light. McKinney is wearing a white feathery tutu, ballet shoes, and standing on toe. With the palms of her hands pressed together as if in prayer, she is smiling and looking very saintly.

Manhattan Serenade (1929)

Around the same time that *Hallelujah* premiered in Los Angeles, McKinney was in the studio shooting *Manhattan Serenade*. Part of MGM's Colortone Revue Series, this often-overlooked short film is a rare moment in American cinema history. Nina Mae McKinney's segment in *Manhattan Serenade* apparently marks the first time a black woman was given the Ziegfeld Girl treatment by a Hollywood studio—in glorious Technicolor, no less.

Directed by Sammy Lee, former choreographer for the *Ziegfeld Follies*, *Manhattan Serenade* is a biracial look at New York entertainment of the 1920s. The film features black and white shots of New York interspersed with musical numbers in Technicolor. The first color sequence represents the white entertainment of the *Ziegfeld Follies* and features the Brox Sisters and a chorus line. Harlem is the subject of the second color sequence, and it features Nina Mae McKinney in dazzling chorus girl regalia.

Warner Bros.' *On with the Show* (1929), a white cast film, which includes two songs performed by Ethel Waters, was advertised as "the first 100% natural color, talking, singing, dancing picture." *Manhattan Serenade* might just then be the first film to include an all-talking, singing and dancing all-black revue in color.[42] *Variety* deemed *Manhattan Serenade* a "first class short" and referred to McKinney not by name but rather as "an attractive high brown girl [who] does some hot warbling and a little cooching."[43] In 2014 *Manhattan Serenade* was preserved by the George Eastman House in New York.

They Learned About Women (1930)

The sequence from McKinney's performance in *Manhattan Serenade* was inserted into the feature film *They Learned About Women*, starring vaudeville actors Gus Van and Joe Schenck, brother to Loew's executive Nicholas Schenck. McKinney, who is uncredited, sings and dances to "Harlem Madness," another Tin Pan Alley tune. Immediately preceding her performance, Van and Schenck, who barely move from their spots on the stage, perform the same song in a large concert hall.

Aside from the fact that both performances take place on a stage, and an occasional shot of the same audience, McKinney's short insert is an obvious splice job that was not originally part of the film. There is no introduction to the performance other than a title card. Then, all of a sudden, an exuberant McKinney appears. Accompanied by two male hoofers and a chorus line, McKinney bursts into song. The preceding stiff performance by Van and Schenck in black and white must have, literally, paled in comparison to the "Harlem Madness" segment as it was shown in its original Technicolor.

The surviving segment, available in context on DVD, is in black and white, but is spectacular nevertheless. It offers an inkling of what black revues of the early 20th century would have been like and why they were so popular with mainstream audiences. This was the first and last time Nina Mae McKinney would be seen on film in an all-out, energetic production number, wearing abbreviated, dazzling attire.

Within a couple of years McKinney's fleeting moment of fame in Hollywood would be over. In April 1930, Elisabeth Goldbeck authored an unfavorable report on the star for *Motion Picture Classic* magazine. Goldbeck's article described McKinney as someone who "imagines she has made the big jump from the black world to the white" and alleged that she had repudiated African Americans. Because the popularity for all-black films was merely a fad, Goldbeck said, McKinney would soon find herself living in a "world between."[44] McKinney reportedly filed a libel suit against the magazine and its author. True or not, Goldbeck's article suggests that McKinney was striving to be on par with whites and that her image was encroaching upon the limits of racial decorum.

Not unlike the studios, Goldbeck betrayed a preference for African Americans that fit within the earlier established, non-threatening types. Just a couple of months after her article on McKinney, Goldbeck wrote a glowing report on another black actor who achieved star status in those early days of Hollywood, Lincoln Perry. More popularly known as Stepin Fetchit, Perry became a success in Hollywood by playing the caricature of the shiftless, dim-witted black man. He was, according to Bogle, the "archetypal coon."[45]

Of Perry, Goldbeck wrote "he typifies his race" and he embodies all "the traits and talents that legend gives to colored people," including their "joyous, childlike charm, their gaudy tastes, their superstitions."[46] At the Hollywood premiere of *Hallelujah*, Nina Mae rose from her seat to shake hands and receive congratulations from such industry notables as Irving Thalberg and his wife, Norma Shearer, Charlie Chaplin, Jack Benny, and Vidor. At the opening of his big film, *Hearts in Dixie*, Perry, on the other hand, was nowhere to be found because he was "was upstairs in the gallery"—where blacks were permitted to sit in a theater, if allowed in at all—where, he said, he belonged.[47]

Goldbeck was right about one thing. Hollywood's interest in all-black-cast films was short-lived. So, too, was MGM's interest in McKinney. In August 1930, *The Chicago Defender* reported that McKinney was still under a long-term contract and that MGM had no intention of releasing her.[48] Just two months later, *Variety* disclosed that after a year of being idle, MGM had finally let the actress go.[49] McKinney and her mother returned to New York in October. According to Harry Levette, during her last few months in Hollywood, McKinney was involved in numerous "scandals and escapades."[50] When she and her mother left Los Angeles, Levette quipped, "The town will get quiet now. Nina Mae and her mamma have gone."[51]

By November, at the age of 17, McKinney was rumored to have married and divorced three times.[52] Amidst the bad press, and under the management of talent agent William Morris, Jr., in December 1930, McKinney set sail on the S.S. *Bremen* with her aunt, Alice Crawford, for a three-month overseas trip that included engagements in Paris, Berlin, Cannes, Belgrade, Monte Carlo and London.[53] While in Paris, McKinney attended the French premiere of *Hallelujah*.[54] She was also rumored to have had an affair with Kagatjita Singh, Maharaja of Kapurthala, whom she first met in Hollywood. McKinney returned to New York in 1931, and within a few months she was in the Warner Bros. studio shooting her next feature film.

Safe in Hell (1931)

Directed by William Wellman, and produced by a Warner Bros. subsidiary, *Safe in Hell* was released three years before Joseph Breen joined MPPDA. Nevertheless, the film's title alone might have elicited some kind of scrutiny from the Hays Office.[55] With its lurid themes of sex, adultery, murder, executions, and disregard for the law, this was just the type of picture that the Hays Office sought to banish. Indeed, after 1934, *Safe in Hell* was kept out of theaters.[56] In addition to providing an instance of pre–Code Hollywood, *Safe in Hell* is also a model of the good-girl/bad-girl dichotomy and the whore turned Madonna.

The trailer for *Safe in Hell* describes it as "the Story of a little girl—who tried so hard to be good—and the world wouldn't let her." The "little girl" is Gilda, played by former Ziegfeld Girl and silent film star Dorothy Mackaill. Having fallen upon hard times, Gilda became a prostitute while her sailor boyfriend was out at sea. When the boyfriend returns, she confesses her sins. Not only does he forgive Gilda, he wants to marry her. There is another problem, though. Gilda is connected with the murder of her ex-boss. Gilda's boyfriend takes her to a Caribbean island where he marries her and then goes back out to sea. For the remainder of the film, Gilda is a born-again virgin, who martyrs herself to remain that way. Despite its transgressions at the beginning of the film, *Safe in Hell* spends most of its time trying to restore to white womanhood the honor it had at first taken away.

In this era of indifference toward the Production Code, Wellman also disregarded Hollywood convention, casting Nina Mae McKinney in an important supporting role that fully integrated her into a predominantly white cast. Wellman is also said to have been gracious enough to let McKinney speak in "normal" language, as opposed to a black dialect.[57] Even looking at it today, McKinney's manner of speech seems very natural, especially when compared with Mackaill's character, Gilda, who lapses into a gangster dialect whenever her bad-girl side comes out.

As Leonie, a Creole lady from New Orleans, McKinney plays a part that is quite possibly a Hollywood first. Leonie is the keeper of a hotel on an extradition-free Caribbean island that is a safe haven for criminals. Before Gilda arrives there, several unsavory men have already taken up residence at Leonie's hotel. In her position at the hotel, Leonie serves others, but she is neither maid nor mammy. Leonie is alluring, but she is not a jezebel. She sings in this film, as well, but she is not an entertainer. McKinney is also given a few comic lines, which she delivers to great effect, but her character is neither lame brained nor a buffoon. Simply stated, Leonie is not a type; she is a person.

Writing for *The New York Times*, Mordaunt Hall said McKinney was "about the most entertaining item" in *Safe in Hell*, and he referred to Leonie's position at the hotel as "barmaid."[58] Hilda See of *The Chicago Defender* also applauded McKinney's performance in the film and wondered, "why [McKinney] does not appear just a bit more." See described Leonie as a "boarding housekeeper."[59] While Leonie does serve drinks and generally cater to the hotel's guests, we never see her cooking, washing a single dish, doing laundry, or making a bed. Leonie, who sets her room rates as she pleases, and apparently answers to no one, is much more than a barmaid or housekeeper.

The only other employee at the hotel is Newcastle, the bellhop, who answers to Leonie whenever she sings his name. Newcastle, who has a British accent, and is played by African American actor Clarence Muse, also transcends stereotyping in this film. Perhaps in 1931 it would have been impossible for a reviewer, black or white, to see McKinney's role in a white-cast film as anything other than a servant. From a contemporary vantage point, however, Leonie appears to be the hotel's proprietor, or at least its manager.

On this island, and in this film, where just about anything goes, McKinney as Leonie does not have to hide her appeal as a black woman. Her hair is never wrapped up in a scarf. She is seen to have several wardrobe changes, wears jewelry, flattering dresses, and high-heel shoes. Her clothing neither conceals nor tantalizes. When we are first introduced to Leonie she is wearing large hoop earrings, a necklace, bangles on her wrist, and a loose blouse that that falls down on one side exposing her left shoulder. This is just enough to let us know that Leonie is an attractive woman, but it is subdued, especially when compared to Gilda's introduction in the opening scene. This shot begins with a close-up of Gilda's feet. Then the camera pans all the way up her legs to gartered thighs, revealing that Gilda is wearing a robe draped loosely over her lingerie.

While Gilda's loose sexual behavior in the beginning of the film has to be spelled out with clothing, dialogue, and action, the nature of Leonie's sexuality is more implicit. For example, when Gilda and her boyfriend arrive at the hotel, Leonie assumes that something untoward is occurring. When she offers the couple an over-priced "one-night" rate, it is understood that Leonie has no problem profiting from, or being complicit in, the assumed illicit behavior. Later, Leonie asks Gilda why she doesn't take up with one of the wealthy men staying in the hotel. Gilda replies, "Oh nothing you would understand. I made a promise." Through its dialogue, the film assumes that Leonie could never comprehend commitment to a monogamous relationship. When it comes to virtue, a white ex-prostitute automatically trumps a Creole hotel manager.

Gilda's status as white woman is emphasized several times during the film, most noticeably with the use of soft-focus close-ups. The script's dialogue also reinforces Gilda's whiteness. When she first arrives at the hotel, all the residents are eager to make her acquaintance because, as one of them remarks, "she's the only white woman on the island." In another scene, one of the men reassures Gilda that they believe in protecting people who visit their island, "especially the ladies—more especially the white ladies."

Despite the film's obvious attempts to draw a distinction between Leonie and Gilda, there are moments when Leonie comes ever so close to capturing the sensual gaze of both the audience and the men in the film. The most conspicuous instance of this is when McKinney sings "When It's Sleepy Time Down South." This song about the bucolic South was written by Clarence Muse and was added to the script specifically to afford McKinney the opportunity to sing.[60]

Tempering the effect of the gaze in this scene, Leonie performs a domestic task. As her guests take their evening meal, Leonie sings and moves around the table as she pours them each a glass of wine. At the end of the song, one of the men proposes a toast to Leonie, "whose eyes are as soft as her voice." Leonie seems embarrassed at the attention and exits while the men still have their glasses raised up high. Just above their glasses the camera moves to a shot of Gilda standing on the landing above in party attire. With this shot, order is re-established; the gaze is returned to the white heroine.

Because *Safe in Hell* liberates its black characters in significant ways, it must find other means to restore the proper racial order. It also does this to Newcastle when Egan, one of the hotel residents, is frustrated by Gilda's rejection of his advances. Egan takes his anger out on Newcastle, punching him in the face, and knocking him down a small flight of stairs. The scene ends with Newcastle on the floor and the hotel guests laughing.

In another scene, when Egan tries to put Leonie in her place, there is a slightly different outcome. When he asks for a brandy, Leonie gently reminds Egan that brandy doesn't sit so well with him. Egan responds by shouting very loudly and directly at Leonie's face: "BRANDY! ARE YOU DEAF?!" Leonie replies, calmly at first, "I can just hear you,

MR. EGAN," and storms off in a huff. Here, Leonie gets the last word. She also gets the last laugh, not for being the butt of a joke, but for resisting Egan's aggression with both dignity and humor. This brief interaction is representative of Nina Mae McKinney's role in *Safe and Hell*. Though she might not be extolled for her chastity like her white counterpart, surrounded by a cast of assassins and scoundrels, Leonie maintains her kindness, elegance, humor, and dignity throughout.

Pie, Pie, Blackbird (1932)

Not long after the release of *Safe in Hell*, McKinney was back at the Warner Bros. Vitaphone studio to shoot *Pie, Pie, Blackbird*, a short film that features her with Eubie Blake and his orchestra and the very young Nicholas Brothers. A harbinger of things to come, *Pie, Pie, Blackbird* primes the actress, at only nineteen years of age, for the part of a mammy. In the short span of ten minutes the film also presents McKinney as a singing jezebel.

In the opening scene, McKinney is immaculately poised, but there is no mistaking the apron over her checkered dress and the kerchief on her head. The Nicholas Brothers, whom she refers to as "pickaninnies," enter to inquire about the pie she is baking. Miss Nina explains through song that she's making a blackbird pie because "the master" says it's the sweetest kind of pie. Inside the pastry, Eubie Blake and his orchestra, dressed in chef's outfits, play jazz.

Very soon, McKinney's other half appears in an elegant evening gown. In "Everything I've Got Belongs to You" she sings about giving up her two-timing ways. McKinney's movements atop Blake's piano are constrained, but she uses her voice, eyes, and facial expressions in such a way that when she offers "everything" we know what she means. The Nicholas Brothers conclude the short with dancing that is so hot it burns up the pie and everyone in sight.

Variety felt that much more could have been done with *Pie, Pie, Blackbird* if McKinney would have been permitted to feature throughout. It also compared her performance in the second half to Helen Morgan, the white actress who played tragic mulatto Julie in Jerome Kern and Oscar Hammerstein's original Broadway run of *Showboat*.[61]

Around this time, it was reported that Nina Mae McKinney was married again. This time, it seems, the rumor was true. McKinney's new husband was Jimmy Monroe, brother of Clarke Monroe, who was owner of the Uptown House, a Harlem nightclub that became prominent during the formative years of bebop jazz. Jimmy, who would later marry Billie Holiday, was generally known as a hustler. In her autobiography, Holiday claimed that the song "Don't Explain" was written after he came home with lipstick on his collar. Holiday also said that it was Monroe who first introduced her to smoking heroin.[62] In addition to taking on the role of husband, Monroe, it was reported, was also McKinney's manager.

With no film roles forthcoming, McKinney sought work in the theater and acquired a part in *Ballyhoo of 1932*. This predominantly white-cast show had a short run on Broadway and included the comedian Bob Hope. Supported by a white chorus, McKinney had only one song, "Love, Nuts, and Noodles," which, according to the *Afro-American*, she performed "a la Africaine" wearing little more than two satin monkeys attached onto her gyrating hips. The review also declared it had seen much better from McKinney in

Harlem floorshows, prior to her success in *Hallelujah*.[63] In what, by this time, had become a common lament of McKinney's work, a review in the *Brooklyn Daily Eagle* noted that her appearance with its "proper, or perhaps improper undulations" was much too brief.[64]

Ballyhoo of 1932 closed in November, after a three month-run. In December, McKinney was headed back to Paris on the S.S. *Bremen* for an appearance at Chez Florence.[65] Two months later, she was on her way to London for a "half colored and half white" show at the Leicester Square Theatre titled *Chocolate and Cream*. McKinney was the main attraction of the chocolate half of the show, which was set on a Mississippi plantation.[66] That same month, from an experimental BBC studio, Nina Mae McKinney became the first black person to appear on British television.[67]

At London's Trocadero Cabaret in April, among a cast of white performers, McKinney was the star of *Revels in Rhythm*. A Pathé newsreel reveals that *Revels in Rhythm* had an eerie grand finale. Looking quite chic in a white tuxedo and top hat, McKinney presents a stark contrast to the white chorus girls who accompany her, dressed as black men in black tuxedos and top hats. Taking blackface from mocking to the macabre, the women's disguises are completed not with dark makeup but with ghoulish zippered blackface masks.[68]

It was at a 1934 performance in Athens, Greece that McKinney was billed as "The Black Garbo." For the most part, throughout 1933 and 1934, however, she worked a rigorous schedule of theater and nightclub dates in Great Britain. For many of these performances McKinney was accompanied by pianist Garland Wilson. McKinney was one of the most popular black artists in Britain at this time and part of an elite group of entertainers that included the musical duo Layton and Johnstone, the comedy team of Scott and Whaley, and the actor Paul Robeson.[69] In 1934 McKinney starred with Scott and Whaley in the low-budget British short film *Kentucky Minstrels*. A musical revue that featured both black and white entertainers, it was released in the United States as *Life is Real*. In Pittsburgh it played as a companion film to *Imitation of Life* (1934).[70] That same year McKinney and Robeson were contracted to make a feature film together for London Film Productions.

Sanders of the River (1935)

Based on Edgar Wallace's novel and directed by Zoltan Korda, *Sanders of the River* tells the story of Commissioner Sanders, a British civil servant assigned to keep the peace among Nigerian tribes in Africa. The film combines actors and studio scenes with actual footage of African people and landscapes. Paul Robeson plays Bosambo, chief of one of the tribes under Sander's watchful eye. Bosambo is an escaped prisoner and a bit of a rascal. When it comes to "Lord Sandi," he is also a fawner. The commissioner takes a liking to the cunning tribesman and confers upon him a position of chief. Nina Mae McKinney stars as Lilongo, Bosambo's wife.

Under Sander's direction, Lilongo was rescued by Bosambo during a slave raid led by King Mofolaba. When Sanders takes leave to England, the African king seizes the opportunity to exact revenge upon Bosambo for intercepting that raid. Mofolaba's men kidnap Lilongo and transport her to his village. Bosambo follows and is captured too. It is left to Sanders, who is called back from Britain, to save Bosambo and Lilongo and restore the peace. Sanders returns and fires machine guns on Mofolaba's men. Bosambo kills

Mofolaba with a spear to the chest. For being a loyal servant to the British Crown, Sanders makes Bosambo the new King of the River.

Much was written about the fact that McKinney's overall deportment in *Sanders of the River* makes her look out of place among the film's other authentic and inauthentic Africans, including the half-naked Paul Robeson, who romps about in animal skins and feathers. From London, one source found her "somewhat too sophisticated for a native African." Andre Sennwald of *The New York Times* said she was more like a "Harlem night-club entertainer than a savage jungle beauty." *Variety* reported that McKinney had been abroad too long to be recognized as American and also noted that she didn't fit in. Nancy Cunard said that Europeans wondered if McKinney was even black.[71]

Underlying criticism in this vein is the idea that McKinney, with her light complexion, smooth, pulled-back straight hair, and occidental facial features, was either too nearly white or too beautiful to be read as a black woman. Fay Jackson, Hollywood correspondent for the American Negro Press, wrote that McKinney displayed a kind of beauty that movies rarely associate with black people.[72] In this respect, McKinney's performance might be viewed as a sign of progress and a cause for celebration. Her beauty, however, is offered at the expense of the other black women in the film, and therefore, any celebration must be tempered.

Sanders of the River, like many films that send British men off to Africa, insists that its white hero is celibate.[73] Commissioner Sanders certainly has no interest in African women. He interacts frequently with Lilongo, but his concern for her, as well as the other Africans, is like that of a father. In reality, of course, whether by rape, concubinage, consent, or as a means to survive, the "sailors, soldiers, and merchant adventurers who laid the groundwork for the British Empire," and to whom this film is dedicated, cohabitated and had sex with African women.

Mixed race children that were born as a result of these unions were considered an embarrassment to the British Empire and were often disavowed by their white fathers. For many African descendants of these British adventurers, the absence of white fathers and being labeled illegitimate is a stigma that has repercussions to the present day.[74] The fact that British men were attracted to African women is broached ever so carefully in Wallace's novel, but avoided altogether in Korda's film. Yet, Lilongo, embodied in the flesh of McKinney, evokes this history that the film attempts to suppress. *Sanders of the River* simultaneously avoids, and begs, the question of mixed race.

Commissioner Sanders' celibacy extends not just to African women but to white women as well. He has been in Africa for ten years. When Sanders returns to England he is supposed to stay for a year and get married. But his leave ends after only a week, and we are never introduced to the fiancée. In fact, there are no white women in this film. Consequently, in *Sanders of the River*, Nina Mae McKinney assumes the role of the white woman, or at least the position usually reserved for white women, that of romantic heroine. Aside from being white, the traditional romantic heroine possesses the "feminine" attributes of passivity and dependence. She is the object of man's pursuit and is inclined toward matters of love and marriage.[75]

When the film begins, Bosambo has five other wives in another village and nine other women who also want to marry him, but when he meets Lilongo he chooses to marry her under the white man's custom of monogamy. Lilongo is shown as a loving mother, and though she is strong-willed, she yields to her husband. This is established

Nina Mae McKinney and Paul Robeson are a loving husband and wife in the London Film Productions feature *Sanders of the River* (1935).

when the couple disagree on how to raise their son. When Lilongo eventually gives in to Bosambo's way of thinking, she whines, "You're full of cunning, and you do just what you like with me." Lilongo's kidnapping and rescue also position her as a quintessential damsel in distress. Her salvation is dependent not only upon her black husband but also her white "father."

All things considered, compared to the other Africans in this film, McKinney's Lilongo fares quite well. The same cannot be said of Paul Robeson's character. Watching Bosambo today, one can't help but feel embarrassed for the gifted actor. When he first signed on for the film, Robeson had envisioned a production that would lend dignity to and greater understanding of Africans. He was, therefore, disappointed with the end result.[76] Some mainstream critics praised the film's artistic merits, and the British Institute of Amateur Cinematographers awarded it a gold medal.[77] Others condemned the film as propaganda for the British Empire and found Robeson's role to be nothing more than an African Uncle Tom.[78]

Nina Mae McKinney returned to Hollywood and MGM at the beginning of 1935 to shoot *Reckless* (1935) starring Jean Harlow and William Powell. Victor Fleming, who would later be known for the *Wizard of Oz* (1939), directed. The trailer for *Reckless* gives McKinney star billing. Granted, she is the last person mentioned, after child star Farina (Allen Hoskins) of the *Our Gang* short film series. Nevertheless, the trailer offers a promise that McKinney will be seen doing something worthwhile. Evidently most of her shots were cut, and the film failed to deliver on its promise. McKinney is in the film, along with Garland Wilson, but one has to watch carefully to find her. Disgruntled by the film's misleading marketing campaign, and out of fairness to its readers, the *Afro-American* decided to eliminate McKinney's name from its advertising of the film.[79]

Later that same year McKinney appeared in the 26th edition of the *Cotton Club Parade*. Produced by Ted Koehler and staged by Leonard Harper, the show featured Emmett "Babe" Wallace, Juano Hernandez, Flournoy Miller, Mantan Moreland, and McKinney's heir apparent, Lena Horne. McKinney sang "Good for Nothin' Joe," which was recorded six years later by Lena Horne.

McKinney teamed up with Babe Wallace again in *The Black Network* (1936), a Warner Bros. short film that tells the story of a black radio network. In it, the wife of one of the network's sponsors wants to replace McKinney and insists on performing herself. Nina Mae and Babe get riled and quit the show. The Nicholas Brothers are dancers and numbers runners. Nina Mae and Babe's numbers win and they become wealthy. Before quitting the show, McKinney performs "Half of Me Wants to Be Good." Needless to say, her other half wants to be bad. The song's lyrics, which speak of one minute wanting to find salvation and the next wanting to be low down, bring to mind her role as Chick in *Hallelujah*. The short ends with the sponsor and his wife in poverty while Wallace and McKinney strut around Harlem's Sugar Hill neighborhood in their finery. *Variety* considered McKinney's singing in *The Black Network* a highlight.[80]

When McKinney returned to England in 1937, she became one of the first entertainers to be given her own variety show on the newly launched BBC television service.[81] That same year it was reported that she was seeking a divorce from Jimmy Monroe.[82] By 1938 McKinney announced that she had a new lover/manager, Jack Evans. It was around this time, too, that McKinney declared she would not accept any maid roles.[83] Just a few years earlier, McKinney had also said she was tired of playing the "hell-cat" type.[84] It seems that McKinney was looking for film roles that exceeded the narrow confines of Hollywood's definition of black womanhood, and in 1938 she turned her attention to race movies.

In the early 20th century, black-cast films for segregated, or de facto segregated, audiences became known as "race films." In response to the derogatory images of *The Birth of a Nation* and other pictures produced by the major film studios, leaders of the African American community had called for, among other things, the formation of a black film industry that could respond to the indictments of mainstream movies. Against the odds, from a system of overt racism and a position of relative poverty, black filmmakers appeared and produced movies that contributed to the construction of an early twentieth-century African American identity. Between 1915 and 1950, over 150 independently owned film companies were formed and approximately one-third of these companies were completely black-owned.[85]

Nina Mae had first been considered for the Million Dollar Productions race film *The Duke Is Tops* (1938), but illness prevented her from taking the role opposite Ralph Cooper, and Lena Horne got the part instead.[86] Ralph Cooper had arrived in Hollywood in 1936 under a contract with Twentieth Century–Fox to replace the ailing dancer Bill Robinson in a Shirley Temple film, *Poor Little Rich Girl* (1936). Once Cooper got there, Fox decided they did not want him for the part and instead Cooper taught Shirley Temple and other white stars their dance routines.[87] In another Fox film, *White Hunter* (1937), his name appeared in the screen credits, but the light-skinned Cooper, whose looks did not conform to Hollywood's idea of a black man, was nowhere to be found in the film.[88]

With the aid of financing from white entrepreneur Harry Popkin, Ralph Cooper helped form Million Dollar Productions, which produced several black gangster films, including *Bargain with Bullets* aka *Gangsters on the Loose*, which Cooper wrote, directed and starred in. *Bargain with Bullets* made history as the first independently produced all-black-cast films to be purchased by the Loew's Theatre chain.[89] Aside from Cooper, Horne and McKinney, other well-known actors who appeared in Million Dollar Productions films include Louise Beavers, Jeni LeGon, Dorothy Dandridge, Lorenzo Tucker, and Mantan Moreland. Nina Mae McKinney appeared in two Million Dollar Productions films, *Gang Smashers* and *Straight to Heaven*.

Gang Smashers (1938)

Harry Popkin's brother Leo Popkin directed Nina Mae McKinney in *Gang Smashers*. McKinney plays Laura Jackson, an undercover law enforcement agent. Unbeknownst to Laura, also working undercover for the police is Lefty Wilson, played by Monte Hawley. Lawrence Criner is Gat Dalton, head of the Harlem racketeering gang that the two agents are trying to bring down.

It is no coincidence that *Gang Smashers'* three principal actors, McKinney, Criner, and Hawley, are all light-skinned. The irony of many race movies is that the black identity they represented was performed by actors who looked white. In much the same way that the light-skinned chorus girl was as an alternative image to blackface, the light-skinned actor of the race movie offered a reverse image of the type of blacks that Hollywood preferred, particularly the tom, coon, and mammy. Much like the chorus girl of the stage, the light-skinned actor of the screen stood for urbanity, assimilation, and progress.

Dedicated to "those colored men and women of the Intelligence Service," the story for *Gang Smashers* (also known as *Gun Moll*), provided by Ralph Cooper, is a relatively simple one. Laura poses as a singer in Dalton's nightclub and uses both her talent as an entertainer and her sex appeal to attract Dalton's attention and gain the gangster's trust. After Laura has made some inroads with Dalton, Lefty Wilson shows up to help the racketeers increase business. Lefty and Laura, unaware of each other's role, develop a romantic interest on the side. Eventually Lefty's cover is blown, and Dalton and his gang take him for a ride so they can execute him. Laura flags down the police and a car chase ensues. When the bad guys' car crashes, Lefty manages to subdue Dalton and hand him over to the police. Lefty and Laura are left alone to begin their romance on the back of a horse-drawn carriage.

Million Dollar Productions gave McKinney top billing in *Gang Smashers*, and it also gave her the more expansive role she seemed to be looking for. In *Gang Smashers*, her only true star vehicle, Nina Mae McKinney does it all. As the girlfriend of a gangster and a nightclub singer, she is at first perceived as a bad girl. When her true identity is discovered, she is revealed to be a good girl. As the object of both Dalton's and Lefty's affections, Laura is a romantic heroine, and as a gun-toting policewoman, she is also an action heroine. In addition to singing during the especially entertaining nightclub scenes, McKinney laughs, swings to the music, and seems to be genuinely enjoying herself as she conducts Phil Moore's orchestra.

With the aid of Popkin's West Coast experience and connections, *Gang Smashers* had it its premiere at the Million Dollar Theatre in Los Angeles, a venue where, ordinarily, the patronage was overwhelmingly white. The black press heralded *Gang Smashers* as the first independently produced all black-cast film to open at a major theater.[90] Before

Nina Mae McKinney does it all, including finding romance with co-star Montey Hawley, in the Million Dollar Productions race film *Gang Smashers* (1938).

its opening, *The Pittsburgh Courier* reported that the downtown Los Angeles debut would establish that black-cast films could draw an integrated audience.[91] This certainly proved to be the case in Los Angeles where patrons lined up at the box-office daily, beginning at 10 a.m., and the theater's 2,300 seating capacity was maxed out every night. Breaking all prior house records, the film was held over for three weeks.[92]

As for the film itself, a reviewer for *The Pittsburgh Courier* found the entire premise of a world in which black people head gangs and police departments implausible. Nevertheless, he deemed the film's production values to be above par, and Uncle Tom, he was happy to report, was "gone with the wind."[96] Back in Los Angeles, the local branch of the NAACP endorsed *Gang Smashers* as a film that would instruct youth that crime doesn't pay.[97] With the success of *Gang Smashers*, it was predicted that McKinney would be re-established as an A-list actress.[98] That didn't happen. McKinney's other extant race movies were not of the same caliber as *Gang Smashers* and feature her in less significant

Based on its West Coast success, Popkin negotiated a deal with the RKO Theatre chain—which typically screened only white-cast films—to have the film presented at three of its Harlem theaters.[93] At the 116th Street Regent Theatre, *Gang Smashers* was only the second all-black-cast film to play there.[94] In Philadelphia, *Gang Smashers* was at the center of battle between owners of two theaters that were playing the film at the same time. After an unsuccessful attempt at using the legal system to prevent his competitor with first-run rights from screening the film, the owner with second-run rights threatened to sue both Million Dollar Productions and the other theater.[95]

roles. In *Straight to Heaven* child singer Jackie Ward was the star. *The Devil's Daughter* (1939), which was filmed in Jamaica, is a poor remake of *Ouanga* aka *The Love Wanga* (1936), starring Fredi Washington.

The Maid Years

With its entry into World War II, and the threat of European fascism, the United States was thrust into a new race consciousness. In 1942, six months after the bombing of Pearl Harbor, President Roosevelt established the Office of War Information ("OWI"), the federal agency that would be responsible for disseminating information on the progress of the war as well as propaganda in its support. The OWI, which took a special interest in the movie industry, established a bureau in Hollywood and concluded that African Americans would be likelier to support the war effort if they saw themselves portrayed more graciously.

At the same time, executive secretary of the NAACP Walter White, hoping to advance his crusade to broaden the range of film roles for African Americans, attempted to capitalize on this new consciousness. White travelled to California and met with Hollywood insiders and studio executives. White also managed to forge an informal alliance between the OWI and the NAACP. The wartime scarcity of film stock, combined with the promise of integration and equality emanating from Hollywood, ultimately spelled disaster for the independent race movie, which seemed out of touch with a changing society.[99]

Hollywood's wartime interest in African American representation was short-lived. While it benefited a few black entertainers, most notably Lena Horne, for others, like Nina Mae, it marked a setback and the beginning of the end. When McKinney returned to Hollywood in 1944, she appeared in a string of films that cast her in bit parts as a maid. In *Together Again* (1944) and *The Power of the Whistler* (1945), McKinney plays essentially the same character. In the former she works in the bathroom of a nightclub and escapes out the window when the club is raided. In Lew Leonard's *The Power of the Whistler*, part of *The Whistler* film noir series, McKinney plays Flotilda, backstage maid to a white dancer, Constantina.

Brief and uncredited, McKinney's role in *The Power of the Whistler* is a reminder of the complex and multifaceted real-life relationships white women performers had with their black maids. In the early 1920s, for example, when dancer Ida Forsyne's career stalled, she was hired by Sophie Tucker. A singer, actress, and comedian of Eastern European descent, Tucker established a name for herself as a top-notch "coon shouter" by performing in blackface and adopting a Southern accent.

Similar to McKinney's maid costume in *Together Again* and *The Power of the Whistler*, for the stage, Ida Forsyne dressed in a black dress and a white apron. At the end of Tucker's act Forsyne would dance to whip up applause for her employer. Offstage, Forsyne was Tucker's personal maid as well. Mae West also shaped her image in contrast to and in combination with black women and black maids. West sometimes mimicked the dance moves of African American women, and in her movies, she was served by an all-star lineup of black maids, including Louise Beavers and Hattie McDaniel. Like Tucker, Mae West also employed black maids offstage.[100]

McKinney is also a maid in the noir style thriller *Dark Waters* (1944), but she's not a very dutiful one. Her character doesn't clean or dust and treats her employers

From jezebel to maid, Nina Mae McKinney discusses her role in Columbia Pictures' *Together Again* (1944) with director Charles Vidor.

with disdain. At first one hopes this might be an act of subversion, but her behavior is explained when it's revealed that the family that she works for has murdered her former employers. Though she was only in her early 30s at the time, a review of *Dark Waters* referred to McKinney as "the Lena Horne of her day," a has-been, in other words.[101] In *Night Train to Memphis* (1946), McKinney's maid is an entertaining straight woman to Nicodemus Stewart, who played Lightnin' on the television version of *Amos 'n' Andy*.

In *Danger Street* (1947), yet another film noir mystery, one gets the impression that director Lew Leonard was trying to provide McKinney with a modicum of dignity and a little more screen time. Her character, Veronica, actually gets to come out of her maid costume into an elegant evening gown, and the gown turns out to be a clue in solving the murder. Demonstrating that she is far from an asexual or obsequious mammy, Veronica, clad in the beautiful dress, refuses to be sequestered with other residents of her employer's estate because she has a date.

Pinky (1949)

By the late 1940s, the Second World War was over, and so too was the government's interest in propagandizing the African American. Nevertheless, questions about equality remained, and postwar audiences were primed for films that explored real social problems. Favorable box office receipts in 1947 from *Gentleman's Agreement* and *Crossfire*, films that tackled anti–Semitism, signaled to Hollywood that stories about American bigotry were of interest to audiences. Of course, the status of Jews, who were well represented in the top ranks of Hollywood's power structure, and that of African Americans, who had no power at all, was quite different. Even so, 1949 saw the release of several films attempting to deal with discrimination aimed at African Americans including *Home of the Brave*, *Lost Boundaries*, and *Pinky*.

Home of the Brave recounts the prejudices a black American soldier is subjected to at home and in the army. *Lost Boundaries* and *Pinky* take up the phenomenon of blacks passing for white, or "passing." *Gentleman's Agreement* and *Pinky*, both produced by Darryl Zanuck and Twentieth Century–Fox, are often described as being part of the "message" movie cycle. Unlike *Home of the Brave* and *Lost Boundaries*, *Pinky* is set in the South. Based on the Cid Ricketts Sumner novel *Quality*, it tells the story of a young, light-skinned African American woman, Patricia "Pinky" Johnson, raised by her pious granny, Aunt Dicey, in a shack that once served as slave quarters. Aunt Dicey's shack abuts the "big house" owned by the slaveholder's heiress, Miss Em.

Pinky moves North to attend nursing school, discovers that she can pass for white, and falls in love with a white doctor. Wishing to escape her actions, Pinky returns to the South after many years away and is dismayed to find that her grandmother is still doing laundry for Miss Em and other white folks. Pinky also learns about the reality of being black. As a favor to Aunt Dicey, Pinky uses her nursing skills to care for the dying Miss Em. Out of the newfound respect she has for Pinky, Miss Em bequeaths all her property to her. When Miss Em dies, a family relative contests the will in court. Pinky prevails, but the Ku Klux Klan has the last word when they burn the house to the ground.

Director Otto Preminger brought *Quality* to Zanuck's attention in 1948.[102] Zanuck liked the story but selected John Ford to direct. When Ford could no longer continue, with the cast and script already set, Zanuck brought in Elia Kazan, director of *Gentleman's Agreement*. Dudley Nichols was hired to write the screenplay. After several rewrites, Zanuck sent a draft of the script to New York to be critiqued by Walter White, his daughter Jane White, and NAACP staff. In addition to his position as head of the NAACP and his interest in black representation in Hollywood, White had yet another attribute that made him uniquely qualified to vet this script about a black woman who passes for white. The NAACP leader himself had passed for white.

Between 1918 and 1927, the fair-skinned, blue-eyed Walter White travelled the United States extensively, most notably throughout the South, sometimes passing as a white man to investigate lynchings and race riots on behalf of the NAACP. It was this bravado that contributed to the organization's ability to bring national awareness to the atrocities of lynching. It also helped White rise to the top ranks of NAACP leadership. Around the same time that *Quality* was published, Nobel Prize–winning author and friend of White's Sinclair Lewis wrote *Kingsblood Royal*. Walter White was the inspiration for the novel's main character, a married white banker who suddenly discovers he has African American blood.[103]

Though the term "passing" can refer to the crossing of any line that divides social groups, it is most often used as shorthand for blacks passing for white. In the late 19th and early 20th century passing was a particularly recognized phenomenon that captured the interest of many authors of fiction. Passing for white could take on various forms. There was complete passing in which one disavowed black family and friends to cross the racial line permanently. Inadvertent passing, as in the case of Lewis' protagonist in *Kingsblood Royal*, occurs when the person is unaware of his or her black ancestry. Being taken for white and making no effort to correct the "mistake" is also considered inadvertent passing. There was also part-time passing, as in the case of Walter White, who passed for white to investigate lynchings. Like the character Pinky, other people passed part-time white when they went North for work and became black again when they returned to the South for a visit.[104]

White and NAACP staff members were critical of the *Pinky* script. Apparently angered or frustrated, Zanuck responded to their criticism by deleting the story's only black radical character, Arch McNaughton. Described in the novel as a "small yellow man," McNaughton is a newspaper reporter from New York whose black mother was personal maid to his white father's wife. While Miss Em and Aunt Dicey represent the conservative, old ways of the South, Arch represents change: desegregation and equal rights through activism and political process. When the two viewpoints collide in a face-to-face dialogue between Arch and Miss Em, it is one of the novel's more informative moments.[105]

Torn between the interests of the film industry's power brokers, Southern racist attitudes, and the opinions of the NAACP, Zanuck hired Jane White as a technical advisor to help provide some balance to the film's script. Philip Dunne, a white man active in the Civil Rights Movement, was also added to the writing team. In a *New York Times* article, Dunne declared that with regard to the problem of racism, the final script, though not altogether neutral, presents no singular point of view as the definitive answer. "We neither deny nor condone the bitter fact of racial prejudice," he said.[106]

The script and the film, however, follow the same line as Sumner, whose novel suggests that the best solution to the "Negro problem" is not one of radical change or activism but rather acceptance, accommodation, and continued segregation. With the deletion of the Arch McNaughton character, *Pinky* dismisses activism as a possible response altogether, making the film seem even more supportive of segregation than the novel upon which it is based. The film's conclusion, which opts to turn Pinky's newly inherited estate into a medical clinic for blacks as opposed to incinerating it, is kinder perhaps, but it toes the segregationist line.

The most glaring evidence of the film's stance on segregation is not in the script but rather in the casting of a white actress, Jeanne Crain, for the title role. Responding to the casting choice, actor Frederick O'Neal, who plays Aunt Dicey's neighbor, Jake, pointed out that the film was doing the very thing it was preaching against. Fredi Washington, who fifteen years earlier played a young woman who passed for white in *Imitation of Life*, declared that choosing a white woman for the part would greatly weaken the film's social impact. Washington further denounced *Pinky*'s producers for denying those actresses who have been consistently turned down for roles because they are too fair-skinned an opportunity to compete for a role for which they would be perfectly suited. *The Chicago Defender* named several experienced black actresses who could have played the part of Pinky, including Jane White, Hilda Simms, and Janice Kingslow.[107]

At the time *Pinky* was in pre-production, Jane White, in addition to helping with the script, had already appeared on Broadway. Her first role, in 1945, was in *Strange Fruit*, a play based on Lillian Smith's novel about an interracial romance. In 1948, she had a part in the short-lived production *Insect Comedy*. Ten years after the release of *Pinky*, White finally landed her first major Broadway role as Queen Aggravain in the musical comedy *Once Upon a Mattress*. At her audition, producers were impressed with her talent but worried that Jane looked too "Mediterranean." Consequently, the actress agreed to "white up," or use white makeup, so as not confuse the audience with matters of race. In 1964 White reprised the role in a televised version of the musical.

Over the years, Jane White grew accustomed to being rejected for parts because she was either too black for white roles or too white for black roles. By the late 1960s, White decided that she would no longer accept roles that involved whiteface makeup.[108] Jane White won two Off Broadway Theater Awards, the second in 1971 for Sustained Achievement. She also received a Los Angeles Critics Circle Award in 1989. Her appearances in film include *Klute* (1971) and *Beloved* (1998).

Another light-skinned actress, Hilda Simms, first made a name for herself in *Anna Lucasta*, a stage production with an interracial history of its own. Originally written with a Polish-American family in mind, Phillip Yordan's play did not receive notoriety until 1944 when the American Negro Theater decided to produce it with an all-black cast. Frederick O'Neal made his Broadway debut in *Anna Lucasta*, as did Simms in the title role.

As a result of its success, *Anna Lucasta* went from Harlem to Broadway, where it had a run of 950 performances. It also marked the first time Broadway audiences saw a play with an all-black cast that did not deal with issues specific to race.[109] In 1949, the play was adapted for the screen featuring a white cast, and nine years later it was remade with an all-black cast that included Eartha Kitt, Sammy Davis, Jr., and Frederick O'Neal. Simms, who was convinced that her film career had been stymied by Hollywood's blacklist, made only two films, *The Joe Louis Story* (1953) and *Black Widow* (1954).

When *Anna Lucasta* moved to Chicago, Janice Kingslow became Simms's understudy and she took over the role in 1946. In a 1950 essay titled "I Refuse to Pass," Kingslow related her own experience as a light-skinned actress to that of the character Pinky. Unlike Pinky, however, when presented with the opportunity to pass for white, Kingslow declined. The actress claimed that an unnamed man from a major Hollywood studio promised her a long-term contract on the condition that she change her name and disavow her black heritage.[110]

Kingslow's telling of this incident nine years later in *Ebony* magazine is slightly different, but what remains consistent is that she was practically guaranteed stardom if she would only agree to pass for white or at least agree not to identify as black.[111] Though she was desperate for money, Kingslow was unwilling to seek fame at the cost of publicly disowning her life experience and her family. Kingslow was in the cast of *Here Comes Tomorrow*, America's first all-black radio soap opera. She also worked as a writer at NBC.

Like Jane White, Kingslow found that her skin color was a detriment to finding work as an actress, and like Simms, by the early 1950s, she discovered that she had been blacklisted. In 1957 Janice Kingslow entered a state mental hospital. Two years later, writing about her challenges, Kingslow acknowledged that many factors triggered her mental illness. Attempting to survive as a black artist in white America was among them.[112]

Director Elia Kazan had his own ideas about who should play the part of Pinky. He felt that they had capitulated in *Gentleman's Agreement* by having Gregory Peck, the perfect model of the white American male, play the part of a Jew. He didn't want to do the same thing in *Pinky*. Kazan thought that a beautiful, black actress should play the role, and he recommended Dorothy Dandridge.[113] There's no evidence that McKinney was ever considered for the title role, but she, too, could have been a contender.

We can only imagine what a more compelling film *Pinky* might have been if an African American actress had played the lead role. Production Code and Southern attitudes aside, Zanuck was advised that even liberal Northern white audiences would not tolerate love scenes between a black actress and a white man. A white actress, Jeanne Crain, took on the role of Pinky.[114]

Kazan, at first, had difficulty working with Crain. Her face, he discovered, remained inexpressive under all dramatic circumstances and "she floated through her role without reacting." Rather than being impatient with Crain or asking her to change, the director decided he would make use of her emotional vacuity. Kazan determined that Crain's numbness, especially when compared with an otherwise lively cast, would perfectly represent Pinky's situation as a victim of her racial ambiguity.[115] While it is still difficult to find Crain credible as a black woman—even one who can pass for white—Kazan's adeptness earned Jeanne Crain a Best Actress Academy Award nomination. Oscar nominations also went to Ethel Waters for her role as Aunt Dicey and Ethel Barrymore as Miss Em.

As unconvincing as Crain's racial performance is, in deference to Kazan's approach, we might consider both Janice Kingslow and Walter White. Kingslow was admitted to a mental hospital, out of touch with reality, in a catatonic state brought on, at least in part, from the stress of racial discrimination.[116] As for Walter White, many people, both black and white, found his real-life "performance" of blackness improbable. In contrast to Pinky, though, when the NAACP leader passed for white, he did so to help achieve equality for black Americans, oftentimes risking his own life.

Furthermore, whether travelling as salesman for a black insurance company, investigating lynchings, or rising to the top ranks of the NAACP, White would have to have known how to generally relate well with other blacks, a trait that seems lacking in Crain's portrayal of Pinky. Pinky, in effect, is much like the tragic octoroon of antebellum fiction who grew up unaware of her black blood until the day she learned she was not only her father's daughter but his chattel as well. In Pinky's case, however, audience sympathy was not for the spectacle of a near-white woman being treated as a slave but rather for a *real* white woman being treated like a black person.

Nina Mae McKinney plays Rozelia, Jake's girlfriend, a woman who, in Sumner's novel, has skin the color of "burnished copper." Rozelia functions as a contrast to Pinky. She is perhaps the young woman Pinky might have been were it not for her white skin and her Aunt Dicey's determination to raise her just like a white child. Sumner's writing, which brings to mind at times the style of Thomas Dixon, Jr., consistently likens Rozelia to a variety of animals and takes pains to emphasize her menacing sexuality. Rozelia's mere presence, for example, is like "a cat's fur rising" or "owls crying in the still of the night," and her clothing, though prim and proper, only served to intensify the "savage exultation of her body."[117]

Pinky, who looks white and was raised like a white child, was conceived in the pre–Civil War mold of the tragic octoroon, while Rozelia is patterned after the sexually dangerous mixed race woman of the early 20th century. When Pinky pays a visit to Jake to retrieve money owed to Aunt Dicey, the disparity between the two women comes into sharp relief. Rozelia is furious when she discovers that Jake has taken her money and given it to Pinky. She confronts Pinky, demands the return of her cash, and then conveniently happens upon a knife to threaten her with. A police car pulls up and Rozelia hides the weapon in her stocking. In both novel and film, Rozelia is subjected to a search and ordered by police to lift her dress. In the novel, Rozelia makes an erotic production out of this incident, lifting her dress in "little twitches that kept time with the almost imperceptible swaying of her hips." Pinky is astonished when she observes that Rozelia is actually enjoying herself.[118]

Jane White's advice to omit this part of the scene from the film went unheeded.[119] The search incident remained but with the sexuality downplayed somewhat. McKinney's Rozelia is clearly not having a good time, but the sight of Rozelia pulling up her dress and a shot of her exposed thigh and a knife concealed in her stocking was sufficient to convey the sexual deviance so clearly spelled out in *Quality*. After the police have figured out that Pinky is "colored," she is forced to undergo to a similar inspection.

As opposed to Rozelia's encounter, which represents sex and danger, Pinky's search evokes sympathy for the indignities that a white Negress must endure. Rozelia, albeit begrudgingly, is an active participant in the search. She pulls up her dress and exposes herself for all to see. Pinky's involvement, on the other hand, is totally passive and handled with complete discretion. Because Rozelia is characterized as threatening, the treatment she receives at the hands of the police seems justified. For Pinky, it's an insult.

Despite problems of exhibiting the film in the South, *Pinky* was the second highest-grossing film of 1949. Bosley Crowther of *The New York Times* declared it one of the year's best pictures.[120] In the black press, reception was somewhat divided. Some found the film's Southern slice of life realistic. *The New York Age* declared it the best film on the Negro question to date.[121] Others were offended by the film's stereotypes and the casting of a white woman in the title role. Walter White took exception not only to the stereotype of the domineering mistress and faithful mammy but also the film's impression that blacks are resigned to their subordinate place in society. A critic for the *California Eagle* argued that Nina Mae McKinney's scene was a "low and dirty characterization" that implied all black women were accustomed to carrying razors in their stockings and pulling up their dresses on command.[122]

Little is known about Nina Mae's McKinney career or personal life after this point. Her final film, *Copper Canyon* (1950), was a Western set just after the Civil War starring Ray Milland and Hedy Lamarr. McKinney's uncredited character, Theresa, is a certified, bandana-wearing mammy. During the 1950s, *Jet* magazine reported sporadically on the former star. She attempted a comeback in 1953 at Small's Paradise in Harlem. In 1954, she was headed to Japan for a USO tour and in 1958 she wanted to publish her autobiography.[123] Before her death in 1967, Nina Mae McKinney, it was rumored, was working as a maid.

3

Fredi Washington

Paradox of Black Identity

Black am I? All right, I am black.
I'll show him what a black girl can do!
—Fredi Washington as Clelie in *The Love Wanga*

A pioneer in dance, film, and television, Fredi Washington began her career as a chorus girl with the touring company of *Shuffle Along*. Washington eventually transitioned from dancer to stage and screen actress, playing romantic leads opposite such eminent figures as Paul Robeson, Duke Ellington, and Cab Calloway. Washington's most prominent role was in the film *Imitation of Life* (1934). As Peola, a young woman who passes for and desperately wants to be white, Washington epitomized early Hollywood's modern tragic mulatto. Like Peola, the fair-skinned, green-eyed actress was light enough to pass for white, and like the character she played, Fredi Washington was also a direct heir to the American racial paradox exposed in *Imitation of Life*, wherein white had become black.

This paradox of racial identity in America developed during slavery. In the years leading up to emancipation, after centuries of racial mixing and sexual depredation, it was becoming ever more evident—visibly and statistically—that slavery's mixed race population was rapidly growing. Whites, it seems, had grown accustomed to increasing slavery's numbers through the enslavement of their own progeny. By the 19th century, with the transatlantic slave trade ended, selling whiteness that resided in bodies deemed *essentially* black was commonplace in the domestic slave trade. Proponents of slavery, however, were in denial about the increasing whiteness of their beloved institution and were unwilling to contend with it directly.[1]

Beginning in the 1830s, privileged men of the South began formulating the "proslavery argument," a collection of lengthy, persuasive documents which might be summed up as follows: slavery is a necessity of civilization; whites are suited to freedom; and black people, inferior, subhuman beings, are uniquely equipped by God for servitude. Despite its reliance on racial identity, and the volume of writing put forth, the proslavery argument never quite addressed the question of where mixed race people fit in.[2]

Implicit in the classification of mixed race people was application of the "one-drop" or "hypodescent" rule, a legal standard that assigned to mixed raced persons the status of the subordinate group.[3] Thus, anyone with an African ancestor, anywhere or at any time, in one's family lineage should be considered black. The one-drop rule still could not explain—according to the proslavery movement's own racial reasoning—why mixed race people with the assumed white blood of freedom flowing through their veins could be considered slaves. The hypodescent rule, nevertheless, served its purpose.

In the antebellum South, the one-drop rule functioned to keep all mixed race children born to slave women under the control of the slaveholder, thus ensuring a steady supply of labor, continued indulgence of sexual desires, and the maintenance of white supremacy. For whites to have defined mixed race children as anything other than black would have been a major threat to a system that provided the white male ruling class with great social, economic, and sexual power.[4]

Though legally classified as black, illegitimate and enslaved mixed race offspring, in comparison to the black population at large, sometimes benefited from their white familial ties and skin color. As opposed to their darker brothers and sisters who were often relegated to physical labor in the fields, mulatto slaves were more likely to be put to work as house servants. As a consequence of this more intimate contact with their masters, mulattoes were exposed to a way of life that they sought to emulate and imitate, and they were sometimes afforded social, economic, and ancestral privileges generally unavailable to the black masses.

Among free blacks, mulattoes also constituted a disproportionate percentage of the black population. In 1850, for example, mulattoes made up 11 percent of the total black population and 36 percent of free blacks. In the lower South, where Fredi Washington was born, the correlation between mixed race and freedom was even greater. Seventy percent of the free black population was mulatto.[5]

In the period before and immediately following the Civil War, the beneficiaries of these privileges, the aristocrats of color and the "mulatto elite," became the leaders of the black community. During Reconstruction, there were twenty black congressmen and two black senators in Washington, D.C. All but three were of mixed race, and some were very light.[6]

The 1927 film *Scar of Shame*, which takes up the subject of caste distinctions, points out that skin color was not the only prerequisite for membership in the upper strata of black society. This silent race film stars chorus girl Lucia Lynn Moses as a young woman who, despite her light complexion and marriage to a member of the mulatto elite, fails to gain permanent entry into her husband's class due to her lack of respectable family connections. Well into the 20th century, family name and ancestry were considered highly important to upper class blacks.

After the Civil War, owing to the great fear of miscegenation, Southerners became fiercely intolerant of anyone who was not distinctly black or white. Free mulattoes who might have once been treated with a modicum of acceptance were increasingly alienated from whites. In response to the escalating hostilities, upper-class mulattoes had no choice but to abandon their dream of assimilation with whites and strengthen their ties with blacks.[7]

The cultural and physical melding of blacks and mulattoes that occurred during and after Reconstruction was the genesis of a new people who came to be known as the "New Negro" and by the early 20th century their nerve center was Harlem. When Fredi Washington arrived in New York, blacks and mulattoes alike were celebrating the New Negro and, by default, embracing, along with whites, the one-drop definition of who is black in America.[8] Though her image at times resisted it, in her "personal" life, Fredi Washington was among the Southern-born mulattoes to proudly proclaim this new black identity.

Fredericka Carolyn Washington was born on December 23, 1903, in Savannah, Georgia. Less than half a century before her birth, a planter who had mismanaged his inheritance made Savannah the site of the largest recorded sale of human beings in the history of the United States. Among slaves and their descendants this event became known as the "weeping time" for the unimaginable grief caused by the break-up of homes and families and the incessant rain that fell during the two-day period in which 436 men, women, and children were auctioned off.

Although before the Civil War, most of its black population was enslaved, Savannah was also home to a small but prosperous free black community. In Savannah, like other cities of the South, free blacks considered themselves a caste apart from slaves.[9] After the war, these mostly mixed race, free blacks and their descendants made up a large portion of the old aristocrats of color. Stemming from the class structure instituted under slavery, what accounted for prestige in the black community immediately following the war was not necessarily wealth or occupation but rather ancestry, family name, and skin color. Consequently, aristocrats of color were known to possess detailed knowledge of their ancestors on both sides of the racial divide. Although they tended to distance themselves from the black population at large, the black upper class also considered it their duty to "elevate the race."[10]

What is readily known of Fredi Washington's family history suggests that she was neither part of the black masses nor a member of the uppermost strata of Savannah's black community. The actress once recalled that growing up, any discussion of the circumstances that led to her family's skin color was off-limits.[11] Perhaps her family's silence on the subject was a reaction to the recent hostilities aimed at mulattoes by whites, but it also contradicts the sense of pride aristocrats of color took in their mixed heritage.

It is likely that the Washington family, who resided next to a white fire chief in a mostly-white neighborhood, occupied an elite status a rung or two below the aristocrats of color.[12] Census records from 1910 identify six-year-old Fredericka and the rest of her family, including parents Robert and Hattie and three siblings, as "mulatto."[13] Robert worked as a porter, part-time barber, and postal worker, professions that carried with them a measure of prestige within the black social structure of the day.[14]

Fredi's childhood in Savannah was disrupted in 1915 when her mother passed away. When her father remarried, she and sister Isabel were sent to be educated at a convent and Catholic boarding school for black and Native American children in Pennsylvania. While they were at the convent their stepmother died, and Robert married for a third time. All told, Washington had nine siblings, who all favored each other because the women her father chose to marry all "looked alike."[15]

When the two sisters reached their teens, Fredi moved to New York to live with her aunt and maternal grandmother. Isabel returned to the South. After marrying and having a child at sixteen, Isabel later joined Fredi in New York and pursued her own career in show business until she married pastor, future congressman, and member of Harlem's mulatto elite Adam Clayton Powell, Jr.

As a concept, Harlem was a black haven, and for many, it was an improvement over their previous living conditions. In reality, life in Harlem was tough. Blacks lived in overpriced, overcrowded boarding houses that often lacked sufficient heat and hot water and where it was not uncommon for rats, bedbugs, and garbage to be left unattended.[16] To help make ends meet, Washington dropped out of school to find work. With the help of her father, who had also come to New York by then, she eventually found a job as a typist and bookkeeper at the black-owned company Black Swan Records. There, Washington made the acquaintance of entertainers such as Mamie Smith, Revella Hughes, and Ethel Waters.[17]

Lured by the prospect of doubling her income, Washington in 1922 decided to try out as a chorus girl. She had no prior experience singing or dancing, but her youth, light skin color and lithe physique certainly fit the chorus-girl bill. Washington auditioned for dancer and choreographer Elida Webb and won a spot with the touring company of *Shuffle Along* where she found herself at the opposite end of the Happy Honeysuckles chorus line from Josephine Baker. The two women became friends, and when Baker was derided by other chorus girls, it was Washington who came to her defense.[18]

That same year Fredi Washington made her first screen appearance in the silent film *Square Joe*. A race film directed by J. Harrison Edwards, *Square Joe* was shot in Harlem and featured the great boxer Joe Jennette as an innocent man wrongly accused of a crime. During its three-day premiere at the Roosevelt, *Square Joe* played to capacity audiences. Marion Moore, daughter of *New York Age* publisher, played the female lead. Little is known about Washington's role in the film, but she did receive mention in a *New York Age* review.[19] Though Washington preferred acting over dancing, dramatic opportunities were few and far between. After *Square Joe*, it was back to dancing in New York nightclubs and cabarets, including Club Alabam.

Located in midtown, Club Alabam offered its white patrons the Harlem cabaret experience without the hassle or expense of travelling uptown.[20] In 1925 *Variety* deemed the Club Alabam floorshow *the* best in and around New York. The shows included provocative numbers like "The Slave Market," with a "hoochie-coochie" slave girl who tries to tempt a prospective buyer. Though the show's performers were black, all imaginings of race were represented. Another popular scene was titled the "Apache's Den." In addition to her place in the chorus line—a "corking set of Creole 'lookers'"—Washington became known for her specialty dancing. One such dance was called the "Jazz of Pash." Another featured a bullfight scene, in which she was the "bull."[21]

In 1926, Washington's talent caught the attention of Lee Shubert, who recommended her to theatrical producer Horace Liveright for a part in the play *Black Boy*. After convincing Liveright that she was indeed black and then reading for him, Washington got the only female role in a racially mixed cast that featured Paul Robeson in the lead. With her role in *Black Boy*, Fredi Washington became Broadway's first sexually dangerous mulatto.[22]

Loosely based on the biography of Jack Johnson, the boxer who had a predilection for prostitutes and white women, *Black Boy* is the story of a naive drifter who becomes a heavyweight champion. Washington had the part of Irene, a prostitute idolized by Black Boy because she is white, or so he thinks. Not only does Irene betray Black Boy, the play's ending also reveals that Irene has been passing for white.

Variety opined that this plot twist and the casting of a black actress who looks white was a compromise made for those white audience members who would have been offended by the sight of an interracial couple.[23] Worried that her reputation as dancer might hinder her chances at acting, Washington was billed in the play as Edith Warren. Several reviewers, including one from the black newspaper *The Pittsburgh Courier*, described Edith Warren as a white actress, and some playgoers wrote letters protesting the interracial love scenes between Washington and Robeson.[24]

During *Black Boy*'s brief one-month run Washington and Robeson began an affair that, despite long separations and Robeson's marriage, lasted more than twenty years.[25] It was around this time that Washington also made the acquaintance of Otto Kahn, a millionaire investment banker and patron of the arts. Kahn thought Washington's "frisky Charleston" dance was a highlight of the play and suggested that she give up acting and return to dancing.[26] Kahn was also of the opinion that race was the only obstacle preventing Washington from becoming a great star. He thought the actress looked French and advised her to adopt a French name—in effect, pass for white. As her story is often told, Washington ignored the advice of Kahn and others who told her she should pass. Nevertheless, it seems that Otto Kahn might have had some small influence on her career.

Soon after meeting Kahn, Fredi Washington formed a dance partnership with Al Moore, a mixed race native New Yorker whose father was Italian. One of the team's first engagements was at Le Perroquet de Paris ("The Parrakeet"). The ultra-posh midtown Manhattan nightclub, which was owned by Otto Kahn's son, featured French-made mural panels, mirrored dance floors, and hanging cages with live parrots. "Al and Freddie" soon came to be known by the French-sounding moniker "Moiret et Fredi" and developed choreography in the ballroom dancing style known as adagio.[27]

Moiret et Fredi, the first African Americans to perform at New York's swanky St. Regis Hotel, were considered among the top dancers in their class.[28] Still, there was not much demand from audiences, black or white, for an elegant, formally dressed, light-skinned dancing couple and, following in the footsteps of other black entertainers, Moiret et Fredi decided to try their act in Europe.[29] At the end of 1928, after two years of performing in such places as Paris, Berlin, Monte Carlo, and London, weary of touring, Moore and Washington returned to the United States.

For a short time after their return from Europe, Moiret et Fredi continued their act together in nightclubs and theaters. In 1929 they replaced the ballroom dancing team of Paul and Thelma Meers in *Hot Chocolates*. An all-black revue staged by Leonard Harper, and which originated at Connie's Inn, *Hot Chocolates* had made its way from Harlem to the Hudson Theatre on Broadway. Moiret et Fredi were also seen in the Broadway production *Great Day*.

The year 1929 was also the year that Fredi Washington had her first experience with a major Hollywood studio. In Paramount's early sound film *The Letter*, based on a William Somerset Maugham short story and set in Singapore, Washington and sister Isabel had uncredited roles as dancers in an opium den. The three dancers in this scene are wearing what appear to be Southeast Asian-inspired masks, thus visual confirmation is not possible, but the spectacle certainly fits with the way in which Fredi and other dancers played with race at the Club Alabam. Yet another achievement for the Washington sisters in 1929 was their separate appearances in musical short films directed by Dudley Murphy. Isabel had a part in *St. Louis Blues*, starring blues singer Bessie Smith, while Fredi was featured in *Black and Tan*.

Black and Tan (1929)

Produced by RKO, a major studio of the day, this all black-cast short film features Fredi Washington as a chorus girl who dances herself to death to the music of composer and bandleader Duke Ellington. The film's writer and director, Dudley Murphy, was a former American expatriate who had lived in Paris during the 1920s. Upon his return to

New York, Murphy, affected by the verve of Harlem, wanted to make sound films featuring the music of black composers. Murphy sought out Carl Van Vechten, the man whose entrée to Harlem was facilitated by Walter White and whose passion for blackness helped bring white attention to the Harlem Renaissance. For Washington, *Black and Tan* provides an example of the dancing for which she was so well known. For Ellington, it was his first onscreen appearance and his most substantial acting role.

A native of Washington, D.C., Duke Ellington was born in 1899, a time when the nation's capital was the center of the black aristocracy. Just below the aristocratic families was a large class of businessmen, professionals, and government workers, which was middle-class by white standards, but considered elite in the black community. This elite society into which Ellington was born was not unified but rather highly stratified. A white observer of the city's black social structure noted that its caste system was as strong as the Brahmin's.[30] Ellington recalled that he didn't know how many black castes there were at the time, but he did know that he and his cousins were not supposed to mix carelessly with those outside of their own.[31] But associating with blacks outside their circle, exploring and revering blackness, is exactly what distinguished Ellington and other members of the mulatto elite during the Harlem Renaissance from their parents and grandparents.[32]

The title of this short film is derived from "Black and Tan Fantasy," a tune Ellington composed with trumpeter James "Bubber" Miley and first recorded in 1927. Originating in the American South, the term "black and tan" initially referred to a coalition of black and white men that sought to include African Americans in the Republican Party. Eventually the term evolved from its political context to include broader social and sexual interracial connotations.

For Ellington, "black and tan" referred to the nightclubs in New York and other cities across the country where people of different races could interact in ways generally not tolerated in other social circumstances.[33] Distinct from venues like the Club Alabam or the Cotton Club, which featured black entertainment for white audiences, patrons of the black and tans were racially mixed. With contrasting themes derived from European classical music, jazz, and the blues, the Ellington and Miley tune "Black and Tan Fantasy" is wholly suggestive of this merging of racial and cultural boundaries.

Duke Ellington was the love of Fredi Washington's life. While Ellington was married, he and Washington had a passionate affair that finally ended when Washington realized Ellington was not going to marry her.[34] Ellington's son, Mercer, in a memoir about his father, makes mention of the connection between the song "Black and Tan Fantasy" and an affair Ellington had with a "very beautiful and talented" unnamed actress. The affair, he said, was the cause of his parent's break-up. Throughout his life, Mercer states, his father wrote compositions inspired by the various women in his life. "Sophisticated Lady" relates to Ellington's wife and Mercer's mother, Edna. "Black and Tan Fantasy" memorializes the "death of love and the end of his affair with the actress,"[35] presumably Fredi Washington.

In the film *Black and Tan*, Fredi Washington and Duke Ellington essentially play versions of themselves. Ellington is a musician, and Washington, his love interest, is a dancer who wants to help her man succeed. The action begins in a Harlem apartment where Ellington and trumpeter Arthur Whetsol, both dressed in suit and tie, are practicing the opening section of "Black and Tan Fantasy." Just a few months before filming *Black and Tan*, Ellington had fired James Miley, the trumpeter with whom he co-wrote the song. Arthur Whetsol, a boyhood friend of Ellington's, was his replacement. Had

Miley not been fired, perhaps he would have had the part of trumpeter. The use of Whetsol, however, who had a lighter complexion than Miley, and, like Ellington, had a genteel upbringing, contributes significantly to the racial politics of the film.[36]

The practice session is interrupted when two men arrive to repossess Duke's piano. The illiterate, comic repo men present a striking contrast to the well-groomed musical aficionados. The appearance of Fredi Washington, who arrives just moments later, punctuates that difference. Ellington, Whetsol, and Washington personify the New Negro of the Harlem Renaissance, while the piano movers, played by Alec Lovejoy and Edgar Connor, represent the old, non-threatening, familiar types. Fredi forestalls the repossession by offering the movers some gin. To Ellington and Whetsol, she announces that she's found them all a gig. Duke reminds her that she shouldn't dance because of her heart condition, but Fredi is determined to do it anyway.

As opposed to a black and tan club with a racially mixed clientele, the nightclub scene that follows is suggestive of the Cotton Club, where blacks performed for white audiences and where Ellington was employed at the time. Onscreen, while he and the Cotton Club orchestra play, actual Cotton Club acts, the Five Hot Shots and Cotton Club Girls, perform. In between these two numbers, Washington makes her appearance as a featured solo dancer. Fredi dances to "Cotton Club Stomp" but partway through she collapses and is carried offstage.

The manager insists that the show must go on and six chorus girls take the stage. In the midst of their routine, Ellington abruptly quits playing so that he can attend to Fredi on her deathbed. Fredi's last wish, to hear "Black and Tan Fantasy," is granted by Ellington, who is supported by his orchestra and the Hall Johnson Choir. As Fredi draws her last breaths, the last thing she sees is Ellington's face, which gradually loses focus and then fades out.

The love story of Fredi and Duke in *Black and Tan* is straitlaced and tender. Dignified romance between black actors had been depicted in race movies, but in a film intended for consumption by mainstream audiences, it is possibly a first. Their apparent monogamous relationship provides a stark contrast to the cruel love triangle in Murphy's other short film of the year, *St. Louis Blues*. In the press, *Black and Tan* received favorable reviews. *Variety* deemed both the music and the cinematography worthwhile attractions and noted that it had more "jazz heaven" in it than *Jazz Heaven*, the white-cast feature film it accompanied.[37] *Black and Tan* was named to the National Film Registry in 2015.

Before making her next significant appearance on film, Washington appeared again on Broadway in *Sweet Chariot* (1930), *Singin' the Blues* (1931), and *Run, Little Chillun* (1933). *Sweet Chariot*, inspired by Marcus Garvey and his Back-to-Africa movement, featured Frank Wilson in the role of Marius Harvey. Fredi Washington was Lola, a secretary enamored with Harvey, her boss. Although the play survived only three performances, *The New York Sun* reported that Washington had "some good moments as Harvey's nearly-white secretary," and *The New York Age* rated her work as excellent.[38]

With a run of 45 performances, *Singin' the Blues* fared much better. Music and lyrics were by Jimmy McHugh and Dorothy Fields with performances from Eubie Blake and his orchestra. Washington's sister, Isabel, was the female star, a nightclub singer. Fredi played her sister's jealous rival, a character described by one reviewer as a "Lenox Avenue gold-digger who lies and cheats and spies."[39] Part melodrama, part musical revue, *Singin' the Blues* also featured Mantan Moreland and Lucia Moses as well as Frank Wilson as Isabel's fugitive lover. Sammy Lee was the choreographer. Singing and dancing were the highlights of this show, which *The New York Times* described as "picturesque and pungent." The *Afro-American* declared that Fredi Washington, who had "all the ease, poise and grace of a veteran actress," made "an elegant bad woman."[40]

The most successful of Washington's stage productions during this period was Hall Johnson's *Run, Little Chillun'!* Its plot presented a conflict between Christian Baptists and practitioners of African paganism, called the Pilgrims. As the strumpet Sulamai, who had dalliances with men on both sides of the religious fence, Washington was torn between the "civilized" and the "primitive." After having an affair with Jim, married son of the Baptist pastor, and convincing him to attend a meeting of the Pilgrims, Sulamai takes up with the pagans' leader, Brother Moses. Jim is reconverted and returns to his family. When Sulamai attempts to repent and seek the love of Christ she is struck dead by a bolt of lightning. Much of the critical attention for this work focused on Johnson's composition and arrangements, which gave prominence to the Negro spiritual.

When *Run, Little Chillun* ended, Fredi reunited with director Dudley Murphy and actor Paul Robeson for the independent feature film *The Emperor Jones*. That same year Washington married Lawrence Brown, a trombonist in Duke Ellington's orchestra. Apparently, the marriage was contrived by Ellington so that Washington would have a reason to travel with the band and remain close to its leader.[41] When her marriage ended in 1948, however, it was Washington who accused Brown of being unfaithful with numerous women.[42]

The Emperor Jones (1933)

Based on a Eugene O'Neill play that made its debut in 1920, *The Emperor Jones* stars Paul Robeson as Brutus Jones, a convict who escapes from prison to become the ruler of a Caribbean island. Robeson had already acted the part of Brutus Jones on stage in London and again in a 1925 Broadway revival. Fredi Washington's appearance in the early part of the film, as the prostitute Undine, is part of a reference to Harlem that provides backstory to the circumstances that led Brutus Jones to prison.

Censorship of *The Emperor Jones* began even before the film was finished. After seeing early rushes, the Hays Office was concerned that Washington would be mistaken for a white woman. Consequently, Washington's scenes with Robeson had to be redone with her wearing dark makeup. The resulting effect left Washington looking a little eerie, thereby accentuating her position as the bad woman. Censorship continued after the film was finished, including the deletion of a shot in which Brutus Jones strikes and kills a white prison guard as well as other scenes from the final act in which Jones is alone in the jungle experiencing a mental breakdown.[43]

While *The Emperor Jones* was still in production, *The Pittsburgh Courier* contrasted it with *Hallelujah*, assuring readers that there would be no ridiculous scenes involving a minister who stops in the middle of a sermon to chase after his lover.[44] While that proved to be true, the film's early scenes are nevertheless reminiscent of *Hallelujah*. Like its predecessor, *The Emperor Jones* has a male protagonist who leaves his Southern home and a good, dark-skinned woman behind. During his travels, Brutus, like Zeke, encounters a fast, light-skinned woman who stands for the seamy side of urban life.

Much like Nina Mae McKinney's Chick, Fredi Washington's Undine is a two-timing gold-digger. Undine's character, however, is the entirely unsympathetic, depraved mulatto. After Jones dumps her, Undine physically attacks his new girlfriend and then exits the picture. Both the protagonists of *Hallelujah* and *The Emperor Jones* run into trouble over a craps game in which someone winds up dead and they are both sentenced to work on a chain gang. At this point the two stories diverge. Mainstream reviewers generally praised *The Emperor Jones* as an artistic achievement for Robeson and the filmmakers.[45]

Cab Calloway's Hi-De-Ho (1934)

In her next short film, *Cab Calloway's Hi-De-Ho*, Fredi Washington starred opposite singer, dancer, and bandleader Cab Calloway. Cabell Calloway III was born in Rochester, New York, in 1907. His mother was a music teacher, and his father was a lawyer. His family later moved to Baltimore where his father had grown up, and Calloway lived out a good deal of his childhood in the home his grandparents had owned since before the turn of the century. Calloway's parents were not wealthy, but the family home where they resided was located on Druid Hill Avenue, a segregated neighborhood where many of Baltimore's black elite lived. Instead of following his father's career path and becoming a lawyer, Calloway quit college to enter show business.[46] By 1931, Calloway and his band had replaced Duke Ellington's orchestra as resident band of the Cotton Club. By the late 1930s, Calloway had one of the most successful black bands of the swing era.

In *Cab Calloway's Hi-De-Ho*, Fredi Washington was upgraded from a Pullman porter's prostitute in *The Emperor Jones* to Pullman porter's wife. Despite the seeming elevation in status, her character, never referred to by name, remains less than honorable. In this short film produced by Paramount Pictures, Calloway is on tour with his band when he makes the acquaintance of Washington's husband, Sam. The Pullman porter confides to Calloway that his wife is a "steppin' out fool" who loves jazz. Calloway advises Sam to keep his wife entertained at home while he's away with the purchase of a name brand radio that "brings the leading radio artists into your home."

Sam purchases the radio and, secure in the knowledge that his wife will no longer need to step out, he goes back out to work on the railroad. When Washington turns on the radio to listen to Cab Calloway, she is transported to a table at the Cotton Club where Calloway and his orchestra, along with five chorus girls, are performing "The Lady with a Fan." After the number is over Calloway joins Sam's wife at her table. In the shot that immediately follows, Washington and Calloway are back at her apartment making out on the sofa when Sam returns home unexpectedly. Calloway hides in the bedroom. With gun drawn, Sam orders the intruder to come out. As instructed, Calloway—and his band—come out of the bedroom and exit the apartment peacefully.

As fanciful as this story is, with respect to Calloway, it does have some basis in fact. The first scene and musical performance takes place on the sleeper car of a train. In actuality, when touring, Calloway and his band often travelled by train. To avoid the indignities of traveling in the segregated South, both Cab Calloway and Duke Ellington chartered their own Pullman sleepers. Calloway was known to bring along his own staff of valets and a limousine that was stowed in the baggage car.

Radio, which features prominently in this film, is the medium that made Calloway a national star. His shows from the Cotton Club were broadcast nationally by NBC, and his was the first black band to be invited to appear on the Lucky Strike Dance Hour. His talent and showmanship aside, Cab Calloway's straight hair, which he tossed about wildly, and his light skin might well have contributed to his ability to transcend racial boundaries. Attesting to his crossover appeal, Calloway's recording of "Minnie the Moocher" was the first by a black artist to sell over a million copies.[47]

Imitation of Life (1934)

In Universal's *Imitation of Life*, Fredi Washington played Hollywood's most iconic mixed race character, Peola, a mulatto who desperately wants to be white. After the film was released, "Peola" soon became a popular slang epithet among African Americans for light-skinned black women who were not quite black enough.[48] Based on a novel by Fannie Hurst and directed by John Stahl, *Imitation of Life* marks the first time a major studio cast an African American actor in the role of a black person passing for white. Even to this day, the actress is one of only a handful to have earned this distinction. With Washington's performance as the anti-heroine Peola, *Imitation of Life* stands out as the flagship of passing and mixed race tragedy in film.

At the time of its release in 1934, *Variety* declared that *Imitation of Life* was the first film to take up the tragedy of being born to "a white skin and Negro blood."[49] Seven years earlier, however, Universal released *Uncle Tom's Cabin* (1927), Harry Pollard's epic silent film adaptation of Harriet Beecher Stowe's 1852 novel. In Stowe's novel, Eliza Harris is a

Lobby card for Universal's *Uncle Tom's Cabin* (1927), featuring Margarita Fisher as slave and tragic octoroon Eliza Harris and James Lowe as Tom. Author's collection.

light-skinned slave who crosses not only racial lines but also gender lines. Eliza passes as a white man to gain her freedom while her husband, George, passes as a Spaniard.

The story of Eliza's passing in *Uncle Tom's Cabin* brings to mind the true story of fugitive slaves Ellen and William Craft, who in 1848, with Ellen posing as a slave master and William as her slave, fled from their bondage in Georgia to freedom in the North. Although their narrative, *Running a Thousand Miles for Freedom*, was not published until 1860, the Crafts' story was well known and began circulating in abolitionist lectures and newspapers shortly after their escape.

Passing is avoided altogether in Universal's film version of *Uncle Tom's Cabin*. Nevertheless, the tribulations of a near-white family of slaves (played by white actors) remain central to the film's storyline. Several years before *Uncle Tom's Cabin*, Oscar Micheaux, the prolific African American director and producer of race movies, addressed invisible blackness and various forms of passing in such films as *The Homesteader* (1919), *The Symbol of the Unconquered* (1920), and, later, *The Exile* (1931) and *Veiled Aristocrats* (1932). In 1938 Micheaux released *God's Stepchildren,* his response to *Imitation of Life*. Before Micheaux, as discussed in the Introduction, white filmmakers took up the woes of light-skinned blackness in films like *The Sealed Envelope* (1912), *The Debt* (1912), and *The Octoroon* (1913).

Imitation of Life, therefore, was not the first picture to examine the tragedy of being born to "a white skin and Negro blood," but it was the first big Hollywood feature to address the phenomenon of passing, prefiguring by more than a decade the message movie cycle, which included the films *Lost Boundaries* (1949) and *Pinky* (1949). To find an actress who could pass for white in *Imitation of Life*, Stahl began an exhaustive search in Los Angeles. The *California Eagle* reported that Stahl was looking for a "young girl who must be of Negro blood but must be absolutely white—a 'throwback' of several generations in which there has at some time been a white father!"[50] When the search was extended to New York, Fredi Washington tested for the role. Some months later, while in Los Angeles, the actress was summoned to Universal and offered the part.

During negotiations Washington confounded studio executives by refusing to sign the industry's customary long-term contract, which offered actors a steady income in exchange for complete control over their career. Such contracts required them to act in whatever film the studio chose for them, allowed the studio to loan them out to other studios, and precluded them from participating in other acting opportunities, such as in theater, radio, or television. Keenly aware of the limited and demeaning screen roles reserved for African Americans, Fredi Washington had no interest in becoming a contract player. In the end, she managed to negotiate a one-picture deal with Universal.[51]

Claudette Colbert, who went on to win an Oscar for *It Happened One Night,* released earlier that year, enacted the role of young widow and mother Bea Pullman. Rochelle Hudson played the part of Bea's daughter, Jessie. Louise Beavers, an actress whose mammy portrayals rival that of Hattie McDaniel, also had an important role in the film. Although she was only a year older than Fredi Washington, Beavers was cast as Peola's mother, Delilah. Like Bea, Delilah is a widow. Mainstream critics of the day declared that Beavers stole the picture from Colbert, the intended star. "No one, white or Negro, has given a better performance this year on the screen," said one reviewer. *Variety* described Beavers' performance as "masterly" and said it was "one of the most unprecedented personal triumphs for an obscure performer in the annals" of the motion picture industry.[52]

The story in *Imitation of Life* begins with a fortuitous meeting between the two mothers, Bea and Delilah. This chance encounter results in the two women and their children taking up residence together, with Delilah serving as Bea's maid in exchange for room and board. At breakfast one morning Delilah shares the ingredients of her secret pancake recipe with Bea. Bea markets the recipe and fashions herself into a tycoon.

With her newfound fortune, Bea lives a lavish lifestyle, sends Jessie away to private school, and hosts posh parties. Delilah, with her 20 percent share of the business, could have easily purchased her own home and retired, but instead she insists on continuing to serve Miss Bea and maintaining their joint living arrangement. Consequently, Peola is raised in an environment from which she is essentially excluded, even though she looks and has been groomed to act the part.

The primary action in *Imitation of Life* revolves around the white heroine's climb to success and her attempt at romance. The real interest of the film, and the theme for which it is best known, is found in the subplot of the dark-skinned maid and her near-white daughter. The crux of this storyline is Peola's refusal to accept the racial identity imposed upon her, an identity that is incongruent with both her skin color and her experience. Yet, despite the emphasis on Peola's appearance, the question of how she came to be phenotypically white is neatly avoided. All that the film reveals is that Peola's father was "a very, very light colored man."

In the novel upon which the film is based, the question of Peola's ancestry is also evaded, but the author at least declares that the character has white blood flowing in her veins.[53] If the filmmakers had attempted to acknowledge or elaborate on the origins of this white blood, the PCA, presumably, would have deemed it a violation of its prohibition against miscegenation. *Imitation of Life*'s only reference to mixed race as a legacy of slavery occurs subliminally with the music that accompanies its opening credits, "Nobody Knows the Trouble I've Seen," a spiritual song rooted in slavery.

From the late 19th century into the early 20th century, a significant number of Americans of mixed European and African descent chose to pass over to whiteness. The impetus for passing arose in a society of great inequality, and in which one part of a person's ancestry was deemed real, essential, and defining, while other parts were considered accidental or insignificant. Passing was often perceived by whites as a threat, and those who passed were often considered dishonest tricksters.[54]

In *Imitation of Life*, lacking any historical context, Peola's "trouble" and her desire to escape from blackness is seen as personal rather than political, and it first rears its ugly head when Peola and Jessie are still children. On their way to school one day, Jessie has insulted Peola by calling her "black." Young Peola, played by child actress Dorothy Black, returns home and throws a tantrum. Crying uncontrollably, Peola renounces her blackness. "I won't be black.... You, it's because you're black. You make me black," she says to her mother. Peola's reaction, which on the surface seems a little neurotic, is better understood when one looks to the scene's source material. When the same incident occurs in Hurst's novel, instead of "black," Jessie uses the "n-word."[55]

The film doesn't actually show Jessie's offense. We only hear of it from Peola after the fact. Peola's on-camera reaction to an off-camera abuse is, by default, exaggerated. When Bea attempts to scold Jessie for hurting Peola's feelings, Delilah interrupts her to deliver the film's most didactic lines on racism. "Oh, t'aint her fault, Miss Bea. It ain't your'n and it ain't mine." Delilah then turns away from Bea and delivers a piece to the camera. "I don't know rightly where the blame lies. It can't be our Lord's. It's got me puzzled." Peola blames her mother for her anguish while the unequivocally black Delilah assures audiences that no one is to blame, not even God. According to the logic of both novel and film, either black people—simply for being black—are responsible for a system of inequality enforced through rigid racial categories or, as Delilah claims, no one is at fault.

Not long after the name-calling incident Peola is caught passing for the first time. During an unannounced visit to her school by Delilah, Peola is outed to her white teacher and classmates. A shamefaced Peola exits the classroom. "I hate you," she tells her mother. That we see only the white world Peola wishes to join, and never the oppression that she shuns, reinforces the notion that Peola's problem is personal. When she was a child, Peola's desire to be white comes across as impudence. As a young woman, instead of being understood as someone who wants the same social opportunities and treatment afforded to whites, Peola seems motivated by either a loathing of blackness or a fetishization of whiteness.

All grown up, Peola, now embodied by Fredi Washington, still can't accept her blackness. Positioning her dilemma as an individual pathology rather than a social ill is furthered in Bea's grand party scene. While merriment ensues upstairs, Delilah and Peola are relegated to their living quarters downstairs. Peola is restless and moody. When her mother asks what's wrong, Peola looks into a mirror and declares that she wants to be white, like she looks. Delilah pleads with her, "Can't you get it out of your head?" This

In Universal's *Imitation of Life* (1934), Fredi Washington's iconic tragic mulatto Peola desperately wants to be white. Her mother, played by Louise Beavers, plans to send her to a school in the South where she can learn how to be black.

self-examination in the mirror and Delilah's response work together to suggest that, in addition to her flawed character, Peola has a defective psyche.

As it turns out, Peola can't get it out of her head. At Bea's suggestion, Delilah sends her daughter to a black college in the South, where she could get a good education and, more importantly, learn how to be black. Before long, Delilah receives word that Peola has left the school. With Bea's help, Delilah tracks down Peola to a restaurant where she's been working as a cashier—and passing for white. Peola tries hard not to acknowledge her mother's presence, but it's no use. Delilah insists on making herself known. Thwarted by Delilah once again, Peola decides to leave for good. She tells her mother, "You mustn't see me, or own me, or claim me or anything."

The pain of being disowned by her daughter is too much for Delilah, who soon succumbs to illness. At Delilah's glorious funeral, Peola returns, guilt-ridden and repentant. She cries out in the street for her dead mother and makes her way toward the horse-drawn hearse into which Delilah's casket is being placed. Sobbing, Peola holds the casket close and asks for her mother's forgiveness. As Bea approaches, Peola wails, "Miss Bea, I've killed my own mother." This is the last time we see Peola.

In a subsequent scene, we are informed that Peola has decided to go back to the black college, just as her mother would have wanted. Universal's solution to Peola's mixed race trouble is to first blame the victim, then punish her for defying society's norms, and then guilt her into compliance. In the novel, Hurst's answer to the mixed race question is equally unsympathetic. Hurst allows Peola her whiteness, but with preconditions. Peola may marry her white boyfriend, but to diminish her as a potential threat to American society, and ensure that her black ancestry will be neither discovered by her husband nor passed on to unwitting future generations, she must move to Bolivia and undergo sterilization.[56]

Fredi Washington's Peola, most often described as a tragic mulatto, also has traits of the tragic octoroon. Isolated from other blacks, Peola was raised as a white child in the home of her mother's white employer. Like her counterpart of pre–Civil War fiction, in terms of speech, style, deportment and physical appearance, Peola is a carbon copy of white femininity. The residence where Peola was raised is a contemporary substitute for the plantation home of the slaveholding father. For all intents and purposes Peola is white. Only the presence of her mother, literally and conceptually, betrays Peola's African heritage.

Like that of the antebellum tragic octoroon, Peola's situation was not representative of the black population at large, but it brought attention, nevertheless, to the inequities of race and aroused some white sympathy for blacks. In the mainstream press, even though it was dubbed a "tearjerker" and a "woman's picture," *Imitation of Life* was generally considered a strong picture with superb acting. *Variety* even ventured to say that the film might contribute to greater tolerance and respect between the races.[57]

Dissenting from popular opinion, Andre Sennwald of *The New York Times* found the film's ideas shallow. Speaking to the stereotyped depiction of Peola, Sennwald commented that the screenplay was "content to suggest that all black women who are light enough to pass are doomed for unhappiness."[58] That the representation of blackness in *Imitation of Life* is problematic did not go unnoticed by black critics, either. In his critique of both the novel and the film, Sterling Brown, for example, noted that "it requires no searching analysis to see in *Imitation of Life* the old stereotype of the contented Mammy, and the tragic mulatto; and the ancient ideas about the mixture of the races."[59]

African Americans supported *Imitation of Life* enthusiastically at the box office, but commentary by *New York Age* critic Vere Johns suggests that inside the theater, black audiences were not enamored with the film's representations. Johns saw the film twice, first in a predominantly white theater, then at a black theater. At the first viewing he was annoyed by the laughter of two African American women. When he saw the film with an all-black audience, he found that the laughter was widespread. They laughed at Delilah for "being so dumb and illiterate," and they jeered Peola for wanting to be white.

Yet, for its absence of plantation caricatures, and for attempting to examine racial injustice, other critics, including Vere Johns, Fay Jackson and Harry Levette, chose to look past the film's hokum and deemed it a triumph and a sign of progress—onscreen and off. Writing for *The Pittsburgh Courier*, George Schuyler declared that not only had it had "a profound effect on the white South," *Imitation of Life* was a "landmark in the history of the American theater."[60]

After the release of *Imitation of Life* Washington was obliged to respond to moviegoers who wondered to what extent the actress was like Peola. The character was "created by white people and it is their conception not mine, of the problems that our girls face when they are light enough to pass," she said.[61] Washington further claimed that she did not relate to Peola's problems and that she had never passed for white nor did she have any desire to do so. There is no question that Washington was proud of her black heritage. However, when it came to getting more for her money, better accommodations, or access to public places from which she would otherwise be barred, Fredi Washington had no problem taking full advantage of her white skin.

When asked in an interview what happens when she goes into a white hotel or a white restaurant, Washington replied that nothing happens: "I just go in, if it's a hotel, and get a room; or if a restaurant, I eat."[62] When travelling through the South with Duke Ellington and his band, Washington was known for purchasing ice cream from whites-only ice cream parlors. Once outside the ice cream shop, to the dismay of white onlookers, she would hand out the ice cream to all the band members.[63] Washington did not consider such instances of being taken for white as passing because, unlike Peola, she did not want to be white nor did she wish to cut off ties from her black friends and family.[64]

In the decade that followed, *Imitation of Life* continued to play in community theaters without incident. However, in 1945, more than ten years after its original release, the city of Atlanta banned the film because it found its "treatment of the racial question contrary to the good order of the community."[65] In 1959 the film was remade starring the non-black actress Susan Kohner as Sarah Jane, a hypersexualized version of Peola.

The Love Wanga (1935)

Long before the black mamas of the blaxploitation era—before Marki Bey entreated zombies to settle the score against whites in *Sugar Hill* (1974)—Fredi Washington was using voodoo to exact racial revenge in *The Love Wanga*. Also known as *Drums of the Jungle, Drums in the Night, The Crime of Voodoo,* and *Ouanga,* this voodoo thriller, made in association with Paramount Picture's foreign subsidiary, was written, directed, and produced by George Terwilliger, a protégé of D.W. Griffith.[66]

It would be easy to dismiss Terwilliger's film for its inferior production values.

Conceptually, however, *The Love Wanga* was ahead of its time. As the second zombie film ever made, after *White Zombie* (1932), it is the first to feature black characters not simply as catatonic bodies risen from the dead but as the story's central figures. Most notably, *The Love Wanga* unabashedly represents interracial desire and ventures to show Fredi Washington throwing herself at one white actor and kissing another.

Although *The Love Wanga* was ready for exhibition before filming had even started on *Imitation of Life*, due most likely to its volatile and taboo subject matter—voodoo as witchcraft, miscegenation, and black revenge—Paramount decided not to release it in the United States. In 1935 it was released in Britain, and while there remains some question as to whether the film should be classified as foreign or American, according to *Variety*, this was the first time a major studio had premiered an American picture overseas.[67]

It would be another six years before the film was seen in the United States. *The Love Wanga* received its seal of approval from the PCA in September 1941, during Joseph Breen's brief hiatus from his role as PCA chief. Although certain parts were censored, and it was released without credits, it is remarkable that the film was approved at all. Breen's absence probably accounts for this atypical loosening of PCA standards.[68]

Set in Haiti, *The Love Wanga* stars Fredi Washington as a mixed race plantation owner who has a foothold in two racial communities. As a landowner and businesswoman, Clelie Gordon is on par, economically, with the whites. As a high voodoo priestess, she also wields power among the blacks. Clelie is undeterred by social propriety, and her dogged pursuit of neighboring white planter Adam Maynard makes something of a fetish out of whiteness. When Adam rejects her and decides to take a white wife, Clelie attempts to use voodoo to stop his marriage. While Clelie is busy chasing after Adam, she is also rebuffing the advances of Adam's mulatto overseer, LeStrange.

Sheldon Leonard, the Jewish actor who went on to have a successful career in Hollywood and television as a writer, actor, and producer, plays the part of LeStrange. It's hard to tell if Leonard wore dark makeup for this "blackface" performance, but given the film's second-rate production values, Washington's fair complexion, and Leonard's seemingly natural and somewhat swarthy complexion, cosmetic blacking up might have been deemed unnecessary. Dark makeup or not, next to Fredi Washington, Leonard seems to fit right in, and his portrayal of the mulatto overseer is actually one of the least outlandish aspects of this film.

The documentary style with which *The Love Wanga* begins turns quickly into camp. An early scene features Fredi Washington at the center of a voodoo ceremony wearing what looks like a costume from her former chorine days. Surrounded by West Indians, singing, chanting and drumming, Washington dances in front of a fire and is soon joined by six other women who also look like they just stepped off a chorus line. At the end of the ceremony a love charm or ouanga is bestowed upon Clelie for her protection.

The action next takes us aboard an ocean liner where Clelie is stalking Adam upon his return from New York with his fiancée, Eve. Clelie manages to get Adam alone and confesses her love. Adam expresses his affinity for Clelie, but she belongs with her own kind, he says. He also informs Clelie of his plans to marry Eve.

Once back in Haiti, LeStrange tries to get Clelie to forget about Adam by reminding her that his "master" is going to marry a white woman. Clelie, trying to prove that she is just as white as Eve, makes an exhibition of her face and hands and then as further proof rips open the top of her dress. The sight of Clelie's décolletage incites LeStrange to take her in his arms, which leads to moments of lustful hugging and kissing. At first Clelie is taken in by the passion, but when the faint sound of voodoo drums begins, she pulls away. Having come to her senses, Clelie puts LeStrange back in his place and calls him "black scum."

Although this love scene is certainly one of the earliest instances—if not the first—of a white actor and a black actress kissing in an American feature length film, it was not intended to be interpreted as interracial. Technically, therefore, it was not a violation of the Production Code, but it is certainly in conflict with the spirit of the Code. Release of the film without credits probably helped conceal this "real" act of miscegenation, which presumably would have been rejected outright by the Hays Office if the black actress were visibly black and the white actor unmistakably white.

After Clelie's first voodoo caper fails, she raises two bodies from their graves to help her kidnap Eve for a sacrifice. Meanwhile, LeStrange, angered by Clelie's rejection, vows to outvoodoo his voodoo priestess. When LeStrange attempts to rescue Eve, Clelie shoots him. Although fatally wounded, LeStrange manages to snatch Clelie's love charm from her. He follows her to the sacrificial ceremony where Clelie is about to deliver a fatal knife strike to the white woman.

Clelie spies LeStrange and becomes unnerved at the sight of him setting fire to her ouanga. She runs off into the bush where she discovers LeStrange's voodoo handiwork: a female corpse garbed in one of her own dresses and hanging from a tree. According to voodoo lore, if Clelie can't recover her clothing, she is doomed to die in awful agony. LeStrange, who is about to succumb to his gunshot wound, doesn't have time to wait and watch Clelie drive herself mad trying to get her dress back, so he strangles her to death.

For its overt representation of miscegenation, for placing two mixed race characters at the center of a story, and for transforming the mulatto's racial frustration from tragedy into terror, *The Love Wanga* might be called the anti–*Imitation of Life* and Clelie might be considered Peola's alter ego. In Clelie we find the sexuality and animus that in Peola's character had to be suppressed. Peola was denied a love interest of any color. In what appears to be the earliest instance of the biracial love triangle, Clelie has two lovers, one black and one white.

Although Adam and Clelie never kiss, there are intimate moments between the two, including a very suggestive one in which Clelie, while begging Adam to love her, gets on her knees, places her hands on Adam's waist, and presses her head into his abdomen. Thus, in *The Love Wanga*, the specter of miscegenation moves beyond that which is merely implied by the corporeal identities of either Peola or Clelie to that which is openly expressed in the relationship between Clelie and Adam.

Both Peola and Clelie chase after whiteness, but when it becomes evident that their efforts have been in vain, the outcomes are very different. When Peola decides to return to the black college, as her mother would have wanted, she does so out of grief, guilt, and shame. As this important moment is revealed by other characters and takes place offscreen, Peola is, in effect, silenced, and her acceptance of blackness is also an acceptance of the white social order. When a similar moment occurs for Clelie, it takes place onscreen, and with an anti-white vengeance: "Black, am I? All right, I am black. I'll show him what a black girl can do!" When Clelie decides to own her blackness, she resolves to take revenge against white supremacy and to be as badass as she can be.

For all its daring, in the final analysis, *The Love Wanga* is a product of American racial ideology. Miscegenation, though front and center, remains taboo; the mixed race woman is a dangerous jezebel, and even the name given to the mulatto overseer—LeStrange—implies that mixed race people are unnatural. Despite Clelie's brazenness, power and centrality, the story's action ultimately works to defend white womanhood and restore the white couple—Adam and Eve—as the normative pairing. For their strangeness, both mixed race characters must die, but Clelie, at least, put up a good fight.

In 1936 Fredi Washington, along with numerous other actors and musicians including Rex Ingram, Ham Tree Harrington, Noble Sissle, W.C. Handy and Ada Brown, helped found the Negro Actors Guild of America (NAG). Bill "Bojangles" Robinson was named its honorary president in 1938, Noble Sissle its president and Washington its executive director and secretary. NAG was formed to create fellowship among black entertainers, but it was open to whites as well. The Guild was mainly a benevolent organization, but it did help actors negotiate contracts with producers and also acted as a casting agency. In her role as executive director, Washington, who remained active in the Guild for over a decade, was also on guard against discriminatory practices in the entertainment industry.

One Mile from Heaven (1937)

For her final appearance on the big screen, Fredi Washington returned to Hollywood in 1937 to make *One Mile from Heaven*, yet another problem picture that, like *Imitation of Life*, predates the message movie cycle. In this Twentieth Century–Fox comedy-drama directed by Canadian-born filmmaker Alan Dwan, Washington gives her best screen performance as a devoted mother of a little white girl. After a newspaper reporter questions the mother-daughter relationship, a white woman is revealed to be the girl's biological mother, and the case is heard in juvenile court. There are very few films that tackle black-white interracial custody battles. Among them, *One Mile from Heaven* appears to be the first.

At the heart of any interracial custody battle lies the question of placing children across racial lines, a practice sometimes referred to as transracial adoption. In the United States transracial adoption, which did not emerge until after the Second World War, initially referred to the placement of nonwhite children with white adoptive families. As the number of white children available for adoption decreased, adoption agencies were forced to reevaluate their "matching" philosophy, central to which was the principle of racial matching.

That transracial adoption, as originally conceived, was not intended to include the placement of white children with black adoptive parents is poignantly depicted in the film *One Potato, Two Potato* (1964). This independent film, which was nominated for a Best Writing, Story and Screenplay Oscar, tells the story of a white absentee father who returns to sue his ex-wife and her new husband, a black man, for custody of their white child.

In the 1970s, as transracial adoption was gaining popularity, the National Association of Black Social Workers came out against the adoption of black children by white families, stating that such placements compromised the child's racial and cultural identities. Some twenty years later, around the time that federal laws were evolving, once again, to remove barriers to transracial adoption, Paramount released *Losing Isaiah* (1995), starring Halle Berry as a mother who fights to regain custody of her black child from its white adoptive mother, Jessica Lange. In 2014 Kevin Costner and Octavia Spencer were grandparents dueling over custody of their mixed race granddaughter in *Black or White*.

One Mile from Heaven is based on a true story from the Denver court of Judge Ben Lindsey, a pioneer in the field of juvenile delinquency and family law. In *The Revolt of Modern Youth* (1925), Lindsey recounts some of the cases that came before him, including one in which an African American woman claimed to be the natural mother of a golden-haired, blue-eyed little girl, referred to as the Koudenhoffen baby. The woman, who is described by Lindsey as a "dark mulatto" and a "typical southern Mammy," was married to a fair-skinned white man and thus attributed the girl's skin color to her husband.[69]

Eventually, it was discovered that the child's actual birth mother was a white woman, unmarried at the time she became pregnant. When the baby was born, the doctor declared it dead, and the attending nurse took it to the mulatto woman to dispose of. But the baby was still clinging to life, and the mulatto woman decided to raise it as her own. In the end, the child was placed in the care of her birth mother and father, who had since married. The foster mother was paid a settlement and allowed to visit the child.[70]

In the film adaptation, the mulatto woman is Flora Jackson, played by Fredi Washington. Avoiding any further interracial entanglements, Flora has no husband, black or white; she's a widowed seamstress. Her daughter, Sunny, is played by Joan Carroll, a Shirley Temple look-alike. Bill "Bojangles" Robinson, the tap dancer whose most emblematic moments on film were as faithful servant to Shirley Temple characters, is Flora's boyfriend, Joe, a tap-dancing policeman. Claire Trevor, who would later win a Best Supporting Actress Oscar for *Key Largo* (1948), is Tex, a reporter who knows how to take care of herself in a press room dominated by men.

When Tex's male peers from competing newspapers send her out after a fake story, she finds herself in the racially segregated neighborhood of Maple Heights where Flora and Sunny reside. Tex perceives the relationship between Flora and Sunny to be unusual. Sensing she might have a real scoop on her hands, Tex takes her suspicions to her editor who refers the matter to juvenile court.

At the initial hearing Flora insists that she is Sunny's mother but is unable to provide proof, and the case is postponed. When Tex's article about the case appears in print, the scheming male reporters look for a way to discredit it. They visit Flora and Sunny and steal a photograph of mother and daughter, which leads to information that seems to confirm Flora is the birth mother. The new information is printed in the rival newspapers along with the stolen photo.

At a nearby prison, a convict recognizes the published photo of Sunny as the daughter of a deceased friend. He makes plans with gangsters on the outside to extort Barbara Harrison, the deceased friend's former wife and biological mother of Sunny, who has since remarried into wealth. Tex singlehandedly foils the gangsters and their plan and delivers Barbara to juvenile court just in time for the second hearing.

Barbara, who thought her child had died in a car accident, has a birth certificate to which Sunny's footprint is compared. Barbara is deemed the biological mother and the judge orders that Sunny be returned to her. Flora is devastated. Here, as elsewhere, the film gives license to Washington to express the tragedy of her character's situation. Tragedy is immediately turned into triumph, however, when Barbara asks Flora to come live with them as the child's "nurse." The film concludes with a children's party held at Sunny's new lavish home for all her black friends from Maple Heights.

Fredi Washington is involved in an interracial custody battle in the Twentieth Century–Fox feature, *One Mile From Heaven* (1937). From left, Howard Hickman, Claire Trevor, Joan Carroll and Fredi Washington.

One Mile from Heaven treats its black characters, especially Flora Jackson, with a rather humane touch that is uncharacteristic for this period in Hollywood. Flora is the perfect mother. Her speech and dress are indistinguishable from that of the film's white women, and the film takes an extremely sympathetic position to her plight as the woman who stands to lose the child she has cared for since infancy. While racist assumptions caused the case to come before a judge in the first place, race is never mentioned by the judge. In fact, at the moment just before Tex bursts into court with Barbara, it seems that, lacking any information to the contrary, the judge is about to declare Flora the child's mother.

Around the same time that *One Mile from Heaven* was released, newspapers reported the case of a New York judge who permitted Serena Alves, an African American woman, to retain custody of the white child she had reared since infancy.[71] Like Flora's case, the situation was more akin to foster care than adoption. Nevertheless, this was during a time when mixed race families were viewed as a step toward integration and, therefore, a threat. In keeping with legislation aimed at maintaining segregation, prevailing social attitudes, adoption agency practices, and the law combined to present near-absolute restrictions to transracial adoption. For the most part, placement of children across racial lines was inconceivable, even more so if the child was white.[72]

The judge's decision in the Alves case seems highly unusual for the time. In the Koudenhoffen case, upon which *One Mile from Heaven* is based, Judge Lindsey had decided from the outset that the child must be brought up by whites. Before the birth mother even came forward, he was in the process of arranging an adoption to a white family.[73] Ultimately, Flora, like the character upon which she is based, must relinquish custody, but race is never uttered by the judge and, therefore, within the film's diegesis, it appears to be irrelevant to the case.

One Mile from Heaven dabbles heavily in integration, but pursuant to the Production Code, on the surface, anyway, it avoids miscegenation. There are, for example, no sex relationships depicted between the black and white races. Yet the viewer is still invited to contemplate miscegenation with the mere presence of Fredi Washington and to think about it further when Flora maintains that Sunny is her child and hospital records seem to prove it. Later we learn that Flora had a baby that died, but for a while it does seem that Flora is telling the truth, which would make Sunny a very light-skinned mulatto. If that were the case, it also follows, before Flora's position is disproved, that viewers might wonder if Sunny is the biological child of Flora and a white man.

The appearance of integration on the surface and miscegenation just below was apparently of no concern to the "coast-to-coast previewing committees" that reported through the office of Will Hays. For the third quarter of 1937, they selected *One Mile from Heaven* as one of the eight outstanding studio offerings.[74] The film's race-mixing did not go unnoticed, however, in the South. In response to *One Mile from Heaven* and *Artists and Models*, also released in 1937, Southern independent theater owners passed resolutions against mixed race cast films with any semblance of "social equality." In *Artists and Models* the white comic actress Martha Raye dons blackface and intermingles with other blacks, including Louis Armstrong. In 1938, in response to this ban on "social equity" films, college students from Greensboro, North Carolina, launched a theater boycott that spread to other cities.[75]

Although *One Mile from Heaven* takes a rather progressive stance on race relations, there are signs embedded in the film throughout that reflect the prevailing racial ideology. Blacks live in a segregated neighborhood, for instance. Flora and Joe are a couple, but their romance is downplayed. We never hear them speak of love or see them do anything more than hold hands platonically. Implying that romance is the domain of whites, despite the announcement of Joe and Flora's engagement at the film's ending, at least two critics reported that the film had no love interest at all.[76]

Furthermore, when Tex first observes Flora and Sunny, the notion that racial categories are firm and immutable is also exposed. The only clue to Flora's blackness is the fact that she resides in Maple Heights—as does Sunny. Yet, absent any other supporting evidence, such as skin color, pattern of speech, or knowledge of other family members, Tex is able to determine that Flora is "colored" and Sunny is white. In reality, of course, when it came to mixed race people, whites possessed no special ability to detect blackness in the face of evidence to the contrary, and within the context of early 20th-century adoptions, color confusion was not uncommon.

Southern-born white author Lillian Smith's personal experience with racial confusion was the impetus for her opposition to segregation and the inspiration for her captivating novel *Strange Fruit* (1944). When Lillian was just a child, a black family moved to her town with their adopted white-skinned daughter, Janie. The townspeople, who assumed that Janie was white, took her from her adoptive parents and placed her in the care of the Smith family. Some time later, after Lillian and Janie had bonded, it was decided that Janie really was black and she was forced to leave.

Historian Ellen Herman also cites early 20th-century cases of racial confusion, including one in which a dark-skinned girl of Italian descent was deemed unworthy of adoption because white families perceived her as "colored." In another case, a Jewish couple that had unknowingly taken a half-black, half-Jewish baby into their home was later persuaded to surrender it to a "colored home."[77]

Many reviewers noted that Bill Robinson and Fredi Washington were the highlights of *One Mile from Heaven*.[78] *Modern Screen* said that Washington was deserving of "acting honors" and that she resembled Sylvia Sidney, the white actress of Russian descent who donned yellowface makeup for the lead role in a 1932 version of *Madame Butterfly* opposite Cary Grant.[79] Referring to the film's subject matter, *Variety* opined that the filmmakers "skate on pretty thin ice." Of Fredi Washington, the reviewer said that she was "splendid" and had "real acting ability."[80] For its time, *One Mile from Heaven* is remarkable for imagining a racially mixed family and suggesting that (outside the master-servant relationship) racial difference is compatible with love and belonging.

One Mile from Heaven was Fredi Washington's last film, but the actress continued to work in the theater until the end of the 1940s. In 1939, Washington took leave from NAG and returned to Broadway in *Mamba's Daughters*. This story about three generations of Southern black women was written by Dorothy and Du Bose Heyward, who also wrote the play *Porgy*. The big star of *Mamba's Daughters* was Ethel Waters, who was born in 1896 and began show business at the age of 15. In the early 1920s, while she was under contract with Black Swan Records, Waters was, reportedly, the nation's highest paid salaried African American recording artist.[81] As early as 1929, Waters appeared as a specialty number in the Warner Bros. feature *On with the Show*.

A critical point in Waters' career came at the Cotton Club's spring 1933 edition, when she was asked to sing the newly penned Harold Arlen and Ted Koehler tune "Stormy Weather." Waters' rendition of "Stormy Weather" was so successful that it became her trademark, and the notice it received earned her a part in the white musical *As Thousands Cheer*, which marked the beginning of her crossover Broadway career.

In *Mamba's Daughters*, Waters was Hagar, a plantation worker, and Fredi Washington was her illegitimate daughter, Lissa. Hagar refuses to name the father of her child and, due to unfortunate circumstances, Lissa is raised by her grandmother, Mamba, away from the plantation where Hagar toils. Lissa grows up in the city with the manners and culture of a white girl. As a young lady, on a visit to the plantation to see her mother, Lissa is raped. The assault results in a child that dies at birth. The play ends with Mamba killing her daughter's assailant and then herself. With financial assistance from NAG and Fredi Washington, *Mamba's Daughter*'s set designer Perry Watkins became the first African American scene designer for a Broadway show.[82]

In June of that same year, when television was in its experimental stage, NBC offered Waters her own show. *The Ethel Waters Show* featured comedy, songs, and sketches. It also included a dramatic scene from *Mamba's Daughters*. Along with other members from the cast, Ethel Waters and Fredi Washington made broadcast history when they reenacted a scene from the Broadway play, which, according to *Variety*, was the "standout of the bill."[83]

In an attempt to link the struggle for equality in the United States with the fight against fascism in Europe, in February of 1942, two months after the United States entered World War II, Fredi Washington's brother-in-law, Adam Clayton Powell, Jr., founded the militant Harlem newspaper *The People's Voice*. Fredi Washington went to work for *The*

People's Voice in the spring of that year as a public relations representative. The following year, she became the paper's theatrical editor. In the succeeding years Washington waged an all-out war of words against racist representations in the theater and film and the concurrent lack of opportunities for blacks.

Casting problems owing to her light skin aside, Washington's position as spokesperson for racial progress combined with her NAG duties and activism would have made acceptable roles extremely hard to come by. Nevertheless, Fredi Washington appeared on Broadway again in 1946 with Rex Ingram, Emmett "Babe" Wallace, and Sidney Poitier in a black-cast revival of *Lysistrata*, based on the 4th-century-BC Greek comedy by Aristophanes.

As a means to bring about peace, the title character, Lysistrata, persuades the women of Greece to withhold sex from their husbands and lovers until a truce in the war can be made. Writing for *The New York Times*, Brooks Atkinson thought the players retained the basic idea of the Aristophanes' comedy and noted that Fredi Washington and Mildred Smith in particular raised the "temperature of the play to a point that can be noticed and appreciated."[84] In 1949, Washington made her second television appearance as an atypical maid "who had more intelligence than other members of the household" in *The Goldbergs*.[85]

In 1952 Fredi Washington retired from the entertainment business and married dentist Dr. Hugh Anthony Bell from Stamford, Connecticut. In 1975 she was inducted into the Black Filmmakers Hall of Fame. Fredi Washington passed away in 1994 at the age of 90.

4

Lena Horne

Separate and Unequalled

*It was an accepted fact that any scene I did was going to be cut when the
movie played in the South. So no one bothered to put me in a movie where I
talked to anybody, where some thread of the story might be broken if I were
cut. I had no communication with anybody.*[1] —Lena Horne

From the time she entered show business, Lena Horne was regarded as an exceptional beauty. A Depression-era child of Brooklyn's black bourgeoisie, Lena was just sixteen years old in 1933 when she started working at the Cotton Club, the famed Harlem
establishment where black entertainers performed for white audiences. Within two years,
Horne had worked her way up from the chorus line to become a featured player and
earned renown as one of the Cotton Club's most prized lookers.[2]

In 1935 Lena got a job with Noble Sissle who, nearly fifteen years after *Shuffle Along*,
had become a successful bandleader. Sissle helped Lena improve her singing. He also
helped her acquire the affectation of a "lady." Irrespective of the racial indignities that he
and his band were routinely subjected to on tour, Noble Sissle insisted that those in his
employ behave themselves at all times. For the male band members, this meant no smoking, no raised voices, or swearing anywhere around the job. For Lena, it meant learning
how to walk, speak and carry herself genteelly. It meant countering every stereotype that
whites held about black women.[3]

In 1940, when she was hired by saxophonist and bandleader Charlie Barnet, Horne
became one of the first black singers to join an all-white swing band. Soon after, she met
Barney Josephson, white owner of Manhattan's Café Society, New York's first openly integrated nightclub, where the likes of Billie Holiday, Hazel Scott, and Sister Rosetta Tharpe
performed and where Paul Robeson was a frequent customer. Under Josephson's tutelage,
Lena continued to hone her craft and her persona. Through her association with Josephson, Robeson, and others in the Café Society orbit, Horne also started to develop a sense
of racial identity and an interest in Civil Rights.[4]

Lena Horne was not necessarily the most talented performer at Café Society, but she
certainly managed to grab more than her fair share of notice.[5] In 1941 Horne came to the
attention of impresario Felix Young, who offered her a chance to appear in a revue at his
Hollywood nightclub. Horne was unsure about the offer because it meant uprooting her
life from family and friends in New York. At the urging of others, however, she took the
job and moved to Los Angeles.

Among those who had urged Lena to move to L.A. was Walter White, the Civil

89

Rights activist and NAACP leader who since 1940 had been campaigning Hollywood studios to revolutionize their depictions of blacks in film. With her Eurocentric beauty, bourgeois heritage, and genteel mannerisms, Lena Horne was, Walter White believed, just the right person to establish an alternate image for black women in film, an image other than that of the maid, whore, or buffoon. Thus, it was a historic moment when, in 1942, Lena Horne signed a long-term contract with MGM that stipulated she would not have to take on the stereotypical roles customarily assigned to black performers of the day.[6] MGM held up its end of the contract by walking a tightrope between advancing racial equality and pandering to Jim Crow.

Originally a character from a minstrel show, "Jim Crow" was the name given to the "separate but equal" laws enacted by almost every former Confederate state following the *Plessy v. Ferguson* decision of 1896. In 1892, Homer Plessy, a Louisiana Creole who was one-eighth black and seven-eighths white, attempted to sit in a railroad coach reserved for whites. When asked by the train conductor about his racial identity, Plessy confessed that he was "colored," which resulted in his arrest.

Plessy fought his arrest all the way to the Supreme Court in 1896 and lost. Without ruling directly on the definition of race, the majority decision in the case of *Plessy v. Ferguson* not only held up the one-drop rule but established the concept of "separate but equal." The Supreme Court ruled that separate facilities, if equal, were not a violation of the Constitution. Therefore, in public accommodations, such as schools, railroad cars, and drinking fountains, states could legally segregate blacks from whites. Under conditions that could hardly be called equal, segregation continued in the South well into the 1960s.

It was during the latter years of Jim Crow, in the midst of the Second World War, that Lena Horne arrived in Hollywood. Many black entertainers had been there before her, but Horne was the first to be given the complete movie star treatment which, along with the long-term contract she signed with MGM, included custom designer gowns, eating in the stars' section of the studio commissary, associating with studio brass, and long sessions devoted to determining how to best light and make her up.[7]

Lena Horne appeared in more than fifteen feature films, the majority of which were completed for MGM between 1942 and 1956. In some instances, Horne was displayed as an "exotic" Latina or West Indian. Sometimes she was situated between black and white, and at other times she was an imitation of a white woman. Never did Lena Horne appear as a maid or buffoon, and only once, in the all-black musical *Cabin in the Sky* (1943), was she cast as a temptress.

While *Cabin in the Sky* certainly did much to confirm the actress's sex appeal, the "bad girl" label did not stick. The "lady" would ultimately win out. Horne's second principal role during her MGM years was in the other all-black musical of 1943, *Stormy Weather*. In this picture, for which she was on loan to Twentieth Century–Fox, Horne starred as singer Selina Rogers opposite old-timer Bill Robinson.

These two essential Lena Horne films, released just months apart, during the Second World War, were the first all-black musicals to come out of mainstream Hollywood. It is no coincidence that at this time the Office of War Information (OWI), a federal agency of the U.S. government, had set up a bureau in Hollywood and taken an interest in film as a means for obtaining support of the war effort, especially among African Americans. Lena Horne's Hollywood image emerged on the one hand as a means to appease African Americans, and on the other, it was contrived primarily for consumption (and sometimes lack thereof) by whites.

After *Stormy Weather* and *Cabin in the Sky*, MGM relegated Horne to cameo roles in specialty acts that, albeit magnificently produced, bore no significant relationship to the story line of her films. A closer look at these films reveals the evolution of the African American specialty act in Hollywood from a musical interlude that was added to enhance what was often at best a pedestrian film and increase its box office draw to a musical segment that was designed to be readily subtracted from a film should it happen to insult the sensibilities of Southern censors threatened by any move toward an appearance of equality on screen.

In her earliest musicals, Horne has, at least, some relation to or contact with other members of the cast: fellow performers, an audience, or occasionally a minor character in the film. Later, even though MGM continued to revere the Horne image, the studio isolated Horne more completely, to the point that essentially no one ever shared the frame with her. Taken on the whole, Horne's position in MGM's white musicals reflects a separation not only from whiteness but from blackness as well. Indeed, separation and absence loom so large within Horne's early image that productions in which she did not appear, such as the films *Cairo* (1942), *White Cargo* (1942) and *Show Boat* (1951), as well as the 1946 stage productions of *Show Boat* and *St. Louis Woman*, also take on significance.

The exclusion and onscreen segregation proved frustrating to Horne both as an artist and an individual. With regard to her star image, the isolation contributed to an aura of perfection. Unlike other screen goddesses of the day, including fellow MGM contract players Hedy Lamarr and Ava Gardner, Horne escaped characterization as a wanton woman or femme fatale. As a sex symbol, Lena Horne was visible but not accessible.

Referring to her early cabaret performances, Horne once remarked, "I was there to be had, but not too much."[8] The same might be said of Lena Horne's Hollywood career. In most of her films, after being momentarily glorified and objectified, she abruptly disappears. As such, Lena Horne's Hollywood image was impervious, and her characterization as a lady was beyond reproach. Beautiful, elegant, poised, and insulated from the action in her films, Lena Horne was a movie star unlike any other. She was separate and unequalled.

Lena Mary Calhoun Horne was born in Brooklyn, New York, on June 30, 1917, to Edwin ("Teddy") Horne, Jr., and Edna Scottron, both of whom were products of Brooklyn's black elite. Lena's maternal great-grandfather, Samuel Scottron, born free in New England, was a former Union soldier and a pillar of Brooklyn's black community. Samuel's wife, Anna Maria, was Native American, born to an Algonquian tribe. Samuel and Anna Maria had six children, including Edna's father, Cyrus. Edna's mother, Louise Ashton, had been raised by her Haitian- or perhaps African-born, French-speaking grandmother.[9]

At the time Lena was born, Teddy and Edna were residing with Teddy's parents, Cora Calhoun Horne and Edwin Horne. Cora Calhoun, Lena's paternal grandmother, was a college educated, black aristocrat. Born in November 1865, she was the granddaughter of Nellie Calhoun, a household cook for the wealthy Calhoun family. With investments in agriculture and minerals, not to mention slaves, the Calhouns were among America's earliest tycoons. Nellie's owner, Dr. Andrew Bonaparte Calhoun, was the nephew of John C. Calhoun, the slavery apologist and vice president of the United States who served under both Quincy Adams and Andrew Jackson.[10]

Nellie gave birth to two Calhoun children who, according to Lena's daughter, Gail Lumet Buckley, "clearly had a white father or fathers." One of those children, Cora's father, Moses, was born in 1829. When the Civil War ended, Moses married Atlanta Mary Fernando, a Louisiana Creole woman who looked white and was fifteen years his junior. Moses and Mary took up residence in Atlanta and had two children, Lena's grandmother, Cora, and her great-aunt and namesake, Lena Leo. Moses prospered as a grocer and restaurant owner. With a thriving business, an attractive family, and an esteemed family name, Lena Horne's great-grandfather, Moses, was the epitome of a black aristocrat.[11]

Cora Calhoun graduated from Atlanta University in 1881, and in 1887 she married Edwin Horne (née Edwin Horn). A native of Tennessee, Edwin Horne was the son of a blue-eyed British white man and a Native American woman. Having decided that, on the whole, the lot of African Americans was marginally better than that of Native Americans, Edwin's parents opted for a "mulatto" over an "Indian" identity for their children. Edwin became a spokesperson for his adopted race at an early age, and by the time he was twenty-one he had entered politics. Edwin and Cora had four sons, including Lena's father, Teddy, who was born in 1893. Three years later, with *Plessy v. Ferguson* decided and the political hopes of the black South dying, Edwin and Cora joined the Great Migration and moved to New York.[12]

It was in the Brooklyn neighborhood where the Hornes settled that Lena's parents, Teddy and Edna, met. On the surface, theirs seemed like a perfect match. The two children of the black bourgeoisie had grown up together and known each other all their lives. In reality, though, neither was ready for the responsibility of marriage and a child. Edna was spoiled, badly educated, and a fantasist. Teddy, unlike his brothers, rejected gentility and middle-class morals and had decided to use his ample charm and charisma in pursuit of pleasure and illicit gains.[13] Teddy abandoned Edna when Lena was just three years old, and the couple later divorced. Shortly after Teddy's exit, Edna also left the Horne household to pursue her dream of becoming an actress.

With both Teddy and Edna gone, Lena became Cora's responsibility. Lena spent a good deal of her childhood with her paternal grandparents and was very much influenced by them. Cora and Edwin were early NAACP supporters. The year before Teddy left, a photo of baby Lena Horne, touted as one of the organization's youngest members, appeared in the October 1919 issue of the NAACP's newspaper.[14] On and off, Lena also stayed with her mother, who lived something of a vagabond lifestyle. In the early 1930s, Edna took off for Havana, where she met her second husband, Miguel Rodriguez, a white Cuban army officer. With a civil war brewing in Cuba, Edna soon decided to return to America with Rodriguez in tow. The couple rented an apartment near Cora and Edwin so that Lena could live with them and continue her schooling in Brooklyn.

Cora was not pleased by Edna's reappearance and made it known that she disapproved of Lena living in an interracial household. Edna, in turn, swore that Cora would never see her granddaughter again—even in death. True to her word, when Cora died in 1932, Edna forbade Lena from attending the funeral. Lena ran off anyway and made it to the entrance of the funeral home, where Edna finally caught up wither her. Edwin Horne, who passed away seven years later, never forgave Edna for the scandalous scene that ensued at his wife's funeral.[15] Just one year after Cora's death, Lena was supporting her mother and stepfather, working as a dancer at Harlem's Cotton Club.

Though often associated with the Harlem Renaissance and black achievement, Harlem of the 1920s and 1930s also had its seamy side. Around the same time that blacks were being recognized for their intellectual, artistic, and social contributions, the National Prohibition Act was passed. The resulting restriction on alcoholic beverages, combined

with a developing new black culture, made Harlem a fertile playground for white criminals like the British-born gang leader and Cotton Club owner Owney Madden.

When Madden's gang was in search of a suitable Harlem location to entertain white
downtowners and serve them bootleg beer, they settled upon a failing supper club owned
by former heavyweight boxing champion Jack Johnson. Madden's people made a deal
with Johnson, under which the gang would operate the business and Johnson would
remain as a front man. Madden was in prison for manslaughter at the time and was not
personally involved in this transaction. Nevertheless, despite his confinement, Madden
maintained tight control over his syndicate.[16]

The first thing Madden's people did when they took over the supper club was to
change the name from Club Deluxe to Cotton Club. They also expanded its seating capacity to 700 and updated the décor to reflect a "jungle" motif. The entertainment, it was
decided, would be fast-paced revues, staged in an extravagant Ziegfeld style. Lew Leslie,
who later gained fame with his Blackbird Revues, was hired to produce. Jimmy McHugh,
who was later joined by Dorothy Fields, would do the songs.

Restrictions that applied to female entertainers were also instituted. Chorus girls,
for example, had to be light-skinned, at least 5'6" in height, and able to carry a tune.
When it came to male entertainers, only their ability mattered. Skin color was not as
important.[17] And then, of course, there was the club's "whites only" policy. Black patrons
were considered undesirable and most were refused entry.

The Cotton Club had its grand opening in 1923, the same year Madden was released
from prison. The business flourished until 1925, when it was closed for violation of Prohibition laws. When the Cotton Club reopened in 1927, it had hired Duke Ellington's band.
Originally called the Washingtonians, the band soon changed its name to Duke Ellington's Jungle Band. In 1929, when CBS began broadcasting Cotton Club performances
nationwide, both Ellington and the club became famous.

By the time Lena Horne auditioned for the Cotton Club chorus line in 1933, Cab
Calloway's orchestra was the house band, Prohibition had been repealed, and the club
had relaxed its "whites only policy" enough so that black Harlem gangsters and family
members of the performers, like Lena's father, could get in.[18] By this time, too, the Cotton
Club had hired its first dark-skinned chorus girl, Lucille Wilson, who later married trumpeter Louis Armstrong. When Lena was hired at age sixteen, she was one of the youngest
dancers on the chorus line. Edna became the quintessential stage mother and kept close
tabs on her daughter's virtue.

Owing perhaps to her mother's persistence, right from the start, Lena was never just
a chorus girl. Often she was taken off the line and given another assignment.[19] For example, in the spring of 1934, toward the end of her first Cotton Club run, Lena was asked
to step in for an absent cast member and appeared in her first featured spot. The number was performed with Avon Long, who went on to become a famous Broadway dancer.
Long sang the love song "As Long as I Live." Lena was primarily there for decoration, but
she sang a few lines, too.

In the fall of 1934, the number with Long was reprised with Lena as the principal. It was during this, twenty-fifth edition of the Cotton Club Parade, that Lena was
spotted by Laurence Schwab. The Broadway producer was looking for someone to play
a light-skinned "quadroon girl" in his new play, *Dance with Your Gods*. Lena took the
part, skipping the first Cotton Club show every night and hurrying back uptown to make
the last two shows. *Dance with Your Gods*, a voodoo thriller set in New Orleans, lasted

only a week. Nevertheless, the experience put Lena on Broadway and was proof that she was beginning to make a name for herself. In that same year, Lena also had a brief and uncredited appearance in the musical short *Cab Calloway's Jitterbug Party*.

After *Dance with Your Gods*, Edna realized that her daughter might succeed in show business where she had failed. She determined, therefore, that Lena should quit the Cotton Club. Horne's final revue was the twenty-sixth edition, which opened in the fall of 1935. Choreography was by Leonard Harper and Elida Webb. On the heels of her success in *Sanders of the River*, Nina Mae McKinney was the show's big-name star. *Variety,* however, was far more interested in Lena Horne, predicting that the "maduro-shaded ingénue," whose beauty made it tough for the other members of the company, would surely be grabbed for the movies. Working opposite her was the "nice-looking" Emmett "Babe" Wallace.[20]

Horne found her opportunity to leave the Cotton Club when in January 1936 Flournoy Miller convinced Noble Sissle to audition her for his band. "I don't see why Noble wanted me," Horne confessed in her autobiography. "I couldn't sing jazz and I couldn't sing the blues. All I could do was carry a tune." Sissle, who was himself bourgeois, liked the way Horne looked and the way she carried herself, and she was hired. Edna stayed by her side, and Lena continued to support her and her stepfather. Life on the road with a touring orchestra in Jim Crow America was not easy. They travelled by bus, had to enter their engagements through the back door, and as they were barred from staying in hotels, they often had no idea where they would spend the night.[21]

Lena soon began to dream of marriage, in part as a way to escape the grind of the tour but also as a means to have some personal and sexual freedom.[22] In late 1936 Lena's father, Teddy, introduced her to Louis Jones, a young man from Pittsburgh with political ambitions who was looking for a respectable wife. Lena was smitten. By January 1937 the couple was married, and Horne, it was said, had retired from show business. In December 1937 Lena gave birth to her first child, Gail. Four weeks later Horne received an offer to co-star in her first feature film. As the newlyweds were desperately in need of money Lena came out of retirement and flew to California.

The Duke Is Tops (1938)

Lena Horne's first feature film appearance came opposite Ralph Cooper in the Million Dollar Productions race film *The Duke Is Tops*. Horne wasn't the filmmakers' first choice for a leading lady, however. Ralph Cooper, who was also a producer for Million Dollar Productions, wanted Nina Mae McKinney as his co-star, but the actress had fallen ill.[23] Cooper and his wealthy white business partner, Harry Popkin, would get McKinney for their next picture, *Gang Smashers* (1938).

When Horne arrived in Hollywood for filming of *The Duke Is Tops* Ralph Cooper thought he'd made a mistake. Cooper told a postpartum Lena that she was too fat to be his leading lady. Lena pleaded with him, as she desperately needed the money. Reluctantly, Cooper agreed to keep her on as singer and main character Ethel Andrews.[24] Cooper plays title character, Ethel's manager and love interest, Duke. Other Million Dollar Players include Monte Hawley as talent scout George Marshall, Neva Peoples as Ethel's comic buddy Ella, and Lawrence Criner as Doc Dorando, a "doctor" in a travelling medicine show. Also among the cast are numerous musicians, chorus girls, singers, and dancers, including innovative tap dancer Willie Covan. From the mid–1930s to the 1940s, Covan was an MGM dance instructor who taught and coached the likes of Eleanor Powell, Gregory Peck, and Mae West.[25]

It was on the set of *The Duke Is Tops* that Lena Horne first met Phil Moore, the film's music arranger. Moore had studied music at the University of Washington and Cornish School of Music. After *The Duke Is Tops*, he tried in vain to get a job with MGM as an orchestrator. MGM wouldn't hire him as an orchestrator, but they did give him a job as rehearsal pianist. When Lena signed with MGM, Moore became her rehearsal pianist. He also assisted Horne with her recording career. Moore coached a number of other stars as well, including Ava Gardner, Judy Garland, Mae West, Marilyn Monroe and Dorothy Dandridge. Eventually, Moore did graduate to orchestration at MGM and became the first salaried African American arranger-composer at a major Hollywood studio.[26]

When *The Duke Is Tops* begins Ethel is experiencing some measure of success touring the South as a specialty act in a revue titled *Sepia Scandals*. The name of this fictional revue, undoubtedly a reference to George White's long-running, white-cast, Ziegfeld-like series of *Scandals* shows (1919–1939), suggests that *Sepia Scandals* is a brown version of a white show. Horne, whose singing style here is closer in sound to white singers of the day such as Irene Dunn or Helen Morgan than it is to contemporaneous black singers like Billie Holiday or Ella Fitzgerald,[27] is *Sepia Scandal*'s most prominent imitator of whiteness.

George Marshall, a talent scout from New York, thinks he can make Ethel into a big star. "She's a cinch for the big time," he says. At first, both Ethel and Duke decline Marshall's proposal. Not wishing to stand in the way of Ethel's success, however, Duke changes his mind and then persuades Ethel to take the offer by falsely claiming he's been handsomely paid to release his interest in her career. Heartbroken, Ethel heads North to start a solo career.

While Ethel is on the road with her new management, Duke attempts to organize a show without her, but it's a flop. Short on funds, Duke puts his entertainment experience to work in Doc Dornado's travelling medicine show. Together, Duke and Dorando make a successful team peddling the doc's universal elixir. One night, while listening to the radio, Duke learns that Ethel's career is faltering. He quits Dorando and returns to his sweetheart's side. Duke revamps Ethel's show and makes it a big hit.

Filming for *The Duke Is Tops* was completed in ten days, and by March 1938, Lena was back home with her family in Pittsburgh. When Lena failed to attend a special Pittsburgh NAACP charity opening for the film in June, an article in *The Pittsburgh Courier* came down harshly on both the star and her film. *The Duke Is Tops* "shows a lack of expert direction and carelessness about detail," wrote the anonymous reporter. The article also called Horne's acting ability into question and accused her of choosing to attend a white film downtown over the Pittsburgh opening of *The Duke Is Tops*. In her autobiography, Horne said that the reason she didn't attend the opening was because her husband wouldn't let her. She also claimed that she was never paid the full salary promised, and when, after she had become a movie star and the film was re-released as *The Bronze Venus*, she still never got paid.[28]

One week after it accused Lena Horne of snubbing the premiere and her race, *The Pittsburgh Courier*, by way of its Hollywood correspondent Earl Morris and local journalist William Nunn, had a change of heart. Both reviewers said that *The Duke Is Tops* was the best "colored" picture they'd ever seen. Morris declared it a racial achievement because it had "no 'Uncle Tom' bandana" sequences. He also praised all the entertainment acts, including Horne's singing. With regard to Willie Covan's dancing, Morris said, "All the hullabaloo over Fred Astaire should belong to Mr. Covan." Indeed, Fred Astaire was also once a client of Covan's at his Hollywood dance studio. William Nunn thought that Horne was "the best looking sepia star" he'd ever seen and said she had a voice of "surprising sweetness."[29]

Other black newspapers were also enthusiastic about *The Duke Is Tops,* including the *California Eagle,* which declared Horne to be the "first woman to appear to advantage in colored-produced films." A reviewer for *The New York Age* thought that representation of the relationship between Horne and Cooper was superior to anything else done in a "colored" picture. Harry Levette also gave the picture high marks, calling it a "class-A" production. Cooper, Levette said, was a real actor far removed from playing a stereotype, and Lena, with her beautiful face and voice, was very successful and sure to make future triumphs.[30]

After returning to Pittsburgh, Lena was wooed by Howard Gumm, a real New York talent agent. Horne was referred to Gumm by founding member and executive secretary of the Negro Actors Guild Fredi Washington. Gumm wanted Horne for a part in Lew Leslie's *Blackbirds of 1939* revue. Described as a disappointing colored imitation of a white revue, *Blackbirds of 1939* opened on Broadway in February 1939 to lukewarm reviews and closed eight days later.[31] Of Lena's contributions to the show, Brooks Atkinson, theater critic for *The New York Times,* declared that with the right guidance, Horne would be a winner.[32]

When Lena returned to her family in Pittsburgh, she was unhappy in her marriage but decided to give it another chance. One year later, in February 1940, Lena gave birth to a son, Edwin Fletcher ("little Teddy"), but her relationship with Louis did not improve. In fact, the birth of Lena's son marked the beginning of the end of her marriage to Louis Jones. With money borrowed money from her stepmother, Lena left Pittsburgh and returned to New York. When she informed Louis that she'd be back to get the children, he told her, "You can take Gail, but you'll never get Teddy."

Back in New York, Lena reached out to Harold Gumm. Together, agent and client discovered that Lena Horne did not fit the prevailing image of black womanhood. "Why, she looks like a sun-tanned white girl," said one club manager. "She sings like a white girl," said another. "But she doesn't sing the blues," and so it went. George White, producer of the *Scandals,* said it was foolish of Lena to attempt to make it in show business as a black woman. White told Gumm that they shouldn't admit she's "colored" and that she should adopt a Spanish name and learn a few Spanish songs.[33]

Eventually Lena was put in touch with saxophonist Charlie Barnet, the white bandleader considered among the earliest to integrate the otherwise all-white swing band. Barnet, whose idol was the African American tenor saxophonist Coleman Hawkins, came from a wealthy family. His parents were disappointed when he chose the saxophone over a law degree.[34] In early 1941, Barnet hired Lena as singer for his band. When Lena called to tell her father the good news, he was outraged. The idea of his daughter traveling around the country with twenty or more white men infuriated him.[35]

Life on the road with a white band was different than travelling with Sissle's band. With Sissle, every band member was black and Jim Crow was meted out across the board. With Barnet's band, according to Horne, every stop was unpredictable. If they showed up at a white-only hotel, sometimes after some discussion with the hotel manager, Lena would be allowed to stay. At other times, she would not, and they would leave to find other accommodations.

In his autobiography, Charlie Barnet remembered those times a little differently. Both he and Horne agree that when the band was scheduled to tour in the South, Horne was given paid time off. When they travelled elsewhere, however, Barnet recalled that there was never any problem getting Horne into their hotels. Whenever they suspected that there might be trouble, their manager would approach the hotel clerk, request their rooms, jabber to Horne in "Spanish doubletalk," and then remark to the clerk that their "Cuban singer would like a single room with a bath." According to Barnet, this worked every time.[36]

By the spring of 1941, Lena had left Barnet and found a gig as a soloist with Barney Josephson, owner of New York's Café Society. With a desire to overturn segregation in nightclubs as well as counter mob ownership, Josephson had opened Café Society in 1938. Unlike other interracial "black and tan" clubs, which were illicit, or at least covert, Josephson envisioned a jazz club where blacks and whites could work together on stage and sit together in the audience, a club where integration was not only out in the open but was its main selling point. Café Society, which was also known for its leftist politics, was just such a place.[37]

One of the first to perform at Café Society was Billie Holiday. One night, a high school teacher, Abel Meeropol, asked Holiday to sing a poem that he had written and set to music. It was called "Strange Fruit" and it was about the lynching of African Americans in the South. Holiday was reluctant to try the song, and when she finally did, she thought she'd made a mistake. No one applauded at first. Then one lone person started to clap. Soon others followed until everyone was clapping.[38]

After that Billie Holiday sang "Strange Fruit" at the end of every set. Not all Café Society patrons appreciated the song, though. Some walked out when they heard it. On one occasion, a woman who had apparently witnessed a lynching as a little girl cried out, "Don't you dare ever sing that song again. Don't you dare." "Strange Fruit" transformed Holiday's career. When she recorded it in 1939, it reached number sixteen on the record charts.[39] Sixty years later, "Strange Fruit" was declared the song of the century by *Time* magazine.

Barney Josephson first saw Lena perform with Charlie Barnet at New York's Paramount Theater. Although he knew Lena was black, from where he was seated, he couldn't tell that she was not white. "She was not a jazz singer," he said, but he thought she had potential, so he hired her. Referring to her first rehearsal with Josephson, Lena described herself as being less aware of racial stereotypes than her new boss. As she started to sing "When It's Sleepy Time Down South," Josephson interrupted to ask if she knew what the song was really about and if she thought that blacks in the South were really as content as the song depicted.[40]

Lena quickly realized that the song paints an idyllic picture of America's plantation past, so she switched to Latin numbers, which she did very well. Afterward, however, Josephson advised her not to do the "rhumba stuff," either. Because of her ambiguous looks, he told her, she could be anything, Brazilian, Cuban, or Spanish. He then he asked her if she was trying to pass. Lena was offended by the question, but Josephson had wanted to shake her up.[41]

Barney Josephson appointed himself Lena's coach and mentor. He wanted to present Horne as a "Negro performer," which meant she would sing jazz standards. Further, to alleviate any racial confusion on the part of the audience, Josephson decided that she should sing at least one blues song in every show. "When you sing the blues," he told

Horne, "they'll think, well, I guess she is [black]."[42] Josephson also thought it would be amusing if Lena sang the blues because she was so beautiful and no one would expect that a man would mistreat or desert her.[43] "It's almost satire to hear you sing the blues," he told her.[44]

In addition to its offering of musical talent, Café Society was also a favorite hangout of black middle-class intellectuals, including Lena's uncle, Frank Horne, who, after serving as dean and later president of a Georgia college, had been recruited to Washington, D.C., where he served in a number of federal positions and appointments dedicated to racial equality. Through Uncle Frank, Lena made the acquaintance of luminaries such as Romare Bearden, Ralphe Bunche, E. Franklin Frazier, and Sterling Brown, just to name a few.[45]

Another frequent visitor to the club, and Horne's boyfriend for a brief period, was heavyweight boxing champion Joe Louis. White bandleader Artie Shaw also claimed to be a paramour of Horne's while she was at Café Society. In June 1941, the two made a record together. Horne, Shaw said, wanted to marry him, but he told her that it would be the end of their careers.[46]

It was at Café Society that Lena developed a friendship with Paul Robeson and was introduced to Walter White. Lena and Paul had been raised in the same Brooklyn neighborhood, though Paul was Lena's senior by almost twenty years. From Robeson, Lena learned about her family history, including the fact that her grandmother, Cora Calhoun Horne, had helped him get his scholarship to Rutgers. Robeson made Horne feel proud of her family background and helped educate her on racial issues. Walter White was also an old friend of Cora Horne's and upon meeting Lena had pronounced her a "winner." Both he and Robeson pointed out to Horne that by virtue of her color and history, her responsibilities to her race would be great.[47]

Boogie-Woogie Dream (1944)

During her stint at Café Society, Lena Horne also found time to make her next screen appearance in the independent short film *Boogie-Woogie Dream*. Written, directed, and produced by filmmakers with leftist political leanings, *Boogie Woogie Dream* did not find distribution until 1944, three years after it was made, by which time Horne was a big star. Set in a nightclub with mural-covered walls, *Boogie-Woogie Dream* is entirely suggestive of Café Society. In addition to Lena Horne, the film features Teddy Wilson and His Orchestra, the house band during the latter part of Horne's Café Society engagement. Boogie-woogie pianists Albert Ammons and Pete Johnson, who often shared the Café Society bill with Horne, are also part of the cast.

Boogie-Woogie Dream is a fanciful tale that begins with Teddy Wilson and his orchestra concluding the evening's final set. The last patrons to leave are a couple of finely dressed talent scouts, a Mr. Weathercoop and his female companion. Weathercoop remarks that he didn't find what he was looking for. Just as they are about to exit, the woman ducks into the ladies' room to powder her nose so Weathercoop takes a seat. Meanwhile, in back of the club, Lena Horne is washing dishes, Pete Johnson is tuning a piano, and Albert Ammons is hanging wallpaper.

Horne starts singing about wishing she could sing the blues in an evening gown instead of polishing glasses. Out front, Weathercoop's companion has rejoined him. Soon enough, Lena's wish comes true. From a cloud of smoke, she emerges wearing a sleek, long dress. Ammons and Johnson, outfitted in new suits, play their original composition "Boogie-Woogie Dream." Horne follows, singing "Unlucky Woman," a blues song penned by the British-born composer Leonard Feather. Here, Horne is not the stiff imitation of a white woman that she was in *The Duke Is Tops*. She talks differently, sings differently, and her movement, though still contained, is less constrained. Her rendition of the blues is sweet and perky but captivating nevertheless. Josephson's efforts to transform Horne into a black performer had apparently succeeded.

With its fantasy theme and female singer transported from the kitchen to the footlights, *Boogie-Woogie Dream* brings to mind Nina Mae McKinney in the Warner Bros. short film *Pie, Pie, Blackbird*. Yet, with respect to their attitude toward black entertainers, the two films are far apart. *Pie, Pie, Blackbird*, with its plantation references and insistence on presenting Eubie Blake and his band as comical figures, cashes in on the popularity of black entertainment while refusing to elevate its opinion of black people. *Boogie-Woogie Dream*, on the other hand, attempts to respect the artists and their talent. Ironically, *Boogie-Woogie Dream* is the closest Lena Horne ever came to playing a maid on screen, but there is nothing demeaning or stereotypical about her role or those of the other musicians.

Boogie-Woogie Dream concludes with another cloud of smoke and everyone returning to their original positions. The phone rings. On the other end is an unnamed Hollywood studio looking for the two talent scouts. Weathercoop and his companion reassure the caller that they've been working all night and that they've found what they were looking for. Horne, Ammons, and Johnson are elated when they are invited to Weathercoop's office at the studio for an audition. For Ammons and Johnson, with respect to a future in the movies, *Boogie-Woogie Dream* was just that—a dream. This was evidently the first and last time the two boogie-woogie pianists would appear on film.[48] For Horne, however, *Boogie-Woogie Dream* is prescient. Within six months of its production, Horne would audition for MGM and sign her landmark contract with the Hollywood studio.

Around the time Lena Horne was making *Boogie-Woogie Dream*, she received news that Felix Young, a Los Angeles transplant, wanted her for a revue he was planning. A reputed compulsive gambler, Young had moved to Hollywood from New York in the 1920s and found work as producer for both Paramount Pictures and Universal Studios. In the 1930s Young purchased the Trocadero, which was one of L.A.'s most popular nightclubs, especially among film stars. In late 1939, just days before he was convicted of assaulting his attorney, Young unexpectedly closed the Trocadero.[49] Two years later he had plans to restart the club, with an opening lineup that, in addition to Horne, would feature Duke Ellington's band, Katherine Dunham's dance company, and Ethel Waters.

Lena was reluctant to take the offer because it meant moving to the West Coast. She was happy at Café Society and didn't want to uproot Gail. The move also meant that she would be farther away from little Teddy, who was with his father in Pittsburgh. Barney Josephson didn't want her to take the job, either. Others, however, felt differently. Influential people, Horne said, asked her to take the job. Teddy Wilson and the musicians in his band told Horne she had to go. She was being given an opportunity to become a big star. Ellington advised her "not to be selfish" and to let the whole world benefit from her radiance. NAACP leader Walter White also urged Horne to go. Because her image ran counter to Hollywood's prevailing mammy image of black womanhood, White thought that Horne would make a great weapon in the fight against racism. On October 19, 1941, Horne played her last night at Café Society.[50]

The bombing of Pearl Harbor on December 7, 1941, interfered with Young's plan to reopen the Trocadero. Instead, he leased a smaller space and would call it the Little Trocadero. While in Los Angeles, waiting for the new club to open, Lena spent time with Duke Ellington. It was through Ellington that she met Billy "Sweet Pea" Strayhorn, the gifted composer and arranger who would prove influential in both her personal and professional life. Strayhorn spent most of his career in service to Ellington and was responsible for a number of notable compositions, including the Duke Ellington Orchestra signature tune "Take the A Train." Horne said she loved Strayhorn from the moment they met. She wanted to marry him, but Strayhorn was gay. Nevertheless, Horne considered Strayhorn her soul mate, and her friendship with the composer lasted until his death in 1967.[51]

While in limbo, Lena also spent time with the members of Katherine Dunham's dance company, who were staying in a house not far from Lena's apartment. Horne seemed intimidated by the dancers. The discipline required by their medium, on the one hand, and the freedom of its expression, on the other, she said, made her feel that she wasn't good enough for them.[52] Like Horne, the dance company's founder Katherine Dunham had already made a name for herself before Hollywood beckoned. Born in Chicago in 1909, Dunham was the daughter of an African American man from Tennessee and a French-Canadian woman descended from Canada's indigenous people and European settlers.

In 1938, Dunham, already an acclaimed dancer and choreographer, earned a master's degree from the Department of Anthropology at the University of Chicago. Her thesis focused on the dances of Haiti. Dunham's contribution to dance cannot be overstated. She introduced African and Caribbean dance and culture to dancers and audiences in America and across the globe and developed pedagogies for dance that today are taught throughout the world. In 1940, Dunham collaborated with George Balanchine, now considered to be one of the greatest choreographers in the history of ballet, for dances in the Broadway musical *Cabin in the Sky*. Dunham also played one of the production's main characters, Georgia Brown, and her dancers were an integral part of the cast.

Dunham's relationship with Hollywood began shortly before Horne arrived on the scene. Her first film, *Carnival of Rhythm* (1941), was intended to be an authentic portrayal of Brazilian folk life.[53] The Technicolor short features Dunham and her dance company performing her choreography. The following year, Dunham had a specialty number in *Star Spangled Rhythm* (1942), a Paramount Pictures war musical with Bob Hope and Bing Crosby. Dunham's song and dance, which she did with a zoot-suited Eddie "Rochester" Anderson, was considered one of the liveliest spots in the show.[54] *Star Spangled Rhythm* and her spot one year later in *Stormy Weather* earned Dunham celebrity status. Although Horne claimed that hers was the only photograph to hang in the barracks of African American soldiers, the *Afro-American* had been publishing photos of a number of women as pinup girls, and in 1943, in addition to Lena Horne, Katherine Dunham was deemed a favorite.[55]

By the time the Little Troc opened in January 1942, Ellington and most of the other acts had moved on. Horne and Dunham's dancers were the only ones left on the bill. The new venue, however, proved too small for the dance troupe. Horne was left alone on the bill, and with Phil Moore's accompaniment, she became an instant hit. Four or five nights a week people pushed their way into the club to hear Horne sing straight versions of familiar numbers. To nightclub owners, who were used to audiences chatting and eating during their best floorshows, Horne was revolutionizing the business. "Even though she didn't claw down the walls like a dusky Betty Hutton or send temperatures up to heaven," said *The New York Times*, everybody stopped whatever they were doing and listened.[56]

Within a couple of weeks after Horne had opened at the Little Troc, Roger Edens of MGM came calling. Edens, who had first heard Lena sing at Café Society, was a composer and arranger for Arthur Freed's production group. The Freed Unit, as it was known, was responsible for films that epitomized the Golden Age of Hollywood musicals, including *The Wizard of Oz* (1939), *Show Boat* (1951) and *Singin' in the Rain* (1952). To some, Roger Edens and the Freed Unit were synonymous.[57] Horne auditioned for Freed first and then for the big man, MGM head and cofounder L.B. Mayer.

In addition to her New York and L.A. agents, Horne claimed that she summoned her father to Los Angeles to help with the negotiation of her contract. She also consulted Walter White, and it was he, most likely, who set the ground rules for Horne's hiring. Early in 1942, Lena Horne signed a contract with MGM that stipulated she would not have to do "illiterate comedy" or play a cook or other parts usually assigned to African American performers.[58]

The signing of Horne's contract came during a time of increasing black political awareness in the United States. America's reaction against the racism of Nazi Germany initiated debate concerning its own brand of racism at home. In March of 1942, *Variety* reported that Walter White, after a meeting with Darryl Zanuck and other production chiefs, had declared that major Hollywood studios would be adapting to the times by eliminating old racial stereotypes from their films.[59]

In her autobiography, penned with Richard Schickel, Horne wrote that she agreed with White; establishing a new image for black women would be an important goal for her. White's concern, and hers, too, she went on to say, was that while waiting for her first big role she might be forced to play a maid or a jungle type.[60] In the same autobiography, contradicting her stated aim and the myth that she would never play a maid, Horne comes across quite matter of factly when describing her first MGM screen test.

Horne's maiden MGM screen test was for *Cairo* (1942) starring Jeanette McDonald and Robert Young. Horne and Eddie "Rochester" Anderson were being considered for parts as their servants. "It was a good role," Horne said. "The maid was to be just as flippant and fresh as anyone. She was a human being, not a stereotype."[61] As fate would have it, though, the screen test flopped. In an attempt to match Horne's light complexion with Anderson's dark skin, the studio applied dark makeup to Horne with disastrous photographic consequences. In the end, Ethel Waters and Dooley Wilson played the servants and the studio called upon makeup designer and cosmetics industry kingpin Max Factor to create a shade of makeup that would make Horne look as dark as possible without making her appear grotesque. The makeup was named "Light Egyptian."[62]

That Horne coveted the role of a "jungle type" in *White Cargo* (1942), another film that was in the works around the time she signed with MGM, further reveals both a scarcity of suitable roles for the new star and an early ambivalence toward challenging stereotypes.[63] *White Cargo*, originally adapted from the 1912 novel *Hell's Playground*, tells of the dangers British men faced on the African continent during colonial times. That danger was not climate, nor disease, nor wild animals. In *White Cargo*, the danger that lurks for the white man in Africa is the Black Eve, the native woman who leads white men to their downfall. The man foolhardy enough to "mammy palaver" with the Black Eve will be shipped back home a useless wreck—nothing more than white cargo!

In *Hell's Playground*, the heroine was a full-blooded African.[64] When Leon Gordon adapted the novel in 1923 for his stage production *White Cargo*, the female character came to be of mixed British and African ancestry and was given the name "Tondelayo." In MGM's *White Cargo*, Tondelayo is played by Hedy Lamarr, the Austrian-born actress known for her extraordinary beauty and her scientific contribution to digital communications. When she was still a teenager, Lamarr appeared in the Czechoslovakian film *Ecstacy* (1933), which also earned her the distinction of having the first onscreen orgasm in a non-pornographic film. In Hollywood, after signing with MGM, Lamarr was branded an exotic femme fatale. *White Cargo* was not her first mixed race role. In her second MGM film, *Lady of the Tropics* (1939), Lamarr starred as a French-Vietnamese half-caste woman.

In keeping with the spirit of Gordon's play, throughout most of MGM's *White Cargo*, Tondelayo is presumed to have a mixed black racial heritage. One character describes her as the "chocolate Cleopatra," and alluding to her in-between racial status, another exclaims that she is "too high and mighty for the natives and too smart for the white man." However, when one of the Brits, Mr. Langford, wants to marry Tondelayo, the resident padre makes the surprising revelation that Tondelayo has no "Accra" blood at all. Her father was Egyptian and her mother a low-caste Arab. Langford's response to this news is equally astonishing. "Get that! I'm marrying one of us," he says. In any event, the casting of a white woman as the mixed race African vamp, who in the end is revealed to have no West African blood, was apparently sufficient to pass muster with the Hays Office and its proscription of miscegenation.[65]

Horne, whom *Variety* once referred to as a "dusky Hedy Lamarr," wanted the part of Tondelayo and resented the studio for not giving it to her. She was further dismayed when she heard that Lamarr had worn *her* Light Egyptian makeup. According to Horne, the use of Lamarr and other white actresses for mixed race roles was an unfortunate side effect of the makeup's creation. In her autobiography, Horne said, "They used it on white actresses they wanted to play Negro or mulatto parts." This meant there would be even less work for black actors with whom, she also declared, she was already in trouble.[66]

Horne's assertion that her Light Egyptian makeup took jobs away from black actors is somewhat dubious since, owing to the Hays Code and the inherent prejudices of the day, major studios had little interest in representing mixed race characters in prominent roles. More likely, Horne's comment is directed at Hedy Lamarr in *White Cargo* and another role she later coveted, that of tragic mulatto Julie in MGM's 1951 remake of *Show Boat*. When the studio announced that Ava Gardner would play the part of Julie, Horne once again felt slighted.

Horne was right about being in trouble with other black actors. Veteran performers who were making a living playing stock roles, like mammies, porters, and sharecroppers, resented Walter White's intervention with the Hollywood system and their livelihood. As White's protégée, they resented Lena Horne, too. Chief among White's detractors was Clarence Muse who criticized White for meeting only with producers and ignoring the actors and their labor union. According to Muse, White, in his crusade to humanize the portrayal of African Americans in films, was trying to "white-wash" the black image.[67]

On April 8, two weeks after its report on Walter White's meeting with studio executives, *Variety* announced that MGM had just purchased the rights to the Broadway musical *Cabin in the Sky*. On that same date, *Variety* also noted that Lena Horne would appear in her first MGM film.[68]

Panama Hattie (1942)

Lena Horne's first part for MGM was in the war propaganda film *Panama Hattie*. This uncredited role, in which Horne is introduced as herself, has no speaking part and is seen only in musical numbers that are not integral to the white-cast plot would set the standard for Horne's position in MGM films. Horne was not singled out for such treatment, however. This was the case for many African American entertainers who appeared in Hollywood pictures during the 1940s. Nonetheless, in *Panama Hattie*, the placement of Lena Horne's musical numbers is more cohesive than it is in many of her later films.

Based on Cole Porter's 1940 Broadway production of the same name, *Panama Hattie* is a musical comedy about white American émigrés and servicemen in the Central American country of Panama during the Second World War. Although Panama's population is predominantly non-white, with the exception of specialty numbers by Horne and the Berry Brothers, black and brown people are invisible in *Panama Hattie*. Ann Sothern, the title character Hattie, is a nightclub singer. Red Skelton, Rags Ragland, and Ben Blue are American sailors who watch over her. Deadpan comedienne Virginia O'Brien also stars as Hattie's pal.

Panama Hattie was first completed in the fall of the previous year. When it didn't rate well with preview audiences, MGM tried to fix it. In addition to reshooting scenes, new musical sequences directed by Vincente Minnelli in his filmmaking debut were added. Among the new additions are two numbers featuring Lena Horne. The first, near the start of the film, is "Just One of Those Things," a torch song from another Cole Porter musical, *Jubilee* (1935). Horne's second number, near the end of the film, is "The Spring," a song about a hybrid Harlem dance with a Spanish-Caribbean influence. The song's title is a contraction of Spanish Swing.

The music for "The Spring" was written by Phil Moore. Moore's soon-to-be wife, Jeni LeGon, co-wrote the lyrics with Alfred Legou. Considered to be the most gifted female tap dancer of her generation, Jeni LeGon had come to Hollywood several years earlier. In *Hooray for Love* (1935), she tap-danced with Bill Robinson. Jeni LeGon even had a contract with MGM, but she was let go after she outdanced Eleanor Powell during a preproduction performance for what would have been her next film, *Broadway Melody of 1936*.[69] LeGon served as Lena Horne's dance coach for "The Spring." In an interview with Horne's biographer, LeGon recalled that Lena's dancing "wasn't very good," but "I taught her what to do."[70]

Conspicuous on drums in "The Spring" sequence is Leo Watson, whom composer turned critic Leonard Feather called the greatest scat singer of them all.[71] Watson doesn't sing, though. Instead, while Horne dances and sings, at times with a West Indian lilt, Watson mugs and clowns on a set of drums that intermittently glides in front of the star. A second drummer, on bongos, chatters to Horne in Spanish and playfully competes with Watson for Horne's attention.

Capturing the greater share of Horne's notice in this number are the Berry Brothers,

a flash dancing trio of siblings that bears comparison with the more famous tap dancing duo the Nicholas Brothers. In the fall 1938 edition of the Cotton Club Parade, the two
rival dance teams appeared on the same bill for the first and only time. Herman Stark,
who was responsible for the show's programming, was also the Nicholas Brothers' manager. Stark put the Nicholas Brothers somewhere in the middle of the show and the Berry
Brothers last. To establish their superiority, the Berry Brothers were thus challenged to
come up with a new and thrilling end to their routine.[72]

The Berry Brothers' finale for this Cotton Club show entailed two of the three brothers sprinting up twin flights of stairs at opposite sides of a balcony that was about twelve
feet above and behind the bandstand. Once atop the balcony, the two brothers leaped
over the heads of Cab Calloway's orchestra to land in perfect unison in a "leg-breaking"
split on either side of the third Berry Brother who, at the same time, was coming out of a
back somersault and also landed in a split.[73] A similar performance by the Berry Brothers
can be seen at the beginning of *Panama Hattie*, although there is only one flight of stairs,
which all three brothers ascend before leaping over the band. The breathtaking dance that
the Nicholas Brothers would execute five years later in *Stormy Weather* brings to mind
the Berrys' acrobatic stairway antics.

In the sartorial semantics of Hollywood, "The Sping" ostentatiously styles Lena
Horne as an exotic Creole. The top she wears reveals, ever so carefully, her midriff and
mid-back. Her skirt has an outer layer made of lace, which is decorated with pom poms.
Accessorizing the ensemble are large conch shells worn as earrings and bracelets. The
largest shell is attached to a bandana placed atop her head. Earlier in the film, Hattie is
also revealed to dress to excess, a faux pas easily recognized by the eight-year-old daughter of her fiancée. The young girl, therefore, goes about snipping off pieces of Hattie's
dress until it becomes more respectable. Horne, of course, gets no such intervention.
Nevertheless, in typical Horne style, she carries off the garish look with grace and is
poised throughout.

When Lena Horne first signed with MGM, one of America's premier gossip colum-
nists, Louella Parsons, reported that she was from the West Indies.[74] After *Panama Hattie*
was released, according to Horne, a number of white people wrote the studio to inquire
about their new Latin discovery. While there might have been some confusion about
Horne's identity among whites, there didn't seem to be any among blacks, although some
did accuse the star of trying to pass.[75]

To many African Americans Lena Horne's presence in *Panama Hattie* was a revelation and a source of dignity. Just months before the film was released, the *California Eagle*
commended Horne for her "race pride" and predicted that her appearance in the film
would "make you feel that democracy for all is fast arriving." After the film was released,
for being black, beautiful, and not hidden under shapeless plantation period dress, *The
Pittsburgh Courier* declared that Lena Horne in *Panama Hattie* was Hollywood's first test
of accepting a new type of American.[76]

For white critics, *Panama Hattie* didn't measure up to the Broadway version. Some
found it dull, with tunes loosely strung together, and not much of a story line. Among
them, Howard V. Cohen of the *Pittsburgh Post-Gazette* thought that Lena Horne, the
Berry Brothers, and Virginia O'Brien were the only worthwhile parts of the film. Cohen
described Horne as a "coffee-colored" sultry singer "around whom no thermometer is
safe." Writing for *The New York Times*, Bosley Crowther said Horne trilled a rhumba
"with plenty of spark."[77]

Around the same time that NAACP leader Walter White was busy trying to convince Hollywood studios to update their portrayals of blacks, the U.S. government created the Office of War Information (OWI) to disseminate information about the war through the use of press, posters, radio, and motion pictures. When the OWI set up a branch in Hollywood, it embarked on a propaganda effort aimed at gaining national support for the war.

The OWI had a special interest in African Americans, and it hoped that by employing more blacks in the film industry and improving the way in which they were portrayed, it could convince them that the war was their fight, too. Lena Horne's biggest films, *Cabin in the Sky* and *Stormy Weather*, were a response to OWI and NAACP pressure to diversify black roles.

Cabin in the Sky (1943)

Cabin in the Sky is Vincente Minnelli's first credited directing project. It is also Hollywood's first all-black musical and the only black musical to come out of the prestigious Arthur Freed Unit. As such, it employed a host of star-studded entertainment that in addition to Lena Horne included Ethel Waters, Eddie "Rochester" Anderson, Louis Armstrong, and Duke Ellington. For Horne, *Cabin in the Sky* is one of the few films in which she has a speaking part and it was her only acting role with MGM. Horne also had two musical numbers in *Cabin in the Sky*, "Life Is Full of Consequences" and "Honey in the Honeycomb." A third number, "Ain't It the Truth," which featured Horne singing in a bubble bath, was cut from the final version.

The Broadway musical upon which the film is based opened at the Martin Beck Theatre on October 25, 1940, and closed after 156 performances in March of the following year. The book was written by Lynn Root and lyrics by John Latouche. The production was staged by the ballet choreographer George Balanchine. The stage show was only a moderate box office success, but it was considered an artistic and critical hit and garnered a fiercely loyal following.[78] After it closed in New York, *Cabin in the Sky* was introduced to a broader audience when it traveled the country.

The Broadway show starred Ethel Waters as Petunia, the pious and doting wife of Little Joe Jackson, a backwoods gambler played by Dooley Wilson. Katherine Dunham was Georgia Brown, the seductress vying for Little Joe's affections. Dunham and her dance troupe made up roughly one-third of the stage cast, and though she was not credited, Dunham co-choreographed with George Balanchine. Dunham's collaboration with Balanchine, the fusion of ballet and black dance vernacular, marked a crucial moment in dance. Perhaps the best example of this occurred at the beginning of the second act, in the show's biggest dance number, "Egyptian Ballet."[79]

"Egyptian Ballet" is a dream fantasy that takes place in the Jacksons' backyard while Petunia is away at the store. Before Petunia left, she and Joe had just finished singing "My Old Virginia Home on the Nile." While Little Joe is sleeping, Georgia Brown takes advantage of the opportunity to entice him. From behind a clothesline hung with laundry, bedsheets parted to reveal dancers dressed in brief costumes. Dunham made her entrance wearing an Egyptian costume made from tie-dyed East Indian scarves with a floss-fringed loincloth that fell to the floor and a headdress copied from that worn by Nefertiti.

Commenting on this scene, Dunham said that she wanted to take her troupe out of the plantation stereotype inherent in "My Old Virginia Home" and find a way to escape some of the racism that she and her dancers would naturally feel appearing in a production that was "audacious and new." Dunham described the "Egyptian Ballet" as both an escape from Virginia back to Africa and a subtle merging of the two experiences.[80] In the press, Katherine Dunham's significant contributions to *Cabin in the Sky* were largely ignored and mostly reduced to the heatedness of her wiggling and strutting. Ethel Waters was deemed the show's star and given credit for holding it together.[81]

Waters reprised her role as Petunia in MGM's adaptation of *Cabin in the Sky*. Her husband, Little Joe, was played by Eddie "Rochester" Anderson, and the role of Georgia Brown went to Lena Horne. Katherine Dunham was not associated with the film, but a few of her dancers were, including Archie Savage who was the film's uncredited dance director. Rex Ingram, also from the stage cast, returned, dressed in black, as both Lucius and his son Lucifer Jr. Louis Armstrong was Lucifer's personal trumpeter and Mantan Moreland one of his idea men. Representing God and dressed in a white marching band uniform is Kenneth Spencer as the Lord's lefthand man, the General. On the night that the film's action comes to a head, Duke Ellington and his band are the main attraction at the local gambling club, Jim Henry's Paradise.

For the most part, it seems, the film is fairly true to the stage production, except that in the film most of the action is presented as a dream.[82] Petunia, a faithful servant of the Lord, wants to get into heaven. Her husband, Little Joe, doesn't have much use for religion, but he does have a soft spot for sweet Georgia Brown, a singer at Jim Henry's. One night, things get out of hand at the gambling club, and Little Joe is shot by Domino

Lena Horne is manipulated by Rex Ingram's fleshly devil in MGM's *Cabin in the Sky* (1943).

Johnson, a natty high-stakes gambler from out of town. Little Joe's life is left hanging in the balance. At home, lying in bed, he dreams that God and Lucius are vying for his soul. God sends down the General and gives Little Joe six months to qualify for entry into heaven. The Devil dispatches Lucifer Jr. to thwart him.

In the battle for Little Joe's soul, Georgia Brown is the Devil's pawn. When we first meet Georgia, she is in her bedroom, unaware that Lucifer Jr. is there with her. As Georgia moves about her abode, in various states of dress and undress, Lucifer reclines comfortably on her bed. Using his supernatural powers, he persuades Georgia to pay Little Joe a visit. Georgia exits and eventually finds Little Joe at home alone. Joe manages to resist Georgia's charms, but when Petunia comes home and discovers the two together, she becomes enraged and sends her husband away. Separated from Petunia, Little Joe cashes in on a sweepstakes ticket, received compliments of Lucifer Jr., and spends his time and money on Georgia.

On the final night of Little Joe's six-month reprieve, Domino Johnson, just released from prison, shows up at Jim Henry's. Shortly thereafter, Georgia and Little Joe, dressed in their finery, arrive on the scene in a chauffeur-driven car. After Georgia sings her number "Honey in the Honeycomb," Petunia enters the action, intent on stirring up trouble and collecting her half of the sweepstakes money. Petunia, also decked out in fancy evening attire, declares that she wants to perform and does her own rendition of "Honey in the Honeycomb."

Petunia also flirts and dances with Domino Johnson, which angers Little Joe, and a brawl ensues. During the melee, Petunia sends up a prayer asking for Jim Henry's to be destroyed. Her prayer is answered, but not before she and Little Joe are killed by gunfire, at which point the General appears to inform the couple that Petunia is eligible for heaven but Joe is not. Just then, one of Lucifer's henchmen arrives with a report that Georgia Brown has repented her sins and given all her money to the church. Since her money came from Little Joe, he is cleared for heaven on a technicality.

Cabin in the Sky, Hollywood's first all-black musical, is fourth in the lineage of all-black feature films, after *Hearts in Dixie* (1929), *Hallelujah* (1929), and *The Green Pastures* (1936). All four films have religious themes and, facilitated by their lack of white characters, endeavor to present the Old South in idyllic terms. Furthermore, while these early films don't explicitly depict a Northern city or a mass Northern movement of Southern blacks, their mise en scène, nevertheless, alludes to the Great Migration by way of urban-rural tension. In *Hearts in Dixie* (1929), for example, which was released just a few months before *Hallelujah*, its patriarch Nappus (Clarence Muse) doesn't want his grandson to grow up like his shiftless son-in-law, Gummy (Stepin Fetchit). For Nappus, the Northern city is a place where he can send his progeny to be educated in the ways of white science and freed from the limitations of black folk wisdom.

In the films that followed, *Hallelujah*, *The Green Pastures*, and *Cabin in the Sky*, the tension between urban and rural is more palpable. In these films, goodness and religiosity correspond to bucolic spaces populated by children, mammies, and pious adults, while evil is associated with urbanly styled men and women and their jazz and blues music. Chief among this latter category of people are light-skinned, polyandrous women. The contrast between the men to whom these light-skinned women are primarily connected is one means by which urban-rural tension is illuminated. Such is the case in *Hallelujah*, when Nina Mae McKinney's Chick can't decide if she wants to be with the city slicker, Hot Shot, or the cotton farmer and itinerant preacher, Zeke.

In *The Green Pastures*, Edna Mae Harris had the honor of playing the light-skinned vamp. Harris got her first big break in 1930 when she appeared in the Pulitzer Prize– winning version of *The Green Pastures* on Broadway. On the heels of her success in the film, Harris was on the road in 1936 with Noble Sissle and his company which at the time included Lena Horne.[83] Harris also played stock roles in a handful of Hollywood films and was a star of race films. In *The Green Pastures*, Harris is Zeba, a sexy sinner who sasses De Lawd and plays the wrong kind of music on the Sabbath. Zeba's boyfriend, Cain the Sixth, wears the "flashy garments" of a New Orleans Rampart Street dandy.[84] Cain's romantic rival, a country boy named Flatfoot, on the other hand, dresses modestly, and his nickname, "Big Gorilla," is a racial epithet that announces his lack of sophistication and connection to the simian world.

Although it can be said that in *Cabin in the Sky* Lena Horne took up the mantle from Nina Mae McKinney and Edna Mae Harris, her portrayal of the temptress departs somewhat from that of her predecessors. In their content analysis of early American films, Wolfenstein and Leites describe the "vamp," close cousin of the temptress, as a wicked woman who elicits an outright sexual response. She feigns exclusive passionate attachment to one man but is ultimately unfaithful. The vamp's dangerousness is linked to her sexuality and the intense jealousy evoked by her betrayal.[85]

Wolfenstein and Leites' definition of "vamp" is a perfect fit for both Chick and Zeba. In *Hallelujah*, Chick's sexual agency is foregrounded from the moment she's introduced. At the center of a crowd, made up mostly of men, Chick sings and dances. As she struts her stuff, members of the crowd express their appreciation for her physicality with comments like "What a brown-skin bunch of goodness she is!" When Zeke sees Chick, he is instantly smitten, but Chick only feigns interest in Zeke so that she and her boyfriend, Hot Shot, can cheat him out of his money. Some time later, in spite of her betrayal, Zeke and Chick end up living together. When Hot Shot reappears on the scene, Zeke's jealousy is so great that he fatally shoots Chick and strangles Hot Shot to death.

While Chick uses her sexuality for financial gain, Zeba's motivations are less complicated; she is simply a hedonist. In one scene, Zeba swears to Cain that there's no one else in the world for her and that she has no interest in Flatfoot. Soon after, Cain discovers Zeba and Flatfoot holding hands, and he fatally stabs his adversary. *Cabin in the Sky* also has clashes of violence between its rival men, but with a much different disposition for the seductive mulatto. The first assault, as it turned out, was not fatal and had nothing to do with Georgia Brown or a love triangle. Rather, Domino Johnson shot Little Joe for cheating at dice. The second clash between the two men is brought on by jealousy over a woman, but that woman is Petunia, not Georgia Brown.

In *Cabin in the Sky*, Georgia Brown is associated with two purportedly dissimilar men: Little Joe and Domino Johnson. However, unlike her counterparts of *Hallelujah* and *The Green Pastures*, her association with the two men does not comprise a love triangle. Georgia is romantically linked to Little Joe, but her relationship to Domino Johnson is rather ambiguous. The film certainly alludes to a connection between the two, however, in their one scene together, when Domino speaks, Georgia recoils, and her only concern is for Little Joe's safety. If Georgia had a relationship with Domino, it has either ended or was never serious to begin with. Georgia might be interloper in a marriage, but she does not appear to be an unfaithful woman.

Horne's interpretation of Georgia Brown also seems to diverge from that of Katherine Dunham's stage version of the seductress. Dunham's costumes were certainly more daring, and of her performance, Brooks Atkinson wrote that she strutted with a "brazen coquetry" that was "remarkably heated."[86] Dunham's "Sharp as a Tack" number opposite Eddie Anderson in *Star Spangled Rhythm,* released just a few months before *Cabin in the Sky,* as well as her later appearance in *Stormy Weather* offer excellent examples of the dancer's sultry, commanding presence. Furthermore, in comparing the stage version of *Cabin in the Sky* to the film, a critic for *The New York Times* noted that, even though Lena Horne made a "bewitching temptress," in deference to Joseph Breen and the Hays Office, Georgia Brown had been toned down for the screen.[87]

Before filming of *Cabin in the Sky* had even started, Breen did offer directives to MGM on the depiction of Georgia Brown. With respect to the bubble bath scene, apparently, no specific order came from the Hays Office, but Minnelli, erring on the side of caution, removed it before the premiere.[88] Horne's toned-down Georgia Brown might also in part be attributed to Minnelli's direction and the dynamics on the set. Ethel Waters, who had a reputation for terrorizing fellow cast members, felt animus toward Horne and resented any special attention she received. To contend with Waters' antagonistic behavior, Minnelli instructed Horne to act helpless and babyish.[89]

When compared to her predecessors, Lena Horne's Georgia Brown, who was manipulated by a fleshly Devil and who ultimately repented for her sins, is not inherently wicked and is just a little too naïve to be taken seriously as a vamp. Horne's Georgia Brown is more like another feminine type identified by Wolfenstein and Leites in their study, the "good-bad girl." The good-bad girl is a woman who is essentially good but appears to be bad. As such, the good-bad girl often appears to be involved with a bad man when, in fact, she is not.[90] While Lena Horne's performance in *Cabin in the Sky* can be identified with the jezebel, it also breaks free from stereotype to hint at a broader potential for the representation of black women in Hollywood.

Similarly, Ethel Waters' portrayal of Petunia transcends the mammy stereotype it typifies. When *Cabin in the Sky* opens, Petunia is busy in her front yard with a laundry basket and ironing board, and later in the film, Little Joe buys her a washing machine as a gift. As Petunia, Waters evokes the same portrait of a washerwoman that she portrayed in two early short films, *Rufus Jones for President* (1933) and *Bubbling Over* (1934), as well as her character Dicey in the later film *Pinky* (1949). In the scene at Jim Henry's Paradise, however, Petunia discards her plain housedress and headscarf for a sparkly evening gown and proves to be even sassier on the dance floor than the so-called seductress. Furthermore, at the same time that Minnelli's direction in *Cabin in the Sky* frames Lena Horne as an MGM glamour queen, it regards Ethel Waters as a star in her own right.

Minnelli's celebrity treatment of black stars and his sumptuous, stylized presentation of impoverished black life did little to resolve the problems of stereotype. In mainstream newspapers, *Cabin in the Sky* was largely met with praise and regarded as a step forward in racial equality.[91] In the African American press the picture was charged with catering to the South and being slanderous of African Americans, and it was labeled "an insult masking behind the label of folklore."[92]

Stormy Weather (1943)

At the start of 1943, while MGM was trying to figure out what next to do with its sepia star, Lena Horne was loaned out to Twentieth Century–Fox, where she was cast as singer Selina Rogers in Hollywood's second all-black musical, *Stormy Weather*. Horne starred opposite Bill "Bojangles" Robinson, who played army veteran and hoofer Bill Williamson. Emmett "Babe" Wallace is Williamson's foil, Chick Bailey. Dooley Wilson, best known for his role in *Casablanca* (1942), is Bill's buddy, Gabe. A number of entertainers appear as themselves, including Cab Calloway who performs "Geechy Joe" and "The Jumpin' Jive." Fats Waller sings "Ain't Misbehavin'," and in the film's big finale, the Nicholas Brothers perform their legendary staircase dance routine.

Directed by Andrew Stone, with an adaptation by leftist Hy Kraft, *Stormy Weather* (originally titled *Thanks, Pal*) was supposed to be a thank you to African Americans for their role in past wars as well as a celebration of their contribution to the entertainment world. In his memoir, Kraft wrote that Stone "didn't have a clue" about what he was trying to achieve and that the film's producer, William Le Baron, was "hardly a man of conviction." Consequently, a good deal of Kraft's initial objectives was diluted.[93]

Remarkably, black choreographer Clarence Robinson was given screen credit as *Stormy Weather*'s dance director, and in another unheard-of move, William Grant Still, "the dean of African American composers," was originally hired as the film's music supervisor. Much like Kraft, Still had difficulty conveying a larger vision of blackness to the studio. William Grant Still was born in 1895 in Woodville, Mississippi, and was raised among the black elite. His father and namesake was a music teacher, and his mother, Carrie Fambro Still, was a schoolteacher. When Still's father died, he and his mother moved to Little Rock, Arkansas, where his maternal grandmother, a former slave, resided. Carrie soon found a job teaching, and when she remarried, she and her husband, Charles Shepperson, were included among the highest strata of the city's black community.[94]

Still was raised in a home that was filled with books and musical instruments. His neighborhood, despite state legislated segregation, was racially mixed, and his playmates were white. Still's mother and grandmother, like many aristocrats of color, had intimate knowledge of their family tree, which included black, Native American, Scotch, Irish, and Spanish ancestors. Still, who had studied music at Wilberforce University and Oberlin Conservatory, made a living in popular entertainment, but he was also a serious composer. In 1936, he was heralded as the first black man to have a major orchestral work played before an American audience. Still's best-known work, *Afro-American Symphony*, was completed in 1930.[95]

Irving Mills, who had been in cahoots with Owney Madden during the Cotton Club's heyday and managed the bands of both Duke Ellington and Cab Calloway, was a production advisor for *Stormy Weather*. When Mills asked Still to be a part of the project, he described a film that would document black culture and black achievement on the concert stage, using vocal artists such as the Fisk Jubilee Singers, famous for introducing "slave songs," known today as Negro spirituals, to the world. Just a couple of months into the project, Still disclosed that this concept had been ousted in favor of showcasing the more popular and profitable music associated with vaudeville, minstrelsy and nightclubs.[96]

Still further charged that various department heads, including the film's music director, Al Newman, had "strange ideas" about black music. According to Still, Newman told him that black music should be crude and black dancing erotic. For being "too good," an arrangement the composer had made from a period he knew first-hand was thrown out by Newman. The final straw for Still came when a ballet idealization he created for the film's title song was nixed for being "too polite" and not sexy enough. Not wishing to profit from a production that he believed was diametrically opposed to the welfare of African Americans, Still resigned his position as music supervisor.[97]

The all-black cast aside, *Stormy Weather*, which spans the period between the two world wars, is typical of many early Hollywood musicals in that it's a story about show business. It's also a wartime propaganda film that begins and ends with its characters performing for the troops. Told mostly in flashbacks, *Stormy Weather* recounts events in the life of its main character, Bill Williamson.

The film opens with Williamson dancing with neighborhood children on his veranda. The kids call him "Uncle Bill," an obvious nod to Robinson's role as Uncle Billy in *The Littlest Rebel* (1935), also produced by Twentieth Century–Fox and in which he played Shirley Temple's dancing house slave on a Southern plantation during the Civil War. Robinson appeared in three other Shirley Temple vehicles, *The Little Colonel* (1935), *Rebecca of Sunnybrook Farm* (1938) and *Just Around the Corner* (1938). Film historian Thomas Cripps deemed Robinson's films with Shirley Temple as "the most persistent racial product of thirties musicals," and Bogle described his character Uncle Billy in *The Littlest Rebel* as the "perfect—perhaps the quintessential" Uncle Tom role.[98]

Stormy Weather's first flashback begins with actual footage of veterans of the Harlem Hellfighters regiment being celebrated as heroes by a massive crowd as they parade up the streets of New York at the end of the First World War. Realism is quickly supplanted by a shot of Bill Williamson and Gabe marching in the parade as members of the 369th Infantry. Later that night Bill and Gabe attend a ball held in honor of the servicemen, with entertainment led by the Hellfighters' bandleader James Reese Europe, played by Ernest Whitman. Lena Horne's Selina Rogers is a featured performer at the ball. She sings with accompaniment from Chick Bailey on piano. Selina refers to Chick as her partner, but it soon becomes evident that Chick wants to be more than just Selina's show biz partner.

Selina's brother Clem, who presumably died in combat, was also a Harlem Hellfighter and a friend of Bill's. When Selina meets Bill for the first time at the ball, he presents her with Clem's Croix de Guerre, the medal that, in actuality, was bestowed by the French army upon every member of the Harlem Hellfighters. At this juncture, it seems that Bill might elaborate on some of the infantry's heroics or explain the circumstances of Clem's death. Instead, the camera quickly cuts away to a lighthearted, comic moment with Gabe and his ditzy, gold-digging date. When the scene returns to Selina and Bill, their conversation has ended, and it's time to dance. In any event, Selina and Bill hit it off. Not only does Bill have a connection to her deceased brother, he's also a great dancer. Selina thinks he should be performing on the stage, but Bill has plans to return to his home in the South the very next day, where his old job awaits.

Later, Selina travels with Chick to Memphis, where she and Bill meet again. Chick is scouting talent for his new show in Chicago. Selina, Chick, and their entourage arrive at Ada Brown's club where Bill is a dancing waiter. Chick decides to hire everyone working at the Memphis club, including Ada Brown, Fats Waller, and, reluctantly, at Selina's behest, Bill Williamson. Selina and Bill eventually become a couple, but they break up when Selina chooses her career over Bill's offer to settle down with him. After some years apart, at the film's conclusion, Selina and Bill reunite.

Stormy Weather is the first of the all-black feature films to be set in urban locales, primarily away from the South, making it appear more contemporary in its portrayal of black people. It is also absent the religiosity and good-and-evil dichotomy found in the earlier all-black films. Nevertheless, a preference for old-fashioned stereotypes is

When it comes to courting Lena Horne, Emmett "Babe" Wallace's new Negro (left) can't compete with Bill Robinson's old Negro in Fox's *Stormy Weather* (1943).

betrayed and the tension between rural and urban retained in the relationship between its light-skinned heroine's two suitors, Bill Williamson and Chick Bailey. In the contest between old (Southern/rural) Negro and the New (Northern/urban) Negro, the former, as played by Bill Robinson, who was forty years Horne's senior and the embodiment of an Uncle Tom, wins hands down.

The decision to cast Bill Robinson as the winner of Lena's heart did not go down without a little controversy. In late March of 1943, after filming of *Stormy Weather* was completed, there was a rumor in the black press that, after a private showing of the film, studio executives had deemed the casting of Bill Robinson a big mistake. The movie would have to be reshot, a decision, said one newspaper, that indicated Hollywood didn't want to further "rile Negroes and progressive whites" who had been urging the studios to portray blacks in a more realistic light. A studio spokesman was quoted as saying, "Miss Horne is a young and beautiful girl and should therefore have been teamed with someone the audience would seriously accept as her screen lover."[99]

Within a few days, the story of Robinson's miscasting was refuted by Fox. In support of the denial, Horne, they said, was happy to work with Robinson and that doing so would surely advance her film career.[100] According to Horne's daughter, this was not quite the case. Horne, apparently, loathed Bill Robinson and considered him a big bully on the order of Ethel Waters.[101] At the time *Stormy Weather* was released, *Variety* also reported that there had been some "intratrade concern" about the casting of Robinson opposite Horne. *Variety*, however, thought the "illusion" (of Horne playing opposite someone who was technically old enough to be her grandfather) came off quite well.[102]

Suave, handsome, and of the same generation as Horne, fellow Brooklynite Babe Wallace seems a more suitable match for Lena Horne. The two had crossed paths before when they were cast as a handsome couple at the Cotton Club in the fall of 1935. The following year, Wallace cut a dashing figure opposite Nina Mae McKinney in the Warner Bros. short *The Black Network*. On stage, Wallace had earned a reputation as a singing emcee and at least one source referred to him as a "colored Bing Crosby."[103]

In 1940, Wallace was hired to front the Ella Fitzgerald Orchestra when it toured the United States. Writing for *The New York Age*, critic Harry Kramer said that Wallace, waving his baton in front of the Fitzgerald band, was a "thing of beauty to behold" and that the dancers were torn between gazing at Wallace and dancing to his "fascinating rhythm."[104] In an interview conducted shortly before his death in 2006, Babe Wallace said that he rejected Hollywood's offers to play stock black roles. Wanting to be the next James Cagney, Wallace said that he held out for better parts. Those parts never came.[105]

Although Wallace's character Chick is presented as rival to Bill, there isn't much of a competition. Selina favors Bill right from the start, and the film never really treats Chick as a serious contender for her affections. Having offered audiences a bourgeois character who did not fit the vaudeville, jazz, or Uncle Tom mold, the studio was not about to crown him a hero. Instead, Bailey's character is mocked, emasculated, and excluded from the finale, and Wallace himself, despite having an important part in the film, received no screen credit. Wallace's character was an innovation, nonetheless. Prior to *Stormy Weather*, one had to look to race films, with actors like Lorenzo Tucker and Ralph Cooper, to see similar representations of black manhood. Hollywood did not again welcome a similar type until a decade later, when Harry Belafonte came along.

Lena Horne has four numbers in *Stormy Weather*. "There's No Two Ways About Love" was written for the film. "I Can't Give You Anything but Love" and "Diga Diga Doo" were borrowed from the *Blackbirds of 1928*, the all-black revue that made Bill Robinson a star. "Diga Diga Doo," which caused a near riot when it was performed by a scantily-clad Adelaide Hall fifteen years earlier, is the closest Horne comes in *Stormy Weather* to representing a stereotype. In "Diga Diga Doo," Horne is the "jungle type." However, while Horne is associated with the "primitive" in this number, she also manages to elude it.

Compared to what is known about Adelaide Hall's performance of the song, Horne's version is rather conservative. The lyrics have been truncated and sanitized, and Horne, looking more like a cute showgirl than randy tropical maiden, moves discreetly to the light, playful musical accompaniment. Scanty costumes, tiger-striped leotards and cat ears are saved for the light-skinned chorus girls seated on the floor around her. Halfway through the number, Horne makes her escape, and the mood turns wild and energetic. The music's tempo speeds up, horns blare, the felines come alive, and a "savage" couple, reminiscent of Josephine Baker and Joe Alex, make an appearance with some frenetic choreography.

Horne's other numbers are all performed straight, including "Stormy Weather," which begins her association with the title song. Eventually, "Stormy Weather" would become Horne's signature song, overshadowing Ethel Waters' connection to it, but it would take decades before Horne could own it and think of it as her song, too.[106] Lena Horne's iconic "Stormy Weather" performance takes place in the present. Selina and Bill have been estranged for several years, and the song is the impetus for their reunion.

The setting is a Hollywood nightclub, a big party for the soldiers before they get shipped out. Selina is accompanied by Cab Calloway and his band. During the song's

Lena Horne and Bill Robinson display their costumes for the primitivist "Diga Diga Doo" number in Fox's *Stormy Weather* (1943).

instrumental break, the one over which William Grant Still resigned, she is also joined by Katherine Dunham and her dancers. As they did in the stage version of *Cabin in the Sky*, the Dunham troupe performs a fantasy dream ballet.

The "Stormy Weather" scene begins with a view of Cab Calloway and his band at floor level with the audience. Selina is on an elevated stage behind them, standing next to a window that opens to an urban street scene. Outside the window, a storm is on the way, as evidenced by wind kicking up the dust. Part way through her song, Horne descends a small flight of steps to join the band and partygoers, including Bill, on the floor. Lightning strikes. Selina runs back up the stairs to close the window, and the action moves out to the street scene where Dunham and her dancers appear.

As rain pours down, a handful of pimpish men and loose-looking women pair up to dance a very slow jitterbug. When Dunham strolls onto the set, a man invites her to join him, but she declines. Lightning and thunder strike again, and Dunham looks up. Seconds later, she descends from the clouds, a goddess. Integrating movements from African and Afro-Caribbean ritual dance, Dunham and her troupe perform choreography that is a blend of modern dance and ballet movements.[107]

Dunham called her "Stormy Weather" number "an escapist impression" from the realities of modern black life—namely that of the black urban underclass. Originally, the studio wanted the entire segment to be nothing but hookers and pimps, but Dunham refused.[108] Her rebuff of the man at the beginning of the piece, thus, takes on double meaning. Not only is Dunham declining street life in that moment; she is also saying "no" to Hollywood's conception of blackness, presenting instead a black identity outside the mainstream and ahead of its time.

For Lena Horne, her star turn in *Stormy Weather* was her most ample and significant screen role. Horne's appearance in *Cabin in the Sky* was certainly rare, but not entirely new. Georgia Brown was, after all, a variation on the light-skinned-woman-as-temptress that had played in Hollywood before. *Stormy Weather* marks the first time a black woman character, on par with those played by Hollywood's white glamour gals, had ever been attempted by a major studio. Selina Rogers is not only glamorous, she's independent. She dances a little and sings. She has romantic interests but is not a seductress. Nor is Selina Rogers a woman tempted by the devil. To the contrary, in *Stormy Weather*, Lena Horne is pretty close to flawless.

Released in July 1943, *Stormy Weather* received high marks in the mainstream press for its fun and entertainment value. Before its release, *Variety* predicted it would have "smooth sailing" at the box office. The *Los Angeles Times* reported that it would surely delight music fans and that crowds had stormed the box offices of five theaters to see the film. *The New York Times*, while noting that its scope was too narrow to be a true representation of the African American contribution to entertainment, deemed it a "first-rate" picture.[109]

In the black press, there was also praise for the film. *The Pittsburgh Courier* said it was perhaps "the most progressive, significant, all-out gesture yet made to portray" blacks without the usual clowning or buffooning. In the *California Eagle*, when asked his opinion of the film, African American composer Leon René said, "it was the first time I sat through a showing of an all-colored film and forgot it was colored." Despite all the acclaim, to some proponents of racial equality and integration, the all-black films *Stormy Weather* and *Cabin in the Sky* were a sign of retreat from progress in race relations, little more than Jim Crow films that reinforced the reality of racial segregation.[110]

Within a year of its inception, the Office of War Information came under attack in Congress in part because its position on race relations angered conservatives and Southern racists. Although the OWI's relationship with Hollywood continued until the end of the war, by the spring of 1943, due to drastic reactionary budget cuts, operations were effectively ended, and the agency's efforts to both employ and humanize black people in films abandoned.[111]

In June 1943, just before *Stormy Weather* was set to be released, race riots broke out in Detroit, leaving nine whites and twenty-five African Americans dead and hundreds more people injured. In response to the social unrest, some major studios decided to withdraw from Southern locales the release of films in which blacks could be seen mixing with whites. Other studios voluntarily took shears to their pictures, editing out the parts that some whites might find racially offensive. Fox considered changing its plans for the release of *Stormy Weather* but was ultimately persuaded by black newspaper publishers against it.[112]

The abatement of Lena Horne's film career after the release of *Stormy Weather* coincides with backlash from the Detroit riots, the OWI's retreat from Hollywood, and the increased activities of Southern film censors on the subject of race. The most flagrant of these local film censors was Lloyd T. Binford of Memphis, Tennessee. Binford, who was born and raised on a Mississippi plantation in 1869, served as chairman of the Memphis Board of Censors from 1928 until 1955. In 1950, recalling his youthful memories of black servants on his family's plantation, a tearful Binford told a reporter for *Collier's* that he loved "old niggers" so much so that he had reserved for his funeral two rows of seats in the back for his black friends.[113] The Memphis censor was so notorious that the term "Binfordized," used to denote extreme censorship or outright banning of films, became part of American film industry jargon.

Memphis's conflict over racial representation in the movies flared up with the Detroit riots and the release of *Cabin in the Sky* and *Stormy Weather*. As one part of a larger effort by the city of Memphis to maintain social control during a period of huge instability, beginning in 1943, Memphis declared war on Hollywood films that deviated from the old stereotypes in their representation of African Americans. Before the race riots, as *Cabin in the Sky* was about to be released, city officials worried that it might further upset whites who were already displeased with African Americans entering the wartime workforce. *Cabin in the Sky* played uncut in Memphis. After the riots, however, city officials updated their censorship policy to include racial restrictions.[114]

Films that hinted at "social equality" between the races and films that pictured black characters doing things that the censorship board deemed they would not ordinarily do in real life were not permitted to play in theaters that catered to white or racially mixed audiences. Although it was held up for an entire year, *Stormy Weather* eventually played uncut in Memphis. In other cities, *Stormy Weather* was not allowed to play until censors were assured it would be shown at black and white theaters simultaneously, on the same day and at the same time, so that white theaters would not get black patrons. Normally, white theaters would get the film first.[115]

After *Stormy Weather*, Binford went on a spree, excising a number of blacks from films. For being "inimical to the public interest," scenes involving Cab Calloway and his band were cut from Andrew Stone's *Sensations of 1945* (1944), leaving the rest of the film, according to reviewers, "patched up" and "confusing." Louis Armstrong was cut from the Warner Bros. picture *Pillow to Post* (1945). And even though Eddie Anderson's character was servant to the white lead in *Brewster's Millions* (1945), the film was banned by Binford, who said it was adverse to the "friendly relations" that existed "between the races" in his city and that Rochester (Anderson) had "much too familiar a way about him." Binford had a special animus for Lena Horne and boasted of deleting her in every picture after *Stormy Weather*. Daunted by the draconian censorship practices of Binford and others like him, the major studios regarded these local censors and the communities they served as a market to be catered to.[116]

In 1943, Lena Horne also appeared as a specialty act in the white musicals *I Dood*

It, Thousands Cheer, and *Swing Fever*. Filming for all three projects began in 1942, and all were released before Binford had fully mounted his attack on Horne and other black entertainers.

I Dood It (1943)

As is the case in many of her films, Lena Horne's musical number in *I Dood It* is window dressing to a story that centers on the romance of a white couple. In this case, Red Skelton, a pants presser, falls in love with Constance Shaw, a Broadway star, played by Eleanor Powell. Clocking in at nearly eleven minutes, Lena Horne's extravagant number is more like a film short than a typical specialty act. As directed by Vincente Minnelli, it carries forward the spirit of *Cabin in the Sky*, and like the all-black musical, it has a religious theme. This time around, however, Lena Horne is a real Goody Two Shoes, on God's side, right from start.

"Taking a Chance on Love," the first of two songs featured in the scene, is also borrowed from *Cabin in the Sky*, but the centerpiece song is "Jericho." A retelling of the Bible story of Joshua and the Israelites' conquest of Canaan, "Jericho" became something of a hit after it was performed by Irish-American tenor Morton Downey in the Hollywood musical *Syncopation* (1929). In that earlier rendition, jazz music was on the side of Joshua and his Hebrew God, and it had the power to make the people of Jericho surrender.

For *I Dood It* "Jericho" was transformed into a sprawling narrative with principal storyteller Horne sometimes standing in for Joshua. In this version, too, a trumpet man is responsible for knocking down the walls of Jericho. However, taking its cue from the earlier all-black films, in this updated version of the song, jazz music is more generally associated with evil. Jazz, it seems, is already an inherent part of the sinners' lifestyle before the trumpet man Joshua comes a-blowing.

Sharing the limelight with Lena Horne in this specialty number is Hazel Scott, the gifted pianist who was born in Trinidad and raised in Harlem. Like Horne, Scott was a favorite at Café Society. While Horne was the queen of the original location downtown, when Barney Josephson decided to open a second club, Café Society Uptown, Scott became its resident diva. There was no love lost between the two women, but they did find common ground in their efforts to rewrite Hollywood's depiction of black women.

In *I Dood It*, Horne and Scott, supported by a cast of approximately twenty black singers and musicians, play themselves auditioning for a revue. Their roles, though not particularly imaginative, are indicative of the film industry's fleeting attempt at presenting African Americans with dignity. Both women, for example, are spoken to and are treated respectfully by white men. They are also a stark contrast to the other black women who appear in this film. Butterfly McQueen, best known as the giddy slave from *Gone with the Wind* (1939), has a part as Constance Shaw's maid. In a stage show within the film Shaw plays a Southern belle, and Dorothy Dandridge's mother, Ruby Dandridge, is her mammy.

The insertion of Horne and Scott's musical scene in *I Dood It* is, arguably, the most seamless of all Horne's specialty sequences. Nevertheless, it's a segregated scene that serves as an interlude from the otherwise white action. As a reviewer for *Motion Picture Herald* aptly put it, the black production number in *I Dood It* is "set into the picture, without disturbing the course of the narrative."[117] While Horne, Scott, and the other black entertainers are isolated from the white narrative in this segregated scene, within the scene, Minnelli's staging and blocking work to separate Horne even further. Horne is estranged not only from whiteness but also from blackness. While Scott's relationship to the other black cast members is secure, Horne's, by comparison, is more tenuous.

Hazel Scott, draped in a full-length white fur coat over a black sequined evening gown, is the first of the two women to make her grand entrance. Ironically, at the same time Scott is granted entrance to the theater, its stage manager is trying to eject a white man (Skelton). When Scott arrives, she is accompanied by an entourage of smartly dressed musicians and singers. As the group waltzes through the backstage door, the manager stops Scott to ask what they're all doing there. Scott confidently announces herself and explains that she's there for the audition. Once on stage, Scott is greeted by the white theater owner, Mr. Lawlor, and the two shake hands. Though it's a brief moment and a small gesture, it's just the kind of display that censors like Binford would soon find distasteful and threatening to the social order.

After the group has taken its place at the far end of the stage, Scott launches into her instrumental rendition of "Taking a Chance on Love," incorporating styles ranging from classical, to jazz, to boogie-woogie. While the pianist and her fast-moving finger work are the uncontested focal point of this segment, Scott is, at all times, conspicuously surrounded by a crowd of black musicians and onlookers. Lena Horne, on the other hand, arrives alone, apart from any of the other black cast members. Her entrance, at the

Lena Horne tries not to get too close to those sinners behind the Wall of Jericho in a musical number from MGM's *I Dood It* (1943).

conclusion of Scott's performance, makes Scott something of an opening act and rightly suggests that Horne is the bigger of the two stars.

Sounding a bit coy, Lena apologizes to the cast and Mr. Lawlor for being late because she couldn't find a taxi. These would be the last words of dialogue uttered by Horne onscreen during her MGM years. Horne, too, is dressed exquisitely, in a black fur coat over a white satin dress, the inverse of Scott's color scheme. As he did with Scott, Mr. Lawlor also shakes Lena's hand. After introducing her to the potential investors that make up the small audience, Lawlor directs Horne where to stand and, with a flourish, removes her fur coat. In contrast to the medium camera shots that were used for Scott's entrance, Horne is captured in a wide shot, rendering her delicate and somewhat detached against a gossamer star constellation backdrop.

Horne kicks off the "Jericho" song in the first of several camera shots in which she occupies the frame completely alone. Horne is, in fact, the only cast member in this scene to receive such sustained, isolated attention from the camera. When not pictured alone, Horne is, sometimes, accompanied by a small chorus of four to six men. At other times, she is supported, albeit antagonistically, by Scott and other black cast members who are positioned at the opposite end of the stage. After daintily singing solo for almost a full minute, Horne is interrupted by the goading, spirited scat singing of Scott and her retinue. As Horne moves toward the source of the interruption, it soon becomes apparent that she is physically separated from the other black cast members by a wall—the Wall of Jericho.

Horne is on the side of God, Joshua, and the Israelites. On the other side of the wall are Scott and her party of revelers, the sinners of Jericho. After some resistance from the sinners, a Joshua character appears and blows the wall down with the sound of his trumpet. Only after the wall comes down does Horne join the rest of the black cast. Without acknowledging any of them, she passes her fellow cast members by to assume her position, up front and center, for the scene's conclusion.

Thousands Cheer (1943) and *Swing Fever* (1943)

Lena Horne's final two releases of 1943, *Thousands Cheer* and *Swing Fever*, might well have been added at the last minute in order to cash in on her meteoric rise to stardom following the release of *Cabin in the Sky* and *Stormy Weather*. In *Thousands Cheer*, Mickey Rooney introduces Horne as "a grand artist" whom viewers might remember from *Cabin in the Sky*. In both *Thousands Cheer* and *Swing Fever*, the lighting and set design of her specialty acts are incongruous with the rest of the picture. In neither film does Horne have any dialogue or interaction whatsoever with any other member of the cast. Furthermore, in both films she is wearing the same dress. Apparently, these are scenes that were not shot for a specific production and could have been inserted into any number of films.

As it was in *I Dood it*, Horne plays herself in these two films, only with much less pomp. In *Thousands Cheer*, an all-out war musical, Kathryn Grayson and Gene Kelly are the romantic leads. The film culminates with a lineup of MGM contract players, including Mickey Rooney, Judy Garland, Red Skelton, Lucille Ball, Eleanor Powell, Ann Sothern, Virginia O'Brien and Lena Horne, all putting on a show for the troops. Like Horne, these MGM stars also appear as themselves.

Thousands Cheer was shot in Technicolor and is thus the first time Lena Horne was seen onscreen in color. Horne sings the Fats Waller tune "Honeysuckle Rose." Rather than performing with either of the two all white jazz bands showcased in the film, Kay Kyser's band and Bob Crosby's orchestra, Horne is accompanied by Benny Carter and his band. This identifies Horne as black, yet she never once interacts or even shares the frame with the all-black band. Instead, against a background of luscious deep purple drapes and mirrors, she appears with eight reflected images of herself.

Despite its limitations, Horne's appearance in *Thousands Cheer* was a momentous occasion, a first. With her café au lait skin, perfectly coiffed hair, flawless teeth, dainty steps, and refined hand movements, Lena Horne, a black woman, was presented as a dignified screen goddess in a Hollywood feature film made for and about white people. Writing for *The New York Times*, Thomas M. Pryor said that Horne deserved a "bouquet" for her performance, which he described as "haunting." Horne biographer James Gavin called it one of her "signature moments."[118]

Though not as impressive, and filmed in black and white, *Swing Fever* positions Horne similarly. Horne sings "You're So Indifferent," a tune borrowed from her early stage appearance in *Blackbirds of 1939*. The scene is set at a dinner club where Kay Kyser is the new bandleader. Before introducing Horne, Kyser informs the club's patrons that he and his band have to leave to entertain the service boys at the canteen. Once again, Horne is accompanied by an all-black band. In this number, she often shares the frame with the musicians, and estrangement has been achieved by lighting and camera work. For the most part, all we see of the musicians are disembodied hands on a variety of instruments and figures in shadow and silhouette.

Broadway Rhythm (1944)

Broadway Rhythm, another backstage romantic musical, stars George Murphy and Ginny Simms as the lead couple. Murphy is Jonnie Demming, a Broadway producer, raised in a vaudeville family. Simms is Helen Hoyt, a Hollywood actress, recently arrived in New York, and hoping to land a starring Broadway part. Lena Horne's role as nightclub singer Fernway de la Fer is perhaps her most inclusionary role in a white musical. In the Latin-inspired "Brazilian Boogie," Horne is enveloped in blackness by virtue of the dancers who accompany her. In a second number, the Gershwin song "Somebody Loves Me," Horne is openly depicted with her white audience. Eddie Anderson also has a prominent role as manservant to the Demming family and aspiring talent agent of Miss Fernway and of Hazel Scott, who appears as herself.

With "Brazilian Boogie," *Broadway Rhythm* offers Lena Horne's most rousing musical film performance, and her most zealous attempt at dance onscreen. Much like her number "The Sping" from *Panama Hattie*, "Brazilian Boogie" is a song about a hybrid dance. According to the song's lyrics, written by the white American songwriting duo Martin and Blane, the dance is a "half-breed" because its "mammy was a samba and it's pappy was swing."

Broadway Rhythm also represents Horne's second appearance in Technicolor. MGM took full advantage of its color capabilities in the film and in particular "Brazilian Boogie," which is performed for an all-white audience at a dinner theater called the Jungle Club. In an attempt to woo Hoyt into his heart, and his next Broadway show, Jonnie has invited her to the Jungle Club for drinks. The stage where Horne performs has a red floor and thatched straw walls. Horne is garbed in a yellow halter top with gold braided trim, a long purple skirt slit on both sides up to her thighs, and yellow magnolias in her hair. There are eight leggy chorus girls, all of whom are costumed in mini-skirts and halters. Some wear red skirts and multicolored tops, while others wear mostly gold.

Lena Horne's sexiest onscreen song and dance number, "Brazilian Boogie," in MGM's *Broadway Rhythm* (1944). Press photo.

Horne's attempt at dancing aside, what's unusual about "Brazilian Boogie" is that, in addition to the women dancers, Horne is accompanied by five handsome, lithe black men with whom occasionally she has close physical contact. While the costumes of Horne and the chorus girls are played to the hilt for sex appeal, the colorful attire of the men has the opposite effect. Yellow spats over white shoes, green and white striped capri pants, yellow crop-top t-shirts, yellow gloves, and white and green polka-dot bow ties on bare necks comprise a campy look that tempers any threat of black male sexuality.

Despite the emasculation of her male dance partners, "Brazilian Boogie" is Lena Horne's most sexually overt onscreen musical number. It prompted one reviewer to call it "torrid." Another reviewer, from the *Los Angeles Times*, considered "Brazilian Boogie" one of the film's highlights. Lamenting the lack of originality in the year's recent crop of musicals, Bosley Crowther pointed to "Brazilian Boogie" as one of the few exceptions.[119] "Brazilian Boogie" certainly is an anomaly. Not since Nina Mae McKinney's "Harlem Madness" number in 1930's *They Learned About Women* had a major studio presented a sexy black woman in a white musical and at the center of such an elaborate and exuberant song-and-dance spectacle.

That Horne was given a character name in *Broadway Rhythm* suggests that the studio originally had greater aspirations for her role, as does a duet that Horne recorded with Anderson, which never made it into the film. The duet, "Tete a Tete at Tea Time/ Solid Potato Salad," while illustrating the very real class and representational conflict between the two actors, also hints at a romance between their characters. Horne's second number, "Somebody Loves Me," likewise implies that there was supposed to be some affection between her and her former *Cabin in the Sky* lover.

As opposed to the usual nightclub setting, "Somebody Loves Me" takes place during the day in a brightly lit barn. Horne is auditioning for a show that Demming's father wants to produce. Having shed the Latin hottie guise, Horne now looks quite prim and proper. She stands on a stage, leaning on an old piano, at which accompanist Phil Moore is seated. Anderson is sitting on the stage, too, ogling Horne and mugging as he smokes his cigar. About midway through the song, Horne moves near to Anderson for just a moment and plays with his hat. While the interaction may not seem like much, it signifies the closest that Horne would come to romance in any of her white MGM musicals.

In most of Horne's musical interludes, including "Brazilian Boogie," once she appears on the screen, the presence of a white audience is illustrated by a discreet cutaway shot of a few audience members, or the lead romantic couple. In some instances, as in *Thousands Cheer*, it's apparent that these cutaway shots were filmed at a different time and in a different space from those of Horne's. "Somebody Loves Me" is notable as one of the few specialty acts in which Lena Horne and her white audience, in this case those involved in attempting to mount the senior Demming's production, are filmed and seen together in the same space, in broad daylight, no less. The only other similar scenes in which Horne was conspicuously filmed together with her white audience can be found in *Panama Hattie*, where the audience is somewhat obscured by the dim light of the nightclub setting.

Broadway Rhythm was the first of Horne's films to be censored by Lloyd Binford. The deletion of her scenes by the Memphis censor captured national attention. After *Broadway Rhythm*, it appears that MGM was conceding to the Southern censors and exhibitors who had proposed that scenes implying social equality should be filmed so that they could be deleted without disturbing the picture's continuity.[120]

Two Girls and a Sailor (1944)

In *Two Girls and a Sailor* (1944), Lena Horne has only one unremarkable number, "Paper Doll." A second song, "Trembling Like a Leaf," never made it to the screen. The "Paper Doll" sequence, which takes place at an event for sailors and soldiers, consists mostly of close-ups and medium close-ups. Its primary emphasis is Horne's face, her beauty. Much like in *Thousands Cheer* and *Swing Fever*, Horne is estranged from the all-black band that accompanies her. It's quite a large band, but the musicians are positioned so far behind Horne, she appears to be performing very much solo on a grand stage.

Horne is also detached from her white audience, especially when compared to the preceding acts in which entertainer and audience were amply filmed together. With Horne, after a rather grandiose introduction, she steps out from behind a curtain into the dark. A spotlight comes on to illuminate her, but the surroundings remain dimly lit. At the beginning, a row of soldiers' heads can be seen gathered at the front of the stage in silhouette. After this, any reference to an audience is limited to a few of the aforementioned cutaway shots. The cutaways here curiously illustrate the way in which Horne was "there to be had, but not too much."[121] The white soldier featured in the shot seems completely enchanted by Horne.

Perhaps the most interesting detail of *Two Girls and a Sailor* is that it's the first time Lena Horne's name appears by itself in the opening credits. Hers is not the only name to appear alone. José Iturbi, Jimmy Durante, and Gracie Allen are also billed in the same style. For Horne, however, this individual billing, which on the surface looks like star treatment, might have also been designed as a way to delete her from the picture entirely. A complete erasure could not have been done so neatly in any of her previous white musicals because, with the exception of *Panama Hattie*, for which she received no screen credit, Horne's name appears on the screen next to some of her white costars. Apart from *Duchess of Idaho* (1950), in the remainder of her MGM films, Horne's name would continue to appear separately in the onscreen billing.

Lena Horne did more than just perform for the troops in film. Like many Hollywood movie stars, Horne did her part to support the war effort. Locally, Lena entertained servicemen at the integrated Hollywood Canteen, a club run by volunteers, many of whom, like her, were celebrities. At the canteen soldiers could enjoy dancing and entertainment free of charge. She was also accustomed to performing for the United Service Organizations (USO), which at that time was segregated. In late 1944, when she went on a USO-sponsored camp tour of the South, Horne received a crash course in what she called the "niceties of segregation."[122]

On her way to Camp Robinson, Arkansas, Horne's plane was grounded. No connecting flight was available so she had to ride in a Jim Crow railroad car. Once there, as she was about to go on, Horne looked out at her audience and was furious to see that there were no black faces. After the performance she learned that the fifty black servicemen on post hadn't been informed of her visit and furthermore they were not allowed in the theater. The next day Horne insisted on performing for the black troops in the mess hall. As she sang, German prisoners of war piled into the tent, to the frustration of the black soldiers. Horne was enraged. She stopped singing and asked that the POWs be removed. When her request was ignored, Horne quit the mess hall and the USO. For the rest of the war, she visited only all-black camps and did so at her own expense.[123]

In early 1945, what Horne described as a "rather serious crisis" developed in her relationship with MGM. Arthur Freed had asked Horne if she would like to appear in a Broadway production. The show was *St. Louis Woman*, written by Countee Cullen and Arna Bontemps, poets of the Harlem Renaissance. Freed planned to help finance the Broadway show, which might later be adapted for the screen. Harold Arlen and Johnny Mercer would write the score, and Horne was to play Della Green, a "fancy lady" of late 19th-century St. Louis who becomes entangled in a love triangle.[124]

Horne loved the music, and started practicing some of the show's songs for people at MGM. However, when she received the written script and learned that her character was a "flashy whore," she started having second thoughts about playing the role. Horne was torn between the opinion of black community leaders and the demands of those who had helped advance her career. Ultimately, she turned the role down, and claimed that as punishment, for a few months, MGM withheld permission for her to work in cabarets in between movie work, as she had been accustomed to doing. MGM denied Horne's claim.[125]

Ziegfeld Follies (1946)

In late 1945, for the first time since *Cabin in the Sky*, Horne returned to the Freed Unit for the making of *Ziegfeld Follies*. A tribute to Florenz Ziegfeld and his hugely popular series of revues, *Ziegfeld Follies* was a showcase for MGM's stable. The lineup included, among many others, Fred Astaire, Lucille Ball, Judy Garland, Gene Kelly, Red Skelton, and Virginia O'Brien. *Follies* was considered a departure from the traditional movie musical in that it is a series of specialty acts with no story. As such, it was the perfect picture for Lena Horne.

Originally, there were two numbers planned for Horne. In one, the Gershwin love song "Liza," it looked as if Horne might finally be matched with a suitable onscreen lover. Horne was paired with Avon Long, who had recently made a name for himself on Broadway as the character Sportin' Life in two *Porgy and Bess* revivals. Similar to the act the couple had done together years earlier at the Cotton Club, Horne was serenaded by Long. Horne, garbed in 19th-century period dress, did not sing or speak a word. Because the film was overcrowded with acts, "Liza" never made it to the screen, and any footage of it was likely destroyed in an MGM vault fire. Only stills and Long's audio recording of the song remain.[126]

Horne's extant number in *Ziegfeld Follies*, "Love," another Martin and Blane song, was written especially for her. The setting is reminiscent of "The Spring" except that the location is somewhere in the West Indies, and instead of singing for a white crowd, the nightclub where she performs caters to an all-black clientele. Setting the mood for the song are two women at the bar who get into a brawl, competing for the affections of the same man. Horne does plenty of emoting in this scene of which *Variety* took note, remarking that she could not have looked "more seductive, or be in more torrid voice, with effective acting as well."[127]

Horne's "Love" performance also epitomizes the aloofness that would soon become associated with her image, particularly as it relates to her nightclub persona.[128] As she sings and moves about the bar, Horne makes very little contact, physical or otherwise, with the bar's black patrons. They look at her with expressionless stares, as if she's an oddity. *Ziegfeld Follies* was previewed for test audiences in 1945 and had its nationwide release in 1946. Both *Variety* and the *LA Times* considered "Love" one of the film's highlights. *The New York Times* reported that in Knoxville, Tennessee, Horne's scene had been cut from the film and her name blacked out from all advertising posters.[129]

Ziegfeld Follies and "Love" represent the last time that Lena Horne would appear alongside other blacks in an MGM film. It was also, perhaps not coincidentally, the first time that she worked on a film with Lennie Hayton. A musical arranger for MGM, Hayton, who was Jewish and white, won an Oscar for *Singin' in the Rain* (1952). The two began seeing each other around the time that *I Dood It* was in production. In 1947, three years after Horne's much publicized divorce from Louis Jones was finalized, Lena and Lennie were married overseas. Until 1950, the couple attempted to keep their interracial marriage a secret.

Horne's marriage, according to Gail Lumet Buckley, further isolated her mother from the black bourgeoisie world into which she was born, and thereafter she and her mother "entered the great 'white' world" where they lived "not *as* white people, but *like* white people."[130] Mirroring events in her personal life, in Horne's next film, she would play a mixed race character married to a white man.

Till the Clouds Roll By (1947)

Till the Clouds Roll By, another musical from the Freed Unit, was directed by Richard Whorf with Lennie Hayton as musical director. The film is a biography of Jerome Kern, who composed hundreds of songs for stage shows and films and was the recipient of two Academy Awards. Kern passed away in late 1945 while the film was still in production. In typical MGM style, a cast full of stars are trotted out to perform Kern compositions. Kern had a writing partnership with lyricist Oscar Hammerstein II, and Lena Horne sings two songs from stage musicals created by the duo. Her first number, "Can't Help Lovin' Dat Man," originated in *Show Boat* (1927). "Why Was I Born?" is from the lesser-known musical *Sweet Adeline* (1929). Both songs were originally performed by the white stage and screen actress Helen Morgan.

The first fifteen minutes of *Till the Clouds Roll By* are dedicated to *Show Boat*, the pinnacle of Kern's career. Produced by Florenz Ziegfeld, the original *Show Boat* opened on Broadway in December 1927 and closed in May 1929 after 572 performances. Considered the American musical theater's first masterpiece, *Show Boat*, which is based on Edna Ferber's 1926 novel, is one of the most revived works of the Broadway stage. It has also had multiple runs in London's West End, and there are three Hollywood screen versions (1929, 1936, 1951). *Show Boat*, which begins in the 1880s, is the story of Magnolia Hawks, a young girl who has grown up on her parents' riverboat, the *Cotton Blossom*.

Piloted by Magnolia's father, Cap'n Andy Hawks, the *Cotton Blossom* travels up and down the Mississippi River, bringing entertainment to riverside cities. As a child, Magnolia learned Negro spirituals from Jo and Queenie, two of the *Cotton Blossom*'s black workers. As an adult, she will perform these songs to make a living. Thus, *Show Boat*'s protagonist, Magnolia, is a white heroine who performs blackness. *Show Boat* also has an intriguing subplot concerning a black woman who performs whiteness. Julie, the *Cotton Blossom*'s leading lady, is a light-skinned mixed race woman who has been passing for white. Julie is married to another show-boat trouper, Steve, a white man. Despite Steve's flaws, Julie "Can't Help Lovin' Dat Man" of hers.

When the *Cotton Blossom* docks in Julie's hometown, Julie and Steve learn that the sheriff will be coming to arrest them for the crime of miscegenation. Before the sheriff arrives, in the presence of others aboard the *Cotton Blossom*, Steve takes a knife, cuts Julie's hand, and then sucks blood from it. When the sheriff arrives, Julie admits that her father was white and her mother black, but Steve invokes the "one-drop rule," claiming that their marriage is legal because he, too, has black blood in him. The witnesses to Steve's trick back up his statement. Julie and Steve escape arrest, but since Julie has been outed, they have to leave the *Cotton Blossom*. It's uncertain what happens to Steve, but Julie eventually becomes a hopelessly drunk saloon singer at a club called the Trocadero.

Kern and Hammerstein's musical version of *Show Boat* defied the unwritten rule that blacks and whites should address the audience separately and not share the stage together. The musical also elevated the Julie subplot and directed the audience to see her as tragic as opposed to contemptible. In the novel, for example, when Elly, the show boat's ingénue, hears Julie's confession, she is outraged and threatens to quit if the "nasty yellow" Julie, who had heretofore been her good friend, and Julie's "white trash" husband are not removed from the boat. In the musical, Ellie (formerly Elly) is sympathetic to Julie's predicament, and she is the one who warns the interracial couple that the sheriff is coming, which gives them time for the knife stunt.[131]

Show Boat's treatment of race and the performance of race are central to its original and continuing importance. Music and *Show Boat* scholar Todd Decker notes that while there have been some Broadway musicals that used both black and white performers in numbers, very few have dealt with American racial discrimination, used racially signified music to express the experiences of black and white characters, or given equal stage time to black and white performers. In *Show Boat*, all these elements come together.[132] *Show Boat* is, perhaps, the ultimate interracial Broadway musical.

The *Show Boat* sequence in *Till the Clouds Roll By* perfectly illustrates MGM's ambivalence as it relates to Lena Horne, the advancement of racial equality, and pandering to Jim Crow. In addition to Lena Horne's two musical numbers, near the beginning of the *Show Boat* sequence, at Cap'n Andy's ballyhoo, Horne makes a fleeting appearance with the white cast members. Following Cap'n Andy's introduction of Steve Baker as "the handsomest leading man," Horne is introduced as the "beautiful Julie Laverne." Husband and wife are introduced in succession yet share the camera frame for less than a second. After the introductions, Julie and Steve are physically separated by Cap'n Andy and Virginia O'Brien's Ellie. Instead of cozying up to her husband, Julie sidles up to Ellie for a few seconds and then removes herself from the action.

MGM's abbreviated version of *Show Boat* was the first to imagine that the mixed race character Julie could actually be played by a woman of mixed racial heritage, yet MGM was careful not to commit the crime of depicting the crime of miscegenation onscreen. One curious little detail of the ballyhoo scene symbolizes the racial confusion presented by both Lena Horne and Julie Laverne. After Horne's departure, members of the cast, marching in a parade, carry a poster that bears a rather dark-skinned likeness of the leading lady who was light enough to pass for white.

Horne's second appearance within the mini–*Show Boat* is her mesmerizing rendition of "Can't Help Lovin' Dat Man." In the stage production "Can't Help Loving' Dat Man" is used to hint at Julie's race problem as well as establish her as Magnolia's stage mentor.[133] Julie sings for Magnolia in the kitchen of the *Cotton Blossom*. When Queenie, the *Cotton Blossom*'s resident mammy, hears her singing she wants to know how it is that Julie knows a song that only black people are supposed to know. In *Till the Clouds Roll By*, Horne sings the song entirely out of context. Seated on the dock, next to a bale of cotton, Horne performs alone, the only player in the *Show Boat* segment, black or white, to do so. The focus is her beauty, and the lighting, in contrast to the previous numbers, has suddenly gone dim, making Horne appear just a little too dark to pass for white.

In her autobiography Horne claimed that Jerome Kern personally asked her to play the part of Julie in the 1946 Broadway revival and that MGM prohibited her from doing so as punishment for turning down the part in *St. Louis Woman*. In August 1945, when the revival was first announced, New York's *Daily News* reported that someone reasonably close to the project said that Lena Horne would definitely not play the Julie role, "no

Lena Horne stars as tragic mulatto Julie in a mini version of *Show Boat* from MGM's *Till the Clouds Roll By* (1947). From left, Lena Horne, William Halligan, Virginia O'Brien and Bruce Cowling.

matter who thinks she ought to have it."[134] White actress Carol Bruce would ultimately play the part.

Words and Music (1948) and *Duchess of Idaho* (1950)

In her final two films for MGM, while still under contract, Lena Horne would tip-toe her way across the color line. In *Words and Music* (1948), Horne has two numbers by Rodgers and Hart, "Where or When" and "The Lady Is a Tramp." In *Duchess of Idaho* (1950) she sings "Baby, Come Out of the Clouds." The formula used to present these songs is similar to some of Horne's previous films. In all three numbers, for the overwhelming majority of the time, she is featured alone and there's a lot emphasis on her face.

In both *Words and Music* and *Duchess of Idaho*, as it is in prior films, the presence of an all-white audience is indicated by cutaways to the lead romantic couple. However, in both films, for a fleeting moment, she is also framed with members of her audience. In "Where or When," as Horne makes her entrance, a white woman sitting at a table can be seen at the edge of the audience as well as what looks like a hat check girl in the back. In "Baby, Come Out of the Clouds," for just a few seconds, a white couple to her right can be seen enjoying the performance.

This was not exactly new, of course. In *Panama Hattie*, perhaps because she was uncredited and something of an unknown quantity then, Horne was pictured with a white audience. And in *Broadway Rhythm*, which went into production at the tail-end of the OWI's residency in Hollywood, Horne was also seen briefly with her white audience. In any event, picturing Horne, however fleetingly, together with her white audience signifies the crossing of a racial boundary.

What is even more telling in these two late films is her musical accompaniment. In *Thousands Cheer*, *Swing Fever* and *Two Girls and a Sailor*, Horne was presented as black by virtue of the all-black band that played for her. At the same time, she was also estranged from blackness by being separated from the band in some manner. In *Words and Music* and *Duchess of Idaho* Horne is also detached from the accompanying bands, but this time the bands are all white.

At the beginning of "Where or When" Horne breezes by the all-white band as she moves to her spot. After that, the band is never seen again in that number, nor is it seen in "The Lady Is a Tramp," which immediately follows. In "Baby, Come Out of the Clouds," at first glimpse it seems that there is no band in sight at all. A closer look, however, reveals that Horne is separated from the all-white band behind her by sheer curtains that subtly obscure their presence. With *Words and Music* and *Duchess of Idaho*, Horne had made the transition from being black, but not too black, to nearly white.

In 1949, when MGM announced plans to film an updated version of *Show Boat*, Horne felt that based on her turn in *Till the Clouds Roll By* she should have been a shoo-in. MGM, however, never even considered her for the role. According to Freed, they couldn't have passed Lena off as white.[135] Surely, if MGM, preeminent manufacturer of illusions, really wanted to use Horne for the part of Julie, the studio, which had created a special shade of makeup to darken her image, could have just as easily used makeup and lighting to whiten her pale copper skin tone. Whatever MGM's reasons were for passing Horne over, the Breen Office, which still had influence in Hollywood, would have presented a major stumbling block as the relationship between Julie and Steve was, in and of itself, a Production Code violation, and even more so if Julie were played by a black actress.

Horne's good friend Ava Gardner was given the role of Julie in 1951's *Show Boat*. When she tested for it, the studio used a recording of Lena's voice as a playback. Gardner wanted to do the singing required by the part and practiced for weeks with Phil Moore. At the last minute, a professional singer, Annette Warren, was brought in to dub Gardner's voice. As the scenes were already shot, Warren had to synchronize her singing to Ava's lips. Ava was synching to the playback of her original recording with its phrasing borrowed from Lena Horne's rendition.[136]

Lena Horne desperately wanted to play the role of Julie. Being overlooked for the part was, for her, apparently the last straw. In March 1950, Horne and MGM agreed to cancel their contract. In an interview that same month, Horne said MGM didn't have any upcoming parts for her and she was getting tired of just singing in musicals. She wanted to do straight movie roles, she said, like a laboratory technician or a slave woman who becomes a leader or even a corpse. She didn't care, as long as she could be a pivotal part of the plot. Three months after her split from MGM, Lena and Lennie's interracial marriage was made public. The couple received threats of violence and obscene mail. Hayton built a wall around their California home and bought a shotgun.[137]

Meet Me in Las Vegas (1956)

After five years of singing in night clubs but no movie work, Horne returned to Hollywood for her final hurrah with MGM, *Meet Me in Las Vegas*. Two songs were slated, "If You Can Dream" and "You Got Looks." "If You Can Dream," which was arranged and conducted by Hayton, uses the same blueprint employed in her last two films. After a shot of the all-white band at the start, the camera pans over to Horne and stays on her for the remainder of the segment. Horne is standing alone on stage, looking much like a Barbie doll in silhouette. When the lights come up, Horne, who has literally been put on a pedestal, is barely recognizable as the starlet who had taken Hollywood by storm in the previous decade.

Over the years, performing in nightclubs, Horne used her pain and anger over racial discrimination to develop an image intended to insulate herself from her white audience. "I used to think, I'm black and I'm going to isolate myself because you don't understand me." Horne's façade left her audience with the impression that she was "cold as an iceberg." By the late 1950s Horne said she was "literally freezing to death." All she could feel was her lack of love toward anyone or anything.[138] That iciness comes across loud and clear in "If You Can Dream," which, with its fleeting glance at the all-white band, might be called her white number for the film.

"You Got Looks" was her black number. Here, for the first and only time on MGM celluloid, Horne is pictured together, in full view, with a black band, a quintet. Horne comes down off her pedestal in "You Got Looks" and appears a little more thawed out than in the previous number. Occasionally, glimpses of her former movie self can be seen. By far the more enjoyable of the two numbers, "You Got Looks" never made it into the final cut of the film.

In 1957, Lena Horne was revitalized, temporarily, by a starring role in the Broadway musical *Jamaica*. After so many years of constant travel, Lena was happy to be home in New York. *Jamaica* was originally written for Harry Belafonte, the Harlem-born son of undocumented Jamaican immigrants, whose 1956 calypso album had topped the charts. Belafonte had also just finished working with Dorothy Dandridge on *Island in the Sun* (1957), a film about interracial relationships on a fictitious Caribbean island. When Belafonte became unavailable for *Jamaica*, the leading role was revised to fit Horne.

Jamaica is the story of villagers on a Caribbean island trying to resist the commercialism of the tourism trade. Horne played Savannah, a beautiful West Indian girl who dreams of going to New York. The cast also included Ricardo Montalbán as Koli, Savannah's island suitor, and Adelaide Hall as her grandmother as well as Ossie Davis and Alvin Ailey. Savannah never actually makes it to New York, but she does experience the city in a dream ballet. *Jamaica* and Lena Horne were a big hit. The show opened on October 31, 1957, and closed, after 555 performances, in April 1959. Brooks Atkinson wrote that the show was beautiful primarily because of Horne, whom he said was a "woman of pride and grace who can pour feeling into a song without sacrificing her good manners."[139]

After *Jamaica*, Horne had a letdown. She had desperately wanted a Broadway show. Now that she'd had one, it was back to shuttling from one club to the next. It seemed little had changed. Lena felt no pleasure in her work and fell into a deep apathy. At the same time, she also began to perceive the separation that existed between her and other blacks. "I had lived a long time now in the white man's world," she said. "I was an alien in the world of the average Negro." After a conversation with a former member of the *Jamaica* cast, who could find no work, Lena began to feel that, in retrospect, her breakthrough in Hollywood had made her nothing more than a "false symbol" of progress and that nothing had really changed. A racial anger began to fester.[140]

Lena let some of that festering racial anger loose one night at the Luau in Beverly Hills. Lena and Lennie were at the popular celebrity hangout to meet an old Hollywood friend. When the friend was late, Lennie went to a phone booth to find out what was keeping her. While Lennie was gone, Horne was left alone on the upper level of the dimly lit restaurant. Directly below her sat an inebriated Harvey St. Vincent and his friend Norman Wynne. St. Vincent, an executive for an engineering firm, was demanding immediate service. The waiter assured him that he'd be there as soon as he'd finished waiting on "Miss Horne's table."[141]

Wynne looked up and said, "There's Lena Horne," to which Vincent responded, "So what? She's just another nigger." Horne stood up, told St. Vincent that she could hear him, and asked him to stop. St. Vincent went on to call her a "nigger bitch." Lena lost control and shouted, "This is America. You cannot insult people like that." She then began to hurl things at St. Vincent, a hurricane lamp, dishes, and ashtrays. One ashtray struck St. Vincent on the forehead and left a small cut. When police arrived, neither party wanted to press charges. After the incident, which captured national and international attention, Horne received a lot of mail, mostly from blacks praising her for what she'd done. The Luau incident, and black people's reaction to it, made Horne realize how important it was for her to identify with black people and vice versa.[142]

Horne's racial conflict and racial anger would continue to fester until, after being asked to become a visible part of the Civil Rights Movement, she began to reclaim her blackness. Horne performed at Civil Rights rallies in the South, participated in the March on Washington, and began to identify with Malcolm X. At the same time, she told Lennie that she was "going through some changes as a black woman" and that she needed to sort it out on her own. Her husband had "washed" her, Horne later said. When Malcolm X was assassinated, and Lennie said to her, "those radicals, they're always killing each other off," as though she were another white person, it was a real blow to her. Lennie didn't see her as black and she realized that was part of the conflict she was feeling.[143]

Lena and Lennie separated. Hayton went to Palm Springs and Horne stayed in New York. Horne would claim that eventually they had ironed out their troubles, but according to Horne's biographer, Horne was quite happy for them to continue living on separate coasts. Alone in Palm Springs, Hayton desperately missed Horne and began drinking to excess. In April 1971, Hayton passed away after suffering a heart attack. In April of the previous year, Horne's father had passed away, and in September of that same year, Horne's son, Teddy, died from kidney failure induced by drug abuse.[144]

Death of a Gunfighter (1969)

During her transition from white back to black, in *Death of a Gunfighter*, Lena Horne starred in a role that was heralded as color blind. Produced by Universal Pictures, *Death of a Gunfighter* represents Horne's first and only dramatic role for which no singing was required. Horne can, however, be heard singing the film's theme song "Sweet Apple Wine" at the film's opening and as closing credits roll. The film is a turn-of-the-20th-century western based on a Lewis B. Patten novel. It was directed in the beginning by Robert Totten. Totten was fired during production and replaced by Don Siegel. Neither director wanted credit for the film so the Directors Guild of America gave credit to the fictive, Allen Smithee.

The film's hero, Marshal Frank Patch, is played by Richard Widmark. Lena Horne, now in her fifties, was selected for her role because, according to a studio executive, she was the most attractive, mature woman "of any color." Horne stars as Claire Quintana, a brothel owner and "Patch's girl." In Patten's book, Claire Quintana is thirty years old, Patch is old enough to be her father, and she is simply a saloon owner; the brothel business is left to others in the town. Patten leaves little clues as to Claire's racial identity, but she is certainly not black. Her surname suggests that she could be Mexican, but Claire, who has been previously married, is referred to as "Mrs. Quintana." She could also be a white woman formerly married to someone of Hispanic descent.[145] Race is mostly irrelevant to Patten's novel, and it would be to the film as well were it not for the fact that Lena Horne is one of its stars.

Advance press for *Death of a Gunfighter* said it was the first time in Hollywood's history that an interracial relationship was depicted in a major movie without making any mention of the fact. Lena Horne's role was touted as a model for future color blind-casting.[146] Apart from Horne's real-life identity as a black woman, and a black bartender who works at Claire's establishment and has but two lines of dialogue, there is nothing in the film that would identify Claire as black. And as far as skin color goes, Horne as Claire blends right in with the other white cast members. If nothing else, *Death of a Gunfighter* proves that Lena Horne could be lighted and made up to pass for white.

Lena Horne's role may have been color blind, but others were not, like the Mexican American county sheriff, Lou Trinidad, portrayed by the Italian American actor John Saxon. Upon Trinidad's first appearance, a villainous bar owner, played by Carroll O'Connor, insults him with the epithet "wetback." When he pays a visit to Patch, Trinidad thanks the marshal for giving him a chance ten years ago as deputy when the townsfolk said that they'd rather leave town than take orders from a "greaseball." The film also has a Jewish storekeeper, Mr. Rosenbloom, who suffers anti–Semitic comments.

Despite *Death of a Gunfighter*'s color blind intentions with Lena Horne, some could not help but read her character as black. In his review of the film, Howard Thompson of *The New York Times* wonders why, among a community of "despicable hypocrites," a black woman would be permitted to operate a brothel in the center of this (white) town. In an interview prior to the film's release, Horne herself said that, internally, she interpreted her character as black. "I like to play this role ... thinking inside of me that she is black because it gives me something to identify with." She didn't have to play it that way, Horne said, but it helped give her more empathy with the character. Later, around the time of the film's release, Horne described her character Claire as a "Polly Adler–type."[147] Known as the "Jewish Jezebel," Polly Adler was a celebrated New York brothel owner of Russian Jewish descent.

Lena Horne had come a long way from the days when she could not appear onscreen with whites. Black, white, Mexican, or Jewish, Claire Qunitana, as played by Lena Horne, is a most down-to-earth and dignified madam and, as the film's title indicates, her lover's days are numbered. The townsfolk want to get rid of Patch because his gunslinging ways are outdated, and he might scare off backers willing to invest there. Aware of his impending fate, Patch asks Claire to marry him, and she accepts. Though it's not made known in the film, Patch proposes marriage because he wants Claire to have all his money, and there's no time to make a will. In the film, the marriage has the effect of making an already respectable madam into an even more respectable woman.

Death of a Gunfighter received good reviews, primarily for Widmark's acting. The *Los Angeles Times* called it an "engrossing western of considerable intelligence and pertinence." Lena Horne's performance was also well received. A reviewer for the *Boston Globe* said that she played her part with "charm and dignity." Others noted that even though she had little to do, she did it well.[148]

The Wiz (1978)

It seems most fitting that Lena Horne's final film role was in the all-black musical *The Wiz* (1978). With it, her image had come full circle, from black to white to black again. *The Wiz* is the screen version of Charlie Smalls' stage adaptation of MGM's *The Wizard of Oz*. The stage production opened in 1975, ran 1672 performances, and won a Tony Award for Best Musical. The film, directed by Sidney Lumet, who was Horne's son-in-law at the time, starred Diana Ross as Dorothy, Michael Jackson as Scarecrow, Nipsey Russell as Tinman, Ted Ross as Lion, and Richard Pryor as The Wiz. Horne played Glinda the Good, the good witch of the South. In signature Horne style, she is seen quickly in a shot near the beginning of the film and again for her one number, "Believe in Yourself."

Many critics panned the film citing, among other things, the miscasting of a thirty-something Diana Ross as a twenty-four-year-old Harlem teacher in a role that was originally that of a fourteen year old. Richard Pryor's part, which is about as brief as Horne's, was also disappointing. Nevertheless, *The Wiz* has some stellar performances, including that of Nipsey Russell's Tinman, Ted Ross's Lion, and Mabel King as Evilene. A critic for the *Boston Globe* conceded that despite the film's weaknesses, *The Wiz* is "classy family entertainment." *Variety* was also complimentary to the film, describing the cast as "flawless" and its cinematography and special effects the most memorable.[149]

Audiences and critics especially loved seeing Lena Horne up there again on the big screen. A critic for the *Los Angeles Times* said that Horne was more "youthfully beautiful than seems possible." The *Chicago Tribune* said her rendition of "Believe in Yourself" was electrifying. When *The Wiz* was previewed across the country, and at the opening night premiere, audiences "screamed, hooped, and hollered" when Horne delivered her song. Horne, who was in the audience for the premiere with her son-in-law director, was moved to tears.[150] Horne had come full circle in more ways than one, and *The Wiz* introduced her to a new generation of audiences.

In 1981, at the age of 64, Lena Horne solidified her superstar status and her black identity when she returned to Broadway in the one-woman show *Lena Horne: The Lady and Her Music*. Originally announced as a four-week limited engagement, the musical retrospective of her career ran for over a year with more than 366 performances. Horne was presented with a special Tony Award for the *Lady and Her Music*, which also aired on the PBS *Great Performances* series in 1984.

The recorded version of Horne's one-woman show reveals that for the dialogue portions Horne adopted a sort of jive-talk dialect. In one of her Hollywood segments, dedicated to the part she never got to play in *Show Boat*, Horne eschews her "urban Northern Negro" roots and likens her stints in the South as a child to Ava Gardner's poor, Southern sharecropper upbringing. Numbers representing her Cotton Club days, a highlight of the show, are supported by black singers and dancers. Regarding her audience, Horne said it was the first time a lot of black people had felt close to her. In

Lena Horne comes full circle, concluding her film career as Glinda the Good in the Universal Pictures all-black musical *The Wiz* (1978).

the years that she was singing in lush cafes, many blacks couldn't afford to see her, and even if they could, in many cases, they would not have been granted entry.[151]

Lena Horne gave one of her last concerts in 1994 at New York's Supper Club. The performance, which was recorded and released in 1995 as *An Evening with Lena Horne: Live at the Supper Club*, won a Grammy for Best Jazz Vocal Album. Lena Horne passed away in 2010 at the age of 92.

5

Dorothy Dandridge

Star-Crossed Crossover Star

It has been my fortune or misfortune to suffer both the separateness and the acceptance by the white world. It was my fortune or misfortune to be part Negro and part white, and to be committed totally neither to one nor the other.[1]   —Dorothy Dandridge

Dorothy Dandridge, much like Lena Horne, was known for her crossover sex appeal. Although she was Lena Horne's junior by only five years, Dandridge took up the mantle from her compeer to push racial boundaries even further. In her early films, like *The Big Broadcast of 1936* (1935), Dorothy appeared in uncredited musical specialty numbers with sister Vivian Dandridge and Etta James, who together were known as the Dandridge Sisters. In the early 1940s, Dorothy appeared in several films as either an African maiden or an American maid. After starring as the red-hot seductress Carmen in the all-black musical film *Carmen Jones* (1954), Dorothy Dandridge became the first African American to be nominated for a Leading Role Oscar.

The mixing of European opera and African American subjects in *Carmen Jones*, combined with its provocative theme and fatal ending, became the jumping-off point for the duplicity, hybridity, objectification, and tragedy that would ultimately come to dominate the Dandridge image. After *Carmen Jones*, Dandridge would be featured up front and center opposite white leading men. For the Dorothy Dandridge image, crossing over and interracial sexuality were synonymous.

Dorothy Dandridge grew up not knowing her father, was forced into show business at a very young age, and suffered sexual and physical abuse at the hands of her mother's live-in partner. With her first husband Harold Nicholas, Dorothy gave birth to a child with severe developmental delays. After her divorce from Nicholas, Dandridge apparently became hell-bent on marrying a white man.[2] Dandridge had a string of affairs with white men who were more than happy to have her as a mistress but unwilling to tie the knot.

When Dandridge finally did get a white husband, he physically abused and financially bankrupted her. Furthermore, like all black performers who worked during the era of Jim Crow, even after Dandridge became a crossover star, she endured the humiliation of American segregation and discrimination. To cope with her fears, anxieties, and setbacks, Dorothy became dependent on prescription drugs and alcohol. This dependency, it seems, led to her early demise.

Dorothy Jean Dandridge was born in Cleveland, Ohio, on November 9, 1922, to Cyril and Ruby Butler Dandridge. In her autobiography, Dandridge claimed to be a mix of British, Mexican Indian, West Indian, African American and Spanish. She also declared that her father, Cyril, was the son of a white British man and an African woman.[3] More likely, the British man and African woman were Cyril's grandparents, Dorothy's great-grandparents.[4] Cyril was the son of Florence Looke Dandridge and James Henry Dandridge. Florence, who appeared to be white, was born in Ontario, Canada. Among the residents of her Cleveland neighborhood Florence's racial identity was regarded as something of a mystery.[5]

By the time Dorothy was born, her mother Ruby had already left Cyril and taken Vivian, their first-born child, with her. For years, Cyril sought access to his children through the court system, but Ruby always managed to evade both Cyril and the law.[6] Consequently, the Dandridge sisters grew up without knowing their father. Soon after she left Cyril, Ruby began a domestic partnership with Geneva Williams, a minister's wife and music teacher. While Ruby worked hard to bring home a paycheck, she left Geneva in charge of her children. Geneva was an abusive woman who beat Dorothy and Vivian regularly. She also educated them and began grooming them for show business.

Owing to Geneva's management, Vivian and Dorothy began contributing to the household income at a young age. By the time Dorothy was seven years old, she and Vivian had toured the South billed as the Wonder Children, performing skits, acrobatics, and songs for African American audiences in churches, halls, and barns. One gag, which played on their mixed race looks, involved Dorothy asking Vivian, the lighter of the two, whether she is white or black. After some repartee, Vivian's final response to her sister was "I am white or black," which was met with much laughter from the audience.[7]

Around 1930, in the midst of the Great Depression, work opportunities were scarce and Ruby, who dreamed of being in the movies, decided they should all move to Los Angeles. A few days after their arrival, Ruby took her daughters to meet Clarence Muse, who had recently appeared in *Hearts in Dixie* (1929). Muse's advice to Ruby was to "go back east." Vivian and Dorothy didn't stand a chance in Hollywood, he said, because the girls did not look black enough.[8]

Ruby ignored the actor's advice. Dorothy and Vivian were enrolled in public school, and their show business training continued. When Dorothy was eleven, she worked for a five-month period in Hawaii with the EK Fernandez Circus, where she and Vivian inherited the name "the Creoles." For Dorothy, Hawaii was a much welcome contrast to her travels in the South. The island's racially mixed culture seemed to put the young Dorothy at ease.[9]

Upon returning to the mainland, Dorothy and Vivian were teamed up with Etta James, whom they had met at dance school. The trio became the Dandridge Sisters, and with them Dorothy had her first feature film appearance dancing with Bill Robinson in *The Big Broadcast of 1936* (1935). Other brief appearances in musical numbers followed in *A Day at the Races* (1937), *It Can't Last Forever* (1937), and *Going Places* (1937).

In 1938, when the Dandridge Sisters were invited to perform at the Cotton Club, Dorothy met her future husband, Harold Nicholas. Dorothy was fifteen at the time. Harold was just a teenager, too, but he already had a reputation as a womanizer. During their time at the Cotton Club, Dorothy and Harold got to know each other under the watchful eye of Geneva. When their season at the Cotton Club ended, Dorothy and Harold promised to stay in touch.

In the summer of 1939, on the eve of the Second World War, the Dandridge Sisters were booked to appear at the Palladium in London. Ruby, who by this time was establishing her own acting career, stayed in Los Angeles. Geneva travelled to England with the girls. During this trip Geneva's obsession for monitoring Dorothy's virginity reached its peak. One day in their hotel suite, Geneva ordered Dorothy on the bed and subjected her to a forced vaginal examination. For Dorothy the experience was tantamount to rape and she retaliated with physical blows.

Once back in Los Angeles, Dorothy resumed her courtship with Harold Nicholas. She also decided that she wanted to strike out on her own. The Dandridge Sisters were disbanded, and in the years following, through 1946, Dorothy was busy with stage productions and films. Her first credited, dramatic role came in the Million Dollar Productions race film *Four Shall Die* (1940). In this mystery thriller, Dorothy played heiress Helen Fielding. In *Sundown* (1941), starring Gene Tierney, Dandridge played an African maiden, and in *Drums of the Congo* (1942), she was an African princess.

In films like *Lady from Louisiana* (1941), which starred John Wayne, *Bahama Passage* (1941), *The Night Before the Divorce* (1942) and *Lucky Jordan* (1942), Dandridge paid her dues contending with roles as a maid. She also continued to appear in specialty musical sequences, including the memorable "Chatanooga Choo Choo" routine she did with the Nicholas Brothers in *Sun Valley Serenade* (1941). This was the first time the Nicholas Brothers had incorporated a woman into their act and, according to the *LA Times*, the number was an audience favorite.[10]

In 1942, after four years of dating, Dorothy and Harold finally married. Dorothy tried her best to be a wife and homemaker, while Harold continued working and resumed his dallying ways. The couple's daughter, Harolyn (Lynn) Nicholas, was born in 1943. When it became apparent that Lynn was not developing like other children, Dorothy sought out treatments and answers from the medical community. Dorothy, who always blamed herself for Lynn's disability, eventually conceded that her daughter would require lifelong care and supervision.

Disappointed, perhaps, with her husband's serial infidelity, and her inability to treat Lynn's condition, Dorothy overdosed on sleeping pills and had her stomach pumped twice during her marriage to Nicholas.

Dorothy and Harold divorced in 1950. Motivated by the need to pay the expenses for her daughter's care, Dorothy set to the task of getting back into show business. Dandridge teamed up with Phil Moore, who had been Lena Horne's rehearsal pianist at MGM. Moore decided that Dandridge, like Horne, had what it took to become a crossover nightclub singer and he was eager to mold her.[11] With Phil Moore as her teacher, accompanist, and lover, Dorothy launched her nightclub act, drawing favorable attention from Los Angeles entertainment editor Dick Williams in 1951.[12]

That same year, when Moore learned that his friend Sol Lesser was producing a movie that called for a beautiful jungle princess, he encouraged Dorothy to test for the role.[13] Dorothy tried out and got the part of an African queen in *Tarzan's Peril* (1951). As Melmendi, queen of the peace-loving Ashuba tribe, Dandridge has far more affinity for the white men in this film than she does the African. When Melmendi turns down a marriage proposal from King Bulam (Frederick O'Neal), her village is taken over by the barbaric Yorongan people. When Melmendi insults the king a second time, he orders three of his "savages" to confine her.

At the hut where she is to be held captive, a defiant Melmendi rebuffs the sexual advances of one of Bulam's men, and the other two men grab her. Melmendi resists. Writhing and kicking, she is bound, gagged, tied up, and laid flat on the ground with her arms stretched above her head. It's an erotically charged scene that marks the first time Dandridge is objectified through physical abuse or restraint. Moments later, when the loin-clothed Tarzan enters the hut to rescue Melmendi, we can't help but wonder whom Tarzan would have chosen for a mate were it not for the Hays Code. Although Tarzan had his Jane, the Melmendi role was significant, as it was the first to suggestively cast Dandridge opposite both white and black men.

Tarzan's Peril led to a role with Columbia pictures in *The Harlem Globetrotters* (1951), which was released around the time the first African Americans were able to join the NBA. Dandridge played the sweet girlfriend of an athlete who wants to quit college to play exhibition basketball. Another important connection Dandridge made that year was with Phil Moore's manager, Earl Mills. Mills soon became Dorothy's manager as well, and by the end of 1951, her relationship with Moore had turned strictly professional.

In 1952 Dorothy was offered a part in the MGM film *Bright Road* (1953) opposite Harry Belafonte. By this time Dandridge and Belafonte had begun an on-again, off-again relationship that would last for several years. Early dailies of the *Bright Road* shoot revealed that Dorothy's skin color was too light for MGM's liking. A new makeup was devised to give her more color, and the scenes were reshot.[14] Much like in *Harlem Globetrotters*, Dandridge's character was the sweet girl-next-door type.

After filming *Bright Road*, Dorothy's relationship with director Gerald Mayer turned romantic, but marriage was never discussed, and eventually they drifted apart.[15] By 1953 Dorothy was dating the British actor Peter Lawford, one of the white men in her life who loved her but wouldn't marry her. One of Dorothy's most notorious white lovers was Otto Preminger, who directed her in *Carmen Jones*. In December 1953, Hollywood journalist Hedda Hopper reported that Preminger had plans to bring Oscar Hammerstein's successful 1940s Broadway musical to the screen. Three months later, Hopper reported that Dandridge, upon her return from Las Vegas, would be involved in the production.[16]

The story of how Dandridge got the part of Carmen Jones goes something like this. During her first interview with Preminger, Dandridge learned that he wanted her to read for a supporting good-girl role. The director had already made up his mind that Dandridge was too sweet and too sophisticated to play the hip-tossing Carmen. Upset by his refusal to let her try out for the lead, Dandridge refused to read at all. Preminger finally relented and set a date for her to return and read for the role of Carmen. For her next appointment, Dandridge arrived already in character, looking and acting the part of a floozy. When Preminger saw her, he is said to have exclaimed, "My God, it's Carmen!"[17]

Carmen Jones (1954)

Carmen Jones earned Dandridge unprecedented celebrity status for a black actress or actor in Hollywood. It was a historic moment when, for her portrayal of Carmen, she became the first African American ever nominated for Best Actor or Actress in a Leading Role. In addition to Dandridge's nomination, the film received an Oscar nomination for its musical score. At BATFA and Cannes there were more nominations, and at the Golden Globes, the precursor to the Oscars, there were two wins. *Carmen Jones* did well at the box-office, too. As a black-cast film, its mainstream accolades and popularity made it a crossover event in and of itself, and Dorothy Dandridge was its star-crossed crossover star.

Dorothy Dandridge as seductress in Otto Preminger's all-black musical *Carmen Jones* (1954).

While there are many elements that contributed to the success of *Carmen Jones*, its fusion of European and African American culture is among them. *Carmen Jones* is a descendant of Georges Bizet's 19th-century opera *Carmen*, which in turn is based on a short story by French dramatist Prosper Mérimée. In Mérimée's novella, don José, a

Spanish soldier turned fugitive, tells a French scholar and traveler about his obsession with a tempestuous "Gypsy" woman named Carmen, whom he met while on guard duty outside a cigar factory. After deserting the military, murdering one of Carmen's lovers and then her husband, José eventually kills Carmen.

In Bizet's opera, Carmen's husband no longer exists; a female character, Micaela, was added as don José's girlfriend, and another of Carmen's lovers, Lucas the picador, becomes Escamillo the toreador. *Carmen* first opened in 1875 at the Opéra Comique in Paris to a disapproving audience that found its subject matter too risqué. Three months after *Carmen's* failed premiere, Bizet died of a heart attack, with no inkling that within a decade his opera would be well on its way to becoming one of the most well known in history. By the 20th century, when Oscar Hammerstein II decided to make it into a musical play, *Carmen* had completely shed its lowly origins and was considered the epitome of Western "high culture."

With *Carmen Jones*, Hammerstein took Bizet's music, added his own lyrics, and employed an all-black cast. The setting is the American South during the Second World War, and instead of a cigar factory, Carmen works in a parachute factory. José, now called Joe, is a recently enlisted corporal who wants to go to flight school. Cindy Lou, formerly Micaela, is Joe's wholesome hometown girlfriend, and Escamillo the bullfighter is Husky Miller, the boxer.

The Broadway show, produced by Billy Rose, premiered in December 1943 and ran for over 500 performances. Despite its success with both critics and audiences, more

Dorothy Dandridge leaves her country boy Joe behind to spend time with the more worldly Husky Miller, and his entourage, in Otto Preminger's *Carmen Jones* (1954). From left, unknown, Nick Stewart, Diahann Carroll, unknown, Roy Glenn, Pearl Bailey, Dorothy Dandridge, and Joe Adams.

than ten years passed before Hollywood would endeavor to make a screen version. Rose claimed that almost every major Hollywood studio had tried to purchase the film rights, but he turned them down because they all wanted to use a white cast. Only Otto Preminger, he said, was interested in keeping the all-black casting intact.[18]

Otto Preminger's *Carmen Jones* was the first black musical film to come out of Hollywood since *Stormy Weather* and *Cabin in the Sky*. It was also the first to be shot in Technicolor. The coveted lead roles of Carmen and Joe went to Dorothy Dandridge and Harry Belafonte. The part of Cindy Lou went to trained opera singer Olga James. Joe Adams played boxer Husky Miller. Other noteworthy performers include Pearl Bailey, Diahann Carroll, and Brock Peters.

Shortly before production began, Dandridge started to have anxieties about the film. She worried that she might disappoint the black community by playing a character that many would consider a whore. When Preminger heard Dandridge was having doubts, he drove over to her apartment one evening. By the end of his visit, Preminger, who was married, had persuaded Dorothy to be both his leading lady and his mistress.[19]

From its theatrical beginning *Carmen Jones* was perceived as hybrid entertainment, a clash of "high" white European culture and "low" black folk culture. In the press and in private letters penned by those close to the production, much was made of the fact that *Carmen Jones* would buck the trend of prior black musicals by not "swinging" the score.[20] When it first premiered on Broadway, reviews also noted that although the story had been updated for the 20th century with an all-black cast, it was not a parody and Bizet's music remained intact.[21] *Carmen Jones* is a musical play that was intended as a sincere interpretation of Bizet's opera. As such, it might be described as an all-black musical without black music.

Through the use of film technology and dubbing, Preminger's *Carmen Jones* takes the hybrid nature of the Broadway production a step further. Promotion for the musical play emphasized the fact that the cast was comprised of unknown talent and actors with little theater experience were entrusted to sing their parts. In the film version, the voices of Dandridge, Belafonte, and Adams were dubbed using classically trained opera singers, two of whom were white, the other African American.

Dubbing was not uncommon in Hollywood musicals, but usually dubbed voices went uncredited. With *Carmen Jones*, the names of opera singers Marilynn Horn, Le Vern Hutcherson, and Marvin Hayes were mentioned in reviews of the film and featured along with the actors' names in the film's opening credits.[22] Visually, whiteness was not permitted to permeate the film's black fantasy world. Aurally, however, it was.

Further complicating racial representation in *Carmen Jones* is Hammerstein's libretto. For the most part, the cast delivers its lines in mainstream American English. When they break into song, however, their language becomes inflicted with uses of "dis," "dose" and "dat," resulting in a racial mash-up that reinforces stereotype and draws attention to difference. "Habernera," for example, retitled "Dat's Love," features Dorothy Dandridge lip-synching to the voice of a white woman singing an opera-style European song while at the same time attempting to incorporate a stereotyped African American dialect.

For Hammerstein, African Americans were the logical subjects for his modern version of *Carmen* because they were, he believed, the nearest American equivalent to the "Gypsies" in Spain. Both, he said, express their feelings "simply, honestly, and graphically." And both have rhythm in their body and music in their heart.[23] Hammerstein's generalizations aside, this ethnic minority group, which originated in Asia, does share some historical similarities with African Americans. Most significantly, the "Roma," as they presently call themselves, have a long history of being enslaved. For them, it was a condition that began in southeast Europe in the 14th century and lasted until 1864, just one year before slavery was abolished in America.

The Roma and African Americans also share a history of being stereotyped by the dominant culture, and sexualized images of "Gypsy" and African American women have been similarly situated in direct opposition to the chaste and proper ideal of white womanhood. For 19th-century French audiences, a Spanish locale would have put them on immediate alert for danger and exoticism, as does Mérimée's description of Carmen. On one occasion, Mérimée wrote that Carmen wore a short red skirt and white stockings with holes in them. Her shoulders were revealed and she held a flower in her mouth. According to the soldier don José, where he came from, "everyone would have crossed themselves at the sight of woman dressed like that."[24]

As the sexualized, degraded "other," during the 19th and 20th centuries blacks and Gypsies alike were at the center of race and race-mixing discourse. For Europeans, mating with the Roma was considered taboo, and in some cases, it was against the law. Mixed race Romani people existed, nevertheless, and were thought to combine the worst traits of both races.[25]

It is not surprising, then, that the scientific community's emphasis on racial classification and racial purity, or lack thereof, surface in Mérimée's novel. When Carmen meets the traveler, he asks of her origins, suspecting she might be "Moorish." Carmen informs him that she is a Gypsy, but the traveler calls her racial purity into question, noting that she was prettier than any other Gypsy women he had encountered.[26] It is possible then to read Mérimée's Carmen as a mixed race Romani woman.

In all her various iterations, it seems, Carmen is punished for her dangerous sexuality. The film's first attempt at restraining Carmen comes after she gets into a brawl with another woman at the parachute factory. Carmen is arrested and Joe is ordered to take her to jail. At a similar point in Mérimé's tale, don José allows Carmen to flee. In Preminger's version, when Carmen makes her first attempts at escape, it turns into a spectacle of bondage with Joe chasing after his prisoner, binding her ankles and wrists, and then tossing her over his shoulders.

In due time, Carmen seduces her captor and manages to make a successful escape. This lands Joe in the stockade for a few weeks. The two bide their time until they can see one another again. When the couple reunites, Carmen's flirtatious actions lead Joe to assault his sergeant. Rather than face jail time, Joe runs off with Carmen to Chicago. Once in Chicago, Carmen can't stand being cooped up in a hotel room, and she eventually takes up with Husky Miller, who is in town for a big boxing match. Carmen's actions demand the ultimate punishment. In the film's final scene Joe calls Carmen out as a tramp and then strangles her to death in a broom closet.

Around the time that *Carmen Jones* premiered in New York, *Life* magazine helped elevate Dandridge's status to cultural icon when it featured her decked out as Carmen Jones on the November 1, 1954, issue of its coveted cover. *Life* declared Dandridge the most decorative of all divas to have played the role of Carmen and added that she succeeded brilliantly as a dramatic actress. The *LA Times* thought the film's cast was sensational and said the "vital and surcharged" *Carmen Jones* was the most audacious picture of the year. *Time* magazine, which thought Dandridge played coquettishness to perfection, saw actors who were presented as individuals rather than racial phenomena. In

Dorothy Dandridge meets her fatal end at the hands of Harry Belafonte's Joe in Otto Preminger's all-black musical *Carmen Jones* (1954).

Motion Picture Daily it was noted that Dandridge had a "rare beauty and depth of character" that should warrant future film roles.[27]

The black press also sang Dandridge's praises. According to *The New York Age*, Dandridge had reached a "pinnacle of dramatic achievement," and the *California Eagle* said she was undoubtedly "the screen's best siren to date." Whether pro or con, reviewers were obliged to address Dandridge's brazen sexuality. *The New York Times* described *Carmen Jones* as a "sex melodrama" with Dorothy Dandridge's Carmen standing out as the most notable among a cast of "serio-comic devotees of sex." Echoing that opinion, another critic wrote that Dandridge was "the most aggressive seductress the screen has offered since the Production Code was framed."[28]

The announcement that Dorothy Dandridge had been nominated for a leading actress Academy Award came in February 1955. Dandridge lost out to Grace Kelly, but on the heels of the Oscar publicity she signed a three-year contract with Darryl Zanuck and Twentieth Century–Fox, which required her to make one picture a year. The studio would have priority on her services, but as the contract was non-exclusive, she was free to do pictures with other studios. Both Preminger, who had usurped Earl Mills' influence, and Zanuck envisioned that Dandridge would play the non-black ethnic roles usually reserved for white women. Zanuck considered this a form of racial progress, but it was also confirmation that the studio had no intention of creating non-stereotypical roles for and about black women.

Shortly after Dandridge signed the contract, she agreed to play Tuptim, an Asian slave girl in an adaptation of the Rodgers and Hammerstein's musical *The King and I*

(1956). As it was with *Carmen Jones*, after agreeing to do it, Dandridge started having second thoughts. She didn't want to play a slave. Preminger didn't want her to do the role either, but for a different reason. Following her success in *Carmen Jones*, Preminger believed Dandridge should be regarded as a star of the same caliber as Marilyn Monroe and thought she should accept only leading roles. Dandridge turned the role down. The studio responded by extending her contract for one year and refusing to compensate her for the current year.[29]

Island in the Sun (1957)

Dorothy Dandridge's next film appearance after *Carmen Jones* was in the Darryl Zanuck/Twentieth Century–Fox production *Island in the Sun*. Among an ensemble cast that included Harry Belafonte, James Mason, Joan Collins, and Joan Fontaine, Dandridge played a mixed race West Indian woman who falls in love with an Englishman. It was not a leading role, but it was a pioneering one. With *Island in the Sun,* Dandridge is credited as the first African American actress to appear openly as the object of a white man's affections and desire in a major Hollywood film.

Island in the Sun is based on Alec Waugh's bestselling novel about love, murder, and political unrest on a small Caribbean island. A Londoner by birth, Waugh was a travel writer, novelist, and writer of short stories for U.S. women's magazines. He was also a frequent visitor to the West Indies, and during the twenty-five years before independence, his writings on the Caribbean were influential in the interpretation and neo-colonial rebranding of the West Indies as a tourist paradise. Having been serialized in *Ladies Home Journal* (under the title "Sugar Barons"), condensed for *Readers Digest*, and selected by the Literary Guild and the Dollar Book Club, Waugh's vision of West Indian life reached millions of U.S. readers.[30]

Writing a century and a half before Alec Waugh, Martinique native Médéric-Louis-Élie Moreau de Saint-Méry also significantly affected understandings of the Caribbean and its people. In his *Description topographique, physique, civile, politique et historique de la Partie Française de l'Isle Saint-Domingue* (1797), a two-volume depiction of Saint-Domingue in the period leading up to the Haitian Revolution, Moreau writes extensively on the subject of skin color and its effect on what was once France's chief colony. Using mathematical calculations and charts, Moreau identifies racial types and degrees of blackness that can occur as a result of various interracial pairings. Listed among these are sacatras (seven-eighths black), griffes (three-quarters), marabous (five-eighths), mulattoes (one-half), quadroons (one-fourth), métis (one-eighth), and mamelukes (one-sixteenth). Moreau even declares that in Saint-Domingue one can find "*sang-mêlés*" or "mixed-bloods" with only 1/512 parts of black blood.[31]

Moreau also believed that as mixed race blacks became increasingly white, they became more degenerate. While Moreau acknowledges that there were also people of every shade among the slaves, his examination of mixed race people took place within the context of free people of color who, in the period just before the slave rebellion, were almost equal in number to whites. Moreau also provides physical descriptions and personality traits for his various racial types. The *métis*, for example, was almost the same color and intellect as the white but not as strong. The mulatto man was "well-made and agreeable in form, and very intelligent," but just as lazy as the slave.[32]

To the mulatto woman, whose "entire being is given up to love," Moreau devotes an entire chapter. A sex goddess and whore, the mulatto woman looked down upon men of color and wanted nothing more than to be with a white man. In a society where white women were few in number, similar to the slave woman, Moreau considered the mulatto woman a necessary evil. Moreau's racial theory, which included the idea that interracial relationships caused France to lose Saint-Domingue, would eventually dominate representations of the Haitian Revolution in the 19th century.[33]

Alec Waugh's novel *Island in the Sun* combines elements of Moreau's racial classification theory with a bit of Dostoyevsky's *Crime and Punishment* and puts them together on the imaginary Caribbean island of Santa Marta in the 1950s, the eve of its independence from Great Britain. For centuries on Santa Marta, marriage and intermixing has occurred between the island's white plantocracy and its former, mostly African slave population, resulting in a multihued color caste system.

In confronting this history, Waugh makes reference to Moreau's racial classification system, even lending it divine credence by introducing it through the voice of a religious figure, the island's Archdeacon.[34] While depicting the colonizer as a color blind bystander, Waugh, not unlike Moreau, displaces the source of the island's political, social, and economic troubles and makes "color" the island's biggest bugaboo. Waugh examines this color-burdened society through the lives and romantic affairs of racialized men of the up-and-coming generation.

One of the story's main protagonists is the off-white Maxwell Fleury, son of sugar baron Julian Fleury. Faltering as both a newlywed husband and novice plantation manager, Maxwell seeks to redeem himself by running for a government office in the new political order. His aspirations are complicated by a visiting American journalist who breaks the news that Maxwell's paternal grandmother was a Jamaican woman of some African descent.

Consistent with Moreau's theory, Maxwell with his imperceptible blackness is, arguably, the novel's most depraved character. His "touch of the tarbrush" drives him mad and leads him to murder a man whom he suspects is having an affair with his wife, Sylvia. The chief of police knows Maxwell committed the crime but doesn't have the proof to convict him.

Euan Templeton, heir to a seat in the House of Lords, and son of the island's presiding British governor, along with the governor's aide-de-camp, Denis Archer, represent the "pure" whites. After a tour of military duty in Egypt, the governor's son has just arrived to the island for a brief holiday and is longing for some female companionship. Euan is fascinated with all the mixture on Santa Marta, "every shade of color from sepia to olive gray, every texture of hair … and every variety of profile." He secretly wishes he were there alone, as a tourist, and not as the governor's son, so he could dabble in all the mixedness.[35]

Euan has already received a warning from Denis, however, about the pitfalls of getting involved with Santa Marta women. There are a handful of white women on the island, but they are intent on marriage, which Euan, who plans to attend Oxford in the fall, is not. As for the half-white girls, romance between white men and mixed race women is uncommon, according to Denis, and such liaisons, when they do occur, are clandestine affairs and ultimately unsatisfactory.[36] Denis never explains to Euan why such relationships are unsatisfactory, but the sentiment is certainly consistent with Moreau's warning against miscegenation.

Denis's statement about relations between white men and women of color belies the fact that the Caribbean's mixed race people are a result of widespread miscegenation and that during colonial times the majority of British men had a black or brown mistress. By the 1960s, white men in the West Indies were taking women of color not only as mistresses but also as brides.[37] Ignoring his own advice in favor of what, in fact, was historically commonplace, Denis soon falls in love with a mixed race woman, Margot Seaton. Margot is a drugstore clerk who appears to be a mix of Spanish and Indian. Even though her skin is dark she has no signs of African blood in her appearance.[38]

Margot's Africanness is betrayed, nevertheless, through her behavior and her affinity to Moreau's "seductive mulatto woman." Much like Moreau's mulatto woman, Margot, it seems, wants nothing more than to be with a white man. As soon as she meets Denis, she grows weary of her boyfriend of several years, David Boyeur, and breaks it off with him. On her first date with Denis, Margot is more than willing to indulge Denis's sexual whim. Instinctively Denis knows that he can't woo her like an English girl. Too much talk or any delay on his part with regard to sex would reflect poorly on the power of Margot's charms.[39] Margot also uses her charms on the governor, dancing with him and talking her way into a secretarial job.

Despite Denis's warning about the island's women, Euan becomes engaged to marry Maxwell Fleury's sister, Jocelyn. When Jocelyn hears the news of her Jamaican grandmother, she assumes that the marriage will be called off. The mere thought of having black blood prompts Jocelyn to behave promiscuously. Jocelyn becomes pregnant, which forces her mother to reveal that the man who raised her, Julian Fleury, is not her biological father. Jocelyn is a love child, the result of her mother's affair with a 100 percent Englishman. Racial obstacles are cleared away and Jocelyn can marry Euan without worrying about any future "danger of seeing a colored man in the House of Lords."[40]

Drawn from the lighter shades of Waugh's racial color palette is the one-quarter black Grainger Morris. A native of Santa Marta, Grainger won a scholarship to Oxford and went on to become an attorney. After seven years of stellar success in England as a scholar and athlete, Grainger has returned home to help his people, even though his people seem like foreigners to him now. At Oxford or in London, he was a welcome guest in any home, but in Santa Marta, because of his color, Grainger can't even join the country club. Grainger begins a romance with Mavis Norman, Maxwell's sister-in-law, and one of the white elites.

Representing the unadulterated black end of the racial spectrum is the dark-skinned David Boyeur, a charismatic and egotistical trade union leader who has little to no white blood in his veins.[41] Boyeur is presumed to be modeled after Grenadian labor leader Eric Gairy, who went on to become Grenada's first prime minister when it gained independence from Great Britain in 1974. When the novel begins, Boyeur is dating Margot Seaton and has even proposed to her. After Margot dumps him, Boyeur sets his sights on Grainger's near-white sister and dreams of the day when his light-skinned children will be accepted as white.[42]

The most definitive resolution to each man's respective situation is seen in Maxwell Fleury's case. To avoid being prosecuted for murder, and to save the honor of his family name, Maxwell successfully carries out a suicide by cutlass-yielding-crazed-black-mob. The suicide plan, which involves provoking upstart David Boyeur into first punching Maxwell and then sicking a crowd of striking laborers on him, was also calculated to take down the dangerous labor leader.

Grainger Morris is appointed attorney general, and the prosecution of Boyeur for Maxwell's death is his first important case. While Grainger investigates the case, Boyeur is detained in prison. Grainger elects not to bring charges because he suspects Maxwell had a hand in his own death. Boyeur is knocked down a peg or two but not out. The two British gents are allowed to marry their island women and return to England. Mavis would like to partake in the human smorgasbord as well, but Grainger rejects her because, he says, he could not effectively serve his people if he were married to a woman of any color.

Filmed on the islands of Barbados and Grenada, *Island in the Sun* was Darryl Zanuck's first independent project after stepping down as head of Twentieth Century–Fox. Zanuck still had a contract with Fox, however, under which the studio would provide most of the financing, and he could choose his own subject, directors, and stars. Zanuck hired Alfred Hayes to write the script and Robert Rossen to direct. A former member of the American Communist Party, Rossen had recently been taken off the blacklist after first refusing to testify and then later naming more than 50 names before the House Un-American Activities Committee.[43]

With *Island in the Sun* Zanuck saw the potential to stir up the same kind of controversy and publicity as he had done with *Pinky*. This time around, however, he didn't want to be accused of pandering to bigots by choosing white actors to play non-white roles. Several months before the ban on miscegenation was removed from the motion picture

In Darryl Zanuck's *Island in the Sun* (1957), Dorothy Dandridge, pictured here with John Justin, became the first black woman in a major Hollywood production to appear openly as the object of a white man's affections and desire.

code, Zanuck selected Dorothy Dandridge to play Margot Seaton opposite the British actor John Justin as Denis Archer. In keeping with the novel, the onscreen Margot is not too African. Yet with Dandridge in the role, the character takes on a corporeal connection to the island's African heritage. Harry Belafonte and Joan Fontaine were picked to play the second interracial couple. The Grainger Morris character was deleted from the screenplay, so Mavis Norman (Joan Fontaine) falls for David Boyeur instead.

Harry Belafonte's David Boyeur is a cross between his namesake from the novel and the excised Grainger Morris. He is still the outspoken labor leader, but instead of being an egomaniac and a fraud, the screen Boyeur is dedicated and poised. This hybridization of the Boyeur character combined with Belafonte's own image—his Caribbean-American identity, the mainstream appeal of his Calypso music, and the actor's recent marriage to white dancer Julie Robinson—allows us to read Boyeur as a mixed race character as well, leaving the film without any significant unmixed black characters. James Mason played Maxwell Fleury and Joan Collins is his sister, Jocelyn.

As soon as the film's stars and its theme of interracial romance were announced, there was, as anticipated, an outpouring of outrage. In the South, there were threats of boycotts, Ku Klux Klan protest meetings, and parades at which effigies of Zanuck were burned.[44] A letter to the editor of a South Carolina newspaper declared that if ever a movie deserved to be cancelled before it made it to the theater, this was it. The project, stated the letter, was "another piece of the constant propaganda of the Communists, NAACP, eggheads, et. Al. to destroy the morals of this once proud nation."[45] Though Zanuck was now an independent producer, he remained tethered to Fox, whose executives were getting antsy about the negative publicity. Despite Zanuck's bravado, compromises with respect to the film's racial themes were inevitable.

Dandridge, who looks her most elegant in *Island in the Sun*, has no substantial dialogue. With the Grainger Morris character deleted, that leaves David Boyeur as the sole spokesperson for and about blackness. On the surface, Belafonte, as the charismatic labor leader, cuts an impressive figure. As a symbol of Civil Rights and black resistance, his character can be acknowledged as a victory in the history of representation. Belafonte, however, delivers few meaningful lines and, for the most part, he is used to illustrate the "color problem."

At the governor's garden party, for example, speaking with the American reporter, Boyeur talks about the people's desire for equality, their history of slavery and the backbreaking work in fields that continued after emancipation. Only moments later, the salience of these lines is negated when the reporter asks Boyeur what he thinks is the island's most important problem. Boyeur surveys the crowd at the party and replies, "Color, Mr. Bradshaw, color."

In another scene, rather than an archdeacon, it is Belafonte who makes reference to Moreau's racial theory. At an outdoor market, Boyeur offers to buy Mavis a drink. As they approach the soda vendor there are four little girls standing nearby. Mavis asks Boyeur to buy drinks for them, too. One of the girls is much lighter than the others. When her mother sees what's going on, she takes the drink away from her daughter and leads her away, but not before casting hostile glances at Mavis and Boyeur. When Mavis asks what that was about, Boyeur responds, "There once was a man—don't remember who—drew up 200 classifications of mixed blood on this island." Apparently, this makes sense to Mavis as no further explanation is given or requested.

Compromises were also made when it came to the interracial romances. Prior to the film's release Belafonte predicted that because a black man had never been in love with a white woman onscreen, *Island in the Sun* would be "the most important sociological film ever made."[46] After it was released, Belafonte called it a "terrible picture."[47] So subdued is the relationship between Belafonte and Fontaine that absent any background information, viewers watching *Island in the Sun* today would not know that it's a romantic relationship at all. The two never kiss, touch, or utter any words of affection.

Harry Belafonte and Joan Fontaine make love by sipping from the same coconut in Zanuck's *Island in the Sun* (1957).

It's not even certain if Mavis and Boyeur like each other. In one scene, when Mavis playfully tries on a blackface carnival mask, Boyeur rips it off her face and gives her a menacing look. Elsewhere, Belafonte slices open a coconut and hands it to Fontaine so she can taste the milk. The two actors considered it a subversion when Belafonte took back the coconut and placed his lips exactly where hers had been.[48]

Even though Joyce and Euan are shown kissing, and Maxwell is permitted to force sex upon his wife, in the press Zanuck claimed that the elimination of the usual displays of love in the interracial romances had nothing to do with race.[49] In the case of the Dandridge and Justin pairing, it is apparent, at least, that the two are a couple, but the physical passion described in Waugh's book is nowhere to be found in the film.

When Dandridge read the script for the first time, she was incensed to discover that her character would not be allowed to kiss the man she loves. An ecstatic embrace while slow dancing would have to do. In addition to no kissing, the original script also prevented between the two any mention of the word "love." Dandridge and Justin protested, and Zanuck finally conceded. Justin's character was permitted to say to Margot, "You know I'm in love with you, don't you?"[50]

Both the film and novel conclude with Denis returning to Great Britain with Margot. In the book the couple are married before they leave Santa Marta. Grainger explains to Mavis that if Denis had taken Margot to England as his fiancée, his parents would have tried to stop the marriage. When Mavis questions whether having a dark-skinned wife would impair Denis's career advancement, Grainger uses circular reasoning to explain that Denis won't have a problem with his dark-skinned wife because England has no color prejudice. "Color prejudice only exists in the countries that have a color problem, such as South Africa, the Southern States, and [Santa Marta]. England doesn't have a color problem," says Grainger.[51]

If England has no color prejudice because it has no "color problem," one has to wonder why Grainger imagines that Denis's parents would have objected to their son marrying a woman of color. Nevertheless, in naming South Africa, the Southern States and Santa Marta as the places that have a color prejudice, it becomes very clear that Waugh's "color problem" is not one of black versus white, but rather it refers to miscegenation and a mixed race population.

In Zanuck's film, Margot and Denis leave for Great Britain together, but not as husband and wife. Only the all-white couple, Euan and Jocelyn, is married before the film ends. Margot remains a mistress. With Boyeur, since the nature of his relationship with Mavis is so obscure, his rejection of her at the end of the film is a bit of a non sequitur. He terminates the so-called affair by letting her know that he is devoted only to his race and that the chasm between them is too great. "My skin is my country," he says, adding that they could never marry because one day she might forget herself and call him the "n-word." As for Maxwell, rather than committing suicide, he turns himself in and will likely serve time for manslaughter.

Although somewhat circumspect with its racial themes, *Island in the Sun*, released just three years after the Supreme Court rulings regarding integration of Southern schools, is nevertheless important for its suggestion of black resistance and for opening the door to interracial relationships in Hollywood. Not surprisingly, in many parts of the South, including Memphis, the film was banned. The Memphis Censor Board unanimously decided it was "too frank a depiction of miscegenation, offensive to moral standards and no good for either white or Negro." In Jacksonville, Florida, robed and hooded Klansmen took to the streets in protest of the film. And when South Carolina introduced a bill that would have made showing *Island in the Sun* punishable by monetary fine, Zanuck said he would compensate any theater fined or penalized under such a law.[52]

Despite, or perhaps because of, the censorship and protests, *Island in the Sun* did very well at the box office. Many critics found the island scenery and cinematography worthwhile but were disappointed with its handling of race. *Variety* wrote that the film, which "barely comes to grip" with the race problem, was just candid enough to "offend the South" but would be a disappointment to the North. That same review also noted that on opening night audiences "guffawed" at a critical dramatic moment. Another review found that *Island in the Sun* handled the "explosive theme of miscegenation with amazing ineptness." Writing for *The New York Times*, Crowther declared that Zanuck had failed to produce a film that deals honestly with the subject of race.[53]

In a follow up to his first review, Crowther shared excerpts from a letter sent to him by a reader whose parents were natives of Grenada. The reader wrote, "Only a white American with a fertile imagination and a background in race relations in the United States would write about the West Indies in terms of racial conflict." The reader went onto say that class, as opposed to color prejudice, in the West Indies was strong and that poverty, social welfare, and education were their prime concerns.[54]

Writing from London, journalist Leonard Mosley, who much later in his career would write a biography on Zanuck, said that even though he enjoyed the film, it was a "monument to misguided thinking and messy racial reasoning." Perhaps one of the strongest statements against the film—white supremacists aside—came from Sir Hugh Foot, Jamaica's governor. Foot described the picture as a "morbid mess" and found it offensive for suggesting throughout that the color problem dominates West Indian life. To the contrary, according to Foot, the West Indies handle the problems that arise between people of different races better than anywhere in the world.[55]

To be certain, the Caribbean was not without its racial order. In Trinidad and Tobago, for example, in the period immediately after it achieved its independence from Great Britain in 1962, there were still whites-only country clubs; there were carnival queen competitions that only white women could win; and with respect to employment, darker-skinned people of African and Indian descent were excluded from working in banks, storefronts, and managerial positions in almost all of the (foreign-owned) corporations operating on the island.[56]

Other than *Island in the Sun*, no film offers came from Hollywood. Dandridge had to look outside the United States for acting projects. Around the same time she signed on for *Island in the Sun*, Dandridge had also made a deal with a French producer to star in *Tamango*. By the time filming for *Tamango* began, Dorothy and Preminger were on the outs and Jack Denison was taking on a more prominent role in her life.

Dorothy met Denison while performing in Las Vegas. After every performance, Denison, a m'aitre d'hotel, would send flowers to her dressing room. As a rule, Dorothy did not respond to such gestures, but Denison was persistent and gradually she grew to like and depend upon him. Despite her ongoing relationship with Denison, during the filming of *Tamango*, Dorothy fell for her costar, the German actor Curd Jürgens. Dorothy was dismally disappointed when, after the production was over, so, too, was the romance.[57]

Tamango (1958)

While *Carmen Jones* is a most vivid and near-perfect encapsulation of the Dorothy Dandridge image, it is in the lesser-known *Tamango* that all the salient elements of the star image align. In this Italian-Franco production about rebellion aboard an African slave ship, Dandridge's character, Aiché, is the slave and concubine of the ship's captain. For Aiché, much like Carmen, sex, duplicity, and tragedy are all part of her makeup. What Aiché has that Carmen does not is an explicit connection to whiteness.

Tamango's director, American-born John Berry, got his start in Hollywood. By 1951, Berry, a member of the Communist Party, had fled the United States for France to avoid testifying before the House Un-American Activities Committee. For Berry, who considered himself a champion of black representation and Civil Rights, *Tamango* was an opportunity to speak out against racial discrimination.[58] Filmed in France, *Tamango* was Berry's first film to be shown in the United States after his exile. Upon his return to U.S. filmmaking in 1974, Berry directed the all-black feature *Claudine*, which starred James Earl Jones and earned Diahann Carroll a Best Actress Oscar nomination.

The inspiration for *Tamango* is, coincidentally, another novella by *Carmen* author Prosper Mérimée. Though fictional, Mérimée's tale was informed by the most accurate information about the slave trade that was available at the time.[59] First published in 1829, Mérimée's *Tamango* begins with its title character, a well-known African warrior and slave dealer, bargaining with a slave ship captain off the coast of Africa.

After consuming plenty of brandy together, the two men strike up a deal, which leaves Tamango with about thirty excess slaves. Tamango tells the captain he must purchase the remaining slaves or they will be shot. As his ship is at capacity, the captain declines. True to his word, Tamango shoots and kills one of the slaves and is about to shoot another, when one of his wives, Aiché ("Ayché" in the novella), intervenes. Angered by her interference, Tamango offers his attractive wife to the captain as a gift, and the captain readily accepts.

Upon awakening from a drunken stupor, Tamango realizes what he has done and is heartbroken. He finds a boat, catches up with the ship, and pleads for his wife's return. The captain not only refuses to return Aiché, he captures the African warrior and chains him up with the other slaves. On board the ship, Tamango notices that his wife holds a special place among the captain's domestic servants. She is not chained up like the other slaves and is nicely clad. Aiché eventually manages to visit her husband and takes him a metal file. Tamango uses the file to sever his chains and then organizes a successful revolt.

All the white men are killed, cut into pieces, and thrown overboard, but the slaves' victory is short-lived as none of them know how to sail. They look to Tamango, who only makes matters worse by executing a maneuver that causes the ship's masts to break off. After a few days of hunger, lost at sea in the burning sun, everyone perishes except Tamango. When at last he is rescued, Tamango is taken to Jamaica where he unceremoniously lives out the rest of his life as a government worker and drummer for a regimental band.

During the more than three hundred fifty years of the Atlantic slave trade, there were nearly five hundred documented slave revolts, and likely many more that went undocumented.[60] The mere frequency of these slave ship uprisings refutes the notion that slaves transported from Africa to the Americas were docile, compliant, and resigned to their fate. In the protracted drama of black people's struggle for freedom, slave ship rebellions were the first act.[61] Despite the longevity of the slave trade and the regularity with which insurrections occurred, filmic depictions of the Middle Passage are few and far between.

Twenty years before *Tamango*, two films that depict the Middle Passage came out of Hollywood. Paramount released *Souls at Sea* (1937), and Twentieth Century–Fox, with Darryl Zanuck at the helm, released *Slave Ship* (1937). For films of this time period, the honesty of the scenes, which show slaves chained up, being herded onto a ship, whipped, and huddled together below deck, is rather unexpected. *Souls at Sea* even depicts what might be called a minor revolt when the skipper, in the midst of whipping his cargo, is pulled into the hold by the slaves and ultimately dies from his injuries.

Like *Tamango*, both *Slave Ship* and *Souls at Sea* are set in the 19th century, during the period when the African slave trade had been recently abolished but continued to flourish. In the Hollywood films, the ship captains are reformed slavers, and the narratives are more concerned with establishing the benevolence of their white heroes than with the welfare of the Africans. *Tamango*, on the other hand, presents the Africans not simply as nameless savages but as thinking, speaking and feeling protagonists.

Berry's *Tamango* also differs from Mérimée's tale with Aiché's character undergoing the most significant revision. When Dandridge finally received a copy of the *Tamango* script, she was, once again, infuriated. Rather than a shipboard rebellion, the script she received read like a shipboard sex drama. This time, however, the right to script approval

Dorothy Dandridge travels the Middle Passage as Curd Jürgen's mulatto slave in *Tamango* (1958), an Italian-Franco production about rebellion aboard an African slave ship.

had been negotiated in her contract. Dandridge did not approve, and before filming began, script changes were made.[62] The resulting film vacillates between rendering Dandridge as a tragic mulatto and a martyr in the fight against tyranny.

In the film, Aiché is no longer Tamango's wife. A generation or more removed from her African ancestry, Aiché is explicitly identified as a mixed race woman from Cuba. Her relationship with the skipper, Captain Reinker, played by Curd Jürgens, is now a full-blown interracial love affair. "LOVE AND ADVENTURE AS BOLD AS THE CASTING," was a tagline used in U.S. newspaper ads to promote the film. With interracial desire as a prominent theme, Aiché takes much of the spotlight away from Tamango, so much so that Berry's film might just as well have been named *Aiché*. To be sure, Tamango, played by Alex Cressan, is still a hero in this compelling depiction of the Middle Passage. At the heart of the androcentric action, however, Aiché grapples with her precarious position as a quasi-white woman.

As for Tamango, in Berry's film, instead of participating in the sale of human flesh, he is a noble and proud lion hunter. At first Tamango despises Aiché and calls her "white man's trash," but after a while, he falls for the captain's mistress and wants her on his side. The ship's doctor, Corot, also desires Aiché, although the attraction is not mutual. Corot is an interloper to an otherwise biracial love triangle. In short, Aiché is sought after by the ship's three most powerful men, and her interactions with each of them throw her predicament into sharp relief.

Captain Reinker represents the white/free world to which Aiché is connected by blood and physical proximity but can never truly belong. Aiché, at one point, declares to Corot that the captain has never beat her, branded her, or uttered a mean word to her. "He treats me like a white woman," she says. And yet in a passionate love scene when Reinker kisses Aiché, he gently whispers *not* "I love you" but "I own you."

Tamango symbolizes her black/slave status, the class to which legally she belongs but in all other respects, especially when compared to the Africans, seems woefully out of place. The captain wants Aiché as his near-white slave mistress. Tamango wants her as his black rebel gal. And Corot, who makes advances toward her whenever Reinker is not around, points out her ambiguous position between to the two poles.

In one scene Corot finds Aiché alone in the captain's cabin. As she pours him a cup of coffee, the doctor asks her how she feels when she sees the blacks chained up and turned into slaves. Aiché doesn't want to talk about it. She ignores his question and responds instead by asking Corot if he wants sugar in his coffee. Corot then reminds Aiché that even though she has white blood in her veins she is still a slave, just like the Africans. Unwilling to take the bait, Aiché coolly asks him if he wants milk in her coffee, to which the doctor replies, "Half and half—your color." Corot also undermines Aiché's relationship with the captain and her attachment to whiteness. Later, it is he who informs her that, at the end of the present voyage, the captain plans to marry a white woman.

Upset by the news of the captain's engagement and worried that she might be sold, Aiché taunts her master. As punishment, she is sent below deck to sleep with the African women. Down in the hold Aiché ends up helping the slaves cover up the murder of one of the deck hands. The following night Reinker sends for Aiché and begs her to stay with him. Aiché is conflicted. "I'm a part of them," she says. That makes no difference, according to the captain, because she is not like them, he says. The Africans are noble and willing to die for their cause, he says. She, on the other hand, is just like him: "We don't want to die for anything. We want to live for ourselves." Reinker promises to break it off with the fiancée and to give Aiché her freedom. Thereafter, Aiché decides she wants no part of the rebellion. When Tamango asks for her help, she refuses.

The revolt goes on without Aiché's help. In the mayhem that ensues, Tamango takes Aiché hostage down in the hold with the other African men. She attempts to escape, but one of the slaves holds her back. She begs to be set free and tries to explain to them that she's not a slave anymore. From the deck above, the captain also pleads with Tamango to let her go, promising that no one will be punished if they comply. Eventually Tamango is forced to admit that the slaves are no match for the ship's firepower. He tells his African brothers that they can give up if they want and some of them might live, or they can stay and fight—even if they die, they'll win, because dead men cannot be sold. Moved by his words, one man after another agrees to fight, and they begin chanting and drumming their chains on the floorboards.

At this point, Tamango tells Aiché she is free to go. Surrounded by the African men chanting and clapping, Aiché gingerly makes her way to the ladder. She begins her ascent to the deck, but then hesitates, turns around, and decides to join the slaves in their death chant. Given that Aiché had refused to help them revolt and that only moments earlier she was begging to be set free, her decision to die with the slaves comes as something of a surprise. For many critics, application of the one-drop rule was sufficient explanation for Aiché's change of mind. She had simply decided to side with "her people."

There is no one-drop rule anywhere in the Caribbean that defines mixed race people as black.[63] In all probability, someone like Aiché, a thoroughly Westernized, mixed race Cuban woman, would likely not have considered the African slaves "her people." While

Dorothy Dandridge is taken hostage by Alex Cressan during a revolt aboard a slave ship in *Tamango* **(1958).**

it's impossible to separate Aiché's racial heritage from her position as a slave, her kinship with the Africans has more to do with the latter. Her decision to die with the slaves is not simply about race. When Aiché turns back to join the slaves, she is, in effect, making a declaration that she is not like Reinker, a slaver and linchpin in the brutal and horrific system that assaulted the sanctity of millions of human beings. Rather than living for herself, Aiché decides to die for a cause greater than herself.

In both France, where it was filmed, and in the United States, *Tamango* was a source of controversy. When the film was released in France in January 1958, the country was in the middle of the Algerian war and, just a few years earlier, its colonial efforts in Indochina had come to a bloody end. *Tamango* was seen in France, but in its African colonies it was banned for being too inflammatory. In the United States, *Tamango* had trouble finding release at all. The Civil Rights Movement was afoot, and with *Tamango*'s militant theme and interracial love scenes, no major American distributor would take the film on. When it was finally released in September 1959 by the Hal Roach Distribution Corporation, distribution was limited and the film was shut out of some markets. In the cities where it did make it to the screen, *Tamango* was quite popular.[64]

Tamango was panned by both the *Los Angeles Times* and *The New York Times*, but other papers regarded it more favorably. One of the few reviewers to praise Dandridge's acting was Helen Bowers of the *Detroit Free Press*. Although her performance was "excellently realized emotionally," said Bowers, "she is plainly a woman of the 20th century." Bowers was also in the minority when she connected the dots from *Tamango* to America's present-day racial problems. *Variety*, upon the film's Paris release, predicted that *Tamango* would do well at the box office and praised its excellent production values. Vincent Canby, writing for *Motion Picture Daily*, also complimented the film's production values and thought that the final sequence in which Aiché makes her fatal decision made for particularly good drama. A reviewer for the *Baltimore Sun* was surprised to discover that *Tamango* "is actually pretty good."[65]

William Leonard of the *Chicago Tribune* described *Tamango* as a "skillful adaptation" of Mérimée's novel and named it one of the top five films for October 1959. Leonard also wondered in his review why Hollywood hadn't yet discovered the true story of a successful slave ship revolt that occurred in 1839.[66] That revolt, which Steven Spielberg would bring to the screen decades later, occurred on the slave ship *Amistad*. Forty years after *Tamango*, the release of Spielberg's *Amistad* (1997) proved that slave revolts were still a controversial topic in some places. For Jamaican audiences, *Amistad* was censored, and the opening scene, which depicts a bloody rebellion, was cut.

The Decks Ran Red (1958)

Nearly a year before *Tamango* was released in the United States, Dorothy Dandridge was involved in another shipboard mutiny in *The Decks Ran Red*. The story of the schooner *Harry A. Berwind*, upon which this film is very loosely based, is far more intriguing than this literally whitewashed version. It is also one of the most notable instances of black-on-white shipboard violence to take place in early 20th-century America.[67]

The real-life mutiny aboard the *Harry A. Berwind* took place in 1905 off the coast of North Carolina. Behaving erratically, the *Berwind* attracted the attention of another schooner, the *Blanche H. King*. When members of the *King*'s crew boarded the *Berwind* they found four black sailors, one dead, lying in a pool of blood, one restrained by a rope and chain, and two standing near the rail. It was soon determined that all four of the *Berwind*'s white crew members, including its captain, Edwin Rumill, had been shot, killed, and thrown overboard. The three surviving crew members, Henry Scott, the sailor found tied up, Robert Sawyer, and Arthur Adams, were charged with murder.

Scott, an American, and Sawyer, a West Indian, were described in the newspapers as "full blooded Negroes." Adams, a very light-skinned West Indian, was referred to as "mulatto." Adams and Sawyer claimed that Scott methodically shot and killed the white crewmembers and then shot John Coakley, the deceased black sailor, when Adams, Sawyer, and Coakley tried to summon help from a passing vessel. Scott first maintained that Adams, Sawyer and Coakley were the source of the violence. Later, he changed his story and said that all of the black sailors had planned the murders together. Either way, since black men and murdered white men were involved, the crime was assumed to be racially motivated.[68]

Less than thirty days after the *Berwind* had been rescued, all three men were put on trial for the murders. Adams and Sawyer were tried first and Scott a few days later. The captain of the *King* and its crew had a financial interest in the conviction of the sailors. If all three men were convicted, under maritime law, that left the *Berwind* without a crew, which then entitled the captain and crew of the *Blanche H. King* to a share of the *Berwind*'s cargo as well as a monetary award based on the value of the ship.

In the first trial, the captain implied that all three sailors were involved in the mayhem. At the second trial, Scott reverted to his original story, while the captain offered additional evidence against him. Ultimately, all three men were convicted and sentenced to death.[69] The captain and his crew collected their salvage money, and the captain's wife, who was also onboard at the time of the rescue, was said to be the first woman awarded salvage money stemming from a mutiny.[70]

Henry Scott was hanged in July 1906, but before his execution he confessed that Adams and Sawyer were innocent. The attorneys for Sawyer and Adams persuaded President Roosevelt to issue a stay of execution for their clients and later their death sentences were commuted to life in prison. A couple years after the commutations, Adams wrote a letter to H.B. Warner, a British-born actor, who at the time was enjoying a successful career on Broadway. Warner asked his personal attorney to look into the case. Consequently, in 1912, President Taft commuted the sentences of Adams and Sawyer and granted their freedom.[71]

Based on both the introduction to *The Decks Ran Red* and its trailer, it's evident that the filmmakers wanted viewers to believe that their motion picture depicts true-to-life events. However, this MGM release, written, directed, and produced by Andrew Stone, bears very little resemblance to the facts of the *Harry A. Berwind* case. Stone's version takes place on a freighter named the S.S. *Berwind*. When the film begins, following the mysterious death of its captain, the *Berwind* is anchored in New Zealand. Rattled by the captain's death, two crewmembers, including the cook, have deserted ship.

James Mason, as Captain Rumill, is brought on board as the new skipper. Dorothy Dandridge stars as Mahia, wife of Pete, the ship's newly hired cook. Aside from an Asian crewman, Pete and Mahia are the only people of color aboard the freighter, and other than identifying Pete as Maori, there is no mention of race in the film. Nor is there any specific reference to Mahia's racial identity. Only the film's trailer goes so far as to describe her as a "native" woman.

African American actor Joel Fluellen plays the part of Pete, who refused to take

Dorothy Dandridge stars with James Mason (center) and Broderick Crawford in Andrew Stone's shipboard sex drama *The Decks Ran Red* (1958).

the job as ship's cook unless his wife could accompany him. His function in this film is merely a pretense to justify Dandridge's presence on the ship. With only a few words of dialogue, Fluellen is rarely heard from or seen, and when the mayhem begins, his character is shot down and killed.

While Dandridge might have narrowly escaped a full-on shipboard sex drama in *Tamango*, such was not her fate in *The Decks Ran Red*. As the only woman on board this voyage, Dandridge's sexuality is exploited to the hilt. At various times Mahia is described as "sensuous," "exotically beautiful," "a lush dame," "a well-stacked doll," and "loaded with sex." Every "love-starved" white sailor aboard the *Berwind* is attracted to Mahia. In this film, Dandridge also makes the complete crossover into white territory. Although she is married to a man of color, instead of a biracial love triangle, she's at the center of a lust triangle with two white men, Captain Rumill and LeRoy Martin, one of the mutineers. Martin, a bad-boy punk with slicked-back hair, is played by Stuart Whitman. Broderick Crawford is the other mutineer, Henry Scott.

Dandridge's sexuality is so powerful in *The Decks Ran Red* that it is deemed just as threatening as the savage mutineers, if not more so. The film's trailer, which describes Mahia as "a reckless woman among violent men," advertises that the ship is menaced not by a murderous psychopath but rather "a love-starved crew and a dangerously beautiful native woman." At first, Mahia's presence fits right in with Scott and Martin's plan to fan unrest among the crew. When Martin comes on to or, rather, sexually assaults Mahia,

Pete loses his temper and hurls a knife at Martin's head, missing only by inches. This gets Pete locked up in a cabin and Mahia confined to the bridge. In the end, Mahia transforms her menacing sexuality and uses it for good to save the entire crew and ship.

Perhaps the most significant aspect of Dandridge's role in *The Decks Ran Red* is that it symbolizes a near-complete crossing over. In *Carmen Jones*, while every black man coveted Dandridge, white racial desire was covert. In *Tamango* Dandridge was sought after by men, both black and white, but it was within the highly racialized context of master and slave. In the deracinated world of *The Decks Ran Red*, with the exception of the charade of her Maori husband, Dandridge is given the all-out white-woman treatment. When she embarks on the ship, for example, her entrance acknowledges her star status. All eyes are upon her, and every man on board the ship, whether good or evil, finds her desirable. With actor Stuart Whitman, Dandridge also shares an interracial kiss. It can hardly be considered romantic, though, since in the midst of it the dangerous Mahia shoots Martin in the gut.

Dandridge next starred in the Samuel Goldwyn adaptation of George Gershwin's 1935 opera *Porgy and Bess* (1959). Considered the most famous American opera of the 20th century, *Porgy and Bess*, which is based on DuBose Heyward's novel *Porgy* (1925) and the play adapted from it, is about the residents of a ghetto called Catfish Row. Chief among its residents are a drug addict and prostitute, Bess, her disabled boyfriend, Porgy, and her violent ex-boyfriend.

For its antiquated, stereotyped images of African Americans, protests against the production began almost as soon as it was announced. Early on Dorothy Dandridge and Harry Belafonte were mentioned for the lead roles, but Belafonte wanted nothing to do with it. He turned it down because he found it racially demeaning and advised Dorothy to do the same.[72] Dorothy ignored the advice and signed on for the part of Bess. Sidney Poitier, who ambulates on his knees throughout the entire picture, plays Porgy. Other actors include Sammy Davis, Jr., Pearl Bailey, Brock Peters, and Diahann Carroll. Although mainstream critics loved the picture, it did not do well at the box office.

Porgy and Bess was Dandridge's final Hollywood feature. Afterward, the actress appeared in two foreign films, *Malaga* (1960), also known as *Moment of Danger*, and *Marco Polo* (1962). In *Malaga*, much like in *The Decks Ran Red*, Dandridge is in a love triangle with two white men, Edward Purdom and Trevor Howard, both British actors. Similarly, her character, Gianna, is without a racial identity. Director Laslo Benedek considered the casting of Dandridge as simply an actress and a personality without the mention of race, something of an experiment.[73] Despite her attraction to both men, she kisses neither one, although to further the plot, she does make herself into a prostitute for one night.

In *Marco Polo*, a French production shot in Yugoslavia, Dandridge was cast as Empress Zaire. During pre-production, Dandridge described her role as that of a bored princess with a harem of men. When Marco Polo comes along, she decides to purchase him.[74] *Marco Polo* was plagued with production problems and never released in the United States.

Between wrapping up the filming of *Malaga* and opening of *Porgy and Bess* in June 1959, Dandridge married Jack Denison. Almost immediately, Denison took over management of her career and exploited her for money. A few movie deals were floated, but nothing materialized. By 1960, Dandridge was forced to return to touring night clubs. During this period, Dandridge also tried her hand at regional theater.

Beginning in 1961, Dandridge was cast as Julie LaVerne in three regional productions of *Show Boat*.[75] Dandridge's first turn as Julie came in July 1961 at the Wharf Theatre in

Dorothy Dandridge's raceless character tussles with Trevor Howard in the British film *Malaga* (1960).

Monterey, California. In June 1962, with Norwood Smith, who had played Gaylord Ravenal in a 1948 Broadway revival of *Show Boat*, she appeared in a *Show Boat* production out of Dayton, Ohio. Dandridge's third run at *Show Boat* was in October 1964 with Kathryn Grayson at the Hyatt Music Theatre in Burlingame, California. Grayson had starred as main character Magnolia Hawks in MGM's 1951 screen version of *Show Boat*, and in 1946, along with Lena Horne, she sang in the *Show Boat* segment of *Till the Clouds Roll By*. In all these productions, Dandridge's performance, at best, was considered mediocre.[76]

Citing Denison's physical abuse, in 1962 Dandridge filed for divorce. A year later she filed bankruptcy. Adding insult to injury, in the midst of her bankruptcy proceedings, the woman who had been taking care of her daughter, Harolyn, for the last ten years was no longer willing to do it. After ten years of never missing a payment for her daughter's care, Dorothy was in arrears for two months. For a short time, Harolyn stayed with her. Dorothy, however, was in no condition to take care of a young adult with special needs. Harolyn was placed in a state institution. Dorothy felt that she had failed miserably.

To numb the pain and ease her anxieties, Dandridge began to rely more heavily on vodka, champagne, and prescription drugs. On September 8, 1965, at the age of 42, Dandridge died from an overdose of Tofranil, an antidepressant known to cause suicidal thoughts. Although the coroner declined any attempt to determine whether the overdose was accidental or suicide, Dandridge's close friend Geri Branton felt quite certain that it was the latter.[77]

6

Lonette McKee

Mixed Race Heroine Remix

Actually, I wanted to make her a little blacker. I wanted to play her more realistically. Not as Julie trying to pass as white but just plain Julie—as she is.[1]
                                                                  —Leonette McKee

A musical child prodigy and triple threat in acting, singing, and composition, Lonette McKee was born in 1954 to an African American laborer and his Scandinavian American wife. As a young girl Lonette performed at record hops, dances and small nightclubs in her hometown of Detroit. At fourteen McKee had a regional hit record, and by age sixteen she had written music and lyrics for a film soundtrack. One year later, Lonette McKee achieved celebrity status when she appeared as the dusky half of a biracial singing and dancing duo on the television series *The Wacky World of Jonathan Winters* (1972–1974). Off Broadway, in a one-woman show, McKee tackled the role of Billie Holiday. On Broadway she was Julie in two revivals of *Show Boat*, first in 1983 and again in 1994.[2]

Lonette McKee's career as film actress spans more than four decades and includes more than twenty-five films. A baby boomer, McKee represents an entirely new generation in the progression of this history. Her entrée into Hollywood coincides with the New Hollywood, a period in filmmaking that followed the dismantling of a system in which a handful of major studios controlled every level of the marketplace from production to exhibition. New Hollywood, which began in the late 1960s and lasted through the 1970s, saw the replacement of the Production Code with the MPAA rating system as well as unprecedented amounts of sex and violence on screen.

McKee's first credited film role was a tragic chanteuse in the African American cult movie *Sparkle* (1976). This led to a principal role opposite superstar comedian Richard Pryor in *Which Way Is Up?* (1977). In Julie Dash's short film *Illusions* (1982), McKee played a movie executive who passes for white in 1940s Hollywood. What should have been Lonette McKee's biggest break came two years later when she played a showgirl in Francis Ford Coppola's *The Cotton Club* (1984). Based on Jim Haskins' history of the famous interracial yet segregated nightclub, *The Cotton Club* movie provides an appropriate entry point into the Lonette McKee image.

Although the actress's film career begins in the New Hollywood, Lonette McKee's star image is laden with vestiges of mixed race representation from days gone by: from *The Cotton Club* to *Show Boat* and passing for white, to a propensity for subsuming tragic characters, not to mention an association with Old Hollywood via *Illusions*, and comparisons to Ava Gardner, Lana Turner and Lena Horne. Despite its foothold in the past, however, there are notable instances, as in *The Cotton Club*, when McKee's image breaks free from the shackles of stereotype to represent a wholly new type of mixed race heroine.

In *The Cotton Club*, McKee's character, Lila, though purportedly patterned after Lena Horne, passes for white. In this way, the film connects McKee/Lila not only with Horne but also Fredi Washington and the tragic mulatto as well. *The Cotton Club* departs from the stereotype, however, by positioning McKee as romantic heroine opposite African American dancer and actor Gregory Hines and giving the couple a Hollywood happy ending. This is a momentous occasion in film as it ostensibly marks the first time in a big-budget Hollywood feature film that a black romantic couple was given almost the same priority as its white equivalent—and it was done so with great sensitivity.

Lonette Rita McKee was born in Detroit, Michigan, on July 22, 1954, to father Lonnie, an auto industry worker, and mother Dorothy. Older sister Katherine was born in 1951. A younger sister, Carol, who was born with cerebral palsy, came along five years after Lonette.[3] It seems fitting that McKee, the first actress in this study who is known to have one parent that identified as white and one as black, was born just two months after the Supreme Court decision in *Brown v. Board of Education*. That landmark ruling, which came on May 17, 1954, overturned the *Plessy v. Ferguson* decision of 1896, which had legalized the practices of segregation and "separate but equal" in public accommodations. It would be another thirteen years, however, in *Loving v. Virginia*, before the Supreme Court would declare state laws banning interracial marriage unconstitutional.

The same year that the decision in *Plessy v. Ferguson* was rendered, Henry T. Ford was test-driving his first automobile on the streets of Detroit and the city soon became the center of the nation's automotive industry, hence its nickname the "Motor City" or "Motown." Henry Ford developed a national reputation as the black man's friend, employing him when others would not.[4] During and after the Second World War, with the second wave of migration from the South, Detroit attracted thousands of blacks eager to earn a decent wage. Lonette's father, Lonnie, who was born in Mississippi, might well have been among them.

Many blues artists also moved to Detroit at this time. Hoping to capitalize on these musicians, a significant number of record labels set up shop there. Although Detroit's vibrant blues scene ended in the 1960s, the city remained home to countless record labels in the mid–20th century, including Motown Records, founded by Berry Gordy in 1959. Diana Ross and the Supremes, Marvin Gaye, and the Jackson 5 are just but a few of the artists that helped Berry create what became known as the Motown Sound, resulting in one of the most influential record labels of the 20th century.

Young Lonette McKee grew up in a poor working-class neighborhood of Detroit. At an early age, she started banging away on an old piano and eventually taught herself how to play. Lonette was about nine years old when her mother Dorothy realized that her daughter had a special talent. Dorothy and Lonette started making the rounds together, knocking on one studio door after another, trying to get someone to listen and take notice. It was then that Lonette learned a hard lesson about the cutthroat aspect of the recording business. At ten years old, she heard one of her original tunes playing on the radio. Someone had taken her music and added new lyrics. The song, according to McKee, was a hit for which she received no royalties. Undeterred, Lonette was escorted around town by her mother so that she could play her cute, catchy tunes at local supper clubs.[5]

As a teenager, when she wasn't performing, Lonette attended St. Martin Deporres

High School. In the summer of 1968, she was a regional winner in a "High School Cover Girl" beauty contest. That same year she had a regional hit record, "Stop! Don't Worry About It." At The Pumpkin, a popular club just outside of Detroit, McKee also appeared in a "Soul Review" hosted by the local television dance show *Swingin' Time* (1963–1970). At age fifteen, Lonette wanted to get away from Detroit and the cruelty of her father. "I really hated him," she said. Lonette would remain bitter toward her father until 1985, at which time she re-evaluated her childhood, found compassion for her father, and decided not to judge him anymore.[6]

With her mother's blessing, Lonette quit ninth grade and moved to Los Angeles to join sister Katherine, who was also pursuing a show business career. Kathrine McKee was working as a showgirl on the Las Vegas strip before singer, dancer, and Rat Pack member Sammy Davis, Jr., hired her as mistress of ceremonies for his Vegas nightclub act. Katherine also became Davis's road wife. "He had an open marriage and we were lovers. That's how it went," she said years later.[7] In 1971 Katherine had the title role as a free woman of color in *Quadroon*, an exploitative antebellum B movie that in the spirit of *The Birth of a Nation* (1915), though far more explicit and graphic, accentuates the mulatto and brutal buck stereotypes. Lonette wrote the film's music and lyrics and can also be spotted in the film as an uncredited quadroon extra.

It was surely Katherine's association with Davis that helped Lonette get a job as an intern on the *Bill Cosby Show* (1969–1971). Around this time Cosby also arranged a scholarship for her at a Hollywood acting school.[8] In the spring of 1972, Lonette auditioned for a spot with Greg Garrison's Golddiggers, a white singing and dancing troupe created for the television show of another Rat Pack member, Dean Martin. Garrison, who produced and directed episodes of *The Dean Martin Show* (1966–1974) and countless Martin TV specials, was a Florenz Ziegfeld, of sorts, for television. At the time Lonette auditioned, Garrison had two distinct acts, the Golddiggers and the Ding-A-Lings. The Golddiggers were "clean-looking, all-American girls," mostly under twenty-one years of age. The Ding-A-Lings were slightly older and a little more sexified.[9]

McKee was turned down for the Golddiggers, but then Garrison decided he wanted to use her for something else. He decided to create a third act featuring one white woman, former Golddigger and Ding-A-Ling Michelle Della Fave, and one black woman, McKee. The duo, known as the Soul Sisters, appeared on another of Garrison's television shows, *The Wacky World of Jonathan Winters*. Lonette was the first African American woman to break into one of Garrison's TV dance groups.

To make sure that viewers understood that she was, indeed, black, McKee was required to don a short afro wig and wear dark makeup. "It wasn't demeaning at the time," she later recalled. "I think I was too young to realize what was going on." Years later, however, McKee refused to blacken up for the part of Jackie Robinson's wife in the 1981 Broadway musical *The First*. After the advent of the Soul Sisters, Garrison integrated the Ding-A-Lings by adding Japanese actress Helen Funai and Jayne Kennedy, who would soon become one of the most recognized black women in America.[10]

McKee's tenure on *The Wacky World of Jonathan Winters* was short-lived. Nevertheless, she was on the path toward film stardom at a time when Hollywood was undergoing major change. In the 1960s, in addition to the dismantling of the studio system and the Production Code, Hollywood had to contend with television's growing dominance. It had also experienced a series of big-budget flops. Financially stressed studios began to rethink their methods of operation as well as their target audiences. Further, by the 1970s, in the wake of the Civil Rights Movement and the turbulence of the previous decade, black audiences were fed up with Hollywood's representation of them.

Thus, the 1970s saw a surge in black cast movies that were targeted to black audiences. These films sought to explore new ways to represent African Americans, including subverting or inverting the old stereotypes. Within this 1970s black movie boom can be found the genre known as "blaxploitation." Much like American film noir, blaxploitation is a genre that is difficult to pin down because scholars tend to disagree on which films and what time period it includes. With regard to blaxploitation, some say it is an era that collapsed in the mid–1970s; others have argued that though rooted in the 1970s, the genre is open-ended. Still others would say it refers to all black films released in the 1970s.[11]

If blaxploitation were defined as all black films of the 1970s it would include an uplifting production like *Sounder* (1972), a film which black school children were encouraged to see, was praised by Civil Rights leaders, and was described as "breaking the pattern set by black exploitation movies."[12] *Sounder* was nominated for four Academy Awards: Best Picture, Best Screenplay Based on Material from Another Medium (William H. Armstrong novel); Paul Winfield for Best Actor; and Cicely Tyson for Best Actress. Though there may be no agreed upon definition of the genre, *Sounder* is not a blaxploitation movie.

Perhaps Bogle said it best when he described blaxploitation of the 1970s as movies that were often shot on low budgets, poorly directed, technically inferior, and also played on black audiences' need for heroic figures without "answering those needs in realistic terms."[13] Suffice it to say that not all black films produced in the 1970s are blaxploitation. *Sparkle*, which represents McKee's first credited film role, is another such example. Because he considered it suitable for mainstream audiences, *Sparkle* is one of the films that prompted *New York Times* critic Vincent Canby to predict in 1976 that the end of the blaxploitation era was drawing near.[14] Far from being a black exploitation picture, *Sparkle* is an homage to Berry Gordy and the ladies of Motown.

Sparkle (1976)

Set in late 1950s Harlem, *Sparkle* is the story of three sisters who form a singing group. The story idea came from producer Howard Rosenman who, as a teenager, fell in love with the Motown Sound and considered Berry Gordy his idol. In 1971, Rosenman, who was producing commercials in New York, was introduced to Joel Schumacher, a window dresser for an upscale department store. Because they were both in love with R&B music and the movies, the two hit it off immediately. Rosenman and Schumacher then determined to go to Hollywood and make a movie about the women who provided a soundtrack for their daily lives, the women of Motown: Tami Terrell, Mary Wells, Martha and the Vandellas, and especially Diana Ross and the Supremes.[15]

After doing some research on Motown, Rosenman wrote a treatment. Schumacher eventually wrote the script. Three years after the duo first met, *Sparkle* found a home at Warner Bros. Curtis Mayfield, who was responsible for the iconic *Super Fly* (1972) score, was hired to write the music. For Sam O'Steen, who had experience as film editor on a number of movies including *The Graduate* (1967) and *Chinatown* (1974), *Sparkle* would be his directing debut. After reading the script, O'Steen declared it the best thing he had read in two years. Unlike a lot of prospective directors, O'Steen understood that

Rosenman and Schumacher wanted to make *Sparkle* on a first-class basis, not as a black exploitation movie.[16]

According to Rosenman, *Sparkle* has its basis in films like *Funny Girl* (1968), starring Barbara Streisand, and *Gypsy* (1962), featuring Natalie Wood as the famous stripper Gypsy Rose Lee.[17] As for *Sparkle*'s black cinematic heritage, one can find both race and mainstream films with mixed race/black female entertainers, including *Siren of the Tropics* (1927), *Zouzou* (1934), *Show Boat* (1936, 1951) *The Duke Is Tops* (1938), *Stormy Weather* (1943), *Sepia Cinderella* (1947), and *St. Louis Blues* (1958). The most voyeuristic in this lineage is perhaps Berry Gordy's Billie Holiday biopic *Lady Sings the Blues* (1972), for which Diana Ross earned a Best Actress Oscar nomination. As for Hollywood films that attempt to deal with the trials and tribulations of a black girl-group, *Sparkle* seems to be the first.

It was no great leap for *Sparkle* filmmakers to cast Detroit native and music industry hopeful Lonette McKee in one of its principal roles. McKee plays the eldest sibling, Sister. Dwan Smith was cast as middle sister, Delores, and the role of the youngest sister, Sparkle, went to Irene Cara. Other players include Mary Alice as the girls' mother, Effie, and Phillip Michael Thomas as Stix, their manager and Sparkle's boyfriend. McKee was not the only one whose career was jumpstarted by *Sparkle*. Cara went on to star in *Fame* (1980) and won an Academy Award for co-writing the lyrics to the *Flashdance* (1983) theme song, and Phillip Michael Thomas achieved celebrity as one half of the biracial cop duo in the television series *Miami Vice* (1984–1990).

Compared to many black films of the 1970s, *Sparkle* presents a broad range of urban life, especially when it comes to its women characters. Certainly they are "types," but the film can be commended, nevertheless, for offering them in such a variety. Effie, the girls'

(From left) Dwan Smith, Lonette McKee and Irene Cara star in *Sparkle* (1976), the Warner Bros. ode to the women of Motown.

mother, is a maid, but she is not the happy, good-humored mammy of Old Hollywood. Often weary, but always dignified, her character suggests that her life has not been easy. There's the nosey neighbor, Mrs. Waters, who warns Effie that she better keep an eye on her oldest daughter because she's "busting at the seams." The daughter she's referring to is the light-skinned, sexually savvy Sister. Like Peola in *Imitation of Life* (1934), Sister takes after her "high-spirited" absentee father. Dark-skinned Dolores is the militant one. Delores discourages Sister from straightening her hair with a hot comb and resents the fact that her mother has to work as a domestic. And then there is Sparkle, whose caramel coloring is just right. Sparkle is the ingénue, the romantic heroine, and the one who wins in the end.

Although Irene Cara has the title role in *Sparkle* and is positioned as its literal star, the film's real standout is Lonette McKee. Critics lauded McKee's performance and her screen presence. Writing for *The New York Times*, Richard Eder, who didn't particularly care for the film, found Curtis Mayfield's songs, as sung by McKee, the film's only virtue. A critic for the *LA Times* described McKee as "the most ravishing and innocently brazen" of the three sisters. Canby likened McKee to both the grande dame of Motown, Diana Ross, as well as Lana Turner in *Ziegfeld Girl* (1941). Writing for *The New Yorker,* Pauline Kael compared McKee to Ava Gardner, the white actress who played the mixed race saloon singer Julie in MGM's 1951 remake of *Show Boat*.[18]

McKee's performance in *Sparkle* also brings to mind Dorothy Dandridge's Carmen, especially when the girls appear onstage for the first time. When they perform "Jump," one of several original Mayfield songs, Delores and Sparkle look more like prep school students than entertainers. Sister, on the other hand, is wearing a black sleeveless dress and a big red flower in her hair. When the music begins, expectations established by Sister's clothing are fulfilled with a display of provocative dance moves and a brashness that come as something of a surprise to her sisters and which the male audience members eagerly embrace.

For about two-thirds of the film much of the action revolves around McKee's character. Sparkle idolizes Sister and wants to be just like her. Unfortunately, Sister's radiance captures the attention of Satin, a sadomasochistic drug dealer who will lead Sister down the path of self-destruction. Delores loves her older sister so much that she sleeps with one of Satin's henchmen in order to seek revenge. When her plan backfires, one of the girls' friends winds up in jail instead of Sister's drug kingpin boyfriend. After having spent so much time captivated by McKee, it is a bit of a shock when the film abruptly kills her off.

Sister's death, presumably by drug overdose, and her poignant musical exit evoke all at once the tortured aspects of Dorothy Dandridge, Diana Ross as Billie Holiday, and *Show Boat*'s Julie. In this solo number, set in a dimly lit nightclub, McKee, accompanied by saxophone, piano, and drums, sings "Giving Up," a tune penned by Van McCoy and first recorded in 1964 by Gladys Knight & The Pips. In 1971 Donny Hathaway greatly improved upon the song with his soul rendition. As sung by McKee, "Giving Up" is a heartrending, sepulchral, blues number that signifies more than just giving up on a relationship—it's about giving up on life itself.

By this time Delores has moved away from Harlem to seek better opportunity. With Delores gone and Sister dead, the remainder of the film is dedicated to making Sparkle a star and Stix's shenanigans with white mobsters who want a stake in Sparkle's career. It takes more time than the film allows, however, to adjust to Sister's departure and get used to the idea of rooting for a new heroine. Irene Cara is lovely, but the film is simply not as compelling without McKee.

Sparkle was deemed a box office failure, and reviews of the film were mixed. Kael came out in favor of the film, as did Canby, who declared it "dynamic and entertaining." The *LA Times* said it was a "rich gem" that "glows from start to finish." Other critics found it dull and predictable.[19] Despite its mediocre reception, in the years following its release, *Sparkle* played in neighborhood playhouses and inner-city theaters all over the country and became a favorite of black high school kids. At one particular showing, for example, on New York's Lower East Side in the early 1980s, the crowd foresaw the dialogue and sang along enthusiastically with all the songs. *Sparkle* anticipated films like *Fame, Flashdance*, and *Purple Rain* (1984), and it has achieved historical significance as the first African American cult movie.[20]

After *Sparkle*, films about black female singing groups are still rare. The most highly celebrated of them, *Dreamgirls* (2006), starring Beyoncé, Jennifer Hudson, and Anika Noni Rose, did not come along until some thirty years later. Based on the 1981 Broadway play, the *Dreamgirls* movie so closely resembles the story of The Supremes that, after its release, Paramount and DreamWorks found it necessary to publish ads in Hollywood trade publications apologizing for any confusion related to the fictional record label depicted in *Dreamgirls* and Berry Gordy's Motown.[21]

Two films about black girl-groups were released in 2012, of which an Australian feature, *The Sapphires*, is by far the more interesting. Set in the 1960s and based on the life of co-writer Tony Briggs's mother, *The Sapphires* is the story of a group of Aboriginal young women who take their musical act to Vietnam in 1968. In addition to Briggs, director Wayne Blair, cinematographer Warwick Thornton, and the film's lead women are all indigenous Australians. When the film's opening intertitle announces that until 1967 Aboriginal Australians were not considered human, but were officially classified as "Flora and Fauna," it brings to mind how African Americans were once counted as three-fifths of a person.

The influence that African Americans and the Civil Rights Movement had on Aboriginal people is reflected in *The Sapphires* with opening credits that are superimposed over news footage from the 1960s: the Vietnam War, John and Jackie Kennedy riding in the motorcade on the day of the president's assassination, Aboriginals protest marching, immediately followed by African Americans marching, and the face and voice of Muhammad Ali, the legendary heavyweight boxer who refused to be drafted during the Vietnam War. "The American civil rights movement started a lot of things around the world," director Blair said. "It was a great example of what black people could do. Aboriginal people in my country took that blueprint."[22] The film solidifies its connection to black Americans through its American soul music soundtrack.

A second opening intertitle from *The Sapphires* makes reference to Australia's former Assimilation policies and the resulting "Stolen Generations." Between 1910 and 1970, Aboriginal children were routinely taken from their families and placed in institutions or with white families where they were taught to reject their indigenous heritage and to learn "white ways." Because Australia's Assimilation policies were focused on children who were deemed most adaptable to whiteness, light-skinned and mixed race Aboriginal children were particularly vulnerable to removal. In the film, one member of The Sapphires is part of this "Stolen Generation." The formation of the singing group brings her back to her Aboriginal family as an adult. These references to African American culture and (state sanctioned) passing for white make it easy to relate *The Sapphires* to the pantheon of mixed race representation in American films.

The other black girl-group film of 2012 was a disappointing *Sparkle* remake starring Whitney Houston, in her last film appearance, as the mother, Jordin Sparks as Sparkle, and Tika Sumpter is the middle sister. The role of eldest sibling and tragic mulatto went to mixed race British actress Carmen Ejogo. All of these girl-group films owe a great debt to Motown, Berry Gordy, Diana Ross and the Supremes, and the original *Sparkle*.

Following *Sparkle*, McKee was supposed to appear in the Muhammad Ali biopic *The Greatest* (1977) as Ali's estranged Muslim wife. In late 1976, after the production had started, McKee resigned over arguments with the producer about substandard working conditions and a lack of professionalism on the set. According to her mother, Lonette was not only taking a stand for herself but for others as well. Fellow actors Cleavon Little, Jim Brown, and Richard Pryor praised McKee for her action. Before African American screenwriter Bill Gunn was fired from *The Greatest* he also had trouble with the film's white producers and was forced to deal with a host of racial insensitivities.[23]

McKee walked straight off the set of *The Greatest* and onto the set of *Which Way Is Up?*, a comedy in which she starred as Richard Pryor's mistress. By this time, Lonette had hired African American entertainment lawyer, David Franklin, who was known for acquiring precedent-setting recording contracts and multi-million-dollar movie deals for his black clientele. During the 1970s Franklin was also a political strategist and significant figure on the Atlanta political scene. Franklin's first show business client was Donny Hathaway in 1970. Others included Richard Pryor, Roberta Flack and Cicely Tyson. In 1978 Franklin helped McKee negotiate a five-year record deal with Warner Bros. Records.[24]

In addition to looking after her career, Franklin was also an influential person in McKee's private life. The two were likely involved in a romantic affair, and it was Franklin who prompted McKee to rethink her racial identity. Before she met the attorney, McKee had always identified as "mulatto." Franklin, who was also light-skinned, counseled McKee to see herself the way others do, as a black woman.[25] McKee took Franklin's advice and has since forged an identity and image that is racially mixed and assertively black.

Illusions (1982)

Illusions is a short film written and directed by African American filmmaker Julie Dash. In the summer of 1982, *Illusions* was featured at a black filmmakers' series in New York alongside another short, the student film *Sarah* (1981), written and directed by up-and-coming filmmaker Spike Lee.[26] Julie Dash's interest in film began in 1968, during her senior year of high school, when she attended a film workshop at the Studio Museum in Harlem. After earning a BA in film production, Dash made her way to Los Angeles in the hopes of meeting up with a group of mostly African and African American student filmmakers at UCLA.[27]

Against the backdrop of the Civil Rights Movement and the Vietnam War, these UCLA students, now referred to as the "L.A. Rebellion," were making films far removed from the Hollywood aesthetic, films that gave voice to the concerns, the community, and the ancestry of blacks and other people of color.[28] Dash officially joined the L.A. Rebellion when, after completing a two-year conservatory fellowship at the American Film

Institute ("AFI"), she was accepted into the Master's program at UCLA's School of Theater, Film and Television.

While studying at UCLA Dash earned a Director's Guild of America Award for her student film *Diary of an African Nun* (1977), adapted from a short story by Alice Walker. Between 1978 and 1980 Dash was a voting member of the MPAA's rating board. Dash's first feature film, *Daughters of the Dust* (1991), a period drama about a community of Gullah women from the Sea Islands off of South Carolina, was the first by an African American woman to receive a general theatrical release in the United States.

Illusions is set in Hollywood, California, 1942, the same year that the Office of War Information (OWI) established a bureau there and the year that Lena Horne signed her long-term contract with MGM. At the center of Dash's story are two women who, in very different ways, have to suppress their blackness in order to make a living in Hollywood. Mignon Dupree, played by Lonette McKee, is a studio executive passing for white. Rosanne Katon is Ester, an African American woman who freelances as a voice double for white actresses. Other characters include Mignon's boss and head of the fictitious National Studios, C.J. Forrester (Jack Radar). Lieutenant Bedsford (Ned Bellamy) is the OWI official assigned to the studio. Also working at National Studios are two secretaries, Louise (Rita Crafts) and a young woman identified only as Blonde bombshell (Sandy Brooke).

Toward the end of the film we learn that Mignon travelled to Los Angeles after her husband Julius was shipped overseas to fight in the war. At a party with a friend Mignon overheard a movie producer say, "History is not what actually happened … the real history that most people will remember and believe in is what they see on screen." It was

Lonette McKee plays a studio executive passing for white in Old Hollywood in the Julie Dash short film *Illusions* (1982).

then that Mignon decided she wanted to work in Hollywood, where history was being rewritten. Having toiled her way up from a secretary, Mignon is now one of the few women in the country who has the power to make executive decisions at a film studio.

Mignon may have some authority over the escapist musicals her studio puts out, but she doesn't have the power to greenlight a film. Near the start of *Illusions* Mignon tries to convince Forrester that they don't need any more war films. She wants National Studios to be the first to give the public situations and characters that they can recognize from their own lives. Mignon also wants a chance to produce her own project. With regard to the latter, her boss advises her to leave the producing to the men. What they need, Forrester says, is fewer producers and more good stories. Mignon suggests that they make a movie about the Code Talkers, a group of Navajo Marines who became war heroes when they developed a secret code for transmitting sensitive information in their native language. To this Forrester responds, "Who cares about a group of Indians talking mumbo jumbo? It's a viable story, but there's no audience for it."

Mignon and Forrester head over to the recording stages where there is a bit of a problem. The music track and the picture are out of sync in one of the numbers for their next big release, due out at Christmas. Forrester leaves it up to Mignon and the sound engineer to come up with a fix. The film's white star is on the road with the USO entertaining the troops so reshooting is not an option. The engineer suggests that they use the same woman who recorded the master tapes and see if she can sing and match her voice to the picture. Beyond the sound booth, lights come on in the stage area, and Ester appears. As Ester begins to sing, one of Hollywood's illusions is revealed. Ester is a ghost singer. The singing voice of the white starlet on the screen not only belongs to someone else, it also belongs to a black woman.

Ghost singing in Hollywood was necessitated by the advent of sound. As the silent era came to an end and talking pictures became the norm, studios soon realized that some of their greatest stars were vocally challenged. The all-white musical *Singin' in the Rain* (1952), rated by the AFI as the greatest musical movie of all time, is about this transition from the silent to the talking era and the use of a ghost singer. This film about making a film was co-directed by dancer Gene Kelly, who also stars as leading man Don Lockwood. Lennie Hayton, who was married to Lena Horne at the time, won an Oscar for the film's musical score.

Singin' in the Rain also features Jean Hagan as Lina Lamont, a silent film star whose current picture is being reworked into a musical. The change has been motivated by the popularity of *The Jazz Singer* (1927), the celebrated talking picture about a Jewish singer who performs in blackface. *The Jazz Singer* was not the first talkie, but its huge success influenced the industry's speedy transition from silent to sound. Lina, it turns out, has a voice that sounds more like a cartoon character than a screen goddess, and eventually Kathy Selden, played by Debbie Reynolds, is hired to ghost sing. The movie is a hit, and at its premiere the audience wants Lina to sing. She obliges by lip-syncing into the microphone on stage with Kathy doing the actual singing in back of her, behind a curtain. Midway through the song the curtains are drawn, exposing the ruse, and Kathy is applauded as the film's authentic star.

A bizarre irony of *Singin' in the Rain* is that Debbie Reynolds, who was still in her teens, couldn't manage all the songs. For the number "Would You," Hollywood ghost singer Betty Noyes dubbed for Reynolds who, as Kathy, is dubbing for Lina. Matters became more surreal when Reynold's speaking voice was deemed not right for Lina's dubbed speaking voice. When Reynolds/Kathy is dubbing Hagan/Lina's speaking voice, Hagan's natural voice was used to dub Reynolds/Kathy.[29]

Ghost singing was probably one of Hollywood's worst kept secrets. By the time the talking era had begun in earnest, any number of newspapers had printed articles about it. A topic of debate early on, for example, was whether Lara La Plante, who played Magnolia in the 1929 *Show Boat*, had a ghost singer.[30] One article questioned why a film's action had to be put on a hold just so a ghost singer could warble a tune.[31] Another explained exactly how ghost singing was done.[32] There were also numerous pieces that identified ghost singers, with some even naming names of stars for whom they sang.[33]

Some voice doubles did receive credit for their work, including LeVern Hutcherson, Marilyn Horne, and Marvin Hayes in *Carmen Jones* (1954) as well as Gogi Grant in *The Helen Morgan Story* (1957). As a rule, however, ghost singers like Betty Noyes did not get acknowledged for their work until many years later. Contrary to the outcome in *Singin' in the Rain*, ghost singers generally received no screen credits, and they were required to keep quiet about their work as a condition of their employment. In the BBC documentary *Secret Voices of Hollywood* (2013), India Adams, who ghost sang for Joan Crawford and Cyd Charisse, said that she was "scared to death" to go public because if she did the studios would never hire her again.

Marni Nixon, one of Hollywood's most respected and well-known ghost singers, sang for Marilyn Monroe in *Gentlemen Prefer Blondes* (1953), Deborah Kerr in the *King and I* (1956), Natalie Wood in the multi-Oscar–winning *West Side Story* (1961), and Audrey Hepburn in the Oscar-winning *My Fair Lady* (1964). Nixon said that she, too, had been warned by the studios that if word got out about her ghost singing, they would see to it that she wouldn't work in Hollywood again. "I think they thought it would give away the illusion," she said. In the 1960s, after the Golden Age of Hollywood musicals had run its course, Nixon established a precedent for ghost singers when she hired legal counsel to help her establish rights to royalties from the soundtrack recording of *West Side Story*.[34]

While it's evident that there was a large pool of white singers, men and women, who acted as voice doubles for predominantly white actors,[35] it is more difficult to discern how many African American ghost singers were employed in Hollywood. It's quite possible that studios simply preferred to use white singers. Given the pressure on singers not to go public, it also seems possible that there were black ghost singers whose names have not come to the surface. African American singers who have been acknowledged for their work include LeVern Hutcherson and Marvin Hayes who, in their only credited film roles, sang for Harry Belafonte and Joe Adams in *Carmen Jones*.

Muriel Smith, who had the lead (alternating with Muriel Rahn) in the 1943 Broadway production of *Carmen Jones*, was a credited ghost singer for the Hungarian American actress Zsa Zsa Gabor in *Moulin Rouge* (1952). In *South Pacific* (1958), a film in which every singing voice was dubbed save one,[36] mixed race actress Juanita Hall, who had originated the character of Bloody Mary on Broadway, had the opportunity to reprise her role in the film. Muriel Smith, who had played Bloody Mary on the London stage, did Hall's ghost singing.

Another African American singer known for her voice double work in Hollywood, and quite possibly the inspiration for Ester's character in *Illusions*, is Etta Moten. A late bloomer, Moten was almost thirty years old when she graduated from college with a degree in voice and drama. By this time she was also divorced with two young children.

After graduation in 1931 Moten travelled to New York where she found work on Broadway. *Zombie* (1931), one of her first productions, was a flop in New York, but it toured nationally. When Moten arrived in Los Angeles, Clarence Muse lined up an audition for her with Warner Bros., and she was soon dubbing voices for white film stars, including Barbara Stanwyck and Ginger Rogers. According to family members, Moten received $100 for each job and no film credit.[37]

Etta Moten was supposed to appear in *Bombshell* (1933), aka *The Blonde Bombshell*, starring Jean Harlow. However, just as it was for Nina Mae McKinney in *Reckless* (1935), another Harlow vehicle, Moten's scenes in *Bombshell* ended up on the cutting room floor. Victor Fleming, known for *The Wizard of Oz* (1939), directed both films. Fleming told Moten that she lost the part because she would have stolen the big scene from the blonde bombshell.[38] Nevertheless, unlike a lot of ghost singers, Etta Moten, like the fictional Kathy Selden, got her chance to come out from behind the curtain.

In the early 1930s, almost ten years before Lena Horne's first appearance in a Hollywood feature, Etta Moten was given significant face and voice time in two films, *Flying Down to Rio* (1933) and *Gold Diggers of 1933* (1933). Both roles are considered pioneering for being among the first to expand the way in which black women were represented on screen. In *Flying Down to Rio* (1933), starring Ginger Rogers and Fred Astaire, Moten sang in the "Carioaca," a lengthy, segregated song and dance number that was nominated for a Best Song Oscar. The first half of "Carioca" features white performers. The second part, which showcases black dancers, is kicked off by Moten, who makes her entrance wearing a long dress and a basket of fruit for a headdress. Moten swings her hips decorously to the rhythm as she sings about the dance for which the song is named. Moten's scene is a precursor to *Panama Hattie* (1943) and Lena Horne's performance of "The Sping," a song also named after a dance and which pays homage to the Carioca in its lyrics.

In *Gold Diggers of 1933*, Moten, the film's only black character, sings in the finale, "Remember My Forgotten Man," a song that laments the predicament of war veterans who have been relegated to poverty and homelessness. The number begins with the film's star, Joan Blondell, talk-singing the lyrics. After a couple of minutes, the camera moves up to Moten, who is dressed modestly and seated prettily in the window of a tenement building. As Moten sings, the camera pans over to two other windows through which can be seen the forlorn faces of women of forgotten men, a white-haired lady in a rocking chair and a mother holding a baby.

At the end of the number, when Blondell sings a few lines, some have said she was dubbed by African American opera singer Marian Anderson. It seems just as likely, though, that Etta Moten was Blondell's ghost singer.[39] In any case, it was Moten's performance in "Remember My Forgotten Man" that caught the attention of First Lady Eleanor Roosevelt, and in 1934 Moten became the first black woman to sing at the White House. Two years later, Moten also sang for Brazilian president Getulio Vargas and his wife.[40]

Just like *Singin' in the Rain*, Julie Dash's *Illusions* is a film about making a musical film. Both have a scene in which the sound and the picture in the fictional film are out of sync, and both feature a woman acting as a voice double. As it is in *Singin' in the Rain*, in *Illusions*, the actress who doubles for the star in the fictional film has herself been dubbed in the actual film. When Katon/Ester sings in *Illusions*, she is lip-syncing to the First Lady of Song, Ella Fitzgerald. The use of Fitzgerald's voice, which sets the perfect musical mood for the fictional film's numbers, demonstrates how easy it is to be fooled by the visual image. When the voice is synchronized to the lips of the white movie star, thoughts of Ella Fitzgerald recede. When voice and picture are out of sync, impressions of the great jazz singer return.

Singin' in the Rain obscures Hollywood's history with ghost singers by suppressing the actual contribution of Betty Noyes, while at the same time giving the fictional Kathy Selden credit and recognition for her labor. In *Illusions*, Mignon does go out of her way to make sure that Ester gets the best pay and treatment possible, but in denying its ghost singer public recognition, Dash's film takes the more historically accurate approach. Ester's lip-syncing, however, is not just about Hollywood taking advantage of uncredited singers.

In *Illusions*, Ester's ghost singing is a metaphor for all the various ways in which African Americans have been simultaneously exploited and negated in Hollywood, including but not limited to the use of the black voice without credit; the appropriation of black music and dance; the use of white actors in blackface; the employment of white actors for mixed race roles; the inclusion of African Americans in films in a way that makes it easy to delete them at will; the exclusion of black stories, black history, and black romance because they are deemed unpopular and therefore unprofitable; and the use of black actors in non-heroic, stereotypical and demeaning roles.

As for Mingon's character, the power she has in American culture brings to mind that of the real-life persona of Anatole Broyard, a light-skinned Creole man who passed for white. In 1971 Broyard became a daily book reviewer for *The New York Times*, making him one of the publishing industries foremost gatekeepers. The life that Broyard chose meant that his children did not meet his darker-skinned sibling until after his death nor, with the exception of a couple of brief visits, did they have contact with his light-skinned mother and sister.[41]

Broyard not only avoided associating with black people, he was also anti-black. He told his sister that he had decided to pass for white so that he could become a writer, as opposed to a Negro writer. The paradox of Broyard's life, however, according to novelist Ellen Schwamm, was that concealing his blackness prevented him from becoming a great writer.[42] *The Human Stain* (2003), starring Anthony Hopkins as a college professor passing for white, and the Philip Roth novel from which the film was adapted, were rumored to be based upon the life of Anatole Broyard. In "An Open Letter to Wikipedia," published in *The New Yorker*, Roth adamantly denied the rumor.[43]

Mignon's passing, like Ester's ghost singing, is a metaphor, too. It is symbolic of Hollywood itself, the business of manufacturing illusions. Mignon looks white, but she is not what she seems to be. Whiteness, as the scene with Ester on the sound stage reveals, is not what it seems to be either. At the end of *Illusions*, while Mignon is out of her office, Lt. Bedsford is snooping around her desk and finds a personal letter from her husband, accompanied by a photograph of him with his all-black infantry. When Mignon returns to her office, the lieutenant is waiting there to confront her with his findings. Bedsford is about to ask her why she never said anything about her blackness, but before he can finish his question, Mignon interrupts: "Why didn't I what? Why didn't I report to you that I wasn't a white woman? ... Or why didn't someone stop me before I got so far being who I am, Lieutenant?"

Mignon's passing is unlike that of the real-life Anatole Broyard or the stereotyped fictional mixed race heroine. In fact, Mignon hasn't so much been passing but rather choosing not to disabuse people of the assumptions they have made about her. She has been passing out in the open. Mignon hasn't cut off ties with her family. She speaks with her mother and sister by telephone and doesn't worry about receiving mail from her husband at work. When Ester comes into her environment, Mignon doesn't distance herself. Instead, she acts as Ester's protector, providing tea for her on a sound stage where no drinks are allowed and making sure she gets a monetary bonus for her work. After Mignon's first discussion with Ester, Louise remarks how good she was with her and she never knows what to say to "them." Mignon discreetly outs herself when she replies, "It's simple, Louise. Just speak as you would speak to me."

Mignon is also unlike the fictional mulatto woman who wants nothing more than to be with a white man. To the contrary, she summarily rejects Bedsford's advances. Whereas in other films, when the mixed race woman is discovered passing for white, she might be beaten or otherwise punished for her "deceit," in *Illusions*, there are no such consequences. Though it might be naïve on her part, Mignon doesn't seem a bit worried that Bedsford will say anything or that there will be any repercussions from his discovery. She's not ashamed, and she's not inclined to flee. In fact, Mignon, who was thinking about leaving the film business, has now made up her mind to stay.

Mignon's motive for passing was, at first, self-serving, but her encounter with Ester changed all that. Mignon will continue to pass as a white studio executive, but now she will do it as a voice for African Americans. Her statements in the final moments might be construed as the autobiographical sentiments of the film's writer and director, Julie Dash. When Mignon determines to remain in the film industry, she is not simply referring to Hollywood where National Studios resides. Rather, she is stating her aim to create narratives that will contribute to the cinematic heritage of the nation.

When Julie Dash finished *Illusions*, she immediately began intensive research for her feature film, *Daughters of the Dust*.[44] In 2004, thirteen years after it was released, *Daughters of the Dust* was one of the 25 films selected that year for addition to the Library of Congress National Film Registry, thus ensuring its survival and conservation as part of America's film heritage. *Illusions* was inducted to the National Film Registry in 2020.

In the early 1980s, Lonette McKee caught the attention of casting director Barry Moss, who was working on the Houston Grand Opera (HGO) revival of *Show Boat*. Upon meeting McKee, Moss thought it would be wonderful to have a black woman play the part of tragic mulatto Julie. McKee auditioned and landed the part. HGO's *Show Boat* revival promoted Lonette McKee as the first black actress to play the mixed race character Julie.[45] While McKee was the first mixed race/black woman to portray Julie in a major American theater company,[46] she was not *Show Boat*'s first black Julie.

In 1947, Lena Horne played Julie in MGM's mini version of *Show Boat* in *Till the Clouds Roll By*. In the early 1960s Dorothy Dandridge played Julie in at least three regional productions of *Show Boat*, and in 1971 acclaimed mixed race jazz singer Cleo Laine took on the role in a production of *Show Boat* at the Adelphi Theatre in London. Cleo Laine was born in a suburb of London in 1927. Her white mother was from Swindon, and her father was born in Jamaica. Among Laine's numerous honors are the 1983 Grammy Award for Best Female Jazz Vocalist, and in 1997, she was made a Dame Commander of the British Empire.

The HGO revival of *Show Boat*, which opened in April of 1983 and closed two months later, earned Lonette McKee a Tony nomination for Best Performance by an

Lonette McKee was the first mixed race black woman to portray *Show Boat*'s Julie in a major American theater company. She is pictured here in a 1982 pre–Broadway performance of the Houston Grand Opera's revival of the famous musical.

Actress in a Leading Role in a Musical. Around the same time, McKee's life was said to imitate art when she married Leo Compton, a white backstage doorman she met during a pre–Broadway *Show Boat* run in San Francisco. Of their relationship, McKee said that race was not an issue, "as long as I know I'm black and I know who I am."[47]

The Cotton Club (1984)

Lonette McKee had yet another opportunity to pass for white in *The Cotton Club,* a visual extravaganza inspired by James Haskins' illustrative history of the famous Harlem nightclub. An educator and prolific author, Haskins wrote a number of books on black history for both children and adults. Among his other adult books are the biographies of Richard Pryor, Scott Joplin, and Lena Horne.

The Cotton Club movie was produced by Robert Evans and directed by Francis Ford Coppola, the same duo that worked together with novelist and screenwriter Mario Puzo to bring *The Godfather* (1972) to the screen. *The Cotton Club* had a budget roughly eight times that of *The Godfather* and employed a legion of talented dancers, hoofers, and extras as well as an impressive ensemble cast of actors that, in addition to McKee, included brothers Gregory and Maurice Hines, Richard Gere, Diane Lane, Nicolas Cage, Bob Hoskins, Fred Gwynne, James Remar, and Laurence Fishburne. *The Cotton Club,* it would seem, had all the makings of a big hit, but from beginning to end, Evans' reckless mode of production was at odds with the film's success and its African American theme.

Robert Evans began developing *The Cotton Club* after optioning the rights to Haskins' book in 1980 from Jim Hinton and Charles Childs. The latter was a chemical company executive and longtime friend of Haskins. Hinton and Childs spent two years trying to promote the book as a film but were unable to obtain the necessary financing. "They were not allowed as black guys to do it," Haskins said at the time of the film's release, "so they had to sell it to Bob Evans, who was allowed to do it."[48]

In the 1970s, Robert Evans was associated with a number of successes that, in addition to *The Godfather,* included *Love Story* (1970), *Chinatown* (1974), and *The Marathon Man* (1976). By the end of the decade, however, Evans seemed to have lost his touch, and in 1980, he pleaded guilty to charges of drug possession. Evans hoped that *The Cotton Club* would reestablish his reputation. Robert Evans did manage to make Haskins' book into a movie; without him it would likely have never happened. But even for Paramount's one-time head of production, bringing *The Cotton Club* to fruition was no simple feat. Complicating matters was Evans' determination to move full speed ahead before financing and a script were in place. This contributed to an unusual level of chaos on the set and behind the scenes that is itself worthy of a screenplay.

Despite his Hollywood connections, Robert Evans was unable to generate

Lonette McKee is a singer who passes for white in the Robert Evans/Francis Ford Coppola production *The Cotton Club* (1984).

interest in *The Cotton Club* within the film industry. All the major studios passed. Evans' recent drug conviction didn't help matters. With the financial successes of the 1970s black movie boom apparently all but forgotten, a greater deterrent was the commonly held tenet that films about African Americans don't make money. This, coupled with a general apathy for the great black performers of the 1920s and '30s, meant that Evans had to look for financing outside the film industry. Three years later, after a failed negotiation with a Saudi Arabian arms trader and a deal that fell through with a Texas tycoon who died of a heart attack just one day after committing to bankroll the film, Evans went into partnership with a pair of businessmen from Las Vegas, Ed and Fred Doumani.[49]

At the same time, Evans had also been in search of a bankable male star. Al Pacino and Sylvester Stallone had both declined before Richard Gere finally signed on to play the white male lead. By this time Gregory Hines was already on board as the film's black male star. The signing of Gere, however, meant that the film would evolve into a star vehicle for a white man. Gere, who had played trumpet in high school, wanted his character to be a musician. And so it was that a white cornet player became the hero of a film about African Americans and a nightclub where no white performer had ever played.[50]

After the agreement with the Doumani brothers and the casting of Gere, Orion Pictures signed on to distribute *The Cotton Club* under an agreement in which the studio had no financial obligations until the film was completed. Evans' production woes continued. Likely to make the project look more like *The Godfather* and less like the black musical and recent box office flop *The Wiz* (1978), Evans brought in Coppola, who was also contending with financial struggles of his own. Coppola was initially hired to help fix the original script drafted by Mario Puzo, but eventually he would also direct.[51]

Coppola's first draft focused on the Harlem Renaissance and included Civil Rights marches and readings by black poets. Evans hated it, as did the Doumanis, who promptly suspended pre-production financing, which was already in full swing at $140,000 a week. To keep financing going, Evans sold his Paramount stock, but those funds would soon run out. Around this time, Evans made the acquaintance of cocaine dealer Karen Greenberger, aka Elaine Jacobs. Greenberger, who was interested in investing in *The Cotton Club*, became Evans' lover. When Evans asked Greenberger if she knew any other potential investors, she introduced him to Roy Radin, a small-time theatrical producer. Radin and Evans began talking business, along with the chairman of the National Bank of Puerto Rico. The three men signed a letter of intent to create a production company based in Puerto Rico that would produce *The Cotton Club* and two other movies.[52]

When Greenberger found out about the letter of intent she was livid. She argued with Radin at Evans' New York residence and demanded to be cut in on the deal. Radin told Greenberger that she would get a $50,000 finder's fee, but Greenberger wanted a percentage of Radin's share. Evans, who was starting to have second thoughts about going into business with Radin, apparently sided with his girlfriend. In May 1983, Radin flew to Los Angeles. While he was there, Greenberger called him at his hotel and said she wanted to meet to settle their disagreement over *The Cotton Club*.[53]

The following evening, Greenberger picked Radin up from his hotel in a limousine. It was the last time Radin was seen alive. One month later Radin's decomposed body was found in a canyon near Los Angeles. In the press, the investigation into Radin's death became known as the "Cotton Club murder." In 1988, felony complaints were filed against Greenberger. Three years later, Greenberger and three accomplices were convicted of murder. Evans was also a suspect in the case, but he was never indicted.[54]

Around the same time Evans was in negotiations with Greenberger and Radin, he also met with Coppola, Gere, and Hines at Coppola's estate to come up with a new script. Evans used the revised script to persuade the Doumanis to resume funding of *The Cotton Club*. In June 1983, Coppola agreed to direct. The following month, Coppola hired Lonette McKee after stopping by a New York nightclub called Sweetwater's, where the actress was singing the songs of Irving Berlin and Jerome Kern as well as some original material. The director also brought in Pulitzer Prize–winning novelist William Kennedy to further update a script that would remain in a constant state of flux during most of the shooting.[55]

The end result is a film that is part musical, part gangster, a *Stormy Weather* meets *The Godfather*, if you will, in which blacks became the backdrop of their own story. That being said, to the film's credit, and most likely due to Coppola's direction and input from Gregory Hines, *The Cotton Club* is entirely sensitive to its portrayal of African Americans. Furthermore, even though white action takes precedence over black, there is an evident attempt to give African American characters near equal time.

Pandering, perhaps, to its sibling investors, *The Cotton Club* spins its biracial tale by following the parallel stories of two sets of brothers—one black, one white. Richard Gere and Nicolas Cage are the Irish American brothers, Dixie and Vincent Dwyer. Dixie is a cornet player in the mold of Bix Beiderbecke,[56] and Cage's character is based on Vincent Coll, a mobster who became infamously known as "The Baby Killer." The African American brothers, Sandman and Clay Williams, are a tap-dancing duo, played by Gregory and Maurice Hines. Shortly after the film opens the Williams brothers get their big break when they are hired for the Cotton Club.

Richard Gere (left) is a cornet player and James Remar is mobster Dutch Schultz in the Robert Evans/Francis Ford Coppola production *The Cotton Club* (1984).

Bob Hoskins plays Owney Madden, the Cotton Club owner who once controlled the bootleg business in Manhattan. Fred Gwynne is Frenchy DeMange, one of Madden's closest aides. The Dwyer brothers end up in the service of Madden's Bronx adversary, Dutch Schultz, played by James Remar. Diane Lane, the white heroine, is Schultz's moll and Dixie's love interest, Vera Cicero. Laurence Fishburne is African American mob boss Bumpy Rhodes, a character Fishburne reprised in the film *Hoodlum* (1997) about real-world mob boss Bumpy Johnson. Giancarlo Esposito has a small role as one of Bumpy's hoodlums and Mario Van Peebles can be seen as a dancer in a number opposite Lonette McKee.

Lonette McKee is Lila Oliver Rose, a chorus girl who starts out at the Cotton Club and later passes for white as a singer at Vera's nightclub. McKee's character is patterned after the Cotton Club's most famous showgirl, Lena Horne, although Horne never passed for white. Lila's relationship with Sandman is also suggestive of Dorothy Dandridge, who met her first husband, tap-dancer Harold Nicholas, at the Cotton Club. Lila and Sandman's relationship is far more convincing than Dixie and Vera's, and it atypically positions McKee as a romantic heroine. Furthermore, when compared to Diane Lane's bad girl Vera, who dates a married mobster and is unfazed when he commits a brutal murder right in front of her, McKee's Lila also takes on the role of good girl.

In mainstream films that privileged white characters, seldom, if ever, had there been a black couple given near equal importance to that of the film's leading white couple. According to Coppola, Gregory Hines was responsible for ramping up the relationship between Lila and Sandman and insisting "on a story that had a black man and woman kissing and being in love without it being tawdry."[57] From the time Sandman first meets Lila, whether it's his hypnotic gaze as he watches her dance a steamy routine or begging

Lonette McKee and Gregory Hines are treated with deference as a black romantic couple in the Robert Evans/Francis Ford Coppola production *The Cotton Club* (1984).

for her hand in marriage, his passion for Lila is emphatic. When Sandman and Lila finally make love, the scene acknowledges a keen sensitivity to the way in which black sexuality had been typically handled—or avoided—in mainstream cinema up to that time.

Practices of racial discrimination came into full relief at the Cotton Club, and behind the story of white gangsters, Coppola's film attempts to illustrate the segregation and colorism of the early 20th century. The Cotton Club featured the crème de la crème of black entertainment on stage but with few exceptions catered exclusively to white customers. In its later years, the Cotton Club relaxed its admission policy, slightly. Thus, at an early point in the film, Bumpy Rhodes bemoans the fact that he can't get into a club where his own people are the stars. Near the end of the film, after some years have passed, Rhodes is granted entrance to the Cotton Club.

Clay and Sandman's younger sister Winnie (Wynonna Smith) is depicted as the first dark-skinned chorus girl to be hired at the Cotton Club. In actuality, Lucille Wilson, a Cotton Club girl from 1932 to 1940, was the first woman to successfully challenge the skin-color policy.[58] Wilson later married trumpeter Louis Armstrong in 1942. Prior to Wilson's challenge of the color scheme, most of the Cotton Club girls were light enough to pass for white, and some of them did, including Peggy Griffiths who danced on the chorus line with Lena Horne. Griffiths later married a wealthy New Jersey judge and withdrew from black life altogether. At least two other showgirls achieved some measure of success as white performers in film and on Broadway.[59]

Lila's decision to pass for white is, therefore, plausible, but the scenario begs for more detail. What we do learn about Lila is that father is "colored," her mother is white, and she passes for white for better pay, opportunity, and the privilege of being treated like a human being. One is still left wondering, however, when she passes for white, other than singing at Vera's nightclub, where she goes, what she does and with whom, and what emotional cost, if any, does she bear for doing so?

Even though Lila's character is underdeveloped, she is not a stereotype. She is not a clichéd mulatto. There is no apparent tragedy associated with being mixed race or with passing. Lila is not motivated by hubris, fetishization of whiteness, or a fractured psyche. Much like Mignon in *Illusions*, Lila's reasons for passing are pragmatic, and she does it without shunning blackness or fear of being found out. When Lila disappears, for example, and Sandman tracks her down to Vera's white nightclub, she doesn't reject him as Peola did her mother in *Imitation of Life*. Lila welcomes Sandman with open arms. In the end, as opposed to discovery or fear of white rejection, it is Lila's love for a black man, ergo, love of blackness, that keeps her securely tied to the black community.

As it should be, *The Cotton Club*'s best elements can be found in its musical and dance sequences, even though few, if any, are shown in their entirety. McKee is featured in several of these, including an exotic dance opposite Mario Van Peebles to the tune of Duke Ellington's "Creole Love Song." While passing for white, under the pseudonym Angelina, McKee's character sings "Them There Eyes." Her best number, however, is "Ill Wind," a torch song that was first performed at the Cotton Club by Adelaide Hall for the same 1934 revue in which Lena Horne made her debut. Part of a montage that includes shots of newspaper headlines and white gangs invading the Harlem numbers racket, McKee's rendition of "Ill Wind" easily holds its own against that of others who have recorded the song over the years, including Lena Horne, Dinah Washington, and Ella Fitzgerald. McKee also recorded and sang "Stormy Weather," but the footage was excluded from the film's final cut.

Coppola gives us all-too-brief glimpses of a Duke Ellington character, and Larry Marshall does a fine Cab Calloway impersonation, especially when he sings "Minnie the Moocher." Among *The Cotton Club*'s most impressive performances are the tap dance scenes featuring the Hines brothers, whose grandmother Ora Hines once danced at the Cotton Club. Maurice and Gregory began performing together as the Hines Kids when they were, respectively, six and four years old. Later, when their father joined the act, drumming behind them, they became Hines, Hines and Dad. The two brothers argued a lot, and it was a painful time for all of them when Gregory decided to leave the act in the early 1970s.[60]

Coppola incorporated the Hines brothers' history of discord into *The Cotton Club*.[61] When Clay discovers that Sandman has been lobbying Cotton Club management for a solo spot, Clay feels betrayed and leaves the sibling act. Clay and Sandman eventually reunite in a scene that offers a first-rate, emotionally satisfying song-and-dance presentation of "Crazy Rhythm." Knowing that it mirrors actual events in the lives of the Hines brothers makes the performance all the more touching.

In the style of the traditional musical film, *The Cotton Club* reaches its conclusion with a whimsical finale. The scene moves back and forth from the Cotton Club stage to New York's Grand Central Station. Played for the camera as opposed to a fictional audience, the elaborate musical ending is somewhat discordant with the rest of the film. Given the film's musical inspiration, however, it is at the same time fitting. Owney Madden happily goes back to prison, leaving the rackets in the hands of Italian mobsters. Dutch Schultz is killed, which allows Vera to go to Hollywood with Dixie. Sandman and Lila tie the knot.

As Orion prepared to distribute *The Cotton Club*, lawsuits were filed that not only postponed release of the film for several more months but added further to its prerelease reputation as a project destined to fail.[62] *The Cotton Club* finally premiered in New York on December 2, 1984, and opened nationwide two weeks later to graciously mixed critical response.[63] A number of reviewers, for example, pointed out the film's flaws, including a meandering plot, a lack of chemistry between Gere and Lane, and the emphasis on white gangsters at the expense of the black entertainment. Overwhelmingly, the same critics agreed that the film's strongest element was its vibrant musical and dance numbers.[64]

Both the *Village Voice* and *Variety* declared that *The Cotton Club* was by no means the disaster one might have expected from its production publicity. *Village Voice* further noted that while the film sentimentalizes history, it doesn't distort its essence, including that of segregation and racial exploitation. *Variety* also said the film had more entertainment highs than lows and predicted that it would generate good box office returns.[65] *Variety*'s prediction was not entirely off the mark. During the first week of its nationwide opening, *The Cotton Club* ranked fifth in terms of weekly gross receipts, and in the five weeks that followed, it remained within the top ten.[66]

Nevertheless, in a move that film scholar Jon Lewis describes as mysterious, at best, and devious, at worst, Orion, which was responsible for marketing the film, decided to cut its losses early and turned its advertising dollars toward *Amadeus* (1984), thus ensuring that *The Cotton Club* would be regarded not as an homage to African American entertainers but as a financial failure.[67] Despite Orion's botched release, *The Cotton Club* was nominated for two Academy Awards, Best Art Direction-Set Direction and Best Film Editing. It was also nominated for two Golden Globes, Best Motion Picture and Best Director, and it won a BAFTA for Best Costume Design. *The Cotton Club* soundtrack also won a Grammy for Best Jazz Instrumental Performance, Big Band.

The Cotton Club Encore (2019)

In 2015, Francis Coppola came across an old, prerelease recording of *The Cotton Club*. Even though it was thirty minutes longer than the released version, Coppola found that it played faster and made more sense. He realized that when *The Cotton Club* came out, audiences probably didn't understand the story, so he decided to make a new version of the movie. Because MGM, which acquired the rights to *The Cotton Club*, was not interested in restoring the film, Coppola covered the $500,000 cost on his own. In the new, reconstructed cut, known as *The Cotton Club Encore*, "thirteen minutes were deleted to balance out the black and white narratives, and twenty-five minutes from the old, unreleased version were added."[68]

The Cotton Club Encore premiered at the Telluride Film Festival in 2017 and had both its theatrical and DVD releases in 2019. In October 2019, the film also played at the New York Film Festival. In a Q&A following the film's presentation, Coppola admitted that he had cut the restored scenes from the prerelease version due to pressure from investors who complained that the film was "too long," had "too much tap," and "too many black people." Also, because of the lawsuits that had been filed, the director felt threatened that the film might be taken away from him.[69] The added material to this new version includes more time dedicated to Sandman and Clay as well as heretofore unseen musical numbers that turn Coppola's handiwork into an indisputable musical film.

Among the new numbers are a comical duet featuring Jackée Harry, which the *LA Times* considered "showstopping,"[70] and a brief segment that shows a pair of spot-on Nicholas Brothers impersonators. The *pièce de résistance* and the centerpiece musical number of *The Cotton Club Encore* is Lonette McKee's performance of "Stormy Weather," which *Rolling Stone* called "one of the most devastating covers of the song imaginable."[71] The new film doesn't provide much more depth to the character of Lila Rose. Nevertheless, McKee's performance of "Stormy Weather" establishes her as the film's top female lead.

Whereas in Lena Horne's musical numbers in film, the camera might have cut to a furtive shot of the lead male gazing at her, with McKee, throughout her "Stormy Weather" performance, all the important men's eyes are upon her, Sandman and Clay, Dixie, Schultz, and Owney Madden, who stops what he's doing and remarks to himself, "what a beauty." McKee's "Stormy Weather" number in *The Cotton Club Encore* should also place her in the lineage behind Ethel Waters and Lena Horne of women who will forever be associated with the song.

With the added musical numbers, the musical ending is no longer out of sync with the rest of the film. The restoration of balance between black and white is still not exactly equal, but it definitely makes *The Cotton Club Encore* Hollywood's ultimate interracial musical film.

Brewster's Millions (1985)

Following *The Cotton Club*, Lonette McKee reunited with comic Richard Pryor in *Brewster's Millions*. In this seventh remake of a film based on a 1902 novel by George Barr McCutcheon, Pryor was the first African American to play the title character. In a 1945 adaptation of *Brewster's Millions*, Eddie "Rochester" Anderson, the film's only black character, is a servant to Brewster. That film was banned in Memphis by none other than Lloyd T. Binford because Rochester had an important role and the film portrayed "too much social equality and racial mixture."[72]

This 1980s version would have made Binford turn over in his grave. Richard Pryor plays a minor league baseball player who stands to inherit $300 million if he can spend $30 million in thirty days. With Pryor as Brewster it seems that McCutcheon's story was adapting with the changing times. But even though Brewster is now a black man, his rich great-uncle who bequeaths him his inheritance is still a white man. Given the film's silly concept from beginning to end, did the great-uncle have to be a white man? In any event, Brewster's mother, it turns out, is biracial, which makes him something of a mulatto and perhaps explains his attraction to McKee's character Angela Drake, the straitlaced accountant hired to monitor his spending.

Angela's racial identity is never explicitly addressed, but in addition to what we know about the real-life McKee and in looking at her character's choice in men, a mixed race identity might be inferred. Angela is situated in a biracial love triangle. When she first meets Brewster, she is dating a white man. By the end of the film, Angela has fallen for Brewster.

Lonette McKee once dreamt of achieving a level of fame and celebrity that has eluded so many black actresses in Hollywood. With *The Cotton Club*, it was predicted that Lonette McKee would emerge as a big star. Due in no small part to lack of opportunities, that didn't happen. "I have no illusions anymore about where black women stand in the film industry," the actress said in 1987, "especially a woman like me, who doesn't look very black."[73] Reconciling herself to an entertainment career without superstardom, McKee continued to pursue work where she could find it, on screen, on stage, and in nightclubs.

In 1986 McKee returned to the role of tragic chanteuse in *Lady Day at Emerson Bar and Grill*. In this off-Broadway show McKee played Billie Holiday, the legendary jazz singer whose remarkable talent has often been overshadowed by the lurid details of her personal life. Nicknamed "Lady Day" by her good friend and saxophonist Lester Young, Holiday was raped by a neighbor at age eleven and working as a prostitute by the age of twelve. She also had a reputation for gambling, drinking, swearing and fighting. In the 1940s, Holiday started using heroin, and she was sentenced to one year in prison for drug possession in 1947. Her destructive way of life took its toll, and in 1959, at the age of 44, Billie Holiday died of cardiac failure.[74]

Much like *Lady Sings the Blues*, and the William Dufty biography upon which it is based, reviews of *Lady Day at Emerson Bar and Grill*, which is set in a seedy bar four months before the singer's death, point to an emphasis on the more sordid details of Holiday's life. As it was with *Show Boat*, McKee's personal life was compared to that of her character's. McKee, reports said, was able to evoke Lady Day because she, too, had suffered abuse and racism. She drew on the painful experiences of her life, which included leaving Detroit as a teenager to get away from her cruel father, and a former dependence on violent men, which she attributed to her difficult childhood.[75]

McKee's character Darcey Leigh in Bertrand Tavernier's *Round Midnight* (1986) was also patterned after Billie Holiday.[76] The drug-addicted, tragic star of this film, however, is Dexter Gordon, who plays saxophonist Dale Turner. In *Round Midnight*, McKee is simply the exotic singer who, in the tradition of Lena Horne, appears onscreen briefly to sing "How Long Has This Been Going On?" and then quietly disappears. Around this time,

McKee also had a small part in another Francis Ford Coppola film, *Gardens of Stone* (1987), opposite James Earl Jones.

McKee found work on the small screen as well. In the 1980s she could be seen in numerous television series, including *Spenser: For Hire* (1985), *Miami Vice* (1986), *The Equalizer* (1985) and *Amen* (1989). In the television movie *The Women of Brewster Place* (1989), adapted from the Gloria Naylor novel, and produced by Oprah Winfrey's Harpo Productions, Lonette McKee was part of an ensemble cast that included Cicely Tyson, Oprah Winfrey, Mary Alice, Robin Givens, Jackée, and Lynn Whitfield. In this four-part miniseries about the lives of black women in an urban housing project, McKee took on a different sort of tragic role. McKee plays Lorraine, a troubled woman whose experience of alienation comes not from failing to conform to a particular racial norm but rather from not conforming to the sexual norm.

Lorraine is a lesbian who lives with her partner in Brewster Place. Unlike her partner, Lorraine cannot fully embrace her lesbian identity. She is constantly in fear of being found out and attempts to pass as heterosexual. This results in a fateful argument between the couple, which motivates Lorraine to go out alone one night and culminates in her rape by a neighborhood thug. While still in a state of shock from the assault, Lorraine mistakes one of the film's only decent black men—the project janitor—for her attacker and beats him senseless with a two-by-four.

After divorcing Leo Compton in 1990, Lonette McKee fell upon hard times. Work was scarce and consequently she had no choice but to move to a drug-infested Brooklyn neighborhood where gunfire kept her up at night.[77] It was, perhaps, these hard times that influenced McKee's decision to star in the television movie *Dangerous Passions*. In this clichéd melodrama, which originally aired on ABC in 1990, McKee plays a woman caught in a love triangle with leading men Carl Weathers and Billy Dee Williams.

Ignited by the successes of Spike Lee's *She's Gotta Have It* (1986) and Robert Townsend's *Hollywood Shuffle* (1987), the 1990s ushered in a new wave of black cinema. Much like the race movies of the early 20th century and the black movie boom of the 1970s, this third wave of black cinema began on a shoestring with the efforts of independent black filmmakers. Once it was proven there was money to be made, major studios were eager to commandeer some of the new black-oriented films. The year 1991 alone saw the release of numerous black-themed and black-directed films, both independent and studio-financed, such as *Daughters of the Dust*, *Strictly Business*, *The Five Heartbeats*, *New Jack City*, *Rage in Harlem*, *Boyz n the Hood*, and Lonette McKee's next feature film, *Jungle Fever*, which was written, directed, and produced by Spike Lee.

Jungle Fever (1991)

Jungle Fever is the first of several creative ventures that Lonette McKee had with Spike Lee. Their other collaborations include recording her 1992 album *Natural Love* for Lee's music label and small roles in the films *Malcolm X* (1992), *He Got Game* (1998) and *She Hate Me* (2004). In *Jungle Fever*, McKee stars as biracial woman scorned Drew Purify. Drew is an educated, professional woman and a devoted wife and mother. Her husband, Flipper Purify, played by Wesley Snipes, is an architect. The happily married, bourgeois couple lives in Harlem with their young daughter Ming. When, out of mere racial curiosity, Flipper begins an affair with his Italian American secretary, family harmony is torn apart, and the racially polarized neighborhoods of black Harlem and white Bensonhurst collide.

The woman Flipper has an affair with is Angie Tucci, played by Anabella Sciorra. Angie lives with her father and two brothers in a predominantly Italian American neighborhood of Bensonhurst. If Lee's rendering of Italian Americans in *Jungle Fever* feels somewhat familiar, it's likely because several of the actors, including Frank Vincent, who plays Angie's father, and Michael Imperioli, one of Angie's brothers, appeared just a few months earlier in Martin Scorsese's *Goodfellas* (1990). Vincent, Imperioli, and Sciorra also went on to play extended roles in HBO's successful TV series *The Sopranos* (1999–2007).

Others who apparently walked straight off the set of *Goodfellas* and onto *Jungle Fever* are Joe D'Onofrio, who plays a Bensonhurst "goombah," as well as Debi Mazar and Gina Mastrogiacomo, who appear as Angie's two best friends, Denise and Louise. John Turturro, not from the *Goodfellas* cast but a player in a number of other Spike Lee films, was cast as Angie's jilted boyfriend, Paulie Carbone. Paulie spends his days taking care of his widower father, played by Anthony Quinn, and single-handedly running the family business, a small neighborhood establishment with a newsstand, lunch counter and soda fountain called the Candy Store.

On the African American side, in addition to McKee and Snipes, the cast includes Lee, who wrote himself into the script as Flipper's neighbor and best friend, Cyrus. Lee also cast his then-girlfriend, supermodel Veronica Webb, as his wife and Drew's best friend, Vera. Like Drew, Vera is biracial. Ruby Dee and Ossie Davis are Flipper's parents, Lucinda and the Good Reverend Doctor Purify. Samuel Jackson (who also had a small role in *Goodfellas*) is Flipper's crack-addicted brother, Gator. Halle Berry made her feature film debut in *Jungle Fever* as Gator's crack-whore girlfriend, Vivian. Tyra Ferrell has a part as Orin Goode, a regular patron of the newsstand at Paulie's Candy Store. Though its potential is never fully explored, Orin and Paulie are the parties to a second interracial relationship in *Jungle Fever*.

Until the late 1960s, black-white interracial romance was a scarcity in Hollywood films. On the rare occasion when it was depicted, it was most often shown as occurring between white men and mixed race, typically light skinned women. Films like *Show Boat* (1936, 1951), *Pinky* (1949), and *Kings Go Forth* (1958), which all feature white actresses in the role of a fair-skinned, mixed race woman, exemplify this pattern. With the exception of D.W. Griffith's *The Birth of a Nation* (1915), in which principal black characters are played by whites in blackface, rarely, if ever, did Old Hollywood's depiction of interracial desire involve a black man and a white woman. While *The Birth of a Nation*, like the aforementioned films, features a white actress as the mulatto love interest of a white man, it also has two black men (white actors in blackface)—Gus, the renegade, and Silas Lynch, a mulatto—lusting after white women.

Griffith's various representations of interracial desire in *The Birth of a Nation* serve as a warning against miscegenation. Lydia, the mulatto woman, who is maid and mistress to a powerful politician, is demonized and considered a threat to national security. Nevertheless, her relationship with the white man is presumably longstanding and seemingly secure. When it comes to the pairing of black men with white women, *The Birth of a Nation* rejects any possibility of a relationship whatsoever. Both Gus and Silas are entirely unsuccessful in their attempts to woo women of the opposite race. The outcome for Gus and the young girl who is the object of his affection turns out especially bad. To avoid Gus's advances, the girl jumps off a cliff to her death. Gus is then hunted down by whites and lynched. While the end results of interracial mixing in *Show Boat*, *Pinky*, and *Kings Go Forth* aren't quite as grim, they nevertheless convey the same message: mixed race relationships are an ill-fated taboo.

Island in the Sun (1957) was the first Hollywood feature to employ African American actors in principal roles involving interracial relationships. In addition to the love that blossomed between Dorothy Dandridge and John Justin, the film also purports a relationship between Harry Belafonte and Joan Fontaine. Owing to the times, interaction between the latter couple is so restrained that the two don't even seem to like, let alone love, one another, and ultimately, their relationship, unlike that of the white man and mixed race woman, does not survive. Belafonte fared only marginally better at interracial romance in *The World, the Flesh and the Devil* (1959), in which he, a white man, and a white woman are the only people left alive on the planet. It was not until 1967, just a few months after the decision in *Loving v. Virginia*, that a Hollywood studio presented a clearly discernible and optimistic scenario for a black man and a white woman in *Guess Who's Coming to Dinner* (1967).

Guess Who's Coming to Dinner stars Sidney Poitier and Katharine Houghton as an interracial couple who have to break the news of their engagement to their parents. The action takes place in a single day and culminates in a meal with the couple and their respective parents at the white family's dinner table. Throughout the course of the day, reactions from all four parents are gauged, but the couple's only real concern is the white parents' approval, which they are certain to win given that Poitier's character is a doctor, humanitarian, and Nobel Prize candidate. To top it off, he's also saving himself for marriage. That being said, *Guess Who's Coming to Dinner* marks the first time a black actor kissed a white actress in a major Hollywood picture, an achievement for which both Houghton and the film's director, Stanley Kramer, received death threats.

Shortly after *Guess Who's Coming to Dinner* (1967) came *The Story of a Three-Day Pass* (1968), a fanciful and more convincing representation of a black man-white woman romance. Although *The Story of a Three-Day Pass* is a French film, it deserves mention in this context because its protagonist is a black soldier in the U.S. Army, and Melvin Van Peebles, its writer and director, is African American. Denied opportunities in Hollywood, Van Peebles moved to France in order to pursue a career as a filmmaker. *Guess Who's Coming to Dinner* and *The Story of a Three-Day Pass* were soon followed by the black movie boom and blaxploitation of the 1970s, which turned the taboo of interracial desire on its head. Independently produced films like Van Peebles' *Sweet Sweetback's Badasssss Song* (1971) and *Super Fly* (1972), as well as studio features like *Shaft* (1971), not only coupled their black heroes with white women but also showed, with graphic specificity, the white woman as the black hero's concubine.

When the black movie boom was over, Hollywood went back to be being mostly mute on the subject of interracial relationships. In the decade that followed, John Waters' *Hairspray* (1988) stands out for pairing a black teenage boy with a white girl, while in films like *Brewster's Millions*, *Flashdance* (1983), *Soul Man* (1986) and *Angel Heart* (1987), Hollywood returned to the conventional formula of pairing mixed race women with white men. However, instead of using white actresses, as had been done in earlier decades, the mixed race roles of the 1980s went to biracial actresses like Lonette McKee, Jennifer Beals, Lisa Bonet, and Rae Dawn Chong. Despite this apparent boon for biracial actresses, for the most part, when it came to films featuring black-white interracial desire, the 1980s was a time of dearth. Thus, by the early 1990s, when *Jungle Fever* was released, interracial romance, especially between a black man and a white woman, was once again a taboo in Hollywood.

Jungle Fever, the title of Spike Lee's film, is a term that originally referred to illnesses contracted in and native to the tropics, but at some point, "jungle fever" became synonymous with interracial sexual attraction. "Jungle" alludes to white colonizers and their relationships with black and brown women of the tropics, while "fever" implies that such an attraction is a sickness. Technically, then, "jungle fever" refers to a white person's aberrant sexual desire for a black person. As used by Lee, however, "jungle fever" applies to both participants in an interracial relationship. In the film, when Flipper reveals to Cyrus that he cheated on Drew with a white woman, Cyrus tells him: "You got a big problem, you and her. The both of yous got the fever ... the both of yous got jungle fever." Stevie Wonder contributed a number of original compositions to the film's soundtrack, and his lyrics to the film's title song confirm that in *Jungle Fever*, the fever works both ways.

It's difficult to pinpoint when, exactly, "jungle fever" took on a sexual, interracial connotation. In 1958, more than thirty years before Stevie Wonder, Charlie Feathers, a white American rockabilly musician from Mississippi, also co-wrote and recorded a song titled "Jungle Fever." In it, Feathers sings of looking for his lover among leopards, lions, and "darkies." Nearly thirty years before Feathers, Walter Donaldson wrote the music and MGM executive Howard Dietz penned lyrics to another "Jungle Fever" song, which was performed by the Mills Brothers for the 1934 Civil War movie, *Operator 13*.

With its Civil War theme, depictions of planter society, and a love affair that unites North and South, *Operator 13* was promoted as the successor to *The Birth of a Nation* (1915). With respect to its treatment of blacks, however, the two films are very different. *Operator 13* is entirely lacking in the animosity and vitriol that *The Birth of a Nation* has for its black and mixed race characters. For the time period, the film's unabashed, doting, representation of black-white interracial desire is also a surprising anomaly. *Operator 13* stars Marion Davies as Gail Loveless, an actress who joins the Union army as a spy. Code named "Operator 13," Loveless falls in love with Captain Jack Gailliard, a Confederate spy, played by Gary Cooper. In a variation on the shtick employed in *The Birth of a Nation*, with the aid of burnt cork, Loveless poses as Lucille, a mulatto slave and laundress, at a Confederate encampment.

Davies' comical antics as Lucille might bring to mind Topsy, the buffoonish child character played by a white woman in blackface in *Uncle Tom's Cabin* (1927). Davies' performance is disarmingly affable, however, and Lucille is no pickaninny. Lucille is an undeniable object of desire. At the time of the film's release, one reviewer described her as "a pretty black Topsy," while another reporter declared that it was in the dark makeup that Davies was the most beautiful.[78] Disguised as Lucille, it doesn't take long for Loveless to convince the Rebels that she's just a giddy mulatto with nothing but white men on her mind. Even before Lucille meets Gailliard, she is wooed by another Confederate soldier, Captain Sweeney.

Sweeney's pursuit of the mulatto is out in the open and, with the exception of an elder male slave, entirely unopposed. Sure, the audience knows that Lucille is a white woman in blackface, but within the diegesis, the characters, at least those on the Confederate side, including Sweeney, think Lucille is black. The film has its limits, though. The relationship between hero and heroine cannot fully blossom until after Loveless trades her slave disguise for that of a Southern belle. Nevertheless, even when she is in black-face, it's apparent that Captain Gailliard has a thing for the "pretty colored gal."

The Mills Brothers' captivating performance of "Jungle Fever" in *Operator 13* cleverly masks and accentuates Gailliard's attraction to Lucille. On the surface, because "Jungle Fever" is sung to slaves gathered for a medicine show, it gives the impression that black men are singing an ode to a black woman. "Jungle Fever," however, with its music and lyrics by two white men and its inherent interracial connotation, immediately follows Lucille's second, rather intimate encounter with Gailliard. As the Mills Brothers sing, Lucille appears at the center of the all-black crowd. Her presence, though brief, coincides with the Mills Brothers crooning about reconciling with a dusky, dark-haired, African siren.

Despite giving his film a title loaded with racial meaning, Spike Lee maintained that the interracial angle in *Jungle Fever* was merely a "hook" to get viewers interested. The heart of *Jungle Fever*, he said, is the destruction wreaked upon families by the crack epidemic.[79] To its credit, *Jungle Fever* is one of the few films of the 1990s to deal with crack addiction from the perspective of an African American family, and Gator's story arc, addiction, and strained family relationships are illustrated to great effect. However, looming much larger in *Jungle Fever* than the crack epidemic is the notion that everyone is vexed by the power of race and skin color ideology.

Even before the story begins, the unwieldy hook of interracial tension rears its head. An opening intertitle dedicates the film to Yusef Hawkins, the 16-year-old black teenager from the East New York neighborhood of Brooklyn, who was shot to death after being set upon by a mob of white youths from Bensonhurst, Brooklyn. On August 23, 1989, Yusef and three of his friends journeyed from East New York to Bensonhurst to look at a used car being advertised for sale. When they arrived in Bensonhurst they were confronted by a mob of 30 to 40 young men wielding baseball bats. After being taunted by the mob, Yusef was shot to death.

In the press it was often reported that the Bensonhurst men had been angered that a white girl from their neighborhood was dating a black youth. However, the main catalyst for the violence appears to have been a 17-year-old, crack-addicted white girl and resident of Bensonhurst who had threatened to summon her black and Hispanic friends to beat up on neighborhood whites. Yusef's murder shocked New Yorkers, lit a fire under Civil Rights leaders, and undermined Mayor Edward Koch's bid for a fourth term. David Dinkins defeated Koch in the Democratic primary, and in 1990, he became New York's first and, to date, only African American mayor.[80]

Within the world of the story itself, racial tension in *Jungle Fever* is first revealed early on, at Flipper's architectural firm. Flipper, who has been a valuable member of the company since it was founded, is the only black employee. The African American secretary he once had has moved on, and his bosses have been in search of a replacement. Flipper arrives to work one day to discover that his newly hired secretary is not African American, as he had requested; she is the Italian American Angie Tucci. When Flipper expresses frustration at the hiring decision, his bosses accuse him of reverse racism. Flipper loses the battle with his bosses, and Angie stays. The two get to know one another over late night work sessions and take-out dinners, and before long a rather tepid love affair begins.

Far more impassioned than the so-called fever in *Jungle Fever* are the various reactions to it. Angie's best friends, for example, are divided upon hearing the news. Louise thinks that sleeping with a black guy is disgusting. Denise reasons that it's the 1990s, and there's nothing wrong with it, but she also warns that there will be trouble if Angie's father finds out. When Mike Tucci does catch wind of the affair, he throws Angie out of the family home, but not before battering her with the same kind of crazed anger one imagines might have possessed members of the Bensonhurst mob that killed Yusef Hawkins. "What kind of woman are you? … I didn't raise you to be with no nigger! I'd rather you be a mass murderer," says the father as he brutally beats his own daughter, first with his hands and then his belt.

Mike's rage, and that of the Bensonhurst mob, evokes the history of Italian, and other southern and eastern Europeans who immigrated to the United States in the late 19th and early 20th century. These "new immigrants," as they were called, were not initially categorized as white, nor were they seen as fit for citizenship. As such, they occupied a status in between black and white. While there were certainly instances of new immigrants forming alliances with African Americans, a good deal of them, it seems, soon learned the importance of being "not black." New immigrants consolidated their own identity and status as whites by buying into white supremacy and vehemently shunning black people.[81]

Passionate anti-black sentiment is regularly expressed by a group of "goombahs" that frequent the Candy Store. Illustrating America's racial contradictions and its love-hate relationship with African Americans and African American culture, Vinny (Nicholas Turturro), who is the most vocal of these men, takes advantage of any and every opportunity to denounce black people. Vinny also enjoys blasting the sounds of African American rapper Flavor Flav in his car when he's driving.

Barbs directed at Frankie Botz (Michael Badalucco), another member of the group, also point to the racial history of Italian Americans and suggest that even late into the 20th century they fit somewhat uneasily within the category of whiteness. Early in the film Botz drowns his sorrows in chocolate egg creams over the loss of his Italian American girlfriend to a "pretty boy" with blond hair and blue eyes. "You'd think they'd want their own kind," Botz says as he vents to his buddies. Later on, when Vinny insinuates that Botz's mother is black, Botz becomes enraged. "My mother's not black," he protests. "She's just dark. There are dark Italians. Hey, I'm as white as anybody in here!"

Racially based rhetoric and insults are not limited to *Jungle Fever*'s Italian American characters, either. In one scene, which reads like a response to *Guess Who's Coming to Dinner*, Flipper and Angie are invited to dinner at the home of Lucinda and the Good Reverend Doctor. Before the meal has hardly begun, the Good Reverend Doctor begins condemning Flipper and Angie's affair by relating it to interracial intimacies during the antebellum period. Put on a pedestal by Southern society, he explains, the white woman was "too holy and pure to be touched by any man." Meanwhile, at the end of the day, the white man was down at the slave quarters, "grabbing up every piece of black poontang he could lay his hands on." The Good Reverend Doctor concludes his two-minute diatribe by describing his son's actions as fishing "in the white man's cesspool" and then excuses himself from the table.

When Flipper and Angie go out to eat in public, they are also met with opposition. Lashawn, a waitress played by Queen Latifah, refuses to acknowledge the interracial couple seated in her section of a Harlem restaurant. When she finally does get around to waiting on them, Lashawn rolls her eyes while reading off the daily specials and then impugns Flipper's racial authenticity by recommending that he order the "blackened catfish." Lashawn's reaction to Flipper and Angie would likely have resonated with many African American women who, for decades, have occupied one of the most disadvantaged positions within the relationship market.

Since the 1960s, African Americans have become the most unmarried group of people in the country. This is, in part, because factors such as mass incarceration, violence, educational failure, and lack of economic opportunity have diminished the ranks of black men, thereby contributing to an imbalance between marriageable black men and available black women. Augmenting the man shortage is the fact that in the post–Civil Rights era, black men have become twice as likely to intermarry as black women. Black women, on the other hand, tend to intermarry less than any other minority group. Adding insult to injury, as a study from one of the nation's top dating websites suggests, black women are quite likely the least sought-after demographic in the dating pool.[82]

Even though intermarriage among black men is only part of the story, it seems that for many black women, the sight of a black man with a white woman embodies every obstacle black women face in trying to find a suitable mate and elicits visceral opposition. In a 2010 commentary for *Essence* magazine, African American singer and songwriter Jill Scott spoke to this phenomenon when she wrote of the handsome, wealthy black man she had just befriended and how she secretly hoped he was married to a black woman. When she learned that the man's wife was white, Scott said that she felt her spirit "wince." Scott declared that such a reaction is common among African American women.[83]

In a 1993 essay, in which she vowed to relinquish the wrath she feels toward black man-white woman couples, African American author Bebe Moore Campbell expressed a similar sentiment. Campbell wrote that for many black women, when successful black men date or marry white women, it's like "being passed over for the prom by the boy of their dreams, causing them pain, rage, and an overwhelming sense of betrayal and personal rejection." The hurtful message that black women receive, Campbell went on to say, is one of "blatant sexism and eerie internecine racism."[84]

That hurtful message seems to be at the root of the anger expressed by Angela Bassett's character, Bernadine, in *Waiting to Exhale* (1995). When Bernadine's husband informs her that he plans to divorce her for his white bookkeeper, she says, "I give you eleven fuckin' years of my life, and you're telling me me that you're leaving me for a white woman?" When her husband asks, "Would it be better if she were black?" Bernadine fires back, "No, it'd be better if you were black." Reinforcing the catastrophic nature of the husband's revelation, as the couple is having this conversation, the disturbing humming tone of the Emergency Alert System can be heard playing on a television or radio in the background. Shortly, thereafter, Bernadine, much like Drew, unleashes her rage when she discards her husband's personal effects. While Drew disposes of Flipper's belongings by tossing them out a second-story window and onto the street, Bernadine takes the fury to another level. She transfers the contents of her husband's walk-in closet to his BMW and sets it all on fire.

In *Jungle Fever*, a lengthy and partially improvised scene, which takes place not long after Drew has learned of Flipper's affair, speaks to the animosity some black women feel toward black men and their white women as well as the frustrations that black women experience in the relationship market. The scene, known as the "war council," might well be regarded as the precursor to *Waiting to Exhale*. In it, Drew and four of her girlfriends extemporize on race, class, and skin color as it relates to dating and mating. One of the first issues to come up is the man shortage. "Ain't no good black men out there," says

Nilda (Phyllis Yvonne Stickney), one of the group's more outspoken members. According to Nilda, most black men are incarcerated, addicted to drugs, or gay, and the good ones know they're in demand, so there's no incentive for them to be monogamous.

Nilda is also the one to suggest that, for many black men, being with a white woman is not just one of the perks of prosperity, it's a requirement. "Most of the brothers who have made it got white women on their arms," she says. "In order to go up that little ladder of success, seems like you've got to have 'Miss Thing' on your arm." That white women are also regarded as problematic in the equation is another topic for discussion. "You can't walk down the street with your man without 29,000 white bitches coming on to him," says Drew. Thus, not only does Drew feel rejected because her husband is having an affair, she feels further betrayed because the affair is with a white woman. As if that weren't enough, *Jungle Fever* makes Drew's experience of her husband's betrayal a triple whammy by suggesting that her pain is further intensified because she is biracial and light-skinned.

That Drew's father is white and her mother black is revealed when Flipper visits Drew at her workplace and tries to make amends. As soon as Flipper attempts to speak, Drew launches into a racial tirade: "Well, I guess I just wasn't light enough for you, was I, Flipper? You had to eventually go get yourself a white girl, didn't you?" Drew continues, accusing both Flipper and Cyrus of having a color complex because the only women they have ever dated were light-skinned black women. Drew, it seems, has always suspected that her husband was color-struck and that it was her skin color that attracted him to her. For Drew, Flipper's dalliance with a white woman serves as confirmation of her suspicion and arouses deep-seated racial insecurities.

Drew goes on to recount how she was taunted as child because of her mixed race: "I've told you what happened to me when I was growing up. I've explained to you. I've poured my heart out. I've told you how they called me high yella, yellow bitch, white honky, honky white, white nigger, nigger white, octoroon, quadroon, half breed, mongrel,

Lonette McKee is Wesley Snipes' biracial wife, and a casualty of jungle fever, in Spike Lee's film about interracial relationships, *Jungle Fever* (1991).

and what do you do?" When, in response, Flipper points out that maybe she has a color problem, too, Drew admits that he might be right. "Maybe that's why this hurts me so much," she says.

Later on in the film, mixed race persons are further characterized as being especially disturbed when Angie tries to have a conversation with Flipper about their future and the possibility of them having children together. "No half-black, half-white babies for me," says Flipper, despite the fact that his own wife is biracial. "A lot of times," he goes on to say, "the mixed kids come out all mixed up, a bunch of mixed nuts."

Not only does *Jungle Fever* cast Drew as racially tragic, it also uses her to provide the film with its most sensual moments. Given that Angie's relationship with Flipper is the movie's hook and centerpiece, one might expect more eroticism from the woman who engages in the double transgression of interracial and extramarital sex and whose last name is a pun with the word "tushie" (slang for buttocks). Such is not the case. In her only graphic lovemaking scene, Angie is depicted as a somewhat restrained lover who remains clothed during the entire event.

Drew, on the other hand, is portrayed as a rambunctious lover, and her reputation for making too much noise during sex is the inside family joke. She has two partially nude sex scenes that are like bookends for the film. *Jungle Fever* begins and ends with Drew and Flipper having sex. When we last see Drew, the barriers to Flipper's interracial love affair have won out. He and Angie have parted company. Drew and Flipper have reunited in the bedroom but are not living under the same roof. During their lovemaking, Drew weeps uncontrollably. When it's over, Drew, with her back turned, tells Flipper he should leave. Seemingly unfazed by his wife's grief, Flipper visits with his daughter in the next room, while Drew is left alone sobbing.

Despite a fine acting performance from McKee, *Jungle Fever* reduces Drew to a randy tragic mulatto. It also takes the old line of depicting interracial desire as an ill-fated taboo. What sets *Jungle Fever* apart from many earlier films with interracial relationships is that Lee gives equal time to voicing black opposition as he does to white. Furthermore, as opposed to pairing a white man with a mixed race woman, *Jungle Fever* features a black man and a white woman. As such, Drew is not a participant in the film's interracial desire, but rather, as the child of an interracial marriage and victim of Flipper's infidelity, a bystander to it. Nevertheless, it is Drew, the mixed race woman, who bears the brunt of jungle fever in *Jungle Fever*.

The other victim of *Jungle Fever*'s interracial affair is Paulie Carbone who, as it turns out, is the film's most virtuous male character. At first, Paulie is heartbroken by his girlfriend's betrayal. However, unlike Drew, who during the "war council" declared that she would not date a white man, Paulie is emboldened by the experience and spurred to seek love across racial lines. Paulie asks Orin out on a date. As Paulie makes his pitch to her, Stevie Wonder's "Queen in the Black" plays conspicuously in the background. Here, Lee flips the script on conventional mainstream Hollywood films by making the dark-skinned Orin Goode the film's queen and ultimate prize.

Later on, Paulie risks being disowned by his father and endures a beating from Vinny and his gang just so he can go on a date with Orin. Though beat up and disheveled, Paulie makes his way to Orin's place. Orin invites him in, and the door closes, literally and figuratively, upon the film's other interracial couple. Amidst an onslaught of pessimism, through Orin and Paulie's developing friendship, *Jungle Fever* allows a small sliver of hope for interracial love.

In 1993, Lonette McKee revisited passing for white in *Alex Haley's Queen*. In this television miniseries, starring Halle Berry as the title character, McKee attempts to teach Berry the finer points of survival as a whore in the post–Civil War South. Around the same time, some ten years after her first appearance in *Show Boat*, Lonette McKee was asked to reprise her role as Julie. McKee readily accepted, declaring that this time around, she intended to make Julie a little blacker. She didn't want to play Julie as a character trying to pass as white but rather "just plain Julie—as she is."[85]

As music scholar Todd Decker points out, casting a mixed race woman in the part of Julie altered the character's interpretation. According to Decker, other eminent women who had played the part of Julie, such as Helen Morgan and Carol Bruce, sang Julie as if she were a white woman. Cleo Laine and Lonette McKee, on the other hand, sang Julie black. However, although Laine and McKee both allowed Julie to sing the blues, there was still a difference in how the two mixed race performers handled the role. With Laine, who was known to deflect issues of race and resented attempts by either the press or her management at being stereotyped, her connection to blackness in *Show Boat* was implicit.[86]

In contrast, McKee's relationship to blackness in the 1994 *Show Boat* was emphatic. For example, when one of the characters asks Julie how she knows a "colored folks' song," one critic noted, "McKee doesn't play the anxious tragic mulatto, worried that her true identity will be revealed; instead, she laughs and gaily waves the query away, explaining that her mama taught it to her." McKee also had no problem placing her own personal history in a context side by side that of Julie. In one interview, for example, referring to her own racial heritage, she said, "it's astonishing—I get to play what I am." On another occasion, McKee said that she had never considered passing for white, but she understood Julie as a woman much like herself, "a black woman trying to survive in a racist society."[87]

Unlike any other actress that came before her, Lonette McKee openly expressed Julie's blackness, transforming the role of Julie for late 20th-century audiences. McKee also paved the way for other, more visibly black actresses to play Julie. In late 1995, when McKee left the show, light-skinned pop singer Marilyn McCoo took over amid concerns that her appearance and connection to the all-black pop group 5th Dimension would render her unbelievable as a character that passes for white. After McCoo, Garth Drabinsky, the show's producer, continued to cast black Julies for Broadway, London, and his touring companies.[88]

In the 1990s, as Lonette McKee approached her 40s, she decided take more control over her career by rejecting any roles that she considered demeaning. Around the same time, she also noticed that the scripts she was receiving from agents and mangers were mediocre and uninteresting. In their mid- to late thirties, McKee said, too many gifted women find that plum acting roles are no longer available to them. "We become only wives and mothers on screen, playing only supporting roles to the male leads."[89]

True to these words, in 1992, beginning with Spike Lee's *Malcolm X*, McKee began appearing as a tragic maternal figure. In *Malcolm X* she is Louise Little, mother of the controversial human rights activist, who loses custody of her children and is committed to a mental hospital after her husband is executed by white supremacists. In the television movie *Blind Faith* (1998), McKee plays mother to a teenage boy who is wrongfully convicted of murdering a white boy. In *He Got Game* (1998), her character, Martha Shuttlesworth, is a casualty of domestic violence, survived by her two young children and the husband convicted for her death, played by Denzel Washington.

In *Lift* (2001), McKee's character, a former victim of child abuse, has become a selfish and detached adult. Her daughter (Kerry Washington), a high-end shoplifter, tries to placate her with stolen goods. As mother to the whistleblower in *She Hate Me* (2004), if not tragic, she is certainly bitter about being trapped in a loveless marriage with her aging, diabetic husband (Jim Brown). In the independent feature *Luv* (2012), McKee is both mother and grandmother. Her son, an ex-convict played by the rapper Common, is killed in a gunfight while trying to teach his 11-year-old nephew how to be a man in the streets of Baltimore.

Not all of the actress's roles during this stage of her career have been entirely somber. In the television movie *Having Our Say: The Delany Sisters' First 100 Years* (1999), Lonette McKee was Nannette Logan Delany, known as Mama Delany in the film. Nannette was born free in 1861 to James Miliam, a white man, and Martha Logan, a "free issue" qua-droon woman. While studying at St. Augustine's University in Raleigh, North Carolina, Nanette met Henry Delany, who was born a slave in 1858. The couple married in 1886 and gave birth to ten children, including Sadie and Bessie Delany, the sisters who, at ages 102 and 100, respectively, were the subject of a 1991 *New York Times* article which was followed by a best-selling book, then a Broadway play, and finally the television movie.

According to the Delany sisters, Nannette's great-grandmother, Eliza, and their great-aunt Patricia were the children of a white woman and her slave. The two mixed race children were born while their mother's husband, John Logan, was away from home, fighting in the War of 1812. When Logan returned, he forgave his wife for the affair and raised the mulatto children as his own, alongside the couple's seven white daughters. When Eliza grew up, she became involved with a white man and had four children by him, including Nannette's mother, Martha Logan.[90]

The stars of *Having Our Say* are Diahann Carroll, who plays older sister Sadie and Ruby Dee, who is Bessie. Lisa Arindell and Audra McDonald play the sisters in their youth. Amy Madison is Amy Hill Hearth, the *New York Times* journalist to whom the sisters relay their life story. Sadie and Bessie's grandmother, Martha Logan, is played by Della Reese, and Mykelti Williamson is their father, Henry Delany. McKee's role as Mama Delany is a supporting one, in which she appears in flashbacks as the Delany sisters relay their story to Hearth. Though her character suffers in her later years from the loss of her husband and then dementia, she is mostly depicted, and remembered, as the intelligent, dutiful and loving mother and wife of an early 20th-century black bourgeois family.

In 1999, Lonette McKee also appeared in *A Day in Black and White,* an independent feature written and directed by Jamaican-born filmmaker Desmond Hall. Set in New York City, *A Day in Black and White* is a succession of dialogues about American race relations that brings to mind Spike Lee's *Jungle Fever*. In a scene that debates the merits of Lee's work, Hall, in fact, pays homage to the auteur. *A Day in Black and White*, much like *Jungle Fever*, is mostly concerned with black-white racial relations, and it exposes the prejudices, myths, and beliefs from both perspectives. Hall's deft comedy, however, has a decidedly lighter and more conciliatory tone.

Lonette McKee's character, Viv, also known as "black woman in office," is just that, a black woman who engages in dialogue with two white men in the conference room of a law office. Over the course of their conversation, she champions affirmative action and rappers and comes down against European beauty standards and black women pressing their hair. McKee has often described herself as being pro-black, almost militant. As such, one imagines that "black woman in office" is, perhaps, much like the "real" Lonette McKee, herself.

McKee's role as mother in the *mixploitation*[91] film *Honey* (2003) and its sequel *Honey 2* (2011) reflect the change in attitudes toward mixed race identity that has transpired since the actress first began her film career. *Honey* and *Honey 2* feature racially diverse casts and revel in all that is mixed. In keeping with this formula, the film capitalizes on the interracial aspect of McKee's image, casting her as a non-white but otherwise racially indistinct.

Jessica Alba, the actress who, ethnically, is reported to be a mix of Mexican, Danish, French and Spanish, plays the title character and lead role in *Honey* and McKee's daughter. Like McKee, Alba has claimed she was initially stereotyped into certain roles because of her looks and her perceived ethnicity. In contrast to McKee, however, Alba—who is nowhere to be found in the *Honey* sequel—discovered that the lighter she dyed her hair, the more Hollywood insiders were able to look beyond her ethnicity.[92]

A decisive moment for McKee in this later stage of her career came when her manager sent her a script for the role of a maid. McKee fired the manager and spent the next three years studying screenwriting and learning all that she could about independent filmmaking. The end result was the independent feature *Dream Street* (2010) written, directed, and produced by McKee. *Dream Street* did not find a wide release. Around 2010, McKee moved back to Detroit in order to spend more quality time with her mother and younger sister, and in 2012, she began teaching acting workshops at City College of New York.[93]

7

Jennifer Beals

White But Not Quite

*I know I won't be cast as a Swede or a woman born and raised in the Congo,
but I do have more options than some actresses.*[1]   —Jennifer Beals

The middle child of an Irish Catholic American schoolteacher and an African American grocer, Jennifer Beals became a pop and fashion icon overnight after starring in the 1983 hit movie *Flashdance*. Although universally panned by critics, *Flashdance*, which tells the story of a welder turned ballet dancer, was a critic-proof major marketing event. Not only was it the third highest grossing film of 1983, but its soundtrack was also one of the year's top selling albums and the clothing worn by Beals ignited a fashion trend. Since that time, in both film and television, Jennifer Beals has portrayed a broad array of characters, exhibiting racial identities that range from mixed race to white to Latina to ambiguously ethnic, and she has amassed a body of work unconstrained by a black racial heritage.

Jennifer Beals has always been forthcoming about her African American father and over the years has publicly expressed her fondness for him and his memory.[2] Nevertheless, right from the start, the connection between her image and blackness has been a tenuous one. Regarding her acceptance into Yale, a statement the actress made at the height of her *Flashdance* fame is indicative of this estrangement. "I thought they only took geniuses," she said. "But I was lucky, because I'm a minority, I'm not Black, and I'm not White, so I could mark 'other' on my application, and I guess it's hard for them to fill that quota."[3]

Taken at face value, Beals' statement on getting into Yale is an equal denial of a black or white identity. It is not the denial of one or both parents, but rather a refusal to identify within the prevailing black/white binary paradigm of race, a paradigm inconsistent with the actress's experience. Nevertheless, the statement and the Jennifer Beals image itself have largely been interpreted, especially among African Americans, as a singular rejection of blackness. A 1990 article in *Ebony* magazine, for example, which warned of the dangers of "drifting toward the South African solution to the race question and creating a new racial middle-group," chided Beals for not publicly identifying with the black community.[4]

Beals' alienation from blackness is further evidenced in the roles she has played. Absent from the spectrum of her varied racial representations are characters that identify as black. The racial identities of her numerous romantic partners in film are also telling. Rarely, if ever, has she been coupled with a black actor. Beals and Denzel Washington flirted with intimacy in the feature film *Devil in a Blue Dress* (1995), but unlike in the novel upon which the film was based, nothing came of that flirtation. And in the television movie *The Feast of All Saints* (2001), her character has a sexual liaison with a Creole man played by biracial actor Daniel Sunjata.[5] Overwhelmingly, however, Beals' onscreen lovers have been white men that include the likes of rock star Sting, boxer Ray Mancini, television host Jon Stewart, and actors Matthew Broderick, Steve Buscemi, and Nicolas Cage. Offscreen, the men in Beals' personal life have also been white.

As a further indication toward whiteness, in much of Jennifer Beals' work, including her breakout role in *Flashdance*—within the world of the narrative—race is not supposed to matter. Nevertheless, there are a few noteworthy instances, such as in *Devil in a Blue Dress* and the television movies *The Feast of All Saints* and *A House Divided* (2000) in which race and mixed race come to the fore. Beals has also played biracial characters in a number of television series including *The L Word* (2004–2009), *Chicago Code* (2011) and *The Last Tycoon* (2017). Taken on the whole, however, the actress's work reveals a preponderance of either white or ambiguously "other" characters in Eurocentric situations. Without having to deny her origins or ancestry, Jennifer Beals has eluded the one-drop rule definition of blackness in America. Much like the Irish immigrants from whom her mother descended, she has formulated something akin to a "white ethnic" identity, an identity that is white but not quite.

Jennifer Sue Beals was born on December 19, 1963, in Chicago, Illinois, a city that celebrates Jean-Baptiste-Point Du Sable, a Creole man, as its founder. Du Sable, who was born in Haiti, was the child of an African mother and a French mariner father. The permanent settlement that he established on the western shores of Lake Michigan in 1799 is now the largest metropolis in the state of Illinois. Since its entry into the Union in 1818 as a "free" state, Illinois has been at the center of national politics and its problems have generally been regarded as representative of those that affect the entire nation.

Shortly after its admission into the Union and up until the Civil War, whether slave or free, blacks were prohibited from migrating to Illinois. Fugitive slaves followed the Underground Railroad to Chicago, nevertheless. After the First World War, Chicago, much like New York, became a mecca for African Americans fleeing the poverty and discrimination of the South. Between 1910 and 1940, the black population of Chicago increased multiple times over. Census records of 1940 indicate that Jennifer's father, Alfred Beals, and her paternal grandmother, Susie Ford, were participants in the Great Migration, having journeyed to Chicago from Texas.[6] As the city's population increased, blacks, including those whose ancestors had once lived somewhat freely in various parts of the city, were forced to live in segregated neighborhoods on Chicago's South Side.

Jennifer's older brother Gregory was born in 1958 and younger brother Bobby came along in 1964. In 1963, when Jennifer was born, she and her family were living on Chicago's South Side where Alfred Beals owned a grocery store. Though he was not wealthy, her father managed to take his family on expensive vacations to foreign destinations such as England and Europe.[7] The Beals family lived in the community area known as Chatham,[8] a neighborhood regarded since the 1950s as a stronghold of Chicago's African American middle-class. Chatham has also been home to some of the nation's most successful black businesses.

The Italian, Hungarian, and Irish immigrants who inhabited Chatham in the late 19th century were among the numerous people who, upon first arriving in America, were not welcomed into the category of whiteness, a category that carried with it the privileges of freedom, citizenship and legally defensible rights to property. The process by which the descendants of these new immigrants eventually became white ethnic Americans relied heavily upon the systematic, and often violent, rejection of African Americans.

In the mid–20th century, when blacks started moving into Chatham and other adjoining South Side areas, whites started moving out. In 1950 Chatham was over 90 percent white. By the 1960s, the neighborhood where Jennifer Beals grew up, and was teased by other children who called her "whitey," was over 60 percent black. Though the racial transition in Chatham occurred somewhat peacefully, in other surrounding neighborhoods, the threat of desegregation resulted in riots.[9]

In 1953, violence erupted just south of Chatham, in the all-white community of South Deering, when the Chicago Housing Authority ("CHA") allowed Betty Howard, a very fair-skinned African American woman, to move into the Trumbull Park housing project. The CHA, which maintained an unstated policy that only whites could live in certain projects like Trumbull Park, assumed that Howard was white. For several weeks, in what is known as the Trumbull Park Homes Race Riots, angry whites directed fireworks, rocks, and racial epithets at the apartment of Betty Howard and her husband Donald. Several months later, the CHA reluctantly agreed to further integration by permitting ten more black families to move into the complex. This action resulted in more violence accompanied by a massive police presence.[10]

In 1966, Dr. Martin Luther King, Jr., encountered greater racial hostility in Chicago than he had in some Southern cities. Protesting segregation and housing discrimination, King led hundreds of black and white demonstrators through some of Chicago's white neighborhoods, including South Deering. Police had to be brought in to control the whites that jeered, shouted and threw bottles, rocks, and bricks at King and the protestors. In April 1968, following the news of Dr. King's assassination, more rioting occurred in Chicago, this time by blacks. Thousands of Army troops and National Guardsmen were brought in to quell the violence that lasted for three days.

By the time Jennifer's father passed away in 1974, the racial changeover in Chatham was complete. Ninety percent of its residents were black. It was at this time that Jennifer's mother, Jeanne Anderson, decided to move her family to the city's predominantly white North Side. While Jeanne continued to teach school on the South Side,[11] Jennifer attended the prestigious Francis W. Parker School on the North Side. In this new, mostly upper-middle class white environment, any race-consciousness the young Jennifer had was supplanted by class-consciousness.[12]

Jennifer was thirteen years old when she started working part-time to help earn money for her college tuition. Her first job was at Baskin-Robbins selling ice cream. In the summer of 1979, at age fifteen, Jennifer was cast as an extra in *My Bodyguard* (1980), a film about white high school boys starring Matt Dillon, Adam Baldwin, and Joan Cusack. Though Beals has an uncredited role, her presence is noticeable among an otherwise all-white cast. Absent the star hair and makeup treatment, and benefiting, possibly, from a summer tan, it is one of the few films in which her character looks like a token non-white other.

At sixteen Jennifer decided to try modeling, and by 1981 she was working with acclaimed fashion photographer Victor Skrebneski. In 1982, Jennifer graduated from high school and was accepted into Yale University. Before entering college, Beals auditioned for the lead role in *Flashdance*. When she finally received word that she had won

Jennifer Beals was a token non-white "other" in her first film, Twentieth Century–Fox's *My Bodyguard* (1980). She is pictured with Matt Dillon along with two unidentified blond actresses.

the part, Beals took a temporary leave from Yale and made her way to Pittsburgh for the filming of *Flashdance*.

Flashdance (1983)

In this Paramount production, directed by Adriane Lyne, a teenage welder from Pittsburgh dreams of dancing her way out of the working class. The dreamer is Alexandra ("Alex") Owen, played by Jennifer Beals. Alex is one of three characters who work nights at a local bar called Mawby's while aspiring to transcend their blue-collar environment. Alex's best friend Jeanie Szabo is a waitress who wants to be a professional figure skater. Jeanie's boyfriend and short-order cook Richie Blazek wants to be a big-time comedian. As for Alex, she's an exotic dancer who wants to attend a prestigious ballet school. In the end, only Alex succeeds.

While dancing at Mawby's one night, Alex is spotted by her steel mill boss, the much older, nouveau-rich Nick Hurley, played by Michael Nouri. Hurley pursues Alex, rescues her from an assault, and then uses his status as boss to date her. Alex is offended when Nick pulls a few strings to get her an audition at the ballet school, but she goes to the audition anyway, does an incredibly inspired routine, and earns a spot in the school.

With a working-class heroine who struggles against the odds to pursue her passion, *Flashdance* was touted as a woman's version of both *Rocky* (1976) and *Saturday Night Fever* (1977). Light on narrative, heavy on music and dance, and a biracial actress in the lead, *Flashdance* also has a lot in common with 1980's *Fame* starring Irene Cara. With the aid of Cara's voice, both *Fame* and *Flashdance* won an Academy Award for Best Original Song.

Like Alan Parker, director of *Fame*, Adrian Lyne is a British filmmaker who got his start by directing television commercials. Parker was also one of a handful of directors asked to take on *Flashdance* before Lyne finally agreed.[13] *Fame* begins with auditions at a New York performing arts high school, while *Flashdance* ends with Alex's audition at a Pittsburgh ballet school. Both *Fame* and *Flashdance* represent young people striving to succeed as performers in an urban setting. Where the two films diverge is in how these urban spaces are racially defined.

Fame's version of community is inclusive. In the name of the performing arts, students from barrios, ghettos, working- and even upper-class neighborhoods all come together to dance, act, sing, and make friends. As Coco Hernandez, the black-white-Latina Irene Cara is representative of this pluralistic vision. *Flashdance*, on the other hand, is a world of individualism and exclusivity. From a community singularly identified as white ethnic working-class, Jennifer Beals as Alex Owen attempts to assimilate into the more elite and rigidly European class of whiteness as represented by the insular world of classical ballet.

Although Alex is the prima donna of *Flashdance*, her family history remains sketchy. Alex's mother and father are non-existent. Her closest parental bond is with an elderly mentor, Hanna, a former dancer with the *Ziegfeld Follies*, who speaks with a European accent and encourages Alex to apply to the ballet school. Alex is from Altoona (a

Jennifer Beals is a dancer in Paramount's hugely popular, critic-proof film *Flashdance* (1983).

predominantly white, industrial town in Pennsylvania) and she had a father who once took her to the symphony. She also goes to confession and has a surname that could be of Irish origin. Perhaps, like Beals' mother, Alex is supposed to be Irish Catholic.

Yet, with no family members or other details to confirm Alex's identity, the filmmakers leave room for alternative interpretations. Based on their own identity and experience, viewers have read Alex as French, black/white, black/Hispanic, Italian, white, ethnic, and ethnic Catholic.[14] Alex's teary-eyed confession to Nick that she just can't wait to get on stage so that she can disappear implies some past trauma, though what that might be is never revealed. With the lack of family ties and a hint of tragedy combined with the actress's own biracial background, one might be tempted to read Alex as a black/white character for whom blackness is a recessive trait.

There is certainly a dichotomous tension within Alex's character. At times Alex is doe-eyed and naïve, and then suddenly she is sexually knowing and vulgar. By day, as she works alongside men as a steelworker, Alex is empowered. At night, however, when she performs partially nude for men's visual pleasure, patriarchy is restored and meaningful empowerment negated. Dialogue backstage in the dancers' dressing room confirms that whatever strength the women seem to possess onstage is temporary and fleeting. The only concern, for example, of one young dancer, Tina Tech, seems to be whether or not a guy will call her back for a date. In another scene, when Alex returns to Mawby's one last time to collect her belongings, an elder dancer bemoaning her fate serves as a cautionary tale for Alex.

Although Alex is immersed in a white ethnic world, racial tension is still at play in *Flashdance*. On the one hand, the selection of a black/white actress for a white ethnic role might be considered "color blind" casting and a sign of racial progress. On the other hand, locating these white ethnic, blue-collar characters within a steel mill town both suppresses and evokes a history of black struggle. In cities like Beals' hometown of Chicago and Pittsburgh, where *Flashdance* is set, the definition of whiteness evolved and expanded through the inclusion of new immigrants—from whom Alex's *Flashdance* pals and presumably Alex herself are descended—and the exclusion of African Americans. This simultaneous inclusion and exclusion were especially visible in housing and industrial employment.

The documentary *Struggles in Steel* (2015) recounts the little-known history of black steelworkers and the exclusion and egregious discrimination they encountered in the industry. During the Great Steel Strike of 1919, for example, thousands of black men were brought from the South to the Midwest to be used as strikebreakers against an all-white union that refused black workers. Once the strike was over and the union defeated, the men were abandoned to the streets, with no jobs and no money to get back home.

When black men did manage to get hired in steel mills, they were given the dirtiest, most hazardous, "man-killing" jobs, while the "clean" jobs went to their white peers. After the passage of the Civil Rights Act in 1964 and a 1974 Consent Decree that compelled one company to end its discriminatory practices, conditions gradually improved for some steelworkers. At the very time that blacks started making gains, however, the steel industry was in decline. By 1983, when *Flashdance* was released, steel mills were closing and some black communities were left devastated as a result.[15]

Blackness finds its way to the surface of this blue-collar fairytale in more obvious ways as well. One such instance occurs early on when Alex is working out at a gym with two other dancers, Tina Tech, a blonde, and Heels, the only African American with a speaking part. Once again, Tina is anxious because a man she went on a date with hasn't called her back. Annoyed by Tina's coyishness, Heels tells her to "just get up and call the dude!" Tina possesses the "feminine" quality of passivity, while Heels exhibits a more "masculine," aggressive approach to dating and sexuality. To ensure that audiences understand this difference in attitude is racial rather than personal, Heels punctuates her statement by adding, "I'm glad I ain't no honky."

For her part, Alex is an intermediary. She is neither the passive one, waiting for the guy to call, nor is she an aggressor—at least, not yet. As Alex transforms from an innocent teenager who confesses to her priest that she's been thinking about sex, to having sex with her boss, to playing the seductress, the establishment of traditional gender roles in this scene takes on more relevance.

A more palatable insertion of blackness into the narrative occurs just after the workout scene. As Alex and Jeanie make their way through the streets of Pittsburgh, they happen upon a group of breakdancers. Though brief, this performance by the Rock Steady Crew is considered momentous for hip-hop culture because it introduced large segments of the public to breakdancing for the first time.[16] Although the Rock Steady Crew is a racially mixed group, the origins of breakdancing are generally associated with black youth culture, and the crowd that gathers in this scene to watch them is predominantly African American.

Alex doesn't join in with the street dancers. She stays back to cheer and clap with the crowd. Later, Alex confesses that she is self-taught and has never taken a dance lesson in her life, a trait that coincides with a dominant stereotype that sees African Americans as having "natural" talent. Furthermore, in the film's climactic audition scene, it becomes clear that Alex's dancing is in part street-inspired and that she has appropriated a breakdancer's backspin move for her routine.

An argument between Alex and Nick also seems calculated to evoke a fleeting connection to blackness while marking racial difference at the same time. Their quarrel, about Nick being seen with his ex-wife, occurs at the steel mill in front of an overweight African American woman who operates an onsite lunch truck. The black woman never says a word as the couple's exchange goes back and forth, yet twice she is shown in close-up shooting sideways, bug-eyed glances at Nick until finally Alex bursts out: "Who's the goddamn blonde, Nick?" The sequence invites comparison of Alex to both the African American lunch lady and the blonde evoked in the argument. Visually, it is apparent that Alex does not fit the stereotype of the overweight black woman who functions as comic interloper in Nick and Alex's argument, nor, as we shall soon see, does she fit the image of the ex-wife who is not only blonde but is educated and from a "good" family.

That Alex is not a paragon of white womanhood becomes apparent when Nick takes Alex out to dinner at a posh restaurant. As Nick attempts to regale Alex with stories of growing up poor, Alex "seductively" sucks on lobster and talks dirty to him through butter-moistened lips. Just when Alex decides to play footsy under the table with Nick's crotch, the ex-wife, Katie, appears. Wearing a conservative boat-neck blouse and fur-trimmed hat, Katie, who looks like she just flew in from Reykjavik, presents a conspicuous contrast to Alex who is wearing what looks like a man's tuxedo.

When Katie asks about the couple's first date, Alex removes her jacket to reveal a sleeveless, backless shirt and tie halter-top and proudly declares that she "fucked [Nick's] brains out." For director Adriane Lyne, Alex's sexual assertiveness in this scene was viewed as a reversal of gender roles.[17] Whether or not this is truly a role reversal depends on whether Alex is read as a white woman or a woman of color.

The studio's preferred reading of Alex is that in the tradition of American individualism, she is a woman empowered to succeed in a man's steel-mill world and to follow her dreams. In keeping with Beals' own history of replacing race-consciousness with class-consciousness, Alex teeters not on a dichotomous racial boundary but rather on the boundaries of class and culture. Alex's acceptance into the ballet school means that her lowbrow street dancing will soon be transformed into high art. And the film's Cinderella ending, which has Nick waiting for Alex outside her audition with a dozen red roses, suggests that the time-honored tradition of marrying up might still be

Jennifer Beals is congratulated by Michael Nouri after her inspired audition earns her a spot at ballet school in Paramount's *Flashdance* (1983).

the best way to escape the working class. Much like the new immigrants that came before her, Alex is formulating a new white identity.

While most critics gave *Flashdance* unfavorable marks, a few found words of praise for it. Gene Siskel, who thought that Alex looked a little like Irene Cara in *Fame*, found it a visually attractive, refreshing rite-of-passage story.[18] Peter Travers, in his pre–*Rolling Stone* days, gushed over Beals and thought her performance made the film worthwhile.[19] Many critics, though, saw *Flashdance* as merely an extended version of a music video one might find airing on the newly launched cable station MTV. In fact, the film's success is attributed in part to an "invisible" marketing campaign that included the production of a video for MTV before the film was released.[20] Other critics implied that *Flashdance* was good old-fashioned sexism masquerading as feminism.[21] Writing for *Time*, Richard Corliss made reference to the film's repressed blackness when he noted that, like *Saturday Night Fever* and the *Rocky* films, *Flashdance* achieved success "by taking experiences of black youths and playing them in whiteface."[22]

Within a week of the film's release, Beals stirred up a bit of a scandal when she told a reporter that her body double, Marine Jahan, did all the dancing. Actually, Jahan did most of the dancing. In addition to Jahan, a female gymnast and a male member of the Rock Steady Crew contributed to the final audition scene.[23] Paramount didn't want the public to know that Beals didn't do the dancing.[24] When asked about Beals' comments, Don Simpson, one of the films producers, stated that Jennifer was mistaken. It's fairly easy, however, to spot the body-double shots, especially if one is looking for them. In fact, watching for these inconsistencies is now part and parcel of the *Flashdance* viewing experience.

A couple of weeks after the body-double scandal came another hullabaloo with the news that Jennifer Beals had a black father and a white mother. "I was black, I was white. I was even claimed by Puerto Ricans," said Beals.[25] As it was with the body doubles, one might wonder if the studio would have preferred to keep Beals' family history concealed as well. One of the first public mentions of Beals' parentage appeared in the *LA Times* three weeks after *Flashdance* was released.[26] A few weeks later, Jennifer Beals was claimed by *Jet* magazine,[27] and in November 1983, she was one of three nominees for the NAACP Image Award for Outstanding Actress in a Motion Picture.

Beals, it was reported, wasn't nominated for the Image Award because of her black heritage, but rather because she represented a woman who came from "the wrong side of the tracks" and had struggled to find success. The NAACP further asserted that the Image Awards were created for anyone, black or white, who presents a positive image for minorities.[28] In 1971, it did give its Outstanding Actress in a Motion Picture award to Jane Fonda for her role in *Klute*—and perhaps for her political activism as well. In the early 1970s, Fonda was known for her opposition to the Vietnam War and was outspoken in her support of Huey Newton and the Black Panthers. Later, in the 1980s, Fonda also adopted Mary Lewis, an African American teenager from Oakland. To date, Fonda remains the only white actress to have ever received the NAACP Image Award for Outstanding Actress in a Motion Picture. In 1983 Jennifer Beals won out over Diane Abbott and Pam Grier.

After *Flashdance*, Jennifer returned to Yale to focus on American literature and Italian studies. While there she met and dated Robert Simonds, a student who, at 22 years of age, was launching his own career as a Hollywood producer.[29] During her summer breaks Beals worked on two productions. The first was Shelley Duvall's children's television series *Faerie Tale Theatre*, which aired on Showtime from 1982 to 1987. Beals starred as the oppressed orphan misfit turned princess in the *Cinderella* episode that aired in 1985. Jean Stapleton was her fairy godmother and Matthew Broderick was her prince.

The feature film *The Bride* was also released in 1985. In this remake of *The Bride of Frankenstein* (1935), Beals starred opposite Sting's Dr. Frankenstein as his half-monster, half-human creation. By 1985 her courtship with Simonds had ended, and in early 1986, Beals married writer and director Alexandre Rockwell. Beals graduated with honors from Yale in 1987.

For the next eight years, Beals kept busy working on independent films and television movies. In 1988 she appeared in the boxing film *Split Decisions* starring Gene Hackman. Set in Hell's Kitchen, a New York neighborhood once associated with poor and working-class Irish Americans, Beals played a nurse and working-class, girl-next-door type. That same year she was also seen as Lady Olivia Candioni in *The Gamble*, a foreign 18th-century period drama, which also starred Faye Dunaway and Matthew Modine. In the misogynistic *Vampire's Kiss* (1988), which has been interpreted by at least one film

Jennifer Beals is rock star Sting's half-monster, half-human creation in Columbia Pictures' *The Bride* **(1985), a remake of** *The Bride of Frankenstein* **(1935).**

scholar as a warning against miscegenation,[30] Beals' character, Rachel, is a figurative and literal vamp.

Beals had a small part as a French transvestite in *Sons* (1990), which was written and directed by her husband, Alexandre Rockwell. Other films directed by Rockwell include the Sundance Grand Jury Prize–winning feature *In the Soup* (1992), in which she played a Dominican girl next door opposite Steve Buscemi, and *Four Rooms* (1995), in which she was the wife of veteran actor David Proval. Two other projects during this period that deserve special mention for being so bad they're good are Beals' first television series with a recurring, starring role, *2000 Malibu Road* (1992), and the Lifetime movie *Night Owl* (1993).

Devil in a Blue Dress (1995)

For Jennifer Beals, the third wave of black cinema, which began in the late 1980s and continued into the 1990s, marked a "coming out" of sorts. After more than ten years in the business, Beals attempted her first role as a definitively mixed race character in a film helmed by an African American director, Carl Franklin. When the actress first heard that Hollywood would be bringing *Devil in a Blue Dress* to the screen, she called and she wrote, offering to audition. Beals was determined to play the part of Daphne Monet,[31] a Louisiana Creole woman who moves to Los Angeles, passes for white, and then finds herself at the center of a mystery involving the city's political elite. When auditioning for the role, Franklin told Beals that several of the actresses he had seen claimed to be passing for white in their daily life. Beals told Franklin that she shouldn't be "punished for having always embraced who I am."[32] Beals' campaigning paid off. She got the part of Daphne Monet, which she has affectionately referred to as her "ode to the tragic mulatto gal."[33]

Produced by Sony Pictures subsidiary TriStar Pictures, *Devil in a Blue Dress* is based on the 1990 novel penned by the half-black, half-Jewish author Walter Mosley.[34] The book is first in the Easy Rawlins series about a black private eye. In addition to directing, Carl Franklin also wrote the screenplay. A history major at UC Berkeley in the 1960s, Franklin initially turned to acting as a career. Dissatisfied with the moderate success he found, Franklin enrolled in the directing program at the American Film Institute in 1986. Within a short time, Franklin made a name for himself when he directed *One False Move* (1992), a low-budget cult classic starring Billy Bob Thorton, Michael Beach, and biracial actress Cynda Williams. Like *Devil in a Blue Dress*, *One False Move* also has a miscegenetic plot twist.

In TriStar's *Devil in a Blue Dress* (1995), Jennifer Beals is a Louisiana Creole who passes for white and then finds herself at the center of a mystery in 1940s Los Angeles.

Because it pays homage to the hard-boiled detective fiction of Raymond Chandler and the film noir style of *Chinatown* (1971), *Devil in a Blue Dress* has been described as both "funky noir" and the black *Chinatown*.[35] Its setting is 1948 Los Angeles, and its hero is Ezekiel "Easy" Rawlins, played by Denzel Washington. A World War II veteran originally from Texas, Easy has just been fired from his factory job when a friend introduces him to a suspicious white man, DeWitt Albright (Tom Sizemore). On behalf of a client, Albright offers Rawlins money to help him find Daphne Monet. Don Cheadle also plays an important supporting role as Easy's violent and unstable childhood friend, Mouse.

Much like in *Chinatown*, in the course of Easy's search, people turn up dead, and a sexually taboo secret is exposed. The secret in Roman Polanski's *Chinatown* was incest. In *Devil in a Blue Dress*, miscegenation and pedophilia are the dirty secrets that belong to mayoral candidates Todd Carter and Matthew Terell, respectively. Todd Carter is the rich white man to whom Daphne was engaged until the Carter family found out about her Creole mother and paid her a large sum of money to leave town. Matthew Terell, also wealthy and white, was the one who exposed Daphne's racial identity to the Carter family. To prevent Terell from going public, Daphne purchased photographs of him with young

Denzel Washington's private eye, Easy Rawlins (right), and his unstable friend Mouse, played by Don Cheadle, unravel the mystery in TriStar's *Devil in a Blue Dress* (1995).

boys. DeWitt Albright, who claims to work for Carter but actually works for Terell, hires Easy to find Daphne and the damaging photographs.

By pitting two powerful sexual taboos, miscegenation and pedophilia, against each other, placing them on the same immoral ground, *Devil in a Blue Dress*, novel and film, comment on the way in which miscegenation was once condemned in mainstream society with the same intensity as other sexual taboos that were deemed perverse and unnatural. Far more provocative than the film, Mosley's novel fuses miscegenation with pedophilia and the incest taboo as well. The book's ending reveals that Daphne's father had molested her when she was a child and that her half-brother, Frank Green, had killed him for it. As a storyteller, Mosley is not alone in creating a connection between miscegenation and other sexual taboos, particularly incest. Dating back to at least the 18th century, racial conservatives, moderates, and liberals alike have been impelled to conflate miscegenation with incest and other sexual taboos.[36]

One very early example of merging miscegenation, incest, and child molestation can be found in *Adventures of Jonathan Corncob, Loyal American Refugee*, published anonymously in London in 1787. When the protagonist visits a West Indian plantation, he encounters four generations of mixed race females who have all been fathered by the same white man and are all direct descendants of the same black woman. As each girl reached the age of twelve, the planter-father would take her as his mistress. And with each successive generation, the offspring became lighter to the point where his last child, an infant, who was both his daughter and great-great granddaughter, was white in color. This incestuous practice, Corncob is informed, is referred to as "washing a man's self white."[37]

Thomas Dixon, author of *The Clansman* on which D.W. Griffith's film *The Birth of a Nation* (1915) is based, also took up the theme of miscegenation and incest in *The Sins of the Father* (1912). In this novel, Cleo, a mixed race woman, seduces a member of the Ku Klux Klan, has a daughter by him and then conspires to have the man's legitimate white son fall in love with their illegitimate mixed race daughter. In the end, it turns out that the girl proffered to the son is not his half-sister, but rather a white girl used by Cleo to exact revenge on the Klan member and his family.

This topic was also of interest to D.W. Griffith. His silent film *Broken Blossoms* (1919), which is based on the Thomas Burke story *The Chink and the Child*, intertwines incest, pedophilia, and miscegenation (white/Asian), along with a host of other vices and sexual taboos. Griffith also infamously conflated rape and miscegenation (black/white) with his portrayal of the characters Gus and Flora in *Birth of a Nation*.

In *Within Our Gates* (1920), independent black filmmaker Oscar Micheaux used miscegenation, rape and incest to respond to the charges made against African Americans in *The Birth of a Nation*. Through the character of the light-skinned Sylvia Landry, Micheaux exposed the twisted origins of the jezebel myth and righted historical wrongs by reframing the sexual narrative of the white man and mixed race woman. In one of the film's most striking moments, while Sylvia's adoptive parents are being lynched and burned—for a crime they did not commit—Armand Gridlestone, son of a former slave owner, attempts to rape Sylvia. In the violent struggle that ensues, Sylvia does everything within her power to fend off the attacker. Ultimately, she is spared because a scar on her chest identifies Sylvia to Gridlestone as his own daughter.

A more recent and subtle example of conjoining miscegenation and child molestation is found in the film *Black or White* (2014). After the loss of both his daughter and wife, Kevin Costner finds himself raising his mixed race granddaughter alone. During the custody battle that ensues with the black side of the little girl's family, Costner reveals that his white daughter was only seventeen when she got pregnant, while the African American father was twenty-three. He refers to his deceased daughter as a "goddamn baby" and accuses the black man of "abusing" her. That this revelation takes place in a court of law heightens the criminal aspect of said abuse, as does Costner's statement that he and his wife had chosen not to press charges.

Franklin's omission of the incest backstory in the film weakens the lead female character. In the novel, Daphne's birth name is Ruby Hawkins, and passing as the white Daphne Monet is a means to dissociate from her childhood trauma. Wicked sexuality, which is central to Daphne's character in the book, is also downplayed in the film, especially in its depiction of the relationship between Daphne and Easy. In the novel the two become romantically entangled, and there are scenes of savage lovemaking—always initiated by Daphne. In the film, the romantic/sexual angle is minimized, and there is zero chemistry between Beals and Washington. Despite Daphne's lame attempts at seduction, Easy, it seems, knows better than to mess around with a "white" woman.

Around the time of the film's release it was reported that downplaying the story's romantic component was inherent to Franklin's process of making *Devil in a Blue Dress* his own and a means for the writer-director to concentrate more on the development of Easy's character.[38] Mosley's comments several years later at an event for the Authors Guild Foundation ascribe a rather different reason for eliminating Daphne and Easy's sexual relationship. Speaking about the adaptation of his novel for the screen, Mosley confessed that since he had been paid handsomely for the rights to his creative work, he didn't mind the alterations. Mosley further disclosed that what really prevented the dark-skinned Denzel Washington from kissing the light-skinned Jennifer Beals was the studio's fear of disaffecting Southern audiences.[39]

Consistent with the Beals image itself, in spite of black family ties, Daphne is alienated from blackness. As revealed by Albright when he first hires Easy, although Daphne is presumed white, she purportedly retains a connection with the black community. Daphne, Albright says, likes "jazz, pig's feet, and dark meat." This "predilection" of Daphne's for the company of black people never comes across in the film, though. Aside from her scenes with Denzel Washington, Jennifer Beals is isolated from the African American community around which this film revolves. Rather than catching a glimpse of her, for example, in a black nightclub listening to jazz, we see her hiding out in the whites-only section of an upscale hotel. Although Coretta (Lisa Nicole Carson), an African American woman and one of the first characters to turn up dead, is her good friend, we never see Daphne and Coretta in a scene together, nor do we see Daphne with her gangster half-brother, Frank Green.

We can only imagine that Daphne, because of her mixed racial heritage and ability to pass for white, is able to move seamlessly across the color line. In terms of the film, Easy is the one who travels back and forth from the black neighborhood of Watts to LA's affluent white neighborhoods. Near the end of the film, Easy acts as intermediary in negotiating the final breakup of Daphne and Carter's relationship. In keeping with Mosley's interpretation, both Daphne and Easy, it seems, are endowed with the double racial consciousness. Near the end of Mosley's novel Mouse tells Easy he's just like Daphne. When Easy asks what he means, Mouse replies: "She look like she white and you think like you white."[40]

In the film, with her sexuality and her blackness watered down, there wasn't much for the femme fatale to do. Beals was reduced from a devil in a blue dress to a mere damsel in distress. In terms of its overall reception, Devil in a Blue Dress was the reverse of Flashdance. Devil in a Blue Dress, and the performances of Washington and Cheadle in particular, were generally praised by critics, while Beals' performance was singled out for being less than stellar.[41] And despite the film's overall critical success, it was a flop at the box office. In addition to failing to attract a black youth audience, Devil in a Blue Dress had the misfortune of opening during the same week that the verdict in the O.J. Simpson murder trial was announced, a time when the country's racial tensions were running high.

Devil in a Blue Dress made national news when it was snubbed by the Oscars. The bold headline "HOLLYWOOD BLACKOUT" on the March 18, 1996, issue of People magazine was accompanied by a rather in-depth cover article that exposed Hollywood's institutional racism at every level from the unions to the executives and the Academy. The article was out of character for a magazine better known for celebrity gossip than for being a mouthpiece for racial justice, and not surprisingly, the issue didn't sell well. The article on Hollywood and race, however, which noted that only one of the 166 Academy Award nominees that year was African American, was picked up by other news outlets and received extensive media attention.[42]

The article also named several Oscar-worthy performances that, on a more level playing field, might have been nominated, including Laurence Fishburne for his starring role in Othello (1995), composer Kenneth "Babyface" Edmonds for his Waiting to Exhale (1995) score, and Denzel Washington for his Easy Rawlins portrayal. The most glaring snub, according to *People*, was Don Cheadle who, for his role in *Devil in a Blue Dress*, was named Best Supporting Actor by both the National Society of Film Critics and the Los Angeles Film Critics Association.[43] For her portrayal of Daphne Monet, Jennifer Beals was nominated for another Outstanding Actress Image Award. She lost out to Angela Bassett who won for *Waiting to Exhale*.

In 1996 Jennifer Beals and Alexandre Rockwell were amicably divorced. Throughout the late 1990s, Beals worked consistently, appearing in television series, television movies, and feature films. In 1998 she married Canadian entrepreneur Kenneth Dixon and later had two children with him. By the beginning of the millennium, Jennifer Beals had appeared in over thirty films, and she was ready for more mixed race roles.

Along with the 1990s new wave of black cinema, there came a cycle of mixed race antebellum feature and television films about American slavery that took pains to depict relationships between white men and women of color, typically slaves. These films, which feature mixed race women as lead characters, include the miniseries *Alex Haley's Queen* (1993), *The Journey of August King* (1995), *Jefferson in Paris* (1995), *The Courage to Love* (2000), and *Sally Hemings: An American Scandal* (2000). Also a part of this cycle are two television films featuring Jennifer Beals, *A House Divided* (2000) and *The Feast of All Saints* (2001).

A House Divided (2000)

A House Divided was directed by John Kent Harrison. Its title, a reference to a speech made by Abraham Lincoln in which he declared that the nation could not continue as "half slave and half free," is a perfect segue into this story about Amanda America Dickson, who was both a slave and the beloved daughter of a wealthy white plantation owner. The inspiration for this movie is Kent Anderson Leslie's published dissertation, *Woman of Color, Daughter of Privilege* (1995). Leslie describes Amanda Dickson as a person for whom racial categories did not apply and whose identity was ultimately defined by class.[44]

Showtime's version of Amanda Dickson disingenuously reveals her as woman who rejected her blackness outright. Thus, in *A House Divided*, the factual and the fictional combine to make an excellent fit for the Jennifer Beals image. Beals was, in fact, so interested in Leslie's doctoral thesis that she approached Showtime about making it into a movie. That was when she learned that Sam Waterston, who owned the rights to it, had already pitched it to them. Shortly thereafter, Beals was offered the role of Amanda Dickson.

Leslie's dissertation pieces together oral history and legal records to provide a detailed account of Amanda Dickson's life. Amanda was born in Hancock County, Georgia, in 1849 to David Dickson and his mother's slave, Julia Frances Lewis Dickson. Julia was 12 years old when the 40-year-old Dickson raped her. While Amanda was still a baby the Dicksons took her from Julia to live in her white grandmother's room. Amanda spent most of her childhood in that room, studying, learning to read and write, and doing whatever she was told until the day her grandmother passed away in 1864. According to the African American side of the Dickson family, Amanda's father and grandmother adored her. During Amanda's childhood, David Dickson became the richest man in Hancock County and owned 150 slaves.[45]

Amanda was 16 years old when the Civil War ended. In 1865 she began a sexual relationship with her father's nephew, Charles H. Eubanks, a soldier just returned from the war. Because of anti-miscegenation laws Amanda and Charles could not legally marry in Georgia. Dickson family history suggests that the couple might have married out of state. Soon after their union, Amanda and Charles moved away from Hancock County and set up their own planation home. In 1866 Amanda gave birth to her first child, Julian Henry, and in 1870 she had a second son, Charles Green.[46]

Shortly after Charles Green's birth Amanda returned to her father and the Dickson plantation with her two sons. When her husband came to retrieve his family he was turned away. Dickson treated his grandsons as if they were his sons. He gave Amanda, Julian, and Charles his surname and then took them to New Orleans to have them declared white. When David Dickson died in 1885, Amanda's mother Julia was still alive and living on the Dickson plantation.[47]

While Dickson was alive his relatives were tolerant of his black family. After his death, in order to gain control of his estate, Dickson's white family portrayed his behavior as immoral. Seventy-nine relatives came forward to object to David Dickson's will, which made his mixed race daughter and her children the largest property owners in Hancock County. In 1887, the Georgia Supreme Court upheld a Superior Court decision that ruled in favor of Dickson's will.[48]

By the time her father's will was finally settled, Amanda had taken up residence among Augusta's black elite, where her wealth, family name, skin color, education and deportment would have given her considerable cachet. Amanda became the state of Georgia's wealthiest black person, and shortly thereafter, her sons married into prominent black families. In 1892 Amanda married widower Nathan Toomer, who was described in the mainstream press as "nearly white" and "one of the wealthiest colored men" in the South.[49] Like Amanda, Nathan Toomer was a slave before the war and had benefited from his near proximity to his white master. Amanda's new husband had been the body servant of Henry Toomer, son of a former judge. Nathan Toomer had four children from his first marriage, including his youngest daughter, Mary.[50]

The year after Amanda was married, her 23-year-old son, Charles, became infatuated with his 14-year-old stepsister, Mary Toomer. Nathan and Amanda were so concerned by Charles' obsession that they placed Mary in a Baltimore convent and warned the mother superior that Charles might try to kidnap her. Their fears were justified. Charles did try to kidnap Mary and had somehow convinced his brother- and sister-in-law to do the deed. The kidnapping attempts were unsuccessful, though, and when his in-laws were arrested in Baltimore, Charles showed up to ask the court to assume custody of Mary until he could get a divorce and marry her. The court refused Charles' request and Mary was put back in the care of the convent. Charles was not indicted, but his co-conspirators were.[51]

In June 1893 Amanda and Nathan travelled to Baltimore to hear court proceedings in the kidnapping case. For the return trip to Augusta they purchased two first-class train tickets from the Pullman Company for a section of a sleeper car. Unbeknownst to them, a few days before they purchased their tickets, a railroad manager issued a directive that all Pullman cars on the New York to Augusta line be terminated in South Carolina. When Amanda and Nathan arrived at the Columbia station, their car was disconnected from the train that continued on to Augusta without them. Stranded in the railroad yard in the hot summer sun, Amanda, who already had a frail and nervous constitution, became gravely ill. The following day their sleeper car was reconnected to a train bound for Augusta. Two days later, Amanda Dickson passed away at the age of 43.[52]

As a postscript, Amanda's son Charles Green Dickson eventually got his divorce and is said to have moved to California where he passed into whiteness. Nathan Toomer sued the Pullman Company but did not prevail. Nine months after Amanda's death Toomer married Nina Pinchback, who was the daughter of P.B.S. Pinchback, a plantation owner's mulatto son who could have easily passed for white. For several weeks during Reconstruction, Pinchback was acting governor of Louisiana. He was also later elected to the U.S. Senate, but the Senate refused him a seat. Nathan Toomer and Nina Pinchback had a son, Jean Toomer. Nathan abandoned his new family shortly after Jean was born. Jean Toomer grew up living alternately as white and African American and became an influential poet and author of the Harlem Renaissance.[53]

The events of Amanda Dickson's life, certainly worthy of a miniseries, were adapted by writer Paris Qualles into a feature-length screenplay that focuses on the brief period after David Dickson's death and the legal battle over his will. Sam Waterston is Amanda's father, David Dickson, and LisaGay Hamilton is her mother, Julia. Through flashbacks told by the two women to Amanda's lawyer (Tim Daly) we learn some details of the family's history. Contrary to the documentation and conclusions drawn in Leslie's thesis, *A House Divided* takes a fascinating 19th-century elite mulatto slave/lady and compresses her into a tragic octoroon but with a triumphant ending.

The reworking of Amanda's character begins with her resentment of Julia for abandoning her. Early on, *A House Divided* presents a bloody scene in which Julia attempts to end her pregnancy. Presumably, Amanda does not know her mother tried to abort her, but the implication is that Amanda's feelings of abandonment began in the womb. Concerned by Julia's behavior, Dickson encourages her to have the child and suggests that they move forward and just put the whole rape thing behind them.

After Amanda is born, Julia seems to want nothing to do with her. She refuses to breastfeed her and hands her over to the care of Dickson's mother. While it's impossible to know what kind of arrangements were made behind closed plantation doors, to imply that a slave girl could "give" her child to the family that already legally owned it seems misleading, to say the least. Leslie's research indicates that Julia did breastfeed Amanda. It was only after Amanda was weaned that she was taken from her mother, an event that Leslie describes as another act of violence against Julia that was "as tragic as the rape itself."[54]

Much like some of the tragic octoroon characters of pre–Civil War fiction, in *A House Divided*, the identity of Amanda's mother and her black blood are kept a secret from her. When the war is over, and Amanda wants to marry a white soldier (who is not her kin), Julia insists that Amanda should know the truth. Amanda reacts to the news by denying it. "You are not my mother," she says to Julia. Angered by the secrets that have been kept in her family and her father's refusal to let her marry, Amanda runs off with the soldier to Augusta and passes for white.

When Amanda's boyfriend finally discovers that she is black, he beats her up and abandons her. Amanda manages to make a life for herself away from the plantation. Eleven years later, upon the news of her father's passing, she returns. Once back home she continues to be condescending toward Julia, speaking to her as a lowly servant. Near the end of the film, right before the jury's decision is announced in her favor, Amanda makes peace with her mother.

In reality, Amanda Dickson married her cousin, who must have known she was his uncle's slave-daughter. With her olive complexion, whether she could have passed for white is debatable. Furthermore, according to Leslie, Amanda probably always knew the truth about her mother. Leslie presupposes there was certainly some psychological

Jennifer Beals (left) is the mixed race daughter of a slave, played by LisaGay Hamilton, and a slaveholder in Showtime's Civil War/Reconstruction-era TV movie *A House Divided* (2000).

distancing from her mother on Amanda's part,[55] but her research does not suggest that there was any animus between the two. For many years, she and her mother lived together with Amanda's sons in a home that David Dickson had built for them on the plantation. After her father's death, Amanda gave Julia her majority interest in the home in consideration for the "natural love and affection" she had for her mother.[56]

The stereotyping of the mixed race woman notwithstanding, *A House Divided* differs from similar television dramas, such as the two CBS miniseries *Queen* and *Sally Hemings: An American Scandal*, for refusing to romanticize the sex between master and slave. *Queen*, loosely based on the life of Alex Haley's grandmother, features Halle Berry in the title role. Queen is the product of a relationship between Easter, a slave, played by biracial actress Jasmine Guy, and the plantation owner's son (Tim Daly).

British-born biracial actress Carmen Ejogo plays the title role in the *Sally Hemings* miniseries. Hemings was the slave and half-sister of Thomas Jefferson's wife, Martha Wayles. Hemings, who was described by another slave as being very attractive and "mighty near white," had a sexual relationship with Thomas Jefferson before and during his tenure as president of the United States. The veracity of this version of history has been challenged for centuries, but in 2000, based on DNA results and other historical evidence, the Thomas Jefferson Foundation concluded there was a high probability that Jefferson was the father of all Sally Hemings' children.[57]

In both the CBS dramas, the sex scenes between master and slave are idealized with candles, firelight, soft music, and the slave woman adorned in virginal white. Easter and Hemings are not only portrayed as willing participants in the sexual encounter, they are also depicted as making overtures toward their master. *A House Divided*, on the other hand, makes no attempt to idealize the sexual encounter between the 40-year-old master and his 12-year-old slave. It depicts sexual harassment leading up to the event and shows the encounter itself as a brutal rape. Having depicted the savagery of the master, the remainder of the film is dedicated to redeeming him. In the end, *A House Divided* is more about the white man of privilege than it is the woman of color.

The Feast of All Saints (2001)

Jennifer Beals delved further into antebellum mixed race womanhood in another Showtime production, *The Feast of All Saints*. Based on the 1976 historical novel by Anne Rice, adapted for the small screen by John Wilder, and directed by Peter Medak, the miniseries features a rather impressive cast of mixed race, or phenotypically mixed race, actors that, in addition to Jennifer Beals, includes James Earl Jones, Ruby Dee, Robert Ri'chard, Gloria Reuben, Pam Grier, Jasmine Guy, Eartha Kitt, Nicole Lyn, Daniel Sunjata and Victoria Rowell. Other members of the cast include Ossie Davis, Forest Whitaker, and Ben Vereen.

Set in the 1840s, *The Feast of All Saints* is perhaps the most elaborate onscreen fictional account of free people of color in New Orleans before the Civil War. It's protagonist, Marcel Ste. Marie (Robert Ri'chard), is a young boy who becomes a man during the course of the story. James Earl Jones plays the much older version of Marcel, whose father, Phillipe Ferronaire (Peter Gallagher), is a wealthy white planter. Marcel's mother, Cecile Ste. Marie (Gloria Reuben), was born in Haiti, the daughter of a French plantation owner and a slave. Having escaped Haiti's bloody revolution as a little girl, in New Orleans, Cecile became one of the *gens de couleur libre* ("free people of color"). Like his mother, Marcel is also free, and for him, coming of age in antebellum New Orleans means coming to terms with his blackness.

During the colonial and antebellum periods, a racial order developed in Louisiana, and particularly in New Orleans, that was distinct from the rest of the United States. It was an order that resisted the one-drop rule and resulted in a three-caste social system that included whites at the top, free people of color in the middle, and slaves at the bottom. The racial pattern started with the arrival of French colonists, most of whom were men, and was later reinforced during the years of the Haitian Revolution when thousands of French-speaking refugees from St. Domingue (now Haiti) migrated to the Crescent City. Within this racial order intimate relationships between white males and women of color, while still against the law, were generally more open and accepted than in the rest of the United States.

Beginning in the first half of the 19th century, European travelers to New Orleans, wrote of the city and its racial openness, and from these writings the myth of quadroon balls and *plaçage* emerged. Since the end of the Civil War, authors, historians, and modern scholars alike have bought into the myth and regarded the two institutions as important and complementary aspects of the antebellum racial order in New Orleans.[58] According to this lore, in which "quadroon" can be interpreted as any visibly mixed race woman, quadroon balls and *plaçage* were institutions that developed to satisfy white men's need for interracial sex and which offered mixed race women an opportunity to stake claim to the benefits of whiteness.

The quadroon balls of the myth were dance parties where white men courted prospective mixed race mistresses. While the women of color, dressed in elegant finery, mingled with white gentlemen of means, their mothers waited in the wings. When a young woman was selected, after a period of courtship, the mother and the suitor would negotiate the *plaçage*, a quasi-marital arrangement in which the suitor agreed to provide support for the young woman and any children who might come along as a result of the union. Finally, most of these arrangements were said to be short-lived, lasting only until the man found someone of his own race to marry.

Recent scholarship, which relies on archival sources rather than recycled versions of the traveler accounts, debunks the quadroon-*plaçage* myth.[59] While quadroon balls certainly did exist, they were probably not a precursor to *plaçage*. In fact, the term "*plaçage*" was rarely used before the Civil War, and when it was, it referred to a union between two free people of color. As for quadroon balls, they can be better understood as part of the New Orleans public ball tradition. The inspiration for quadroon balls might have been the "tri-color-balls," which were so named because they were attended by free people of color, slaves, and whites. Tri-color balls, which first started around 1799, were intended for free people of color. White men, however, attended these balls uninvited and danced with mixed race women. Just a few years later, in the same location where the tri-color balls had taken place, the first ball for free women of color was held. Others soon followed suit until eventually a "quadroon ball" could be found almost any night of the week.[60]

In antebellum New Orleans, it is also true that numerous relationships developed between white men and free women of color. These relationships, however, were far more complex and very different from those described in the myth. One study demonstrated that the majority of white men in interracial relationships were not well-to-do planters but rather members of society's middle ranks. As for the women, many of them, as opposed to being economically dependent, brought their own capital to the relationships, while others contributed labor to their partner's business. Furthermore, the relationships were definitely not transitory or casual, many of them lasting for more than ten years.[61]

Another aspect of the quadroon-*plaçage* myth is that mixed race women considered themselves superior, not only to slaves/blacks, but also to free men of color. Therefore, as one travel account wrote, "white gentlemen remained one of [the quadroon's] few options for security."[62] After the 1809–1810 immigration of nearly ten thousand refugees from St. Domingue by way of Cuba, almost three-fourths of the adult free people of color in New Orleans were women. In the marriage market, this demography disadvantaged refugee women and those descended from refugee women the most.[63] It seems likely that the real reason for the number of interracial relationships, especially during the early part of the 19th century, was not due to racial snobbery on the part of mixed race women, but rather that there simply weren't enough free men of color to go around.

While there are numerous films that use New Orleans as a backdrop, rarely have any fixed their gaze upon its antebellum free people of color. Other films to explore this group include the independent blaxploitation-era feature *Quadroon* (1971) and the Lifetime movie *The Courage to Love*. Set in 1835, *Quadroon* features Kathrine McKee as sex object in the title role. *The Courage to Love*, also set in the 1830s, depicts a more pious free woman of color. Vanessa Williams stars as the real-life character, Henriette Delille, foundress of the Catholic order the Sisters of the Holy Family.

Essential to the storyline of *Quadroon*, *The Courage to Love*, and *The Feast of All Saints* is the quadroon-*plaçage* myth. *Quadroon*, in its opening scene, features a poster announcing a quadroon ball. Kathrine McKee's character, Coral, is expected to become a *placée* ("placed woman"), but rejects her fate and chooses instead to fall in love with a Yankee from the North. The real-life Henriette Delille, on whom *The Courage to Love* is based, is said to have been a product of *plaçage* and to have campaigned against it for being demoralizing and degrading. In the film, Delille's mother, played by Diahnn

Carroll, is driven to madness when her partner of many years, Delille's father (Stacy Keach), decides to marry a white woman. In *The Feast of All Saints*, Marcel and his sister Marie (Nicole Lyn) are both products of *plaçage*. Marie grows to despise her mother for being a placed woman and, like Coral and Delille, vows to refuse it for herself.

In *The Feast of All Saints*, it is within this world of quadroon balls and *plaçage* that we find Jennifer Beals and her character, Dolly Rose. In Rice's original version of the story, from the time Dolly left her convent school at age sixteen and began appearing at quadroon balls, she had an endless succession of white men in her life. Her first such relationship was with a man from an old Louisiana family and resulted in the birth of a daughter. After their daughter was born, Dolly was unfaithful and the father left for Europe. He returned only when their daughter passed away. Somewhere amid the white men, Dolly also took up with Christophe Mercier, a free man of color who, after a stint in Paris, returned to New Orleans to start a school for young boys. Christophe comforts Dolly Rose when she is grieving the loss of her daughter. Following her mourning period, Dolly sets herself up in an apartment and turns it into a brothel.

For the most part, the miniseries remains true to Rice's novel, except when it comes to Dolly Rose and her backstory. Rather than being a mother who mourned the loss of a child born to *plaçage*, Beals' character grieves the death of the white man who took her to England so that he could marry her. Her British father-in-law adored her—until he found out about her African heritage. In reality, some interracial couples did, in fact, leave America so that they could legally marry.[64] Yet, having placed Dolly outside the familiar narrative of antebellum America, it immediately pulls her right back in as a light-skinned strumpet who attempted to pass for white.

In both the novel and the miniseries, Dolly Rose's response to her grief is to set up her own bordello. The brothel-mansion of the miniseries, where Dolly Rose provides shelter for wayward women of color and hosts her own quadroon balls is far grander than the one implied in the novel. Nevertheless, in keeping with the myth, *The Feast of All Saints* likens the quadroon women involved in interracial relationships to prostitutes.

That prostitution is a way of life for Dolly Rose is made clear in the miniseries when Christophe (Daniel Sunjata) first returns from Paris and pays a visit to Dolly Rose. During this scene it becomes clear that Dolly and Christophe have a shared history of exchanging money for sex. "You were my first love," Christophe says to Dolly. Christophe then goes on to recall how he saved for weeks to get the money to be with her. Near the end of this scene Dolly lets him know that their next time together won't be free.

Given Dolly's vocation, and when compared to the film's other sex scenes, this scene between Dolly and Christophe is a rather tame one. Nevertheless, it marks Beals' first real sex scene with an African American actor, an acquiescence to blackness heretofore unseen from the actress. While the character of Dolly Rose is a minor supporting role, *The Feast of All Saints* seems to signify a subtle evolution in the racial identity of the Jennifer Beals star image.

After *The Feast of All Saints*, Jennifer Beals took on a handful of television roles that gave her characters a biracial identity far removed from the tragic mulatto. One of the most popular of these was created for the Showtime series *The L Word*, the first television show to revolve around the love lives of gay women. When approached by Showtime to head the ensemble cast, Beals requested a biracial identity for her character and producers obliged. Pam Grier's character, Kit, is Bette's alcoholic half-sister and Ossie Davis plays their ailing father.

The first season of *The L Word* in particular devotes significant time to exploring Bette's biracial identity. One story arc has Bette and her blonde partner, Tina (Laurel Holloman), trying to start a family. After some searching Bette finds them the perfect sperm donor. Tina is taken aback when the perfect donor turns out to be African American. Another episode has a black woman accusing Bette of hiding behind her light skin and denying her blackness.

Following her successful run on *The L Word*, Beals moved over to Fox to play a character whose biracial identity is treated matter of factly in the series *The Chicago Code*. Her character, Teresa Colvin, is Chicago's first female police superintendent. In another Fox series, *Lie to Me*, Beals played Zoe Landau, attorney and ex-wife of deception expert Cal Lightman (Tim Roth). Here, Landau's biracial identity is something of a footnote used to justify a racial story line.

The Last Tycoon (2016–2017)

The quintessential fit for the Beals star image, and arguably the actress's finest performance to date, can be found in the Amazon television series *The Last Tycoon* (2016–2017). In this period drama, based on F. Scott Fitzgerald's unfinished novel, Beals plays Margo Taft, a biracial actress who, similarly to Lonette McKee's Mignon in the short film *Illusions*, passes for white in Old Hollywood. Both women are gutsy, complex characters, but whereas Mignon seems to bypass Jim Crow rather effortlessly, the more ruthless Taft goes to great lengths to bamboozle it. The show's lead male characters were inspired by Louis B. Mayer and Irving Thalberg. Kelsey Grammer plays studio head Pat Brady and Matt Bomer is his whiz kid producer, Monroe Stahr. When his studio experiences financial troubles, Brady attempts to get Margo Taft to star in one of his pictures.

Margo's character, who does not appear in Fitzgerald's novel, is loosely based on the Anglo-Indian actress Merle Oberon, who was born in Bombay to a British mechanical engineer and a Sri Lankan girl, who was just twelve years old in 1911 when Merle was born. Oberon's first big break as an actress came when British director Alexander Korda offered her a small but important role in *The Private Life of Henry VIII* (1933). Oberon married Korda in 1939, and she became Lady Korda when her husband was knighted a few years later. It is believed that Korda concocted Oberon's fake origin story, which negated the actress's impoverished childhood and her Indian heritage. When she lived in England, Oberon would have her grandmother—who up until the actress's birth certificate was made public in 2014 was believed to be Oberon's mother—dress up as a maid and serve tea.[65]

In *The Last Tycoon*, Margo's mother, Lucille, is also obliged to dress up as a maid and act as her daughter's servant. Lucille, played by L. Scott Caldwell, is not Indian but rather African American. Seeing the light-skinned Margo next to the dark-skinned Lucille in a maid uniform invites obvious comparison to Peola and Delilah in *Imitation of Life*, but Margo is no tragic mulatto. Margo is on an intense mission to get as far as she can in the cutthroat world of Hollywood. Margo also wants to make sure that her mother is provided for, and contrary to Peola, she includes Lucille in her life. Margo Taft is Peola reimagined. She is perhaps a heroine that those black audiences of 1934, who jeered at Peola, would very likely have rooted for.

8

Halle Berry

Imitation of Dorothy Dandridge

My struggle has very much been hers, trying to carve out a niche for myself as a leading lady.... I'm still in almost the exact same position she was in.[1]
— Halle Berry

In 2002, for her performance in *Monster's Ball* (2001), Halle Berry made history, becoming the first black woman to win the Oscar for Best Actress in a Leading Role. In her acceptance speech, Berry acknowledged that the win was not just for her. The win, she said, was for her peers as well as her predecessors, specifically Dorothy Dandridge, Lena Horne, and Diahann Carroll. Berry also triumphantly declared that with her win, the door to Hollywood had been opened for all women of color.[2] More than ten years later, after the 2015 Academy Awards, when not a single black actor was nominated for either a supporting or lead role, the actress lamented that her Oscar win "meant nothing."[3] To date, Halle Berry is still the only black woman to win the Leading Role Oscar.

Although she will always be remembered for the historic Oscar win, Halle Berry is probably more widely recognized for her beauty and sexual desirability. "When considering Halle Berry," wrote one journalist, "it is almost impossible not to focus on her beauty." She has "the kind of flawless beauty that would make a bishop kick in a stained glass window," said another. She's been called the "most beautiful woman in the universe," and throughout her career Halle Berry has scored high in polls that rank the desirability of women celebrities. She has made *People* magazine's "50 Most Beautiful People in the World" list numerous times, and in 2003, Berry became the first black American celebrity to top that list.[4] Affirming her status as mainstream sex symbol, in 2008, the men's magazine *Esquire* named Berry "Sexiest Woman Alive."

Berry was fresh out of high school when she began taking advantage of her looks at beauty pageants. Eventually she made it all the way to the Miss World finals, the first black American to do so. After a couple of years working as a model, she decided to try acting. In her very first feature film, Spike Lee's *Jungle Fever* (1991), Berry made the calculated decision to play against her reputation as a beauty queen and model, tackling the role of a crack-addicted prostitute.

Race and mixed race are also prominent aspects of the Halle Berry star image. That she was raised by her white mother and abandoned by her black father has been frequently publicized throughout her career. When she made her debut in films, *Ebony* magazine declared that Berry had overcome "the potentially damaging problem of being born to a Black father and a White mother." Reports that Halle was taunted as a child with mixed race epithets, such as "half-breed," "zebra," and "oreo"—as in Oreo cookie—also abound. Further, Berry has complained of being turned down for Hollywood roles simply because she's black and has also been rejected by black filmmakers for not being black enough.[5]

In the same way that she determined not be typecast for her beauty, Halle Berry decided early on that she would not succumb to the professional pitfalls of being a black actress.[6] Berry's film career began with movies that were part of the new wave of black cinema. After *Jungle Fever*, she appeared in *Strictly Business* (1991), and in 1992, she starred opposite Eddie Murphy in *Boomerang*. Even before *Boomerang* was released, however, the actress made it clear that she had integration and assimilation on her mind. Black films, Berry proclaimed, had performed their function. She was not interested in films like *Boyz n the Hood* (1991) because they are too angry and harsh. The "separatism" that movie exhibits, Berry said, "must not become the norm for black artists who work in the industry."[7]

Despite her disdain for hood films like *Boyz n the Hood*, *New Jack City* (1991), and *Menace II Society* (1993),[8] in mainstream films with predominantly white or integrated casts, Halle Berry would not be averse to playing hood characters inspired by the hood films. In 1995, for example, Berry reprised her role as a crack addict in *Losing Isaiah*. In *Bulworth* (1998), opposite Warren Beatty, she was a streetwise, dreadlocked home girl from Compton, and her Oscar-winning performance in *Monster's Ball* is an even more bleak representation of impoverished black motherhood than that portrayed by Tyra Ferrell in *Boyz n the Hood*.

Berry's first opportunity to portray blackness among an integrated cast came in 1993, when she landed the title role in *Queen*, a television miniseries based on the Alex Haley novel. *Queen* is not only the first production to revolve around Halle Berry; it is the first in which she plays a character explicitly identified as biracial. Berry plays a light-skinned slave, modeled after Alex Haley's paternal grandmother, the daughter of a plantation owner and one of his slaves. A major television event, *Queen* introduced Berry to mainstream America as a near-white, biracial character and marks a pivotal juncture in the development of her career and persona.

Following her induction into the mainstream, Berry began appearing frequently in films with predominantly white or integrated casts, many of which, like *Queen*, associate her image to whiteness in intimate or familial ways. In *Losing Isaiah*, for example, she and white actress Jessica Lange battle over and then share custody of her black son. In other films, including *The Flintstones* (1994), *The Rich Man's Wife* (1996) and *Bulworth*, Berry stars as love interest opposite white actors Kyle MacLachlan, Christopher McDonald, and Warren Beatty, respectively. Later, Berry would go on to appear with Billy Bob Thornton in *Monster's Ball*, Pierce Brosnan in *Die Another Day* (2002) and David Duchovny in *Things We Lost in the Fire* (2007). In her personal life, after her first two marriages to black men ended in divorce, Berry partnered and had children with white men.

Films like *Monster's Ball*, *Losing Isaiah*, *Bulworth*, and *B.A.P.S.* (1997) rely on Berry's characters possessing a black identity, but at the same time play on Berry's racial duality. Her characters function as intermediaries between black and white. In *Monster's Ball*, Leticia is the catalyst for "curing" Hank of his inbred racism. In *Losing Isaiah*, Khaila traverses the boundary between her black ghetto life and that of her baby's adoptive upper-middle class white family. Berry's character in *Bulworth* affords the senator entry into the world of blackness, which he then appropriates in order to tell the truth about American politics. In *B.A.P.S.*, her character is an emissary of racial harmony who also traverses racial and class boundaries.

Berry's flexibility with race is not just limited to black or biracial roles either. *The Flintstones*, for example, was another turning point in Berry's career because it was the first time that she got a significant part that was written for a white woman. Other color blind or assimilated roles in the early stage of her career include *Executive Decision* (1996) and *The Rich Man's Wife* (1996). Berry has also played characters with implicit non-white identities that are neither black nor biracial. In *Race the Sun* (1996), another part that was written for a white actress,[9] and *Swordfish* (2001), her characters are decidedly multiracial.[10]

Later in her career, Halle Berry also appeared in films in which she takes on multiple characters with various racial identities. In *Frankie & Alice* (2010), her character is a black exotic dancer with dissociative identity disorder, and among her alter personalities is a racist Southern white woman. In *Cloud Atlas* (2012), with the aid of hair, makeup and prosthetics, Berry took on several characters with varied ethnicities, including a Maori tribeswoman, a German/Jewish aristocrat, and an Asian male.

What is remarkable about Halle Berry's star image is not simply its filmic array of racial representations, but its ability to accommodate the most stereotypical and degraded images of black womanhood (i.e., *Jungle Fever*, *Losing Isaiah*, and *Monster's Ball*) on the one hand and break away from it on the other. Certainly there have been plenty of actresses who have represented low-down or stereotyped blackness, just as there have been those who eschewed such imagery. Few, however, have been willing, or able, to maneuver from one extreme to the other with such aplomb.

In 2008 Halle Berry was featured in the A&E *Biography* television series. The episode begins by predicting the aspects of her image for which she will ultimately be remembered. In addition to her beauty and the Oscar win, the "tragedies" of her personal life are highlighted. Certain events, the documentary informs, are as "dramatic as the tragedies that she's been through on screen."[11] Clearly, this is media sensationalism. Halle Berry has never been an antebellum slave or married to a man facing execution on death row. Nevertheless, for celebrities, their private challenges are fodder for tabloid and publicity reporting, and in Berry's case, somewhat commonplace troubles have, at times, been amplified as tragedies.

Compounding the so-called tragedies of Berry's personal life is her penchant for playing tortured women in her professional life. Berry is drawn to tormented characters and claims to do her best work when playing them.[12] Tragedy and, more specifically, interracial tragedy are also key aspects of the Berry star image. Some of the actress's most prominent work harkens back to the old stereotype of the mixed race woman. Her role in *Queen*, one of the most anguished mixed race characters to have ever graced the big or small screen, fits Jules Zanger's antebellum tragic octoroon almost to a tee.

Even in films in which her characters are not expressly identified as mixed race, because it is commonly known that Berry is biracial, the stereotype of the tragic mulatto lurks. In *Bulworth*, for example, which hints at a mixed race identity, her character, Nina, is irrationally conflicted. She meets a white man and can't decide if she wants to murder or fall in love with him. Nina's attempt to cross the racial line for love is thwarted by a tragic ending. Berry's character in *Monster's Ball* might also be interpreted as a contemporary tragic mulatto.

In his exhaustive study on blacks in film, *Toms, Coons, Mulattoes, Mammies and*

Bucks, film historian and Dandridge biographer Donald Bogle described Dorothy Dandridge as "the 1950s definitive tragic mulatto."[13] While Queen is Berry's most anguished tragic mulatto, her portrayal of Dorothy Dandridge is a close second. Tragedy aside, *Introducing Dorothy Dandridge* speaks to Halle Berry's ability to masterfully participate in the manufacture and shaping of her own image. Through the promotion and production of *Introducing Dorothy Dandridge*, a new generation was introduced to Dandridge, and the Berry and Dandridge star images became permanently conjoined.

Halle Maria Berry was born in Cleveland, Ohio, on August 14, 1966. She is the daughter of Jerome Berry, an African American, and Judith Hawkins Berry, a white woman of American and British descent. Her parents met at a psychiatric hospital where Jerome was employed as an orderly and Judith as a nurse. Judith was shunned by her family when she and Jerome married in 1964. Halle's older sister, Heidi, was born that same year. Until the age of four, Halle lived with her family in a predominantly black neighborhood of Cleveland's inner city.[14] Like other big American cities of the early to mid–20th century, the black population of Cleveland soared with the Great Migration, of which Jerome, who was born in Mississippi, was a part. By the early 1960s blacks, who made up over 30 percent of the city's population, were contending with poor working conditions, segregated housing and schools, and widespread discrimination.

In 1970, when her parents divorced, Halle moved with her mother and sister to Oakwood Village, a small, racially mixed suburb just outside of Cleveland. Whether it was the inner city or the suburbs, according to Judith, her family never quite fit in. In their mostly-black Cleveland neighborhood they were singled out for being interracial, and in the suburbs, they experienced prejudice for being black. When Halle was 10, her father attempted to reconcile with his family after a six-year absence. It was during this time that she learned he was a violent alcoholic. According to the actress, it was one of the most difficult times of her childhood. Halle was happy and relieved when her mother finally told Jerome he had to leave.[15] Halle Berry would remain estranged from her father until his death in 2003.

From early on, Judith Berry impressed upon her two daughters that even though they had a white mother, because of their appearance, society would see them as black. "They don't know that you're biracial. They don't know who your mother is, and they aren't going to care," she told them. Judith Berry taught her daughters to accept a black identity and to expect the discrimination that goes along with it.[16] Nevertheless, as a little girl, Halle, who was extremely shy, wondered where, exactly, she fit in. At school she found it difficult when children made her feel like she had to choose between hanging out with the black kids or the white kids.[17]

Because her mother didn't know a lot about black history, Berry said that she felt blessed to have had an African American teacher, Yvonne Nichols Sims, in fifth grade. Ms. Sims, she said, was like a "fairy godmother, of sorts," who helped instill in her a sense of (black) racial pride.[18] Fortuitously, Ms. Sims became Halle's guidance counselor in junior high and then again in high school. Among the racially mixed, but predominantly white student body of Bedford High School, buoyed by the confidence instilled by both her mother and her guidance counselor, along with the need to prove she was just as good as the white students, Halle became an overachiever. She was president of her freshman class, editor of the school newspaper, a member of the honor society, and a varsity cheerleader.[19]

In her junior year of high school, Berry's all-out approach came to a halt when she entered the contest for prom queen. After the votes were tallied, it was determined that Halle had defeated her blue-eyed, blonde competition. It was such a decisive victory that Halle and her friends were accused of stuffing the ballot box. To settle the controversy, she and the other would-be prom queen were given the option of either sharing the title or tossing a coin. The girls opted for a coin toss. Halle won and was eventually crowned junior prom queen, but she was convinced that the accusations of cheating were racially motivated: "I thought they accepted me, and then I realized that they accepted me, but not as a symbol of beauty for the school."[20]

As a result of the prom queen controversy, Halle withdrew from extracurricular activities in her senior year of high school. After graduating in 1984, she enrolled in college to study journalism. That same year her boyfriend submitted a photo of her to a statewide beauty pageant. Halle was selected as a finalist, and at the age of 17, she won her first pageant, Miss Teen Ohio. Shortly thereafter she was crowned Miss Teen All-American.

A couple of years later, and out of her teens, Halle Berry became Miss Ohio, USA. At the time, the win was a rare accomplishment for a black woman, but Berry was not the first African American or mixed race beauty queen from Ohio. Twenty-five years earlier, sponsors of Miss Ohio, USA decided to integrate the contest for the first time by allowing one black woman to enter the competition. Their token contestant was the very light-skinned Corrine Huff, who went on to become the first African American woman to wear the crown from Ohio or any state.

Huff, the daughter of an interracial union, was actually the runner-up for the 1961 Miss Ohio contest. Right before the Miss USA competition was to take place, however, the Ohio winner disqualified herself because she didn't meet the minimum age requirement. Consequently, Huff ascended to the Ohio title. As the first black woman to wear a state crown, Huff was also the first to be entered in the Miss USA pageant, where she ultimately placed sixth. In the years that followed, Huff was employed as a secretary for Fredi Washington's ex-brother-in-law, Adam Clayton Powell, Jr. She and the congressman were involved in a highly publicized financial and romantic scandal.[21]

The first black woman to place first and win the Miss Ohio, USA contest outright was Jayne Kennedy, née Jayne Harrison, in 1970. Shortly after winning the title, Jayne wed disc jockey Leon Isaac Kennedy. Intent upon pursuing show-business careers in Hollywood, the couple moved from Cleveland to Los Angeles.[22] Jayne found work right away, appearing as a regular on the popular television series *Rowan and Martin's Laugh-In* as well as *The Dean Martin Show*. Like Lonette McKee on the *Jonathan Winters Show*, presumably to make her racially distinct from her counterparts, instead of her own natural, long, curly hair, on *The Dean Martin Show* Kennedy wore an afro wig.

Leon managed Jayne's career and eventually forged a more prominent role for himself in the business as an actor and then a producer. In 1979, he starred as an incarcerated boxer in *Penitentiary*, a film that made more than $12 million on a budget of less than $300,000.[23] Following the success of *Penitentiary*, in 1981, Leon produced, wrote, and starred in a remake of the 1947 boxing film *Body and Soul,* in which Muhammad Ali had a cameo appearance. Jayne, who by this time had appeared in numerous television shows and blaxploitation films, had a leading role opposite her husband.

Jayne's biggest break came earlier, in 1978, when she became the first African American woman to host a sports broadcast for a major television network. From a pool of seventeen women, most of whom were blue-eyed and blonde, Jayne was selected to replace

Halle Berry owes much to the trails blazed by fellow Miss Ohio, USA beauty pageant winner Jayne Kennedy, who is pictured here with her *Body and Soul* (1981) co-stars Leon Kennedy (left) and Muhammad Ali.

Miss America 1971 (not to be confused with Miss USA) Phyllis George on the CBS sports program *The NFL Today*. After CBS sent a tape of Jayne to their Southern affiliates and none objected, she got the job. Two years later Kennedy was fired by CBS for violating her contract when she joined the cast of *Speak Up America* on rival network NBC. Kennedy claimed that she had been granted verbal permission to do the NBC show during her off months. CBS apparently rescinded its approval.[24]

After the firing, Kennedy remained active in the sports business. In 1982, she became the first female host of the long-running, syndicated television series *Greatest Sports Legends* (c. 1972–1992). During her tenure on the show, Kennedy interviewed the likes of boxer Larry Holmes, basketball star Kareem Abdul Jabbar, and tennis great Ken Rosewall. She also released exercise LPs and videos, was a national spokesperson for Coca-Cola, and won an Emmy for her coverage of the 1982 Rose Bowl Parade. By the mid–1980s, before she remarried and stepped away from the spotlight, Jayne Kennedy was one of the most recognizable and respected black women in America.[25]

Halle Berry owes much to the image of and trails blazed by Jayne Kennedy. Shortly after her Miss Ohio, USA win, Berry acknowledged that Kennedy was something of a role model for her. Berry said that she drew inspiration from the "business-like control" Kennedy had over her life and the manner in which she was able to conquer goals.[26] There are indeed similarities between the two women who both hailed from the Cleveland area and wore the Miss Ohio, USA crown before making their way to Hollywood.

The acting careers of both Kennedy and Berry were built primarily on a foundation of beauty and sex appeal as opposed to a particular talent, dancing or singing. Although their looks opened doors for them, both women believed that their beauty was an obstacle to be overcome. Like Berry, Kennedy had crossover appeal. Television producer Charles Fitzsimons once said that Kennedy had the potential to be a big star because she is "universal" and "goes beyond race."[27] Another significant parallel between Kennedy and Berry was their aspiration to portray Dorothy Dandridge in film.

Interest in bringing Dorothy Dandridge's life to the screen began as early as the 1970s when singer, dancer, actress, and sex symbol Lola Falana expressed a desire for top billing in a Dandridge biopic. Songstress Freda Payne, whom Walter Winchell once described as "the most stunning singing sensation since Dorothy Dandridge and Lena Horne," also wanted to portray the star. In the decade that followed, it was Jayne Kennedy who had plans to star in a Dandridge film.[28]

In 1981, after purchasing the rights to Earl Conrad's biography *Everything and Nothing: The Dorothy Dandridge Tragedy* (1970), the independent production company Cannon Group placed a full-page ad in a Hollywood trade magazine for a film titled *The Dorothy Dandridge Story*. Jayne Kennedy would star, husband Leon would produce, and *Tamango* director John Berry was also associated with the project. When plans fell through and the Cannon option lapsed, Jayne attempted, unsuccessfully, to purchase the rights in her name. Undaunted, a couple of years later, after her divorce from Leon, Jayne optioned the Earl Mills biography *Dorothy Dandridge: A Portrait in Black* (1970). A Dandridge biopic starring Jayne Kennedy never came to fruition, but Halle Berry superseded Kennedy when she purchased the Earl Mills option from Jasmine Guy in 1996.[29]

After Berry won the 1986 Miss Ohio pageant, she went on to the Miss USA competition. Halle was named first runner-up, which secured her a spot in the Miss World pageant. (The first-place winner went to the Miss Universe contest.) Berry, who was the first black woman to represent the United States at Miss World, placed among the seven finalists. The winner of the Miss World competition that year was Giselle Laronde, a woman of mixed racial heritage from Trinidad and Tobago.

Berry did not come out on top at Miss World, but she did exhibit her penchant for going above and beyond to get noticed. At a Miss World luncheon, where contestants were asked to take part in a parade of national costumes, Berry created a bit of a stir when she showed up in nothing more than a bikini with strands of beads and shooting stars. Berry claimed her outfit was intended to show America's "advancement in space." According to the master of ceremonies, in his six years of hosting Miss World, it was the skimpiest costume he had seen. While Berry pranced around in a bikini, "fellow contestants, clad in authentic national costumes that concealed their bodies, cried foul."[30]

After Miss World, Berry quit college and headed to Chicago to pursue modeling and take acting lessons. She eventually moved to New York and signed a contract with the man she once called "her secret weapon," Vincent Cirrincione. The colorful, fast-talking Cirrincione[31] remained her manager for some twenty years. In 1989, she landed a role as a model on the ABC television series *Living Dolls*. The series was canceled after twelve episodes, but within two years she had her first feature film role in Spike Lee's *Jungle Fever*.

In a casting story reminiscent of Dorothy Dandridge and *Carmen Jones*, when Berry first auditioned for *Jungle Fever*, Lee wanted her to read for the part of his attractive bourgeois wife. Halle, however, had something else in mind. She wanted to play the drug-addicted prostitute. Lee thought Berry was "too fine to play a five-dollar crack ho," and she was seen five times before she secured the role. After neglecting to bathe for a week and showing up in character, Berry was finally able to convince Lee and others on the set that she was up to the task.[32] Although it was a small role, Berry handled it competently. More importantly, her willingness to play a low-down version of blackness, the antithesis of a pretty face, suggested to some that she was serious about an acting career.

Halle Berry thus began her film career at the height of the new wave of black cinema. She followed up her appearance in *Jungle Fever,* with two meatier roles in the black films *Strictly Business* (1991) and *Boomerang* (1992). In *Strictly Business* she played a nightclub promotions manager. According to Cirrincione, Berry was initially rejected for the part because the filmmakers said "she wasn't black enough," but when things didn't work out with their first choice they called Halle back.[33] In Eddie Murphy's *Boomerang*, directed by Reginald Hudlin, Berry was Angela Lewis, an art director for an all-black cosmetics firm. Against Robin Givens' vampy character, Berry is the good girl.

Early in her career Berry met and ultimately won the support of Joel Silver, the influential Hollywood producer responsible for blockbusters like *The Matrix* trilogy and the *Lethal Weapon* series. In between *Strictly Business* and *Boomerang*, Berry had a small part

Halle Berry began her film career at the height of the new wave of black cinema in films like Eddie Murphy's *Boomerang* (1992).

in Silver's *The Last Boy Scout* (1991). She played opposite Damon Wayans as an exotic dancer who meets an early, unfortunate death. Other films produced by Silver and in which Berry appears include *Executive Decision* (1996), *Swordfish* (2001), and *Gothika* (2003).

Alex Haley's Queen (1993)

The CBS miniseries *Queen* is based on a book by Alex Haley that was unfinished at the time of his death in February 1992. *Queen* is one of three sequels to the phenomenally popular ABC miniseries *Roots* (1977), based on Haley's 1976 novel of the same name. The other sequels in the saga are *Roots: The Next Generation* (1979) and *Roots: The Gift* (1988). Haley, who won a Pulitzer Prize for *Roots*, was later criticized and successfully sued for plagiarizing large sections of it. Nevertheless, between the book, which is a fictionalized account of his mother's family tree, and the miniseries, Alex Haley and *Roots* are responsible for popularizing modern genealogy and bringing black history into the mainstream. Forty years after it first aired, *Roots* remained the highest rated miniseries ever broadcast.[34]

While *Roots* traces Alex Haley's maternal family tree, *Queen* is about his father's side of the family, specifically his biracial paternal grandmother, Queen Haley. Although the *Queen* miniseries can't quite compare to *Roots*, it was still a major television event in its own right. When it aired in 1993, cable networks were closing in, but the Big Three television networks (ABC, CBS, and NBC) still had command of primetime TV audiences.[35] *Queen* dominated the ratings during the February "sweeps" and was the highest rated movie on any network in four years.[36]

Produced without the involvement of any African American writers, producers, production people or drivers,[37] *Queen* is Berry's first major starring role construed from an all-white perspective. Television veteran John Erman directed, and David Stevens, an Australian screenwriter, wrote the teleplay. Stevens worked with Haley on the script for two years, but Haley died before casting or filming began. After Haley's death, Stevens also completed the *Queen* novel.

With its mass television audience, *Queen* introduced Halle Berry to the American mainstream and therefore represents a pivotal juncture in the development of Berry's career and persona. *Queen* marks Berry's first time playing a title character, no small feat for a role that had to be sustained for the length of the six-hour miniseries. It was also the first time a Berry character was explicitly identified as biracial and therefore, a perfect vehicle for playing up Berry's own mixed race identity.

Numerous reviews and publicity pieces made comparisons between Halle Berry and the mixed race antebellum woman she portrayed. "Like Queen, Berry is a child of mixed heritage," and she spent a portion of her life wondering who she was and where she fit in, reported one TV critic. In another review, Berry was quoted as saying that had she been born one hundred years earlier, *Queen* "could be my story." Christopher John Farley, who later wrote a biography of the actress, wrote that Halle Berry had found "grandma Haley's long-lost respect and identity, and is figuratively, literally, ironically, truly, Queen."[38]

To land the central role of the near-white slave, Halle Berry had to put on white makeup in order to appear light enough for the role.[39] She also had to beat out a number of accomplished biracial actresses, including Jasmine Guy, Jennifer Beals and Lonette

McKee.[40] Guy, instead, plays Queen's mother, Easter, and McKee plays an adulthood friend, Alice. Queen, ages 5–6, is played by Raven-Symoné. Tim Daly is Queen's father.

Her white grandparents, James Jackson, Sr., and Sally Jackson, are played by Martin Sheen and Ann Margaret. Paul Winfield as her black grandfather, Cap'n Jack, is also influential in Queen's life. Other talented actors among the cast include Ossie Davis, Patricia Clarkson, Dennis Haysbert, Danny Glover, and Lorraine Toussaint, just to name a few.

The saga begins on the Alabama plantation, where Queen is born to Easter, a slave, and James Jackson, Jr., the plantation owner's son. Despite the unlikelihood, filmmakers went out of their way to portray the relationship between Colonel Jackson and his slave as loving and committed. Their first sexual encounter onscreen is presented with sentimentality and, more importantly, it is consensual. Producer Mark Wolper, whose father David L. Wolper produced *Roots* and was executive producer of *Queen*, acknowledged the improbability of such a sexual encounter but claimed that Haley had told him it was so.[41]

Halle Berry (left) is the troubled mixed race daughter of a slave, played by Jasmine Guy, and a slaveholder in the Civil War/Reconstruction-era TV miniseries, *Alex Haley's Queen* (1993), which originally aired on CBS.

The *Queen* teleplay, and later the novel, were based on Alex Haley's notes and a 1988 audiotape as well as interviews with Haley prior to his death. According to screenwriter Stevens, Haley told him explicitly that he wanted the relationship between Easter and Jackson Jr. "painted in pastel tones." Yet, in the 1988 audiotape that Haley made for *Queen* producers, the author made no mention of a romantic relationship between his great-grandparents. He did, however, say that his father had told him that "young white men, particularly those of the titled class and level, generally 'broke in' sexually with slave women."[42] At best the relationship between Haley's great-grandparents might be deemed exploitative. More likely, though, it should be construed as rape. Obscuring rape and representing Queen not as the consequence of a gross imbalance of power and social relations but rather as a child born out of love certainly makes Queen and her story more palatable for a mainstream audience.

Queen takes its heroine from her birth before the Civil War, through Reconstruction, to the dawn of the 20th century. Along the way Queen Haley encounters more tragedy than Harriett Beecher Stowe's iconic Eliza Harris. When the senior Jackson dies, shortly before Queen's birth, Jackson Jr. becomes the master. He takes a wife, Lizzie (Clarkson), and the couple soon give birth to a daughter of their own, Jane (Jane Krakowski). After witnessing Queen being taunted by other slave children, Jackson decides that his slave daughter should be brought up alongside his free daughter. In the first of many melodramatic moments, Queen is taken from her mother to go live in the big house. At the time of the handoff, Lizzie instructs Easter to keep her distance from Queen as she doesn't want her learning any "nigra" ways. Queen is given every advantage and trained in all the necessary etiquette required to be a lady's maid.

Around the time of the Civil War, Queen loses both her mother and her grandfather, the only people who truly cared for her and acknowledged her as family. After the war, feeling unwelcome on her father's plantation, Queen ventures out on her own. She meets another light-skinned woman, Alice (Lonette McKee), who takes her in and shows her how to successfully pass for white. Alice also teaches Queen how to accept material favors from white men, but strictly admonishes her not to fall in love because of the danger of being found out. Ignoring Alice's advice, Queen becomes engaged to marry a white man, who beats and rapes her when he learns that she is black. Because Queen's careless behavior has jeopardized her livelihood, Alice sends Queen packing.

On the road and alone again, Queen nearly starves to death. When she happens upon a group of blacks that have set up camp, Queen is met with animosity because they think she's white. Soon enough, Queen finds work and shelter with two white spinsters. While in the women's employ, Queen falls in love with a black man (Haysbert) who abandons her when she gets pregnant. After the child is born, her employers plot to take custody of it so that they can save his soul.

Queen escapes with her baby for yet another Southern destination and fortuitously reunites with the baby's father, who is now a labor leader. At the same time, she also unwittingly goes to work for a Ku Klux Klan family that kidnaps her baby and forces the infant to witness the lynching and burning of his father. After finding the baby safe at the foot of its father's charred remains, Queen moves on yet again.

This time, Queen meets ferryboat captain Alec Haley (Glover), who provides her with the love and security she had been searching for since she left the planation. The couple has a son, Simon (Alex Haley's father). When her boys are grown and old enough to leave home, past traumas are triggered, which leads to Queen setting herself on fire and having a mental breakdown. Queen is committed to a mental institution.

The real tragedy underlying the many hardships Queen has encountered, and which the miniseries places considerable emphasis upon throughout, is the heroine's whiteness. Shortly after Queen is born, her grandfather, Cap'n Jack, twice remarks that "she's white as cotton." Her white grandmother, Sally Jackson, warns her son, "Her life will not be easy. She looks as white as you or I." Mrs. Jackson's comments, in addition to highlighting the color of the baby's skin, reinforce a connection between misfortune and mixed race, implying that a divided racial inheritance is somehow worse than the simple fact of being a (dark-skinned) slave.

Queen's white skin, however, is not just emphasized by others. From beginning to end, Queen herself insists upon her whiteness. Early on, in the scene that causes her father to bring his slave daughter into his home, a group of slave children circle around the young Queen (Raven-Symoné). They taunt her, chanting in unison that she's not white; she's black just like they are. Queen cries out in protest and offers up her body as proof: "I am too [white], look at me." Even as a married and aging woman with two young sons, Queen deems it necessary to declare her whiteness. Upon learning that her son has been beat up and cheated out of money by a young white boy, Queen pays a visit to the offending boy's mother. When the mother refuses to listen, Queen rants, "How much white blood you got in you, huh? As much as me? Look at me! Look at me! I look as white as you do."

This persistent insistence upon Queen's whiteness may very well be intended to fulfill Haley's purported wish to get blacks and whites to acknowledge their shared heritage.[43] However, the series' single-minded focus on Queen's tragic story renders an attitude that seems somewhat indifferent to the plight of the assumed "pure" black slave characters in the film. In this way Queen functions like the fictional octoroon created for 19th-century Northern abolitionist audiences and seems to reveal the same racial arrogance.

Like the tragic octoroon of pre–Civil War fiction, in *Queen*, it is not the despicable treatment of slaves to which the audiences are asked to respond. Rather, what evokes audience sympathy is the spectacle of a near-white woman being forced to contend with blackness and the alienation she feels from being shunned, at times, by both blacks and whites. For her performance in *Queen*, Berry was presented with the Image Award for Outstanding Lead Actress in a Television Movie or Mini-Series.

In July 1992, during the making of *Queen*, Berry became engaged to Atlanta Braves outfielder David Justice. In January 1993, the couple was married. The following year, Berry starred in *The Flintstones*, the first of two feature films based on the popular animated cartoon series. Filmmakers originally wanted actress Sharon Stone to play the part of the vampy secretary, but she turned it down. When Berry got an opportunity to try out, she apparently convinced director Brian Levant that Bedrock should be integrated, and a few days later she was offered the part.[44] *The Flintstones* is another important juncture in her career because it was the first time she got a part that was written for a white woman. It is also the first time Berry appeared as sex symbol for a mainstream audience.

Losing Isaiah (1995)

One of Halle Berry's first leading dramatic roles in a Hollywood feature came in *Losing Isaiah*, a slate of 1990s hot-button issues—crack cocaine, welfare queens, and the rights of birth parents over foster parents—masquerading as a film that interrogates transracial adoption. Berry plays Khaila Richards, a crack addict who presumes that her extreme negligence resulted in the death of her infant son. When, a couple of years later, Khaila learns that her child is still alive, a legal battle ensues as she attempts to regain custody of the boy from the white, middle-class family that has adopted him.

In Seth Margolis's 1993 novel, upon which the film is based, when we first meet Khaila, who is known as Selma in the book, despite a regrettable past as a drug user, she is a likeable and principled young woman on the path to turning her life around. Selma grew up a child of the streets. Her mother, who had moved to New York from the South in the hopes of elevating her standard of living, wound up a prostitute supporting a heroin addiction. Selma's father was a drug dealer who refused to acknowledge her as his own child. Before long, Selma was following in her mother's footsteps.

After Selma became pregnant by one of her many unidentified sexual partners, she abstained, for the most part, from drugs. Nevertheless, Isaiah, whom she named after her father, was born premature, low-weight, and in need of an extended hospital stay. Selma, on the other hand, couldn't wait to get high and checked herself out of the hospital the morning after giving birth. Four weeks later Isaiah was released from hospital into her care. Shortly thereafter, Margaret Lewin, a volunteer baby cuddler at the hospital where Isaiah was born, somehow found out Selma's whereabouts, paid her a visit, and offered to adopt Isaiah in exchange for $25,000. Selma, still using drugs and recognizing that she was in no condition to care for her baby, accepted the proposal.

After spending all the money, Selma decides to get herself straight, finds a job as a nanny for a white family, and enrolls in a literacy class. During one of her reading sessions Selma tells her tutor about Isaiah and says she would like to get him back. The tutor refers her to an attorney who takes her case pro bono. As the legal battle is drawn out to its conclusion, we learn along the way that the Lewin family also has its flaws. While the couple works to maintain their lifestyle, Isaiah is taken care of by a foreign nanny whose visa has expired. Mr. Lewin has also been carrying on an affair with one of his employees, but the biggest shocker is that the Lewins never bothered to legalize their custody of Isaiah. Yet it's the interracial nature of the case that turns out to be the clincher.[45]

Losing Isaiah, the novel and film, were released during a publicly volatile time in American race relations. In 1991, four white L.A. police officers were captured on video brutally assaulting motorist Rodney King during a traffic stop. The video, which prefigured the era of viral cop videos, was the first to have a major impact in a police violence case.[46] When, one year later, the officers were acquitted of any wrongdoing, the verdict sparked five days of violent rioting in Los Angeles, which left more than fifty people dead, more than two thousand injured, and a city torn asunder. Two years later, African American football star and actor O.J. Simpson was arrested in Los Angeles for the murder of his white wife, Nicole Simpson, and her friend Ron Goldman. When his murder trial concluded in 1995, and the verdict was read live on national television, more than half the country tuned in to watch, with viewers, for the most part, rooting for a decision along racial lines.[47]

The 1990s also witnessed a major shift in federal child welfare and adoption policy. During the 1960s, as fewer white babies were available for adoption, there was a dramatic rise in transracial adoptions. By the 1970s, transracial adoptions were commonplace. In response to this trend, in 1972, the National Association of Black Social Workers (NABSW) issued a statement against the adoption of black children by white families. Rooted in an awareness of racism as ideology, institutional practice, and fundamental condition, the statement affirmed the importance of a black child's socialization and identity development within the context of a black family.[48] By the 1990s, while many states allowed transracial placement in foster homes, in most states, officially or unofficially, transracial adoptions were barred.[49]

By the time that *Losing Isaiah* was in production, a powerful backlash to racial matching had emerged. In support of more speedy adoptions, opponents of protective policies for same-race adoptions interpreted racial matching as reverse racism and presented arguments that essentially amounted to a denial of institutional racism in child welfare and the assertion that black parents are simply more prone to mistreat their children. Racial matching policies also became a scapegoat for the surge in the number of children in foster care and awaiting adoption. The real culprit, however, was the federal "war on drugs," its draconian sentencing laws, its hyper-criminalization of black people, and its devastating effects on black families.[50]

A consequence of the backlash against racial matching were the federal laws passed during the mid–1990s that prohibited any adoption agency receiving federal funds from considering race under any circumstances. Further, to address the increasing number of children in foster care, the emphasis in child welfare shifted from keeping families together to keeping children out of the foster care system. This translated into speeding up the adoption process by moving more quickly to permanently terminate birth parents' rights. As African American parents are the most likely to suffer from poverty and institutionalized discrimination and be held accountable for its effect on their children, the restructured child welfare system hit them especially hard.[51]

During this same period, a number of custody cases, which pitted foster parents against birth parents, made headline news. A prominent one was the "Baby Jessica case" in which the birth mother, Cara Clausen, lied about the identity of the birth father when she released her baby to the attorney for the would-be adoptive DeBoer family. Within a month of releasing her baby, Clausen informed the birth father, Daniel Schmidt. The couple then sued for custody, arguing that Schmidt had never signed away his parental rights.

The Baby Jessica case dragged on for more than two years, during which time the DeBoers were permitted to keep the child but could not legally adopt her. In Iowa, where birth parents Clausen and Schmidt resided, one court after another ruled in their favor, so the DeBoers took their case to their home state of Michigan. In 1993, after a ruling by the Michigan Supreme Court, Baby Jessica was returned to her biological parents, and with TV cameras rolling, the nation watched in horror as a screaming two-year-old child was taken from the only parents she'd ever known.

Another high-profile custody battle, known as the "Baby Byron case," focused attention on transracial adoption. In July 1992 Byron Griffin, a prenatally addicted African American infant, was born at a Pittsburgh hospital to LaShawn Jeffrey. Thirteen months earlier, Jeffrey had given birth to a girl, Byrae, also exposed to drugs. By the time Byron came along, Byrae was living with a relative, while another family member, Byron's great aunt, Marion Ellis, had custody of Byron's three brothers. Ellis wanted to take Byron as well but was denied when Allegheny County Children and Youth Services (CYS) discovered lead-based paint on the walls in her apartment. Six days after Byron was born, while Ellis was looking for another apartment, and without her knowledge, Byron was placed in the custody of a white couple, Karen and Michael Derzack.[52]

In November 1992, Byron and Byrae's birth father died in an auto accident. The following month, the Derzacks, who had decided they wanted to adopt Byron, found out that he would be taken from them to be placed with a black foster family. When social workers arrived at the Derzack home, they were met with television cameras that filmed the foster parents refusing to give up the child. This was the start of a five-year tug of war over the custody of Baby Byron. A year later, after Jeffrey had entered drug rehabilitation and was reunited with Byrae, a judge ordered that she also be reunited with Byron. Accompanied by two police officers, CYS succeeded this time in taking the toddler from the Derzacks.[53]

In the months that followed, the Derzacks announced a book deal, which prompted the judge to issue a gag order. They also tried to adopt another black baby and then sued the birth mother when the adoption fell through. Meanwhile, Jeffrey was arrested for prostitution and admitted to using illegal drugs. Although she pleaded with the judge to place her children with family members, at the end of 1994, Byron and Byrae were placed with the Derzacks. The following month, Ellis, Jeffrey and the Derzacks appeared together on the *Maury Povich* tabloid television talk show. Six months later, Jeffrey's parental rights were terminated.[54]

Even after Jeffery was out of the picture, the Derzacks managed to remain in the spotlight, including an appearance on another tabloid show with the second birth mother, the one the couple had sued. By January 1996, it had been discovered that the Derzacks had falsified IRS documents presented to the court and neglected to file tax returns for two years. They had also violated numerous court orders. Consequently, they were not allowed to adopt Byron and Byrae, who were removed from their home for good. Two years later, in December 1997, Byron and his sister were finally adopted by a black couple.[55]

While Byron Griffin was an icon in the debate over transracial adoption, Clausen, Schmidt, and Jeffrey symbolized an adoptive parent's worst nightmare: the return of a birth parent demanding custody. Byron's mother, Jeffrey, was also emblematic of a popular contemporaneous subnarrative surrounding adoption and welfare reform in which black women in particular were represented as drug-addicted, poor, and thus "unfit" as mothers.[56] Against this backdrop, the 1990s saw an increasing number of films that focused on adoption, many of which were made for television and featured birth parents as monsters or ne'er-do-wells.

Among this cycle of films was *Broken Promises: Taking Emily Back* (1993), the story of a baby-bartering homeless couple which aired on CBS. On ABC, in *A Place for Annie* (1994), Sissy Spacek played a nurse who, much like in the film version of *Losing Isaiah*, takes home an abandoned baby from the hospital where she works. Just when the adoption is about to be finalized, the HIV-positive, drug-addict mother returns to create havoc. In *Hush Little Baby* (1994) on the USA Network, Diane Ladd starred as a psychotic birth mother who murders three innocent people in her quest to reclaim the affections of the adult daughter she was forced to give up for adoption years ago.

There was also a movie about Baby Jessica. Less than two months after the child had been returned to her biological parents, the DeBoers sold the rights to their story to Bernard Sofronski, who was a producer for *Alex Haley's Queen*. The DeBoers' side of the famous custody case, *Whose Child is This? The War for Baby Jessica* (1993), was directed by John Kent Harrison and aired on ABC. In keeping with the formula, the DeBoers are portrayed as loving, "fit" parents, while the Schmidts are seen as troublemakers. The following year, Doubleday published Robby DeBoer's written account of the ordeal, *Losing Jessica*.

Within this 1990s pro-adoption, anti-birth parent milieu, *Losing Isaiah* is the only film to tackle transracial adoption. Released by Paramount Pictures, *Losing Isaiah* is a collaborative effort of the former husband and wife team of Naomi Foner, producer and screenwriter, and Stephen Gyllenhaal, a director known primarily for his extensive work in television. Halle Berry is the baleful birth parent Khaila and Oscar-winning actress Jessica Lange is her rival, Margaret Lewin. David Strathairn is Charles Lewin, the adoptive father. Isaiah, the little boy at the center of the custody battle, is played by Marc John Jeffries. Other players include Joie Lee as Marie, a welfare queen and Khaila's one-time roommate, and Samuel Jackson as Khaila's activist attorney. Cuba Gooding, Jr., who plays the boyfriend Khaila has to dump in order to improve her chances of prevailing in court, brings a little levity to this otherwise solemn melodrama.

WHO DECIDES WHAT
MAKES A MOTHER?

JESSICA LANGE
HALLE BERRY

Losing
Isaiah

PARAMOUNT PICTURES PRESENTS A HOWARD W. KOCH, JR. PRODUCTION JESSICA LANGE HALLE BERRY LOSING ISAIAH DAVID STRATHAIRN
CUBA GOODING, JR. AND SAMUEL L. JACKSON BASED UPON SETH MARGOLIS MUSIC BY MARK ISHAM EDITED BY HARVEY ROSENSTOCK, A.C.E.
PRODUCED BY HOWARD W. KOCH, JR. AND NAOMI FONER SCREENPLAY BY NAOMI FONER DIRECTED BY STEPHEN GYLLENHAAL TM & COPYRIGHT © 1995 BY PARAMOUNT PICTURES ALL RIGHTS RESERVED.

COMING TO THEATRES THIS MARCH

Halle Berry fights to regain custody of her black child from its white adoptive mother, Jessica Lange, in Paramount's *Losing Isaiah* (1995).

Although Margolis's novel is not without its plot holes,[57] the author does take pains to present both mothers as sympathetic yet flawed, women. Foner, on the other hand, turns Margolis's novel on its head, stacking the deck in Margaret's favor to wage a full-on assault against black motherhood. Margaret is a saint and savior. Khaila is a monster. A poster for the film duly captures this characterization. In the foreground, Lange, cloaked in white, holds a black baby, partially swaddled in white(ness), to her breast. Her eyes are closed, as if at peace. Upsetting this tranquil vignette, Berry's face looms in the background. Cropped aggressively on both sides, and slightly enlarged, it emerges from darkness, with *Mona Lisa*–like eyes that follow the viewer around.

One of the most significant alterations in the depiction of the two women from novel to screenplay concerns Isaiah's origins. In the book Margaret meets Isaiah doing volunteer work for the hospital as a baby cuddler. After Isaiah is released, Margaret essentially stalks the new mother and persuades her to sell her child. In the film, how the Lewins acquire custody of Isaiah is quite a different story.

At the beginning of *Losing Isaiah*, in the dark of night and in pursuit of her next high, Khaila places her baby in a cardboard box next to the trash. The next morning, garbage men arrive and throw Isaiah in the back of their truck. As the packer blade is about to compress the trash, one of the men notices the baby and shouts just in time to spare Isaiah from certain death. Isaiah is taken to hospital where he is diagnosed with prenatal addiction and where he meets Margaret Lewin, who is not a volunteer but a social worker assigned to his case.

Margaret falls in love with the baby and takes him home to become part of her family. After following the letter of the law, Margaret and her husband are eventually granted permanent custody and legally declared Isaiah's parents. The film absolves Margaret and her husband from any wrongdoing with respect to their custody of Isaiah. Khaila is solely to blame for the predicament they find themselves in.

The change in Margaret's profession, from photographer's agent to social worker, is also worth noting. Not only does this provide her with easy access to another woman's child, it also supports her characterization as savior. As a social worker, Margaret is presumed to be working for society's greater good and to have knowledge pertinent to the care of a child with special needs. Indeed, if Margaret has any faults, it's that she's too absorbed in her benevolent employment and in being the perfect mother to Isaiah. These are good excuses for her husband to have an affair, which is the only remaining blemish on this otherwise perfect family. As for the Lewins' nanny, like Margaret, she has been fully exculpated. In the movie, she is no longer an illegal immigrant.

While playing up Margaret's virtues, *Losing Isaiah* exaggerates Khaila's failings. The film, in addition to casting her as a crack addict, prostitute, and dangerously reckless mother, also brands Khaila a thief and a convict. In what is perhaps Halle Berry's most cringeworthy performance of all time, having returned to the site where she left Isaiah and found him gone, her character becomes unhinged. Khaila enters a convenience store one night and shoplifts in plain sight of the storeowner and a uniformed cop. When she exits the store, the policeman follows, grabs her arm, and asks her to pay for what she's taken. Thrashing, kicking, and mumbling nonsensical rap lyrics, Khaila resists the officer's attempt to detain her. Out of nowhere, another policeman appears, and the two men throw Khaila to the ground, where they empty her pockets and, in addition to pilfered snacks, find drugs.

Khaila's shoplifting spree results in a prison sentence, the length of which is shortened by her participation in a special program, away from the general prison population, with a group made up of other "unfit" mothers who all also happen to be black. Upon her release from prison, Khaila works with a counselor who makes sure she finds a job and a place to live. The counselor also teaches her how to read. In the film, Khaila's attempts at turning her life around are conditions of her release from prison. In the novel, none of this occurs. Isaiah's birth mom never steals or gets arrested, and she decides of her own volition to stop using drugs, to get a job, and to take literacy classes.

In the film, Khaila's counselor also helps her find an attorney, who discovers that even though the Lewins did what was required by law to attempt to locate Khaila while she was in prison, they never did find her. Khaila never signed away her rights, and this seems to be the linchpin that allows the case to move forward. Yet, this fact, once discovered, is never once mentioned in the courtroom scenes.

Instead, the case turns into a debate about transracial adoption, and the film tries to present arguments from both sides. Margaret Lewin, victim of an inhumane legal system, is a color blind savior rescuing a child from pathological blackness. Khaila's attorney, who doesn't much like his client and is more concerned with setting legal precedent, believes that black babies belong with black families, period. Absent a sociopolitical context or any suggestion of racism, blacks like Khaila's attorney who favor racial matching are simply color-obsessed, and unfit mothers like Khaila are the problem.

According to filmmakers, the central questions of *Losing Isaiah* are "Who's to say who is a mother?" and "Should a white person raise a black child?"[58] In going to such extremes to portray Khaila as a monster, what this film really asks, however, is "Should a depraved black birth mother, who threw her baby on a garbage heap so she could go smoke crack, be granted custody of the child, after years have passed, and he's already been legally adopted by a model white middle-class family?" The film's answer to this question is "yes" and "no."

Transmogrifying from drug-addicted monster to graceful beauty, Khaila wins her case and custody of Isaiah. Reminiscent of the Baby Jessica case, the unjustness of the legal system and its decision is driven home when we see Isaiah, kicking and screaming, as he is taken from the Lewins, and further, in the weeks to follow, when Khaila is unable to console the grieving boy. At her wit's end, Khaila calls Margaret and suggests that they co-parent him. When all is said and done, Khaila is still an unfit mother.

Like *Queen*, *Losing Isaiah* was an occasion to bring up Berry's biracial identity.[59] In one article promoting the actress and her film, she was quoted as saying: "I was born in Cleveland with a white mother and a black father." Overlooking the role of her "fairy godmother" and fifth grade teacher, Ms. Sims, Berry went on to say that her (white) mother taught her black history "at a time when it was not easy to learn much about it in school."[60]

In another such article, even though Berry had no experience with the child welfare system or adoption, because she had a white mother, she was said to have instinctively understood the issues at the heart of *Losing Isaiah*.[61] Some reviews commented on her character's remarkable transformation.[62] Janet Maslin noted that Khaila evolved from "derelict to debutante as if by magic."[63] Though the transformation is, perhaps, not entirely believable, because of Berry's beauty, and her concomitant urge to portray its polar opposite, it is nonetheless effective.

A number of critics, though, compelled to compare *Losing Isaiah* to a television weepie, generally liked the film and had praise for the performances of both Berry and Lange.[64] Others found the filmmakers' treatment of such an important social issue troubling. One reviewer called it "blatantly manipulative."[65] "Shouldn't this woman suing to regain custody of her son be charged with his reckless endangerment?" asked another.[66] A critic from *The Village Voice* said it was "a sign of the times when the law finds that black children should be with black mothers, but black mothers have to concede that sharing is the highest form of caring."[67]

By the time she had completed *Losing Isaiah*, Berry was certainly no stranger to "tragedy" on screen. In 1996, "tragedy" became part of her off screen persona as well, when the details of her pending divorce from David Justice played out in the tabloids. Berry went public about how painful the breakup of her marriage was. She was so distraught, she said, that she had even contemplated suicide. In an interview for *Ebony* she spoke of the time she went into her garage with her two dogs, sat in her car, and cried for three hours. In this early version of her suicide story, she stopped short of turning on the car.[68] Later, the actress would assert that she had actually turned the car engine on.[69]

Berry's divorce was also an opportunity to present the star as victim to her failed relationships with men: a romance with Wesley Snipes in 1991 that left her crying all the time; the well-known Hollywood personality, who remains unnamed and who hit Berry so hard that she lost 80 percent of the hearing in her left ear; the dentist who, during her marriage to Justice, sued the actress for money he said he had loaned her while they were together; and another ex-boyfriend who stole her Rolex watch and diamond earrings when they split up.[70]

Though her personal life was in turmoil, professionally, 1996 was a banner year for Halle Berry, especially with regard to her goal of assimilation and color blind films. The actress had principal roles in three films released that year. In the action picture *Executive Decision*, with Kurt Russell and Steven Seagal, Berry played a flight attendant on board a hijacked 747. In the thriller *The Rich Man's Wife*, starring Peter Greene and Clive Owen, she is heir to her murdered husband's fortune. Though it received little attention, for Berry, *The Rich Man's Wife* was a victory because she got to be "colorless for three months and feel what white leading ladies feel every time out."[71] In *Race the Sun*, a family dramedy set in Hawaii, Berry played a teacher to a group of misfit students. While *Executive Decision* and *The Rich Man's Wife* are absent any racial context, except a white one, *Race the Sun* revels in the multiracial diversity that is particular to Hawaii.

Despite Berry's onscreen visibility in 1996, new mainstream roles did not immediately come her way. On the rebound from her divorce and ready for a change of pace, Berry made the curious decision to star in a comedy helmed by an African American director. This was not her first African American comedy. Berry had already appeared in *Strictly Business* and *Boomerang*. In these films, however, her roles were played straight, and the comedy was left up to others in the cast. In *B.A.P.S.*, Halle Berry tackles comedy head on.

B.A.P.S. (1997)

Produced by Island Pictures, *B.A.P.S.*, an acronym for Black American Princesses, is a rags to riches hip-hop comedy about two ghetto fabulous waitresses from Georgia. Berry's character, Nisi, has a knack for hairdressing. Her best friend, Mickey, played by Natalie Desselle, is skilled in the culinary arts. The two dream of opening a business together: a combination beauty salon/soul food restaurant. In search of money to finance their enterprise, Nisi and Mickey leave their lackadaisical boyfriends behind and head for Los Angeles where Nisi will compete in a dance contest for prize money and the chance to appear in a music video with rapper Heavy D. Unfortunately, Nisi has not been bestowed with the gift of rhythm, and her dancing proves to be comically subpar. Their trip to L.A. is extended, though, when a white man dupes them into helping him attempt to bilk his ailing millionaire uncle out of his fortune.

The screenplay for *B.A.P.S.* was written by Troy Beyer (aka Troy Byer). The child of a black mother and a white father, Beyer was a regular on the children's television show *Sesame Street* from the age of three until she was twelve.[72] In 1986, she landed the role of Jackie Deveraux, mixed race daughter of Diahann Carroll and Ken Howard in the primetime soap opera *Dynasty*. Both Beyer and Berry appeared on another popular prime-time soap opera of the 1980s and '90s, *Knots Landing*, Beyer in 1985 and Berry in 1991. In *B.A.P.S.*, Beyer also has a small part as Tracey Shaw, attorney for the millionaire.

B.A.P.S.'s director Robert Townsend had initially set his sights on being an actor. After appearing in the Oscar-nominated film *A Soldier's Story* (1984), Townsend was elated by the experience of working with an ensemble cast of black actors. He felt certain that more roles would come his way. Though offers did come, they were all for stereotypical black man roles: rapist, mugger, or drug addict. Appalled by the limited range of film roles available, Townsend preferred to take jobs in television commercials, where he could at least retain his dignity, playing real characters instead of caricatures.[73]

When Townsend called his friend Keenan Ivory Wayans to commiserate, he discovered that Wayans had been offered the same scripts. The two disgruntled actors talked about what type of roles they'd really like to play, and over the course of a few years, they came up with the script for *Hollywood Shuffle* (1987), the film that, in tandem with Spike Lee's *She's Gotta Have It*, would usher in the 1990s new wave of black cinema. In addition to writing, directing, and starring in *Hollywood Shuffle*, Townsend provided the "guerrilla" financing, using part of his earnings from *A Soldier's Story* and charging remaining expenses to his credit cards. The resulting film is a hilarious satire which takes direct aim at Hollywood's black stereotypes.

Exemplifying the message of *Hollywood Shuffle* is its "Black Acting School" scene, an advertisement for a school where white instructors teach black actors how to act black. The commercial is narrated by Townsend, who appears at the beginning of the scene as a house slave with a Stepin Fetchit affect. When someone says, "cut," Townsend switches to a British accent and explains that playing slave parts did not come naturally to him; it was a craft he learned at the Black Acting School. The school teaches actors how to walk black and also features a language class called "Jive Talk 101." In yet another class, students can learn how to be a street hood, but this class, Townsend cautions, is for dark-skinned blacks only because "light-skinned or yellow blacks don't make good crooks."

Following the critical and financial success of Reginald Hudlin's *House Party* (1990), starring rap duo Kid 'n Play, interest in cashing in on black films and, in particular, black youth and hip-hop culture extended to the release of a number of hip-hop comedies. Frequently within the genre of romantic or sex comedies, these films, which provided a counterweight to the despair and violence of the more serious hood films, were characterized by (comparatively) low budgets, conspicuous soundtracks, and grassroots talent, often farmed from MTV and the Russell Simmons landmark HBO comedy series *Def Comedy Jam*.[74]

Representative of this cycle is *Def Jam's How to Be a Player* (1997). Released just a few months after *B.A.P.S.*, it stars standup comic and former *MTV Jams* host Bill Bellamy as a ladies' man juggling multiple girlfriends. Natalie Desselle has a part as Bellamy's sister. *How to Be a Player*'s script was created in a month by first-time writer Mark Brown and was purchased by Island Pictures, whose six-figure bid beat out competing interests, including that of Twentieth Century–Fox.[75] Other hip-hop comedies emanating from Hollywood at the time include *A Thin Line Between Love and Hate* (1996), starring, written and directed by *Def Comedy Jam*'s original host Martin Lawrence, the Columbia Pictures production *Booty Call* (1997) with Tommy Davidson, Jamie Foxx, and Vivica Fox, and Rusty Cundieff's *Sprung* (1997).

B.A.P.S., which can be located within this cycle of films, also stands apart for its stellar cast, integrationist approach, and treatment of women. One of Townsend's great strengths as director is his ability to assemble an array of admirable talent. With Natalie Desselle, who holds her own alongside Berry, casting was formulaic. *B.A.P.S.* was her first starring role and only her second feature. The casting of Berry, on the other hand, who by this time had established herself as both a credible mainstream actress and a pop culture beauty, did not conform to the hip-hop comedy recipe.

In addition to Berry, other accomplished talent in central roles includes Martin Landau and Ian Richardson. Landau, recipient of an Oscar (1995) and three Golden Globes (1968, 1989, 1995), stars as Donald Blakemore, the millionaire uncle dying of cancer. Ian Richardson, a Scottish-born, classical actor, plays Blakemore's butler, Manley. Richardson won a BAFTA Best Actor Award for his role as the scheming politician Francis Urquhart in the British television miniseries *House of Cards* (1990). His character was the prototype for Kevin Spacey's fiendish Francis Underwood in the Netflix *House of Cards* series (2013–2018).

B.A.P.S. doesn't stray too far from the casting formula, however. It also features a number of young comedians and comic actors. Anthony Johnson, who appeared in *House Party* (1990), *Friday* (1995), and *How to Be a Player*, is Mickey's boyfriend, James. The biracial standup comic Pierre Edwards (aka Pierre), who can be seen in *How to Be a Player* with Desselle and Johnson, is Nisi's boyfriend, Ali. Comedians Bernie Mac and Faizon Love also have small parts. Some of the film's more entertaining moments occur when Nisi and Mickey encounter real-life personalities, such as rappers LL Cool J and Heavy D. R&B singer Howard Hewett, actor Leon, basketball bad boy Dennis Rodman, and former MTV VJ, Downtown Julie Brown also have cameo roles.

B.A.P.S.' costume designer, Ruth Carter, got her start working with Spike Lee on *School Daze* (1988). Her other collaborations with Lee include *Do the Right Thing* (1989), *Mo' Better Blues* (1990), *Jungle Fever* (1991) and *Malcolm X* (1992). Prior to *B.A.P.S.*, Carter had worked with Townsend on *The Five Heartbeats* (1991) and *The Meteor Man* (1993). She was also the designer for Spielberg's *Amistad* (1998), and in 2019, she won the Best Costume Design Oscar for her work in the Hollywood black blockbuster film, *Black Panther* (2018). In *B.A.P.S.*, Ruth Carter is the visionary behind Nisi and Mickey's ostentatious style, which includes one of Halle Berry's most memorable onscreen outfits: a skin-tight, shiny orange PVC jumpsuit.

When our two heroines prepare to leave Georgia and board their flight to L.A., Nisi is decked out in said orange jumpsuit, while Mickey sports a yellow animal print pantsuit. Their look is accessorized with high heels, gold teeth, and exaggerated fingernail extensions. The excess of their flamboyant hair weaves—Nisi's in platinum blonde—rivals only that of the beehive hairdos in John Waters' classic film *Hairspray* (1988). Having made it to the dance competition, Nisi is soon expelled for hitting another dancer with her hair. Exhausted, sweaty, and weaves akimbo, the two women are making plans to return home when they are approached by Antonio (Luigi Amodeo), an Italian chauffeur, who offers them room and board in a Beverly Hills mansion, plus $10,000, to appear in a music video.

Nisi and Mickey are taken to the mansion only to find out from Blakemore's nephew,

Halle Berry (right) and Natalie Desselle are Black American princesses styled by Ruth Carter in New Line Cinema's rags-to-riches, interracial hip-hop comedy *B.A.P.S.* (1997).

Isaac (Jonathan Fried), that there is no music video. There is, however, a part for an actress, with an interracial twist. Isaac wants Nisi to pose as the granddaughter of Blakemore's only true love, Lily. When Blakemore was a young man, his family forbade his relationship with Lily, their housekeeper, because she was black. Isaac convinces Nisi and Mickey that in lieu of Lily, the presence of Lily's granddaughter would comfort his uncle during his final dying days. Isaac's real plan, however, is to take control of his uncle's estate by having Blakemore declared incompetent, using the presence of these two black bumpkins living in his home as proof.

With the offer of an acting job and the hint of an interracial relationship, the role of Nisi suddenly becomes a comfortable fit for Berry's image. Departing from the black-cast format of most hip-hop comedies, the stage is also set for a mingling of black and white reminiscent of the previous decade when popular entertainment such as NBC's sitcom *Diff'rent Strokes* (1978–1986) or John Landis's feature film *Trading Places* (1983) presented isolated black characters living among wealthy white people just for laughs. Most of *B.A.P.S.*'s action transpires during Nisi and Mickey's isolation in Beverly Hills. Townsend, nevertheless, manages to give black and white equal play and makes comic relief function as cultural exchange. Humor is attempted, not just when the black characters acclimate to whiteness, but when whites attempt to accommodate blackness as well.

To prepare for comedy, Townsend had Berry watch episodes of *I Love Lucy* (1951–1957), starring the mistress of physical comedy Lucille Ball and her sidekick Vivan Vance.[76] Nisi and Mickey's antics and their close-knit friendship also bring to mind another iconic television comic duo, Penny Marshall and Cindy Williams, also known as Laverne and Shirley. In fact, the pilot for the sitcom *Laverne and Shirley* (1976–1983), much like *B.A.P.S.*, has its single, callow, working-class heroines accepting an invitation to a mansion and finding themselves out of their element once they get there.

In *B.A.P.S.*, when Nisi and Mickey first arrive at Blakemore's mansion, though impressed by its grandeur, they just can't help but make fun of the artwork, including a Picasso portrait that looks like a friend of theirs "with a bad hair weave!" When they are

Classical actor and BAFTA winner Ian Richardson (left) and Oscar-winner Martin Landau are part of the comic cultural exchange in New Line Cinema's rags-to-riches, interracial hip-hop comedy *B.A.P.S.* (1997).

shown to their bedroom, the bidet in their en suite bathroom is cause for confusion and an opportunity for Berry and Desselle to try their hand at slapstick.

On the flip side of the comic cultural exchange, Manley, the British butler (and epitome of whiteness), is often forced to contend with black situations, like being sent on an errand to purchase rap CDs. One of Manley's funniest bits occurs when Nisi and Ali get into a spat over the telephone. Nisi hangs up on her boyfriend, but he calls right back. When Nisi won't pick up, Manley answers and finds himself functioning as go-between for the couple, repeating dialogue in their vernacular.

Perhaps the most refreshing aspect of *B.A.P.S.* is its regard for women. In *A Thin Line*, *Booty Call* and *How to Be a Player* the action revolves around men. Women— and men, to a lesser degree—function as sex objects. *Booty Call* centers on a bet that Jamie Foxx and Tommy Davidson have concerning who will be first to bed their respective dates, the hypersexual Vivica Fox and her more sexually cautious friend played by Tamala Jones. In *How to Be a Player*, women are merely a string of serial sexual escapades that come in an assortment of flavors. Similarly, in *A Thin Line*, Martin Lawrence's character is a player who makes a conquest out of the wrong woman, a psychotic Lynn Whitfield.

In *B.A.P.S.*, the action completely revolves around two women. *B.A.P.S.* is also conspicuously absent the bawdy sex scenes found in many a hip-hop comedy. As such, it is definitely not a sex comedy, and it's not exactly a romantic comedy, either. Next to its central female friendship, and in keeping with its integrationist theme, *B.A.P.S.* is more concerned with the platonic bonds that Nisi and Mickey develop with Blakemore and his butler than it is the relationships they have with their respective boyfriends. Yet *B.A.P.S.* manages to make romantic heroines out of Berry and Desselle, nevertheless. Near the end of the film, thanks to Manley's intervention, Nisi and Mickey are reunited with their boyfriends. In parallel scenes, Ali and James confess their love to their respective mates and promise to get themselves together.

As its title suggests, *B.A.P.S.* resists the familiar sexual scripts available to black women, positioning Nisi and Mickey not as "skeezers" but rather as "princesses" or virtuous women. That they are of upright sexual morality is confirmed when Mickey, in one scene, naively confesses that she's a virgin. As further evidence of their good moral character, when Blakemore learns that Isaac has been trying to take control of his estate, he offers the women $50,000 each for their trouble. Nisi and Mickey turn down the offer and insist that they are there because they want to be.

When Blakemore dies, the princesses are rewarded for their virtue. Nisi, Mickey, and Manley have all been included in Blakemore's will, while the nephew has been left nothing. With their inheritance, Nisi and Mickey's goal of opening a beauty salon/soul food restaurant becomes a reality. They also have enough money to finance a luxury cab service for their boyfriends. Manley, who could do whatever he pleases, chooses to remain by the women's side to support them in living out their dream.

Writing for the *Washington Post*, Esther Iverem thought *B.A.P.S.* was a "very funny movie" with "a lot of heart."[77] Janet Maslin of *The New York Times* said Halle Berry was funny.[78] Film scholar Peter Matthews, writing for *Sight and Sound* magazine, declared it "disarmingly sweet-natured." These opinions, however, were in the minority. Overwhelmingly, critics hated *B.A.P.S.* in its entirety.[79] Among the most scathing reviews was that of famed critic Roger Ebert, who mistook Berry and Desselle's camp styling for a "vulgar and garish" stereotype.[80]

Most critics failed to see that in *B.A.P.S.*, Robert Townsend offers up something rarely, if ever, seen before in film: a funny black female comedy duo that doesn't need to rely on profanity or vulgarity for laughs. Nisi and Mickey are good-natured, principled, romantic heroines who go for their dreams and value their friendship above all. They are also black women who can't dance or sing, don't use drugs, and don't have baby-daddies. Far from being a hurtful stereotype, Nisi and Mickey are a pioneering one of a kind.

Halle Berry's divorce from David Justice was finalized in June 1997. Earlier that year filming concluded on her next feature film, *Bulworth*. *B.A.P.S.*, with its interracial cast and integrationist theme, might be called a mixed race hip-hop comedy. *Bulworth*, with Warren Beatty as a senator turned rapper, is a white hip-hop comedy. Hailed by critics as a great political satire, *Bulworth* is the first of a handful of comedies to focus on white characters affected by hip-hop and African American culture. Other similarly themed films include *The Breaks* (1999), *Whiteboyz* (1999) and *Malibu's Most Wanted* (2003).

Although *Bulworth* is a comedy, Berry's role opposite Beatty is played straight. As originally conceived, her character was supposed to be a rapper, and according to the actress, she had an aptitude for it.[81] You won't see Halle Berry rapping in *Bulworth*, though. In fact, you won't see Berry do much of anything in this film, but her presence as muse provides Beatty with access to blackness and an excuse to rap.

By the end of 1997, it was announced that Halle Berry would join Larenz Tate, Vivica Fox, and Lela Rochon in the cast of the Frankie Lymon biopic *Why Do Fools Fall in Love* (1998). Berry had also started working on her next project, *The Wedding*.

Halle Berry stars opposite Warren Beatty in Twentieth Century–Fox's white hip hop comedy *Bulworth* (1998).

The Wedding (1998)

The Wedding is a two-part television miniseries produced for ABC by Oprah Win-frey's production company, Harpo Films. It aired during the 1998 Winter Olympics and fared well in the television ratings. During the week of the first episode, it was the most popular non–Olympic broadcast.[82] Charles Burnett, auteur of the critically acclaimed films *Killer of Sheep* (1978) and *To Sleep with Anger* (1990), directed. Halle Berry stars as Shelby Coles, a woman of mixed race heritage on the eve of her wedding. Other members of the cast include Lynn Whitfield as Shelby's mother Corrine, Cynda Williams as older sister Liz, Michael Warren as father Clark Coles, and Shirley Knight as the white

Halle Berry finds herself at the center of a biracial love triangle with Carl Lumbly (left) and Eric Thal in the Harpo Films TV miniseries *The Wedding* (1998), which originally aired on ABC.

great-grandmother Caroline. Berry's two love interests are played by Carl Lumbly and Eric Thal.

Writer and journalist Lisa Jones wrote the teleplay for *The Wedding* based on the novel penned by Dorothy West. At the time of the book's publication in 1995, West was touted as the last surviving member of the Harlem Renaissance. Dorothy's father, Isaac West, born into slavery and emancipated at age seven, was a successful businessman by the time his daughter came along. The product of a privileged, bourgeois upbringing, Dorothy, like many African Americans, belonged to a family that came in an assortment of skin colors. Her mother, Rachel, was light-skinned. Dorothy, on the other hand, described herself as the darkest member of her family and struggled with her appearance. The colorism she perceived within her own family, and within the insular world of the black elite, became a major focus of her writing. According to West biographer Cherene Sherrard-Johnson, West wrote obsessively about skin color for the entirety of her career.[83]

Set in the 1950s, Dorothy West's novel tells the story of the light-skinned Coles family, members of a particular class of the black bourgeoisie that spend summers vacationing in the Oval, an exclusive, racially segregated community located on Martha's Vineyard. Weaving together issues of race, class, and color, West's novel traces the mixed race history on both sides of the Coles' family back to the period before the Civil War. At the center of the story is bride-to-be Shelby Coles who, with "rose-pink skin, golden hair, and dusk-blue eyes," is the spitting image of Caroline Shelby, her white maternal great-grandmother. Shelby's mother, Corrine, is the daughter of a black man and a white woman. Shelby's father, Clark Coles, the great-grandson of a white slave owner, is a doctor.

To her parents' dismay, Shelby is engaged to marry Meade, a white man. Not only is Meade of the wrong race, he is also of the wrong class. Meade is a jazz musician. In the days leading up to the wedding, Shelby is also pursued by Lute, a dark-skinned outsider who has taken up temporary residence in the Oval with his three mixed race daughters, all from different white mothers. Liz's husband, Lincoln, is of the right race, but the wrong color. Contrary to her family's expectations, Liz selected a dark man for a mate, but Lincoln, a doctor, at least belongs to the right class.

Skin color is everywhere in West's novel. Corrine's class stature, for example, gives her the confidence to proclaim her blackness even though she looks white. When Liz became pregnant, she was unhappy that it had occurred so soon after her wedding. Her maternal instincts kicked in right away, however, when she gave birth to a brown-skinned baby, a child who would have to go through life without the protective (white) coloring of the Coles. Clark Coles married Corrine, but he finds women with brown skin, like his mistress, far more beautiful.[84]

As for Shelby, an experience she had as a little girl was pivotal to her identity formation. One summer, Shelby wandered away from the Oval to play with a puppy, and before she knew it, she was lost. When her family noticed her absence, an alarm spread throughout town that a child was missing from the island's colored enclave. With her curly blonde hair and blue eyes, beyond the borders of the Oval, no one made the connection between Shelby and the missing colored girl. When asked by a stranger if she is colored, Shelby says she doesn't know. When asked if she's white, Shelby examines her skin, and decides yes, she must be. By the end of the day, Shelby is eventually reunited with her family. It is only then that she finds out from her great-grandmother that she is indeed colored. This knowledge brings Shelby much relief, not because she was black, but because it meant that "she was something definite, and now she knew what it was."[85]

Halle Berry with her maternal grandmother, played by Shirley Knight, in in the Harpo Films TV miniseries, *The Wedding* (1998), which originally aired on ABC.

Considering West's obsession with skin color, and her description of the Coles as near white, the casting of Oprah's miniseries ought to be considered color blind. As such, the Coles' experience of looking white and being black is negated. So, too, is the dilemma at the crux of Dorothy West's novel. Near the novel's conclusion, Shelby questions why she chose to fall in love with a white man and why she never once had any interest in a black man. Lute's presence in the novel certainly contributes to Shelby's need to self-reflect, but he is not a serious contender for her affections.

In the miniseries, the intraracial conflict has been minimized and is replaced by the more familiar interracial conflict. Shelby, therefore, has no need to examine her inherited racial and social snobbery. Her quandary boils down to a hackneyed biracial love triangle in which she must choose between two men, one black and one white.

Introducing Dorothy Dandridge (1999)

Based on the Earl Mills biography, this Dorothy Dandridge biopic was produced for the premium cable station HBO. Martha Coolidge directed. Shonda Rhimes, who later went on to create such television series as *Grey's Anatomy* (2005–) and *Scandal* (2012–2018), co-wrote the teleplay with Scott Abbott. In addition to Berry, the cast includes Cynda Williams as Dorothy's sister Vivian Dandridge and Loretta Devine as mother Ruby. Brent Spiner is Dandridge's manager Earl Mills, and the Austrian actor Klaus Maria Brandauer plays Otto Preminger.

Introducing Dorothy Dandridge chronicles the well-worn hardships of the actress's life: rape by her mother's lesbian lover, an aversion to sex on her wedding night, the birth of her special-needs daughter, the breakup with Preminger, two failed marriages, racial discrimination, prescription drug use and her untimely death. Squeezed in amid the overwhelming misfortune are a few triumphs, the most prominent of which is Dandridge's appearance in *Carmen Jones* and the historic Academy Award nomination, which is followed by losing the award to Grace Kelly—another misfortune.

To play the part of Dandridge, Berry took dancing lessons for several months. She also intended to do her own singing and hired R&B singer Wendi Williams as a vocal coach. Ultimately, Berry decided it would be better to lip-synch to Williams' voice.[86] The film's singing and dancing scenes are mediocre. In the press, while critics overwhelmingly showed deference to Dandridge's legacy and the film's overt racial message, reception to the production itself was rather lukewarm. A writer for the *Baltimore Sun,* who thought that the movie lacked Dandridge's sizzle, found Berry's performance lovely but shallow. Some critics noted that *Introducing Dorothy Dandridge* was not as dynamic or compelling as it should have been, while others found it superficial and too simplistic.[87]

Halle Berry is not only the star of *Introducing Dorothy Dandridge,* she and Vincent Cirrincione are also executive producers. Of far greater significance than the quality of the film is the fact that Berry was able to bring to fruition a project that had been kicked around Hollywood for two decades and further use it as a means to hitch her wagon to Dandrige's star. In the two years before the HBO biopic aired, Dorothy Dandridge was considered the "role of a lifetime." While there were no Hollywood studios clamoring to produce a Dorothy Dandridge movie, competition was nevertheless hot and heavy.[88]

Aside from Halle Berry, a number of actresses were said to be interested in playing the part of the star-crossed star, including Vanessa Williams, Janet Jackson, Jasmine Guy, Angela Bassett, and Whitney Houston. Three actresses, including Berry, owned rights to different Dandridge biographies. Berry had recently purchased the rights to *Dorothy Dandridge: A Portrait in Black,* the biography penned by Dandridge's manager Earl Mills. Janet Jackson had optioned Earl Conrad's *Everything and Nothing: The Dorothy Dandridge Tragedy* (1970). The rights to Donald Bogle's definitive work, *Dorothy Dandridge: A Biography* (1997), belonged to Whitney Houston, who was in discussions with Disney to coproduce a Dandridge biopic. In connection with the release of Bogle's book, Houston's production company also co-sponsored a Dandridge film retrospective in New York.[89]

As others had done before her, Berry attempted to get her project made in Hollywood. Studio executives agreed that it was a great story but said it would never make any money. "This would make a lot of sense for you," they told Berry, "but no sense for us." Berry was undeterred and savvy enough to know that high quality films were being made on cable television, and, in some cases, reaching larger audiences than theatrical releases.[90] Eventually Berry struck a deal with HBO. *Introducing Dorothy Dandridge* is a signature Halle Berry film. As a producer, she was part of every discussion the network had on the production. This was her baby,[91] and she ensured that it would, indeed, be the role of a lifetime.

Before the film's release, Berry's publicity machine set to work on a campaign to conjoin the Berry and Dandridge images by drawing parallels between the two women. Nationwide, numerous publications reported on the "eerie" similarities. *Newsweek*, for example, spoke of the "eerie coincidence of Berry and Dandridge being born in the same Cleveland hospital."[92] The women's appearance was another "uncanny" similarity.[93] *Variety* reported, "Berry and Dandridge were soul mates of different eras: Each was a lovely, light-skinned African American woman, proud of her heritage."[94] A writer for *The New York Times* said, "Ms. Berry's fine features and poise make her an eerie double."[95]

Ebony magazine reported on a number of "eerie incidents" that occurred during filming of *Introducing Dorothy Dandridge* after Berry brought home one of Dandridge's gowns and tried it on. That the gown fit her perfectly was "eerie," Berry said, and she took it as a sign that she was meant to play the part of Dandridge. *Ebony* took the "eerie" promotion of Berry's film unabashedly to the limit, describing accounts of lights that would flicker, dragging noises that came from Berry's bedroom, and flying objects, all of which occurred after Berry tried on the gown.[96]

Another journalist pointed out that both actresses were "tortured souls,"[97] and Berry's thoughts of suicide after her failed marriage to David Justice became the pretext for comparison to the circumstances surrounding Dandridge's possible suicide. In fact, as her bid to play Dorothy Dandridge ramped up, what Berry originally declared were thoughts of suicide in early 1997 turned into a full-blown suicide attempt. When Berry appeared on *The Oprah Winfrey Show* to discuss the breakup of her marriage, she contradicted the statement she made to *Ebony* earlier that year and confessed that when she went out to the garage and sat in the car with her two dogs, she had the engine running for about fifteen minutes.[98]

Perhaps the most significant accomplishment in this promotion of parallels was the attachment of the discrimination Berry had faced in her career to that which Dandridge encountered during pre–Civil Rights Hollywood. "I can't get a starring role in a film because there aren't any, just like 40 years ago," she said.[99] One critic noted that *Introducing Dorothy Dandridge* was a story that could have been Berry's, "a tale of talent hidden under a smothering blanket of racism."[100] Another journalist hit the nail on the head when he wrote that the film had two messages. Its obvious message was that Dorothy Dandridge could have reached the pinnacle of Hollywood were it not for racism, and its implied message is that Berry is enduring the contemporary equivalent of the same slights.[101]

With the production and promotion of *Introducing Dorothy Dandridge*, the Berry and Dandridge images were successfully conjoined. Through the persona of Halle Berry, critics and audiences witnessed onscreen the heartache Dandridge experienced in her personal life and the discrimination she encountered in her professional life. In media, Berry's personal and career hardships became one with Dandridge's struggles. Vicariously, Berry became the quintessential tragic mulatto—pathetic and emblematic victim of racial injustice—rejected in a bid for an Academy Award because of the color of her skin.

In 2000, the entertainment community came together to begin the process of righting the wrongs that Dandridge and Berry had suffered in Hollywood. *Introducing Dorothy Dandridge* was awarded four Emmys, including one for Outstanding Lead Actress in a Miniseries or a Movie. Berry's performance also earned her a Screen Actors Guild (SAG) award and a Golden Globe. The SAG and Golden Globe award ceremonies are held in the months leading up to the Academy Awards, and both are good predictors of results on Oscar night. *Introducing Dorothy Dandridge* was a television movie, however, and not eligible for Oscar nomination. Thus, on the heels of these important accolades, Halle Berry was in search of another dramatic role.

While her divorce from David Justice was still pending, Halle Berry began dating Shemar Moore, the biracial soap opera star who had a nine-year run on *The Young and the Restless.* Their relationship ended in 1998, and by mid–1999, Berry and R&B singer Eric Benet were an item. Benet accompanied Berry to the August 1999 premiere of *Introducing Dorothy Dandridge.*

Around the same time Berry and Benet began dating, filming started on *X-Men* (2000), the first of the *X-Men* franchise films based on the Marvel comic series. Berry was cast as Storm, the mutant daughter an African American photojournalist and a Kenyan princess descended from a long line of African priestesses who have blue eyes and white hair. The day after she finished *X-Men*, Halle Berry was involved in a hit-and-run car accident in West Hollywood.

During the wee hours of February 23, 2000, Berry drove a rented sport utility vehicle through a red light, hit another car broadside, and then promptly drove to her house two blocks away. Ninety minutes later Berry turned up at the local hospital where she told a police officer about the accident and received stitches for a gash in her forehead. Berry made an official police report the next morning.[102]

Following the collision, while Berry took her circuitous route to the hospital, Hetal Raythatha, the other driver involved in the accident, was trapped inside a smoking, crumpled car wreck. Raythatha was eventually rescued by firefighters and delivered to the same hospital as Berry. As she lay on a stretcher awaiting treatment for her injuries, which included a broken wrist, Raythatha saw the famous actress walk by with a bandage on her head. Days later Raythatha learned that her celebrity sighting was no coincidence and that Berry was the driver of the vehicle that crashed into her.[103]

Berry could have been charged with a felony count of hit-and-run, but because she reported the accident to police and claimed to have been dazed by a head injury, she was indicted for a misdemeanor instead. Raythatha, who filed a civil suit against Berry for negligence, thought that Berry's star status played a role in the district attorney's decision to file the lesser charge.[104] Berry did have attorney to the stars Blair Berk on her side. Berk defended Mel Gibson when he was charged with domestic abuse and has helped the likes of Heather Locklear, Kiefer Sutherland, and Queen Latifah with DUI troubles.[105]

While Berry awaited her court date on the misdemeanor charge, a battle between her representatives and Raythatha's attorney played out on tabloid television.[106] The media attention also brought to light another similar hit-and-run incident, which had occurred three years earlier just a block away from the scene of the later accident. No charges were filed in that case. Berry and the other driver worked out their own settlement.[107]

Reports of Berry's driving troubles sparked gossip that she was a serial hit-and-run artist and became fodder for television's top comedians. When Berry appeared on the *Live! With Regis and Kathie Lee* television show with guest host Howie Mandel, the comedian quipped that Berry had crashed into him backstage and then left the scene. At the 72nd Academy Awards ceremony, host Billy Crystal announced that there would be a sequel to *Driving Miss Daisy* (1989), starring Halle Berry. Chris Rock did a segment entitled "Halle Berry 911" on his late-night comedy show and Jay Leno also did a few gags on *The Tonight Show.*[108]

In May 2000, Halle Berry pled no contest to charges of leaving the scene of a car accident. She was sentenced to three years' probation, fined $13,500, and ordered to perform 200 hours of community service. Raythatha was disappointed by the no-contest plea because it meant that Berry agreed with the facts of the indictment but avoided admitting to any wrongdoing. After three months of silence, and with the criminal case behind her, Berry was back to conducting interviews, attempting to heal the serious blow that had been dealt to her image. In an interview on *Today*, Berry said she had a "very defensible reason" for leaving the scene because her head injury absolved her of any responsibility.[109] In *Ebony* Berry shared that the collision was a complete blank and that she had accepted the opinion of doctors who predicted she might never recall what happened.[110]

While shifting the focus of the collision to her brain injury and total memory loss and away from her culpability, Berry also flipped the script to transform herself from villain to victim. The fallout from the accident was like "being dropped off in hell," she said.[111] Further, the "life-changing ordeal" she had survived wasn't really about a car accident at all but about her facing a fear of abandonment, a fear that she traced back to childhood and the relationship she had with her father.[112] Berry's suicide attempt was also revived.[113]

Berry's newfound notoriety on television and in the tabloids meant that she had also become a victim of media. Naturally, the actress didn't appreciate being made the butt of bad-driver jokes. Berry reportedly broke down in tears at the Oscars when Billy Crystal made his remark, and she almost walked off the set of *Regis and Kathie Lee* after Mandel's wisecrack. "To be joked about almost to your face, that's a hard thing to rise above today," she said.[114] For being hounded by the tabloid press in the days after the crash, Berry also compared herself to Princess Diana, the British royal who was killed in a car accident while being chased by paparazzi.[115] Raythatha found it "very saddening" that Berry was "trying to portray herself as the victim."[116] One year after Berry pled no contest, she settled her civil suit with Raythatha out of court for terms undisclosed.

Before the hit-and-run accident, Berry's persona was, for the most part, untainted. On and off screen Berry had worked hard to maintain a "positive" image and be a role model for young girls, especially young black girls. In particular, she had always passed on any scripts that required nudity. "I thought that if I did nudity, I'd let them down and send the wrong message to those girls," she said. Being publicly condemned and ridiculed, however, freed the actress from worrying about what other people thought of her. After the accident she came to the realization "it's not my job to raise those girls" and she decided it was time to do what she wanted to do.[117]

In late 2000, Berry began working on *Swordfish*, in which she was cast as a wanton spy opposite Hugh Jackman and John Travolta. Though it didn't involve a sex scene, *Swordfish* marks the first time that Halle Berry exposed her breasts onscreen. It was a gratuitous moment for which, it was rumored, she was paid a $500,000 bonus. She didn't do it for the money, though. The scene was important, Berry said, because it helped her get over her fear of nudity. Thus, *Swordfish* is the gateway film to the notoriously erotic action in *Monster's Ball*.

Monster's Ball (2001)

In *Monster's Ball*, Halle Berry stars as Leticia Musgrove, an indigent waitress and mother of a pre-adolescent son struggling to survive in a contemporary rural town in Georgia. Her husband, Lawrence Musgrove, played by hip-hop artist and record producer Sean Combs (aka Puff Daddy, P. Diddy, et al.), is on death row. Berry's leading man, Billy Bob Thornton, is Hank Grotowski, a white racist death row corrections officer who assists in her husband's execution. For the Grotowski men, the job of executioner is a family trade. Peter Boyle, as Hank's father, Buck, is retired from the profession. Sonny, Hank's son, played by Heath Ledger, works alongside his father in the same prison. Following Lawrence's electrocution, Sonny's suicide, and the death of Leticia's son by a hit-and-run driver, Leticia and Hank begin an intimate relationship.

The screenplay for *Monster's Ball* had been in development for several years with at least three different producers before African American filmmaker Lee Daniels got a hold of it. For Daniels, who finally managed to strike a deal to finance the film with Lions Gate, *Monster's Ball* was his first production credit. Daniels would go on to produce and direct such films as *Precious* (2009) and *Lee Daniels' The Butler* (2013) as well as the popular television series *Empire* (2015–2020).

For its representation of impoverished black womanhood, Daniels' film *Precious*, like *Monster's Ball*, earned Hollywood's highest accolade. *Precious* was nominated for a total of six Academy Awards, including Best Picture. It collected two: Best Writing, Adapted Screenplay, and Best Actress in a Supporting Role. The latter went to comedian and actress Mo'Nique for her portrayal of a woman who, alongside her husband, had molested and terrorized their own daughter since infancy. Gabourey Sidibe, the abused daughter and title character, earned a Best Actress in a Leading Role nomination, and Daniels was also nominated for Best Achievement in Directing.

Precious, with its black director and a mostly all-black cast, is a film about African American lives. *Monster's Ball*, despite its African American producer and casting of prominent black celebrities, is decidedly about white men. Marc Forster, born and raised in Switzerland and a graduate of NYU's film school, directed *Monster's Ball*. The film's Oscar-nominated screenplay, which focuses on the Grotowski men, is based on the

(Front, from left) Heath Ledger, Sean Combs, and Billy Bob Thornton in the Lions Gate film *Monster's Ball* (2001).

experiences of its white writers, Will Rokos and Milo Addica. Rokos, a native of Hickory Flats, Georgia, and Addica, who grew up in SoHo, Manhattan, were struggling actors hoping to boost their careers by creating for themselves the roles of a lifetime. Both men came from dysfunctional families, had fathers they didn't really like, and wanted to write something about the cycle of violence in father-son relationships.[118]

Although *Monster's Ball* made history with Halle Berry's Oscar win, it is probably better known for Berry and Thornton's lengthy, graphic sex scene. In this day and age, there is, of course, nothing shocking about cinematic sex. It's not uncommon in Hollywood for women to appear nude or partially nude in sex scenes. Nor is it unheard of for an actress to win an Academy Award for such a performance. Prior to *Monster's Ball*, Jane Fonda received a Leading Role Oscar for *Coming Home* (1978), a film in which she was partially nude, and her character was pictured receiving oral sex. Holly Hunter exposed her breasts in her Oscar-winning role in *The Piano* (1993), as did Gwyneth Paltrow when she won for *Shakespeare in Love* (1998). These scenes are rather conventional, however, and pale in comparison to the one in *Monster's Ball,* which looks more pornographic than mainstream.

What makes the sex scene in *Monster's Ball* seem like a softcore porn flick is that it eschews techniques typically associated with mainstream cinematic sex. Here, we are not presented with the "ideal" (white heterosexual) couple. The man does not make the first move. The action does not take place in the bedroom or some other romanticized setting. There is no soft music heard in the background, and the couple's movement is not restricted or hidden by evasive techniques such as partial clothing, bedding, or shots angled from only the waist up.

Contrary to the conventions of mainstream cinematic sex, in *Monster's Ball*, the couple, a racist white man and a grieving, poverty-stricken black woman, is far from the "ideal," as is the setting, Leticia's shabby living room. Berry, like a woman possessed, begs Hank to have sex with her as she growls the now famous line "Can you make me feel good?" over and over again. Evasive techniques are practically non-existent. Both actors are shown head to toe, completely naked from various angles and focal lengths and in numerous positions on the sofa and the floor. Instead of music in the background, the audio for this scene is comprised of heavy breathing, various grunts and groans, slapping skin, and a creaking sofa.

When *Monster's Ball* was first reviewed by the MPAA it received the NC-17 rating, an outcome that could spell financial disaster for a film. To receive its subsequent R rating, shots from the sex scene had to be cut. While theatergoers in the United States saw the R-rated version, in other countries audiences saw the film uncut. In Canada, for example, a writer for the *Vancouver Sun* seemed smug in the revelation that Canadian filmgoers would get to see two more minutes of "thrusting" that Americans would not see.[119] Even with the shorter, R-rated version, an American critic wrote, "The movie's most memorable moments involve some eye-popping soft-porn action."[120]

In the years following *Monster's Ball*, three more names were added to the list of women who received the Best Actress in a Leading Role Oscar for a part involving nudity or graphic sex. Charlize Theron won for *Monster* (2003), in which she played real-life character Aileen Wuornos, rape victim, prostitute, and one of America's first female serial killers. Kate Winslet scored for her role as a thirty-something former Nazi guard who seduces a teenage boy in *The Reader* (2008). At the 83rd Academy Awards, Natalie Portman received the Oscar for her portrayal of a ballerina for whom hallucinations and reality merge in *Black Swan* (2010). Like *Monster's Ball*, all three films depict sex in "non-ideal" sexual situations. However, in terms of the degree of nudity, what sexual content is depicted, how it's depicted, and for what length of time, only Kate Winslet's turn in *The Reader* might be considered a close second to Halle Berry's titillating and candid sex scene in *Monster's Ball*.

With its Southern setting and moody atmosphere, a black man's execution, and racist white men as arbiters in a system of racialized social control (i.e., the prison industrial complex), watching *Monster's Ball* is like waking up to a bad hangover from an antebellum narrative, in which Halle Berry has been cast as the hypersexual mulatto woman who wants nothing more than to be with a white man. Not surprisingly, however, critics for mainstream sources failed to see the film as a newfangled rendition of a white supremacist fantasy. Roger Ebert interpreted the couple's unlikely relationship as transcending race. *Monster's Ball*, he said, "is not a message movie about interracial relationships, but the specific story of two desperate people."[121]

In keeping with the studio's own interpretation of *Monster's Ball*, a number of critics regarded the film as a story about Hank's redemption, with Leticia as his savior, and he her newfound protector.[122] Nevertheless, not everyone bought into the redemption story. In spite of the filmmakers' attempt to make Berry look plain, as is the case with most of her films, her persona is at odds with the character she plays, and it's next to impossible to forget that you're looking at Halle Berry.

Halle Berry made history when she won the Best Actress in a Leading Role Oscar for the Lions Gate film *Monster's Ball* (2001). Berry and Billy Bob Thornton make an erotic but unlikely couple.

A *Chicago Tribune* critic observed, "If you're trying to show that a character has reformed his racist ways, you need to present a more convincing argument for this than that he enjoys getting together with Halle Berry."[123] To this critic's point, Thomas Jefferson fathered a number of children with his mulatto slave Sally Hemings, who also had a reputation for extraordinary beauty, but that did not move the Founding Father to emancipate her or to stop thinking of black people as inferior, not to mention, Hank's father, Buck, who, upon meeting Leticia for the first time, remarks that he also had a taste for "nigger juice" when he was a younger man.

Nevertheless, *Monster's Ball*'s "hopeful" ending asks us to believe that Hank has made a complete turnabout in a matter of weeks simply because he allowed a beautiful black woman to seduce him. Besides sex, the only thing that Hank and Leticia have in common is that they were both abusive to their deceased children, and one played a part in the execution of the other's spouse. Needless to say, these are not necessarily the makings of a healthy relationship.

Had Berry lost her Oscar bid on March 24, 2002, her part in *Monster's Ball* might have been more easily forgotten and relegated to a footnote in cinematic history. As it happened, though, at the 74th Academy Awards, for her role as Leticia Musgrove, Halle Berry made headlines and history when she became the first African American woman to win the Oscar for Best Actress in a Leading Role. For some African Americans, celebration of Berry's win was tempered by the fact that Leticia Musgrove is the epitome of the jezebel stereotype, the sexually aggressive black woman. This is especially troubling when one considers that of all the white women who have won this Oscar, only a handful, roughly 10 percent, were for roles involving graphic sex. On the other hand, the first and only black woman to win the award was rewarded for what is arguably Oscar's most hypersexual performance to date.

As Berry implied in her speech, many believed, or at least hoped, that the 2001 Oscar ceremony was a sign of racial progress.[124] Before 2001, just six African Americans had received Oscars for acting: Hattie McDaniel, Sidney Poitier, Louis Gossett, Jr., Whoopi Goldberg, Denzel Washington, and Cuba Gooding, Jr. Only Poitier's win for *Lilies of the Field* (1963) was in the leading role category. At the 74th Academy Awards, alongside Berry, Denzel Washington was awarded the Leading Role Oscar for playing a thuggish, corrupt policeman in *Training Day* (2001). Sidney Poitier received an Honorary Award as well in recognition of his remarkable accomplishments as an artist and as a human being. It was the first time in Academy history that more than one African American actor was honored in the same year.

Tom Ortenberg, then president of Lions Gate, who launched the campaign responsible for convincing members of the Academy to vote for Berry, viewed the historic occasion as a night of atonement. "I think Hollywood picked a great time to correct some historic wrongs," Ortenberg said.[125] The Academy has a history of righting wrongs, though it usually applies to individuals rather than an entire class of people. Artists who have been nominated but unaccountably lost the award have sometimes been compensated in later years with a consolatory Oscar.[126]

Denzel Washington was nominated twice for Best Actor in a Leading Role before 2001 and three more times after that. *Training Day*, it could be argued, was his consolatory award for *Malcolm X* (1992). As one critic noted on the eve of the awards, a victory for Washington would belatedly recognize him for failing to win for either *Malcolm X* (1992) or *The Hurricane* (1999).[127] As for Halle Berry, *Monster's Ball* was her first and, to date, her only Oscar nomination. Given the atmosphere of reparations at the 74th Academy Awards, Halle Berry's win, as the actress as much as acknowledged in her acceptance speech, might be considered a consolatory award for Dorothy Dandridge and all the black women that came before Berry who were nominated for but never won the Leading Role Oscar: Cicely Tyson, Diana Ross, Diahann Carroll, Whoopi Goldberg and Angela Basset.

Berry's historic accomplishment was followed immediately by the release of the James Bond film *Die Another Day* (2002) in which she starred opposite Pierce Brosnan as the sexually aggressive Bond girl Jinx. Meanwhile, her personal life was in serious turmoil. By November 2002, the tabloids were full of reports that her marriage to Eric Benet was in crisis and that Benet had been unfaithful. The couple separated in October 2003, and their divorce was finalized in 2005. As it was with her first divorce, the sordid details played out in media, including allegations that Eric Benet was a sex addict, allegations that the singer denied.

Through it all, Berry continued to work, churning out performances in *X-Men 2* (2003) and the supernatural thriller *Gothika* (2003). Halle Berry's star power had reached its zenith. For her starring role in the mega budget film *Catwoman* (2004), she received a paycheck of $12.5 million. *Catwoman* was universally panned by critics, and it bombed at the box office. Berry's performance as the feline superhero earned her a Golden Raspberry Award, more affectionately known as the "Razzie," a mock award that honors the worst achievement in film. Most Razzie recipients don't attend the award ceremony, but Berry showed up to claim her award and gave an acceptance speech to boot.

Following *Catwoman*, Berry earned a third Golden Globe nomination for her performance in the Oprah Winfrey/ABC television movie *Their Eyes Were Watching God* (2005) based on the 1937 novel by Zora Neale Hurston. In 2006, she appeared in the third *X-Men* movie, *X-Men: The Last Stand*, and in 2007 she had top billing and lead roles in *Perfect Stranger* (2007) and *Things We Lost in the Fire* (2007). After that, for the first time in Berry's career, there was a three-year period with no film releases. Nevertheless, Halle Berry remained a favorite subject of the tabloids, which were full of information on her latest relationship.[128]

In 2006, Berry began dating French Canadian model Gabriel Aubry. In 2008 Berry and Aubry gave birth to a daughter. The couple's relationship ended in 2010, with reports of a bitter custody dispute. Media attention continued unabated when, that same year, Berry met French actor Olivier Martinez while filming *Dark Tide* (2012). In 2013, Berry and Martinez married and had a son together. They were divorced in 2016.

Frankie & Alice (2010)

When Halle Berry first heard of this project in 1999, while filming *Introducing Dorothy Dandridge*, she knew right away this was a film she wanted to make.[129] *Frankie & Alice*, like *Introducing Dorothy Dandridge*, is another signature Halle Berry film. Berry is not only the star, she and manger Cirrincione are the producers. After winning the Academy Award, Berry had hoped it would be a lot easier to mount *Frankie & Alice*, but such was not the case. After almost a decade in development, filming finally began in 2008. The film premiered at Cannes to somewhat positive reviews, and in late 2010, hoping for a last-minute entry into the Oscar race, it had a limited release in New York and Los

Angeles.[130] Its wider theatrical release, originally set for 2011, was ultimately delayed until 2014.

Frankie & Alice, a Canadian film, is the tale of an African American woman living with dissociative identity disorder in 1970s Los Angeles. As such, in trademark ambitious style, Halle Berry takes on three characters in this film: Frankie, the host personality, is a black stripper; Alice, an alter personality, is a racist Southern white woman; and a third alter, Genius, is a young child with a high IQ. Phylicia Rashad is Frankie's mother, Edna. Frankie's psychiatrist, Dr. Oz, is played by the Swedish actor Stellan Skarsgård. The film is, purportedly, based on a true story created by Dr. Oscar ("Oz") Janiger (1918–2001), the psychiatrist on whom Skarsgård's character is based. In the 1950s and '60s, before the practice was banned, Janiger was well known for administering LSD to his patients. Berry and Cirrincione chose British filmmaker Geoffrey Sax to direct. Ruth Carter is the costume designer.

The film opens with Frankie at work, dancing in a cage to Marvin Gaye's "Let's Get It On." Although her character is a stripper, nudity in this film is minimal, and it occurs outside the context of the strip club. Nevertheless, Frankie excites her clients with provocative moves, and every red-blooded man in the club clamors around her cage. Later that night, when Frankie decides to hook up with one of the club's black patrons, Alice, one of her alter personalities, emerges. Alice panics at the realization that she's being groped and fondled by a black man, so she strikes him over the head with a picture frame and takes off into the night. Frankie is later found in the street, dazed and confused, and taken to a hospital where she first meets Dr. Oz.

Much of the movie focuses on Frankie's treatment and the platonic bond that she develops with Dr. Oz. Through helping Frankie, Dr. Oz breaks out of a professional slump and is ready to become a better man to his estranged wife. Although Frankie can never be completely cured, therapy with Dr. Oz eventually allows her to lead a more stable and productive life. Key to Frankie's recovery is unblocking a repressed childhood trauma. From the outset, with sketchy flashbacks, this repressed memory and concomitant trauma are hinted at. Near the end of the film, the memory is revealed in its entirety.

Frankie grew up in the South, during the 1950s, in the home of the wealthy, white Prescott family, where her mother was employed as a maid. The Prescotts had two children, Pete and Paige, roughly the same age as Frankie. As children, Frankie and Paige became best of friends. That all changed when the two girls grew into their teens, and Frankie fell in love with Pete. When Paige discovered the affair, she denounced Frankie outright. Frankie and Pete decide to run off together to a place where family, money, and skin color don't matter. On their way to this mythical destination there is a car accident and Pete dies.

At the time of the accident, Frankie was pregnant. After Pete's death, she looked forward to maintaining a connection to him through their baby, whom they had already named Alice. When it's time for Frankie to give birth, her mother, Edna, takes her to a motel and handles the delivery on her own. When Edna saw the baby's white skin, she abruptly exited the motel with the baby in her arms. Frankie never saw the baby again, and she suspects that her mother killed it. At first glance, *Frankie & Alice* seems to imply a connection between mental illness and racial oppression. However, in leaving space to interpret Edna as a baby killer, and the real cause of Frankie's pain, the film lets Jim Crow off the hook and makes the black mom the real villain.

Reviews of *Frankie & Alice* were mixed. A number of critics found fault with the script. In addition to Janiger, two other individuals share credit for the concept, and the picture had a total of six screen writers, all of which suggests a lot of working and reworking to come up with a script that satisfied its producers. As for Berry's performance, some critics were unimpressed; others found it acceptable; and still others thought it was outstanding. Peter Travers described it as Berry's "best and most shattering performance" since *Monster's Ball*. Pete Hammond for *Backstage Magazine* declared that Berry had delivered her "finest screen hour."[131] Berry also thought it was her best work since her Oscar win.[132] As a result of the limited awards season qualifying release in 2010, Berry was nominated for a Golden Globe. She lost out to Natalie Portman for *Black Swan*. An Oscar nomination did not follow.

In *Frankie & Alice*, key elements of Berry's persona—sexuality, race/mixed race, and interracial tragedy—are on full display. In the film's production notes, Berry said she perceived Frankie, and her angry white racist alter, as analogous to mixed race, ascribing to it a state of confusion. "I have a fundamental understanding of the chaos of her situation," she said. Producer Hassan Zaidi said that Berry was meant to play Frankie and was "probably the only actress in Hollywood that could" do so.[133] Certainly there are other actresses who could have played the part, but Zaidi's comment speaks to the way in which *Frankie & Alice* epitomizes the Halle Berry star image.

Chapter Notes

Preface

1. Jennifer Beals, "16th Annual GLAAD Media Awards-Fort Mason Center San Francisco," *Jennifer-beals.com,* June 11, 2005, http://www.jennifer-beals.com/speeches/womensnight2004.php.

Introduction

1. Richard Dyer, *Heavenly Bodies: Film Stars and Society* (New York: Routledge, 2008), 17.

2. Lena Horne and Richard Schickel, *Lena* (New York: Doubleday, 1965), 2, 3, 193.

3. *Stardom: Industry of Desire*, ed. Christine Gledhill (New York: Routledge, 1991), xiii.

4. Richard Dyer, "*A Star Is Born* and the Construction of Authenticity," in *Stardom: Industry of Desire*, ed. Christine Gledhill (New York: Routledge, 1991), 135–136.

5. Dyer, *Heavenly Bodies*, 2–3.

6. *Ibid.*

7. Donald Bogle, *Toms, Coons, Mulattoes, Mammies, and Bucks* (New York: Continuum, 1995), 4–13.

8. Sterling Brown, "Negro Character as Seen by White Authors," *The Journal of Negro Education* 2, no. 2 (April 1933): 193–195.

9. *Ibid.*

10. Jules Zanger, "The 'Tragic Octoroon' in Pre-Civil War Fiction," *American Quarterly* 18, no. 1 (Spring 1966): 63–66.

11. *Ibid.*, 63–67.

12. Anna Shannon Elfenbein, *Women on the Color Line: Evolving Stereotypes and the Writings of George Washington Cable, Grace King, Kate Chopin* (Charlottesville: University Press of Virginia, 1989), 2.

13. Thomas D. Clark, "Introduction," in *The Clansman: An Historical Romance of the Ku Klux Klan*, Thomas Dixon, Jr. (Lexington: University Press of Kentucky, 1970), vi–ix.

14. Joel Williamson, *New People: Miscegenation and Mulattoes in the United States* (Baton Rouge: Louisiana State University Press, 1995), 95.

15. *Ibid.*, 42, 59, 92–95.

16. Clark, "Introduction," xvii.

17. "Controversial History: Thomas Dixon and the Klan Triology," Documenting the American South, accessed September 12, 2020, http://docsouth.unc.edu/highlights/dixon.html.

18. William Mackey, Jr., "Introduction," in *Uncle Tom's Cabin*, Harriet Beecher Stowe (New York: Barnes & Noble, 1995), ix.

19. Clark, "Introduction," xiv.

20. Thomas Dixon, Jr., *The Leopard's Spots* (New York: Doubleday, 1902), accessed September 9, 2020, 198, https://docsouth.unc.edu/southlit/dixonleopard/leopard.html.

21. Fawn Brodie, *Thaddeus Stevens: Scourge of the South* (New York: Norton, 1966), 86; Peter Noble, "The Negro in *The Birth of a Nation*," in *Focus on The Birth of a Nation*, ed. Fred Silva (Englewood Cliffs, NJ: Prentice-Hall, 1971), 126.

22. Brodie, *Thaddeus Stevens*, 18.

23. Thomas Dixon, Jr., *The Clansman: An Historical Romance of the Ku Klux Klan* (New York: Doubleday, 1905), accessed September 9, 2020, 93, https://docsouth.unc.edu/southlit/dixonclan/dixon.html#dixon209; https://docsouth.unc.edu/southlit/dixonleopard/leopard.html.

24. Brodie, *Thaddeus Stevens,* 86–92.

25. Dixon, *The Clansman*, 57.

26. *Ibid.*, 94, 371.

27. Clark, "Introduction," v, xvii.

28. Noble, "The Negro in *The Birth of a Nation*," 125–128; Everett Carter, "Cultural History Written with Lightning: The Significance of The Birth of a Nation," in *Focus on The Birth of a Nation*, ed. Fred Silva (Englewood Cliffs, NJ: Prentice-Hall, 1971), 3–6.

29. *Ibid.*

30. John Belton, *American Cinema/American Culture* (New York: McGraw-Hill, 1994), 14.

31. Thomas Cripps, *Slow Fade to Black* (New York: Oxford University Press, 1993), 41; Bogle, *Toms, Coons, Mulattoes, Mammies and Bucks*, 10; Silva, "Introduction," 11.

32. Noble, "The Negro in *The Birth of a Nation*," 131; Melvyn Stokes, *D. W. Griffith's The Birth of a Nation* (New York: Oxford University Press, 2007), 234.

33. Clark, "Introduction," xii; Carter, "Cultural History Written with Lightning," 133; Cripps, *Slow Fade to Black*, 52–53.

34. Daniel J. Leab, "The Gamut from A to B: The Image of the Black in Pre-1915 Movies," *Political Science Quarterly* 88, no. 1 (March 1973): 53–64.

35. "The Sealed Envelope," Supplement to *The Cinema*, February 12, 1913, 81.

36. Montanye Perry, "The Debt," *Motion Picture Story Magazine*, December 1912, 81–86; G. F. Blaisdell, *The Moving Picture World*, November 2, 1912, 435.

37. "The Octoroon," *The Moving Picture World*, November 15, 1913, 716.

38. George Blaisdell, "In Slavery Days," *The Moving Picture World*, May 10, 1913, 600.

39. Leab, "The Gamut from A to B," 68; "Old Cross Roads a Fine Production," *The Morning Call* (Paterson, NJ), November 23, 1915, 8.

40. "Old Cross Roads a Fine Production," 8.

41. Leab, "The Gamut from A to B," 68; "The New Hippodrome," *The Allentown Democrat*, December 15, 1911, 6.

42. "Mystery Film Adapted from Munsey Tale," *Motography*, September 5, 1914, 327.

43. *Ibid.*

44. "Great Picture at the Temple Today and Tomorrow Only," *The San Bernadino County Sun*, June 10, 1915, 5.

45. Edward Weitzel, "I Will Repay," *The Moving Picture World*, November 24, 1917, 1186.

46. Louis Reeves Harrison, "A Woman of Impulse," *The Moving Picture World*, September 28, 1918.

47. "Has Been Well Done but Is Too Heavy for Present-Day Consumption," *Wid's Daily*, September 29, 1918, 19; P.S. Harrison, "Kildare of Storm—Metro," *Motion Picture News*, October 5, 1918, 2250.

Chapter 1

1. Josephine Baker and Jo Bouillon, *Josephine* (New York: Paragon House, 1988), 97.

2. Jean-Claude Baker and Chris Chase, *Josephine: Hungry Heart* (New York: Cooper Square Press, 2001), 5, 57–74; Bryan Hammond and Patrick O'Connor, *Josephine Baker* (London: Jonathan Cape, 1988), 9–10.

3. Jan Nederveen Pieterse, *White on Black: Images of Africa and Blacks in Western Popular Culture* (New Haven: Yale University Press, 1995), 229.

4. Susan Hayward, *French National Cinema* (New York: Routledge, 1993), 83, 149.

5. Jean-Claude Baker, "My Josephine Baker," *The New York Times*, February 4, 1990, BR1; Baker and Chase, *Josephine*, 13; Bennetta Jules-Rosette, *Josephine Baker in Art and Life: The Icon and the Image* (Urbana: University of Illinois Press, 2007), 53.

6. Baker and Bouillon, *Josephine*, 5.

7. Phyllis Rose, *Jazz Cleopatra* (New York: Vintage Books, 1991), 151; Carl de Vidal Hunt, "How an Up-to-Date Josephine Won Paris," *Pittsburgh Daily Post,* January 23, 1927, 5; Baker and Chase, *Josephine*, 18; Maurice Rochambeau, "Josephine Baker Relates Colorful Story of Her First Appearance Before the Footlights," *The Pittsburgh Courier*, December 14, 1929, 7.

8. Baker and Bouillon, *Josephine*, 38.

9. Baker and Chase, *Josephine,* 16–18, 31.

10. *Ibid.*, 17–18; Rose, *Jazz Cleopatra*, 11.

11. Baker and Chase, *Josephine*, 22–25; Rose, *Jazz Cleopatra*, 12.

12. Baker and Chase, *Josephine,* 36–37.

13. Baker and Bouillon, *Josephine*, 27.

14. *Ibid.*, 28; Rose, *Jazz Cleopatra*, 56–57.

15. Jim Haskins, *The Cotton Club* (New York: New American Library,1984), 16.

16. Langston Hughes, *The Big Sea: An Autobiography* (New York: Hill and Wang, 1993), 62–63, 223.

17. Henry T. Sampson, *Blacks in Blackface: A Sourcebook on Early Black Musical Shows* (Metuchen, MJ: Scarecrow Press, 2014), 114; Cary Wintz and Paul Finkelman, *Encyclopedia of Harlem Renaissance, Volume 2* (London: Routledge, 2004), 792.

18. Nathan Irvin Huggins, *Harlem Renaissance* (New York: Oxford University Press, 1970), 289; Rose, *Jazz Cleopatra*, 55; Haskins, *The Cotton Club,* 18.

19. Baker and Chase, *Josephine*, 59.

20. Wintz and Finkelman, *Encyclopedia of Harlem Renaissance,* 151; Henry Louis Gates, Jr., "The Trope of a New Negro and the Reconstruction of the Image of the Black," *Representations* 24 (Autumn 1988): 129–155.

21. Rose, *Jazz Cleopatra*, 100; Baker and Bouillon, *Josephine*, 27.

22. Jayna Brown, *Babylon Girls: Black Women Performers and the Shaping of the Modern* (Durham: Duke University Press, 2009), 191.

23. Sampson, *Blacks in Blackface*, 6–7; Bernard Peterson, *A Century of Musicals in Black and White: An Encyclopedia of Musical Stage Works by, about, or Involving African Americans* (Westport, CT: Greenwood Press, 1993), 92.

24. "Notice," *St. Landry Clarion*, October 21, 1893, 4.

25. "A Riot in Louisiana," *Lafayette Advertiser*, November 4,1893.

26. Shirley Elizabeth Thompson, *Exiles at Home: The Struggle to Become American in Creole New Orleans* (Cambridge: Harvard University Press, 2000), 8–12.

27. Stephan Thernstrom, *Harvard Encyclopedia of American Ethnic Groups* (Cambridge: Belknap Press of Harvard University, 1980), 247.

28. Peterson, *A Century of Musicals*, 253; Sampson, *Blacks in Blackface*, 62.

29. Baker and Chase, *Josephine*, 57, 68; Baker and Bouillon, *Josephine*, 28–29.

30. Rose, *Jazz Cleopatra*, 60.

31. Baker and Chase, *Josephine*, 74.

32. Stark Young, "Good Negro Musical Play," *The New York Times*, September 2, 1924, 22.

33. Rose, *Jazz Cleopatra*, 61; Aberjhani and Sandra L. West, *Encyclopedia of the Harlem Renaissance* (New York: Facts on File, 2003), 63.

34. Tyler Stovall, *Paris Noir: African Americans in the City of Light* (Boston: Houghton Mifflin, 1996), 20–21; Geoffrey C. Ward and Ken Burns, *Jazz: A History of America's Music* (New York: Alfred A. Knopf, 2000), 66–70.

35. Stovall, *Paris Noir*, 19–20.

36. *Ibid.*

37. Petrine Archer-Straw, *Negrophilia: Avant-Garde Paris and Black Culture in the 1920s* (New York: Thames & Hudson, 2000), 51–56.

38. *Ibid.*, 61–62.

39. Clifton Crais and Pamela Scully, *Sara Baartman and the Hottentot Venus: A Ghost Story and a Biography* (Princeton: Princeton University Press, 2009), 1, 38–57.

40. *The Life and Times of Sara Baartman: The Hottentot Venus,* DVD, directed by Zola Maseko, Philip Brooks and Harriet Gavshon (New York: Icarus Films, 1999).

41. Crais and Scully, *Sara Baartman,* 135; T. Denean Sharpley-Whiting, *Black Venus: Sexualized Savages, Primal Fears, and Primitive Narratives in French* (Durham: Duke University Press, 1999), 22.

42. *Ibid.*

43. Crais and Scully, *Sara Baartman,* 140; Sharpley-Whiting, *Black Venus,* 24.

44. Archer-Straw, *Negrophilia,* 107.

45. Baker and Chase, *Josephine,* 111; Rose, *Jazz Cleopatra,* 5; Ean Wood, *The Josephine Baker Story* (London: Sanctuary, 2000), 79.

46. Baker and Chase, *Josephine,* 4,116.

47. Baker and Bouillon, *Josephine,* 50.

48. Baker and Chase, *Josephine,* 113. Baker and Chase argue that Covarrubias was more than just the inspiration; he was the poster's creator.

49. *Ibid.*, 108.

50. Hammond and O'Connor, *Josephine Baker,* 17.

51. Archer-Straw, *Negrophilia,* 119–120; Rose, *Jazz Cleopatra,* 81.

52. Baker and Chase, *Josephine,* 6.

53. Rose, *Jazz Cleopatra,* 33.

54. André Levinson, *André Levinson on Dance: Writings from Paris in the Twenties* (Hanover, NH: University Press of New England, 1991), 74.

55. Baker and Chase, *Josephine,* 134.

56. Hammond and O'Connor, *Josephine Baker,* 42.

57. Baker and Chase, *Josephine,* 142; Jules-Rosette, *Josephine Baker in Art and Life,* 62–64; Stovall, *Paris Noir,* 92.

58. Rose, *Jazz Cleopatra,* 100.

59. Andy Fry, "'Du jazz hot à La Créole': Josephine Baker Sings Offenbach," *Cambridge Opera Journal* 16, no. 1 (March,2004): 45–47; Rosette, *Josephine Baker in Art and Life,* 62.

60. Maurice Bourgeois, "On the Paris Stage," *The New York Times,* January 16, 1927, X2.

61. Maurice Rochambeau, "Josephine Baker's Need for New Thrill Leads to Her Appearance in the Movies," *The Pittsburgh Courier,* January 11, 1930, 7.

62. Ylva Habel, "To Stockholm, with Love: The Critical Reception of Josephine Baker, 1927–35," *Film History: An International Journal* 17, no. 1 (2005): 127.

63. "At the Lafayette Theatre," *The New York Age,* January 11, 1930, 6.

64. Thomas Cripps, *Slow Fade to Black: The Negro in American Film, 1900–1942* (New York: Oxford University Press, 1993), 211; Baker and Chase, *Josephine,* 163–164.

65. "Guard Josephine Baker," *The New York Times,* February 2, 1928, 23; "Missiles Hurled," *The New York Times,* April 12,1929, 6; Hammond and O'Connor, *Josephine Baker,* 80–82; Baker and Chase, *Josephine,* 154–171; Baker and Bouillon, *Josephine,* 71–83.

66. Wood, *The Josephine Baker Story,* 172.

67. Robert W. Rydell, *The World of Fairs: The Century-of-Progress Expositions* (Chicago: University of Chicago Press, 1993), 62; Patricia A. Morton; *Hybrid Modernities: Architecture and Representation at the 1931 Colonial Exposition, Paris* (Cambridge: MIT Press, 2000), 3.

68. Baker and Chase, *Josephine,* 170.

69. *Ibid.*, 87, 176–196, 245; Baker and Bouillon, *Josephine,* 91; Jules-Rosette, *Josephine Baker in Art,* 63; Hammond and O'Connor, *Josephine Baker,* 91.

70. Sieglinde Lemke, *Primitivist Modernism: Black Culture and the Origins of Transatlantic Modernism* (New York: Oxford University Press, 1998), 113.

71. *Ibid.*, 112; Rose, *Jazz Cleopatra,* 134–135; Baker and Chase, *Josephine,* 174.

72. Spencie Love, *One Blood: The Death and Resurrection of Charles R. Drew* (Chapel Hill: University of North Carolina Press, 1996), 49.

73. Rose, *Jazz Cleopatra,* 136; Baker and Chase, *Josephine,* 174; Wood, *The Josephine Baker Story,* 158.

74. Baker and Bouillon, *Josephine,* 94.

75. James Parakilas, "The Soldier and the Exotic: Operatic Variations on a Theme of Racial Encounter, Part I," *The Opera Quarterly* 10, no. 2 (Winter 1993): 33–37; Fry, "'Du jazz hot,'" 50–51.

76. Fry, "'Du jazz hot,'" 48–68.

77. *Ibid.*, 53–56.

78. Baker and Bouillon, *Josephine,* 97–98.

79. Hammond and O'Connor, *Josephine Baker,* 95.

80. Fry, "'Du jazz hot,'" 57–58.

81. Wood, *The Josephine Baker Story,* 183.

82. Rose, *Jazz Cleopatra,* 164.

83. Baker and Bouillon, *Josephine,* 86–89.

84. Linda Mizejewski, *Ziegfeld Girls: Image and Icon in Culture and Cinema* (Durham: Duke University Press, 1999), 43.

85. *Ibid.*, 2.

86. *Ibid.*, 109–131.

87. *Ibid.*, 131; "New All-Negro Revue: 'Strut Miss Lizzie' by Creamer and Layton at Times Square," *The New York Times,* June 20, 1922, 22.

88. Baker and Chase, *Josephine,* 203; Hammond and O'Connor, *Josephine Baker,* 100; Baker and Bouillon, *Josephine,* 101–103; Robert Baral, *Revue: The Great Broadway Period,* 93.

89. Baker and Chase, *Josephine: Hungry Heart,* 203–204; Baker and Bouillon, *Josephine,* 101–103; Hammond and O'Connor, *Josephine Baker,* 100.

90. Brooks Atkinson, "The Play," *The New York Times,* January 31, 1936, 17.

91. "The Theatre: New Plays in Manhattan," *Time*, February 10, 1936.

92. Hammond and O'Connor, *Josephine Baker*, 99.

93. Rose, *Jazz Cleopatra*, 171.

94. Baker and Chase, *Josephine*, 191.

95. "Paris Resents Treatment of Josephine Baker in America," *Chicago Defender*, January 25, 1936, 8.

96. Rose, *Jazz Cleopatra*, 172.

97. Baker and Chase, *Josephine,* 326.

Chapter 2

1. "Nina Mae Eyes New Romance in East," *The Pittsburgh Courier*, May 14, 1938, 1.

2. Floyd Calvin, "Man Who Built Reputation Because He Knew How to Pick Pretty, Shapely Chorus Girls, Takes Rap at Critics," *The Pittsburgh Courier*, January 15, 1927, 2–1.

3. Norma Manatu, *African American Women and Sexuality in the Cinema* (Jefferson, NC: McFarland, 2003), 58–61.

4. Michael D. Harris, *Colored Pictures: Race and Visual Representation* (Chapel Hill: University of North Carolina Press, 2003), 88–92.

5. *Ibid.*, 88–92, 138.

6. Harris, *Colored Pictures*, 135–138; Patricia Hill Collins, *Black Sexual Politics: African Americans, Gender, and the New Racism* (New York: Routledge, 2005), 56.

7. Frank Manchel, *Every Step a Struggle: Interviews with Seven Who Shaped the African-American Image in Movies* (Washington, D.C.: New Academia, 2007), 321.

8. Fay M. Jackson, "Movies Want Only 'Uncle Tom' and 'Mammy' Types," *Afro-American*, October 12, 1935, 8.

9. Jeanine Basinger, *The Star Machine* (New York: Vintage Books, 2009), 75.

10. "Nina Mae McKinney's Life Highly Romantic," *The Chicago Defender*, February 8, 1930, 7; Ruby Berkley Goodwin, "From 'Blackbird' Chorine to 'Talkie' Star," *The Pittsburgh Courier*, June 8, 1929, 13; 1920 United States Census, Gills Creek, Lancaster, South Carolina; Roll T625_1701; Page 17B; Enumeration District 91; Image: 405. Census records indicate the family name is McKenna.

11. "Nina Mae McKinney Just a Little Girl," *The Chicago Defender*, April 5, 1930, 15.

12. "Tan Town Topics," *Variety*, August 19, 1923, 43.

13. Frank Cullen and Hackman and McNeilly, eds., *Vaudeville, Old and New: An Encyclopedia of Variety Performances in America, Volume 1* (New York: Routledge, 2007), 482.

14. Henry T. Sampson, *Blacks in Blackface: A Source Book on Early Black Minstrel Shows* (Metuchen, NJ: The Scarecrow Press, 1980), 496; "Royal: Midnight Steppers," *Afro-American*, July 30, 1927, 6.

15. "Finding Screen Negroes," *The New York Times*, August 25, 1929, X6; "Highflyers of 1927: Lafayette," *The New York Age*, August 6, 1927, 6.

16. King Vidor, *A Tree Is a Tree* (New York: Harcourt, 1953), 175.

17. "Adelaide Hall Returns to Cast of Blackbirds," *The Chicago Defender*, August 11, 1928, 6; Lewis Theophilus, "The Dance That Dazed Mother," *The Pittsburgh Courier*, November 10, 1928, B2.

18. Stephen Bourne, *Nina Mae McKinney: The Black Garbo* (Duncan, OK: BearManor Media, 2011), 15.

19. Vidor, *A Tree Is a Tree*, 175.

20. *Ibid.*

21. Manchel, *Every Step a Struggle*, 318.

22. Vidor, *A Tree Is a Tree*, 176.

23. "Finding Screen Negroes," X6.

24. Irving G. Thalberg to King Vidor, October 22, 1928; King Vidor to Irving G. Thalberg, October 22, 1928 and October 27, 1928; Irving G. Thalberg to King Vidor, October 27, 1928, all in King Vidor Collection, Performing Arts Archives, Cinema-Television Library, University of Southern California, quoted in Judith Weisenfeld, *Hollywood Be Thy Name* (Berkley: University of California Press, 2007), 38.

25. "'Honey' Brown Not Dead," *The Chicago Defender*, January 5, 1929, 7.

26. Irving G. Thalberg to King Vidor, November 1, 1928, in King Vidor Collection, Performing Arts Archives, Cinema-Television Library, University of Southern California, quoted in Weisenfeld, *Hollywood Be Thy Name*, 38.

27. Sterling Brown and Michael Harper, ed., *The Collected Poems of Sterling A. Brown* (Evanston, IL: TriQuarterly Books, 1996), 111–13.

28. Memo from Colonel Joy, October 4, 1928, *Hallelujah*, Motion Picture Producers and Distributors Association Case Files, Margaret Herrick Library, Academy of Motion Picture Arts and Sciences, quoted in Weisenfeld, *Hollywood Be Thy Name*, 27.

29. Jessye, Eva, "The Actors in 'Hallelujah' Didn't Get Enormous Salaries," *Afro-American*, July 5, 1930, A8.

30. F. James Davis, *Who Is Black?* (University Park: Pennsylvania State University Press, 1991), 133.

31. Weisenfeld, *Hollywood Be Thy Name*, 45; Thomas Cripps, *Slow Fade to Black* (New York: Oxford University Press, 1993), 251–252.

32. "N.Y. Critics See Race Insult in Hallelujah," *Afro-American*, August 31, 1929, 8.

33. Mark Vance, "Harlem, the Black Belt, Laughed in Wrong Spots—Likes Hallelujah," *Variety*, August 28, 1929, 5, 27; Ralph Matthews, "Hallelujah Could Have Been Filmed Right in Baltimore," *Afro-American*, May 31, 1930, 9.

34. "New Ideas in the Audible Films," *The New York Times*, December 15, 1929, X8.

35. Matthews, "Hallelujah Could Have Been Filmed Right in Baltimore," 9.

36. *Ibid.*

37. *Ibid.*

38. "Screen Notables Laud Young Film Star," *The Pittsburgh Courier*, November 2, 1929, A-3; Herbert Howe, "A Jungle Lorelei," *Photoplay*, July 1929, 36.

39. Howe, "A Jungle Lorelei," 36.

40. Michael B. Bakan, "Way Out West on Central," in *California Soul: The Music of African Americans in the West*, ed. Jacqueline Cogdell Dje Dje and Eddie S. Meadows (Berkeley: University of California Press, 1998), 66.

41. Howe, "A Jungle Lorelei," 36.

42. "All-Colored Revue Hit Featured in Centre Film," *Ottawa Citizen*, July 18, 1930, 22.

43. "Manhattan Serenade," *Variety*, July 9, 1930, 19.

44. Elisabeth Goldbeck, "Nina Mae McKinney Libeled in Nasty Magazine Article," *Motion Picture Classic*, March 29, 1930, 22.

45. Donald Bogle, *Toms, Coons, Mulattoes, Mammies and Bucks* (New York: Continuum, 1995), 40.

46. Elisabeth Goldbeck, "Step Tells All," *Motion Picture Magazine*, July 1930, 76, 92–93.

47. *Ibid.*

48. "Nina Mae McKinney Still Under Long Term Contract," *The Chicago Defender*, August 9, 1930, 5.

49. "McKinney Off Payroll," *Variety*, October 1, 1930, 5.

50. Harry Levette, "Behind the Scenes with Harry," *The California Eagle*, November 21, 1930, 10.

51. Harry Levette, "Behind the Scenes with Harry," *The California Eagle*, October 24, 1930, 10.

52. "Did Vivacious Nina Cast a Spell to Win Boy Hubby?" *Afro-American*, November 8, 1930, 9.

53. "Nina Mae Irked by Accounts of Many Loves," *Afro-American*, March 28, 1931, 9.

54. "Nina Mae Takes Paris; Berlin Comes Next," *Afro-American*, January 10, 1931, 3.

55. Thomas Doherty, *Pre-Code Hollywood* (New York: Columbia University Press, 1999), 108.

56. William Wellman, Jr., *Wild Bill Wellman: Hollywood Rebel* (New York: Pantheon Books, 2015), 282.

57. *Ibid.*, 281.

58. Mordaunt Hall, "In a Crook's Retreat," *Thee New York Times*, December 19, 1931, 16.

59. Hilda See, "Nina Mae is Quite an Artist in New Film," *The Chicago Defender*, January 16, 1932, 5.

60. Harry Levette, "Muse Gets Break in Safe in Hell," *Afro-American*, October 17, 1931, 10; Wellman, *Wild Bill Wellman: Hollywood Rebel*, 281.

61. "Talking Shorts," *Variety*, May 31, 1932, 14.

62. Billie Holiday and William Dufty, *Lady Sings the Blues* (New York: Harlem Moon, 2006), 117–121.

63. "Nina Mae in Ballyhoo," *Afro-American*, September 24, 1932, 10.

64. "Ballyhoo of 1932," *Brooklyn Daily Eagle*, September 7, 1932, 18.

65. "Paris Bound," *Afro-American*, December 17, 1932, 5.

66. "Leicester Sq., London," *Variety*, February 28, 1933, 56.

67. Bourne, *Nina Mae McKinney: The Black Garbo*, 59.

68. British Pathé, "London's Clubs and Cabarets: Charles B. Cochrans's 'Revels in Rhythm' at the Trocadero Restaurant, London," April 20, 2018, video,

05:54, https://www.britishpathe.com/video/london-clubs-and-cabarets-trocadero-restaurant/query/revels+in+rhythm+at+the+Trocadero.

69. Bourne, *Nina Mae McKinney: The Black Garbo*, 31.

70. "Life Is Real with Nina Mae McKinney at Granada," *The Pittsburgh Courier*, October 5, 1935, 7.

71. "Paul Robeson Seen in New Korda Film," *The New York Times*, April 3, 1935, 20; Andre Sennwald, "The Screen," *The New York Times*, June 27, 1935, 16; "Sanders of the River," *Variety*, July 3, 1935, 14; "Robeson Film Called Propaganda Justifying British Imperialism," *Afro American*, July 6, 1935, 9.

72. Fay M. Jackson, "Hollywood," *Afro-American*, September 7, 1935, 8.

73. Kenneth M. Cameron, *Africa on Film: Beyond Black and White* (New York: Continuum, 1994), 79.

74. Juliette Milner-Thornton, "Absent White Fathers: Coloured Identity in Zambia," in *Burdened by Race: Coloured Identities in Southern Africa,* ed. Mohamed Adhikara (Capetown: UCT Press, 2009), 186.

75. Manatu, *African American Women*, 58–59; Deborah Cameron and Don Kulick, *Language and Sexuality* (Cambridge: Cambridge University Press, 2004), 48–49.

76. Lindsey R. Swindall, *Paul Robeson: A Life of Activism and Art* (Lanham, MD: Rowman & Littlefield, 2013), 70.

77. Sennwald, "Sanders of the River, a British Film Based on the Edgar Wallace Stories," 16; "Sanders of the River," 14; "Korda Film Wins Medal," 21.

78. "Robeson Film Called Propaganda Justifying British Imperialism," 9; "Africans Believe Paul Robeson Was Tricked in British Film," *The Chicago Defender*, October 5, 1935, 24.

79. "Movie Men Lose by Suppression of Colored Stars," *Afro-American*, August 22, 1936, 13.

80. "Black Network," *Variety*, April 1,1936, 17.

81. Bourne, *Nina Mae McKinney*, 47.

82. Robert G. Law, "Nina Mae McKinney Seeks Divorce in British Courts from Her Hubby," *Chicago Defender*, May 1, 1937, 20.

83. "I Will Definitely Not Play Maid Roles Any Longer Vows Nina Mae McKinney," *Chicago Defender*, April 9, 1938, 18.

84. Ted Yates, "Nina Mae Tires of Playing 'Hell-Cat' Roles, Now She's a Lady in Revue," *Afro-American*, September 7, 1935, 9.

85. Sampson, *Blacks in Black and White*, 2–5; Jane Gaines, *Fire and Desire: Mixed Race Movies in the Silent Era* (Chicago: University of Chicago Press, 2001), 16.

86. "Nina Mae Ill; Ralph Cooper's Film Delayed," *Afro-American*, January 22, 1938, 10.

87. "Ralph Cooper Taught White Stars to Dance; Gave Lena Horne Her First Break," *Afro-American*, June 23, 1945, 8.

88. Sampson, *Blacks in Black and White*, 204.

89. *Ibid.*, 63.

90. "Million $ Pic Held Over Second Week," *California Eagle*, December 8, 1938, 2-B.

91. "*Gang Smashers* to Premiere on Nov. 10," *The Pittsburgh Courier,* October 29, 1938, 20.

92. "Million $ Pic Enters 3rd Big Week," *California Eagle,* December 13, 1938, 10-A.

93. "RKO Theatre Chain to Present 'Gang Smashers,'" *California Eagle,* December 24, 1938, 20.

94. Billy Rowe, "Harlemites Go 'First Nighter' for Sepia Film," *The Pittsburgh Courier,* February 11, 1939, 21.

95. "Negro Nabe Exhibs in Battle Over Pix," *Variety,* July 6, 1939, 6.

96. Rowe, "Harlemites Go 'First Nighter' for Sepia Film," 21.

97. "Griffith, NAACP Prexy Endorses Gang Smashers," *California Eagle,* December 22, 1938, 3-B.

98. John Kinloch, "Reviews," *California Eagle,* December 8, 1938, 2-B.

99. Sampson, *Blacks in Black and White,* 7; Thomas Cripps, *Making Movies Black: The Hollywood Message Movie from World War II to the Civil Rights Era* (New York: Oxford University Press, 193), 129.

100. Jayna Brown, *Babylon Girls: Black Women Performers and the Shaping of the Modern* (Durham: Duke University Press, 2008), 212–216.

101. Louella Parsons, "Jack Warner Pays $75,000 for 'The Wallflower' Play," *St. Petersburg Times,* May 28, 1944, 34.

102. Leonard Mosley, *Zanuck: The Rise and Fall of Hollywood's Last Tycoon* (Boston: Little, Brown, 1984), 237.

103. Thomas Dyja, *Walter White: The Dilemma of Black Identity in America* (Chicago: Ivan R. Dee, 2008), 172.

104. Werner Sollors, *Neither Black Nor White Yet Both: Thematic Explorations of Interracial Literature* (New York: Oxford University Press, 1997), 247–251; Williamson, *New People: Miscegenation and Mulattoes in the United State*s (Baton Rouge: Louisiana State University Press, 1995), 100–105.

105. Cid Ricketts Sumner, *Quality* (New York: Bantam Books, 1947), 103–109, 182–186.

106. Phillip Dunne, "Approach to Racism," *The New York Times,* May 1, 1949, X5.

107. Lillian Scott, "White Is Black in Hollywood," *Chicago Defender,* March 19, 1949, 1.

108. Dan Sullivan, "Determined Jane White Gets Off a Racial Treadmill," *The New York Times,* March 25, 1968, 50.

109. William Grimes, "Hilda Simms, Actress, Dies at 75; Broadway Star of Anna Lucasta," *The New York Times,* February 8, 1994, D22.

110. Janice Kingslow, "I Refuse to Pass," *Negro Digest,* May 1950, 22–31.

111. Janice Kingslow, "Trapped Between Two Worlds," *Ebony,* September 1959, 87.

112. *Ibid.,* 83–88.

113. Mosley, *Zanuck,* 239.

114. *Ibid.*

115. Elia Kazan, *Kazan: A Life* (New York: Knopf, 1997), 375.

116. Vernon Jarrett, "Janice Kingslow's Private Triumph," *Chicago Tribune,* May 23, 1975, 2–4.

117. Sumner, *Quality,* 66–67.

118. *Ibid.,* 69.

119. James Gavin, *Stormy Weather: The Life of Lena Horne* (New York: Simon & Schuster, 2009), 207.

120. Bosley Crowther, "Best Films of 1949," *The New York Times,* December 25, 1949, X1.

121. Bill Chase, "Pinky Best Anti-Bias Film Yet," *The New York Age,* October 1, 1949, 21.

122. Walter White, "Regrets He Has No Words of Praise for Pinky," *Chicago Defender,* October 29, 1949, 7; Robert Ellis, "Hollywood at Dawn," *California Eagle,* October 20, 1949, 15.

123. "New York Beat," *Jet,* February 5, 1953, 64; "New York Beat," *Jet,* February 4, 1954, 65; "New York Beat," *Jet,* February 13, 1958, 64.

Chapter 3

1. Joel Williamson, *New People: Miscegenation and Mulattoes in the United States* (Baton Rouge: Louisiana State University Press, 1995), 72–73.

2. *Ibid.*

3. *Ibid.*

4. F. James Davis, *Who Is Black? One Nation's Definition* (University Park: Pennsylvania State University Press, 1998), 113–114.

5. Ira Berlin, "The Structure of the Free Negro Caste in the Antebellum United States," *Journal of Social History* 9, no. 3 (Spring 1976): 299–300.

6. Davis, *Who Is Black?,* 6–7.

7. Williamson, *New People,* 62.

8. *Ibid.,* 6–7; 123; Davis, *Who Is Black?,* 58–59.

9. Berlin, "The Structure of the Free Negro Caste in the Antebellum United States," 299–300; Williamson, *New People,* 24–27.

10. Willard B. Gatewood, *Aristocrats of Color: The Black Elite, 1880–1920* (Fayetteville: University of Arkansas Press, 2000), 12–29.

11. Norma Jean Darden, "Oh, Sister!" *Essence,* September 1978, 99–105.

12. *Ibid.*; Laurie A. Woodard, "Fredi Washington," *American National Biography Online,* October 2014, http://www.anb.org/articles/18/18-03894.html.

13. Year: 1910; Census Place: *Savannah Ward 3, Chatham, Georgia,* Roll: T624_178; Page 13A; Enumeration District:0063: FHL microfilm:1374191.

14. Woodard, "Fredi Washington."

15. Darden, "Oh, Sister!" 99–105.

16. Jean-Claude Baker, *Josephine: The Hungry Heart* (New York: Cooper Square Press, 2001), 150; Cheryl D. Hicks, *Talk with You Like a Woman* (Chapel Hill: University of North Carolina Press, 2010), 42.

17. Woodard, "Fredi Washington."

18. Baker, *Josephine: The Hungry Heart,* 62, 69.

19. "At Roosevelt Theatre," *The New York Age,* June 17, 1922, 6; "Record Attendance to See Square Joe," *The New York Age,* June 24, 1922, 6.

20. Burton W. Peretti, *Nightclub City: Politics and Amusement in Manhattan* (Philadelphia: University of Pennsylvania Press, 2007), 21.

21. "Fredi Washington of Hall Johnson's Negro Music Play," *The Philadelphia Inquirer,* November 19, 1933, 5; Lou Layne, "Moon Over Harlem," *The New York Age,* July 4, 1935, 4; "Club Alabam," *Variety,* August 5, 1925, 35; "Club Alabam," *Variety,* October 14, 1925, 47; "Club Alabam," *Variety,* May 12, 1926, 58.

22. Cheryl Black, "Looking White, Acting Black: Cast(e)ing Fredi Washington," *Theatre Survey* 45, no. 1 (May 2004): 21.

23. "Black Boy," *Variety,* October 13, 1926, 48.

24. "Fredi Washington," *The Brooklyn Daily Eagle,* March 26, 1939, 36.

25. Paul Robeson, Jr., *The Undiscovered Paul Robeson: An Artist's Journey, 1898–1939* (Hoboken, NJ: Wiley, 2001), 100.

26. J. Brooks Atkinson, "The Play: Pugilism a la Mode," *New York Times,* October 7, 1926, 30.

27. "She Adopted Russian Method Though She Is from Savannah," *The Brooklyn Daily Eagle,* March 5, 1933, 54; "Moore's Dad, Irish; Freddie's, Italian," *The Afro-American,* August 10, 1929, 7; Donald Bogle, *Brown Sugar: Eighty Years of America's Black Female Superstars* (New York: Harmony Books, 1980), 79.

28. Cheryl Black, "Fredi Washington," in *Notable American Women: A Biographical Dictionary,* ed. Susan Ware and Stacy Braukman (Cambridge: Belknap Press of Harvard University Press, 2004), 666.

29. "Many Dance Teams Have Sparkled, Then Faded Out," *Afro-American,* June 1929, 1935, 9; Margo Jefferson, "Vintage Glimpses of a Lost Theatrical World," *The New York Times,* October 20, 1996.

30. Gatewood, *Aristocrats of Color,* 12–29, 46–52; Geoffrey C. Ward and Ken Burns, *Jazz: A History of America's Music* (New York: Alfred A. Knopf, 2000), 49.

31. Mark Tucker, *The Duke Ellington Reader* (New York: Oxford University Press), 10.

32. Williamson, *New People,* 152.

33. Krin Gabbard, *Jammin' at the Margins: Jazz and American Cinema* (Chicago: University of Chicago Press, 1996), 64; David Grazian, *Blue Chicago: The Search for Authenticity in Urban Blues Clubs* (Chicago: University of Chicago Press, 2005), 29.

34. Donald Bogle, *Bright Boulevards, Bold Dreams: The Story of Black Hollywood* (New York: One World, 2005), 131.

35. Mercer Ellington and Stanley Dance, *Duke Ellington in Person: An Intimate Memoir* (Boston: Houghton Mifflin, 1978), 47–48.

36. Gabbard, *Jammin' at the Margins,* 162.

37. "'Black and Tan' with Duke Ellington's Orchestra," *Variety,* November 6, 1929, 19.

38. Bernard L. Peterson, Jr., *A Century of Musicals in Black and White* (Westport, CT: Greenwood Press, 1993), 340; Stephen Rathbun, "'Sweet Chariot' Opens," *The New York Sun,* October 24, 1930, 36; William E. Clark, "'Sweet Chariot' Misses Being an Important Play," *The New York Age,* November 1, 1930, 6.

39. "Savannah to Broadway," *New York Evening Post,* September 28, 1931.

40. Peterson, Jr., *A Century of Musicals in Black and White,* 318–319; J. Brooks Atkinson, "The Play," *The New York Times,* September 17, 1931, 21; "Sisters Star in New Melodrama," *Afro-American,* September 26, 1931, 9.

41. Bogle, *Bright Boulevards, Bold Dreams,* 133.

42. "Fredi Names 8 'Other' Women," *Afro-American,* January 31, 1948, 1.

43. Daniel Eagan, *America's Film Legacy: The Authoritative Guide to the Landmark Movies in the National Film Registry* (New York: Continuum, 2010), 215–216; "Emperor Jones," *Variety,* September 26, 1933, 15.

44. Chappy Gardner, "Paul Robeson and Fredi Washington Play 'Star' Roles," *The Pittsburgh Courier,* June 24, 1933, 6.

45. Eagan, *America's Film Legacy,* 216; "Emperor Jones," *Variety,* 15; Mordaunt Hall, "Paul Robeson in the Pictorial Conception of Eugene O'Neill's Play," *The New York Times,* September 20, 1933, 26.

46. Alyn Shipton, *Hi-De-Ho: The Life of Cab Calloway* (New York: Oxford University Press, 2010), 1–17.

47. *Ibid.,* 48.

48. Earl Conrad, "To Pass or Not to Pass?" *The Chicago Defender,* June 16, 1945, 15.

49. "Imitation of Life," *Variety,* November 27, 1934, 15.

50. "Universal Still Looks for White-Negro Girl," *California Eagle,* January 26, 1934, 9.

51. Bogle, *Bright Boulevards, Bold Dreams,*135.

52. "Imitation of Life," *Motion Picture Herald,* December 1, 1934, 39–42; "Imitation of Life," *Motion Picture Daily,* November 20, 1934, 4; Richard E. Hays, "New Picture at Music Hall is One of Finest," *The Seattle Daily News,* December 7, 1934, 23; "Imitation of Life," *Variety,* November 27, 1934, 15.

53. Fannie Hurst, *Imitation of Life* (New York: Permabooks, 1959), 73.

54. Werner Sollors, *Neither Black Nor White Yet Both: Thematic Explorations of Interracial Literature* (New York: Oxford University Press, 1997), 248–254.

55. Hurst, *Imitation of Life,* 145.

56. *Ibid.,* 243.

57. "Imitation of Life," *Variety,* November 27, 1934, 15.

58. Andrew Sennwald, "The Screen Version of Fannie Hurst's 'Imitation of Life,' at the Roxy," *The New York Times,* November 24, 1934, 19.

59. Sterling A. Brown, "Imitation of Life: Once a Pancake," in *A Son's Return: Selected Essays of Sterling A. Brown,* ed. Mark A. Sanders (Boston: Northeastern University Press, 1996), 288–289.

60. "Imitation of Life," *The New York Age,* February 2, 1935, 6; Vere E. Johns, "In the Name of Art," *The New York Age,* February 9, 1935; Fay M. Jackson, "Fredi Washington Strikes New Note in Hollywood Film," *The Pittsburgh Courier,* December 15, 1934, A8; Harry Levette, "'Imitation of Life' Is Possible

Best Seller," *Chicago Defender*, December 15, 1934,
9; George Schuyler, "Views and Reviews," *The Pittsburgh Courier*, June 8, 1935, 12.

61. L. Herbert Henegan, "*Imitation of Life* White
Folks Play, Says Film Star," *Afro-American*, February
9, 1935, 1–2.

62. Earl Conrad, "To Pass or Not to Pass," *The
Chicago Defender*, June 16, 1945, 15.

63. Sheila Rule, "Fredi Washington, 90, Actress;
Broke Ground for Black Artists," *New York Times*,
June 30, 1994, D21.

64. Ralph Matthews, "Peola Off-Stage,"
Afro-American, November 16, 1935, 8.

65. "Negro Film Is Banned on Revival Attempt,"
The Morning News (Wilmington), October 3, 1945,
10.

66. Russell E. Smith, "The Authors of the Photoplays," *The Book News Monthly* 33 (March 1915).

67. "Par May Show U.S. Film in England Before
Here," *Variety*, February 20, 1934, 13.

68. Ellen C. Scott, *Cinema Civil Rights: Regulation, Repression and Race in the Classical Hollywood
Era* (New Brunswick: Rutgers University Press,
2015), 48–52.

69. Ben B. Lindsey and Wainwright Evans, *The
Revolt of Modern Youth* (New York: Boni & Liveright, 1925), 267–277.

70. *Ibid.*

71. "White Child Is Kept In 'Mammy's' Custody,"
The New York Times, November 21, 1936, 9.

72. Elizabeth Bartholet, "Where Do Black Children Belong? The Politics of Race Matching in
Adoption," *University of Pennsylvania Law Review*
139, no. 5 (May 1991): 117.

73. Lindsey and Evans, *The Revolt of Modern
Youth*, 271–273.

74. Nelson B. Bell, "Eight Film Plays Are Named
Best of Three Months by Will H. Hays National Previewing Committees," *The Washington Post*, September 10, 1937, 12.

75. "Martha Raye 'Goes Colored' and the South
Raises 'Cain,'" *The Pittsburgh Courier*, January 1,
1938, 18; "A&T, Bennett Students Boycott White Theatres," *The Pittsburgh Courier*, February 19, 1938, 3.

76. "One Mile from Heaven," *Motion Picture
Herald*, July 24, 1937, 47; "One Mile from Heaven,"
Motion Picture Daily, July 17, 1937, 3.

77. Ellen Herman, *Kinship by Design: A History
of Adoption in the Modern United States* (Chicago:
University of Chicago Press, 2008), 129.

78. "Fredi Washington 'Steals' Another Movie,"
The Pittsburgh Courier, July 31, 1937, 20; "One Mile
from Heaven," *Motion Picture Herald*, July 24, 1937,
47; "One Mile from Heaven," *The Film Daily*, July 20,
1937, 10.

79. "One Mile from Heaven," *Modern Screen*,
October 1937, 108.

80. "One Mile from Heaven," *Variety*, July 21,
1937, 18.

81. "Black Swan Artist Agrees Not to Marry
Within Year," *The New York Age*, December 24, 1921,
2; "Black Swan Troubadours at Auditorium," *The
Charlotte News*, May 22, 1922, 10.

82. Jonathan Dewberry, "Black Actors Unite: The
Negro Actors' Guild," *The Black Scholar* 21, no. 2
(March–May 1990): 6.

83. "Ethel Waters," *Variety*, June 21, 1939, 32.

84. Brooks Atkinson, "The Play," *The New York
Times*, October 18, 1946, 33.

85. "Sorry Wrong Number," *Afro-American*, February 5, 1949, 7.

Chapter 4

1. Seymour Peck, "Calling on Lena Horne," *The
New York Times*, October 27, 1957, X3.

2. Ed Sullivan, "Broadway," *Daily News*, October
1, 1934, 34; "Harlem, N.Y.," *Variety*, September 18,
1935, 33.

3. Lena Horne and Richard Schickel, *Lena* (Garden City, NY: Doubleday & Company, 1965), 67–68;
James Gavin, *Stormy Weather* (New York: Simon &
Schuster, 2009), 52–53.

4. Horne & Schickel, *Lena*, 117.

5. Gavin, *Stormy Weather*, 89.

6. *Ibid.*, 105.

7. Donald Bogle, *Bright Boulevards, Bold Dreams*
(New York: One World, 2005), 219.

8. John Pope, "Lena Horne," *Lagniappe*, 25 June–1
July, 1977, 3, quoted in Shane Vogel, "Lena Horne's
Impersona," *Camera Obscura* 23, no. 1 (May 2008): 15.

9. Gail Lumet Buckley, *The Hornes: An American
Family* (New York: Alfred A. Knopf, 1986), 63–66.

10. *Ibid.*, 9–15.

11. *Ibid.*, 9–25.

12. *Ibid.*, 29–55.

13. *Ibid.*, 62–74.

14. *Ibid.*, 80–81.

15. *Ibid.*, 112, 113, 136.

16. Jim Haskins, *The Cotton Club* (New York:
New American Library, 1984), 29–32.

17. *Ibid.*, 29–34.

18. Buckley, *The Hornes*, 118; Jim Haskins and
Kathleen Benson, *Lena: A Personal and Professional
Biography of Lena Horne* (Briarcliff Manor, NY:
Stein and Day, 1984), 30.

19. Gavin, *Stormy Weather*, 39.

20. Horne and Schickel, *Lena*, 42, 59–61; "Night
Club Reviews," *Variety*, September 18, 1935, 38.

21. Horne and Schickel, *Lena*, 64; Haskins and
Benson, *Lena*, 38; Gavin, *Stormy Weather*, 53.

22. Horne and Schickel, *Lena*, 72.

23. "Nina Mae Ill; Ralph Cooper's Film Delayed,"
Afro-American, January 22, 1938, 10.

24. Helen Arstein and Carlton Moss, *In Person,
Lena Horne* (New York: Greenberg, 1950), 106–107.

25. Robert Dwan, "A Legend in His Own Feet,"
Los Angeles Times, July 26, 1981, 6.

26. Leonard Feather, "Moore Travels the Long
Way to Success," *Los Angeles Times*, March 10, 1974,
18.

27. Richard Dyer, *In the Space of a Song* (New
York: Routledge, 2012), 117.

28. Horne and Schickel, *Lena*, 91.

29. Earl J. Morris, "All-Sepia Musical Praised By

Morris," *The Pittsburgh Courier*, June 25, 1938, 20; William G. Nunn, "Bill Nunn Believes *Duke Is Tops* Sets Pace for Colored Pictures," *The Pittsburgh Courier* June 25, 1938, 21; Dennis McLellan, "Hedda Brooks, 86; Pianist Known as 'Queen of the Boogie' and a Popular Torch Singer," *Los Angeles Times*, November 23, 2002, B14.

30. John Kinloch, "Reviews," *California Eagle*, June 16, 1938, 2B; Romeo L. Dougherty, "*The Duke Is Tops* is Best All-Colored Production Says Veteran Critic," *The New York Age*, July 23, 1938; Harry Levette, "L. Horne Screens Well," *Chicago Defender*, May 7, 1938.

31. Burns Mantle, "'Blackbirds of 1939' Indicate a Talent Shortage in Harlem," *Daily News*, February 13, 1939, 29.

32. Brooks Atkinson, "Lew Leslie Gets His 'Blackbirds of 1939' Onto the Stage of the Hudson Theatre," *The New York Times*, February 13, 1939, 12.

33. Horne and Schickel, *Lena*, 103–106; Arstein and Moss, *In Person*, 147–148.

34. Geoffrey Ward and Ken Burns, *Jazz: A History of America's Music* (New York: Alfred A. Knopf, 2000), 236, 242.

35. Arstein and Moss, *In Person*, 153.

36. Horne and Schickel, *Lena*, 110; Charlie Barnet and Stanley Dance, *Those Swinging Years* (Baton Rouge: Louisiana State University, 1984), 95.

37. Stephen R. Duncan, *The Rebel Café: Sex, Race, and Politics in Cold War America's Nightclub Underground* (Baltimore: Johns Hopkins University Press, 2018), 40–41.

38. Billie Holiday and William Dufty, *Lady Sings the Blues* (New York: Harlem Moon, 2006), 94.

39. Ward and Burns, *Jazz*, 269–270.

40. Horne and Schickel, *Lena*, 113; Barney Josephson and Trilling-Josephson, *Café Society: The wrong place for the Right people* (Urbana: University of Illinois Press, 2009), 119–122.

41. Josephson with Trilling-Josephson, *Café Society*, 122.

42. *Ibid.*, 122.

43. Gavin, *Stormy Weather*, 84.

44. Horne and Schickel, *Lena*, 114.

45. Buckley, *The Hornes*, 144.

46. Tom Nolan, *Three Chords for Beauty's Sake: The Life of Artie Shaw* (New York: W.W. Norton, 2011), 162–163; Gavin, *Stormy Weather*, 88–89.

47. Horne and Schickel, *Lena*, 120; Buckley, *The Hornes*, 145; Gavin, *Stormy Weather*, 87.

48. Colin Davey, "Boogie-Woogie Dream: A Synopsis," Boogie Woogie Press, accessed December 11, 2020, http://www.colindavey.com/boogiewoogie/articles/bwdream1.htm.

49. "Trocadero's Affairs in Federal and Justice Courts," *Los Angeles Times*, October 11, 1939, II-1.

50. Horne and Schickel, *Lena*, 120–121; Haskins and Benson, *Lena*, 60; Buckley, *The Hornes*, 150. "Lena Horne Leaves Broadway," *The Pittsburgh Courier*, October 25, 1941, 21.

51. Horne and Schickel, *Lena*, 124; David Hajdu, *Lush Life: A Biography of Billy Strayhorn* (New York: Farrar, Straus, Giroux, 1996), 94–96; James Sullivan,

"Q&A with Lena Horne," *San Francisco Examiner*, May 31, 1998, 46.

52. Horne and Schickel, *Lena*, 122.

53. Joanna Dee Das, *Katherine Dunham: Dance and the African Diaspora* (New York: Oxford University Press, 2017), 78.

54. Phillip Scheuer, "Many Stars of 'Rhythm' Just Big Happy Family," *Los Angeles Times*, January 29, 1943, 22; Kate Cameron, "Paramount Stars in Variety Show," *Daily News*, January 10, 1943, 35.

55. Horne and Schickel, *Lena*, 172; Vincent Tubbs, "Soldiers Down Under Asking for Pin-up Girls," *Afro American*, November 20, 1943, 6.

56. Barbara Berch, "Score for Miss Horne," *The New York Times*, November 29, 1942, X4.

57. Mark Griffin, *A Hundred or More Hidden Things: The Life and Films of Vincente Minnelli* (Cambridge: Da Capo, 2010), 57.

58. Horne and Schickel, *Lena*, 134; Haskins and Benson, *Lena*, 68; Gavin, *Stormy Weather*, 105; Kenneth Robert Janken, *Walter White: Mr. NAACP* (Chapel Hill: University of North Carolina Press, 2003), 269.

59. "Better Breaks for Negroes in H'Wood," *Variety*, March 25, 1942, 1.

60. Horne and Schickel, *Lena*, 134.

61. *Ibid.*, 136.

62. *Ibid.*

63. Buckley, *The Hornes*, 156–157; Gavin, *Stormy Weather*, 114.

64. Ida Vera Simonton, *Hell's Playground* (New York: Moffat, Yard and Company, 1912), 320. Simonton describes the character as a member of a powerful Gabonese tribe, who was known to polish her skin until it "shone like rich red mahogany."

65. Thomas F. Brady, "Another Script from the Hollywood Laundry," *The New York Times*, May 17, 1942, X3.

66. "Lena Horne," *Variety*, December 2, 1942, 45; Buckley, *The Hornes*, 157; Gavin, *Stormy Weather*, 2009, 114; Horne and Schickel, *Lena*, 136.

67. Clarence Muse, "Noted Screen Actor Thinks Performers Have Been Ignored," *The Pittsburgh Courier*, September 12, 1942, 20.

68. "Metro's *Cabin in the Sky* Buy May Pave the Way for More Negro Films," *Variety*, April 8, 1942, 3; "More *Panama Hattie* Cast Changes, Remakes," *Variety*, April 8, 1942, 25.

69. Cori Howard, "Jeni LeGon Lived through Hollywood's glamour days," *National Post*, October 8, 1999, B5; David Spaner, "Show Stopper: Jeni LeGon often stole the spotlight dancing with the biggest stars of the 20th century," *The Province*, October 22, 2006, B7.

70. Gavin, *Stormy Weather*, 107.

71. Leonard Feather, "Bessie to Flora," *Los Angeles Times*, February 5, 1984, 60.

72. Marshall Winslow Stearns and Jean Stearns, *Jazz Dance: The Story of American Vernacular Dance* (New York: Da Capo, 1994), 276–277.

73. *Ibid.*, 276–277; Isadora Smith, "Cab Calloway, Nicholas Brothers Reach Their Peak," *The Pittsburgh Courier*, October 22, 1938.

74. Louella O. Parsons, "Eyeing Hollywood," *The Morning News* (Wilmington), February 18, 1942, 21.

75. Horne and Schickel, *Lena*, 140.

76. Freddie Doyle, "Swingtime," *California Eagle*, July 2, 1942, 2B; Billy Rowe, "Beauty of Colored Girls About to Come Into Its Own," *The Pittsburgh Courier*, October 17, 1942, 21.

77. Bosley Crowther, "Panama Hattie—Or What Is Left Over of a Musical Comedy," *The New York Times*, October 2, 1942, 31; "New Films," *The Boston Globe*, October 9, 1942, 25; Harold V. Cohen, "Panama Hattie with Red Skelton," *Pittsburgh Post-Gazette*, September 25, 1942, 10.

78. "Cabin in the Sky," *Variety*, February 10, 1943, 8.

79. Henry T. Sampson, *Blacks in Blackface: A Source Book on Early Black Musical Shows* (Metuchen, NJ: The Scarecrow Press, 1980), 169–170; Carol J. Oja, *Bernstein Meets Broadway: Collaborative Art in a Time of War* (New York: Oxford University Press, 2014), 163; Katherine Dunham, "Early New York Collaborations," in VeVe Clark and Sara E. Johnson, eds., *Kaiso! Writings by and about Katherine Dunham*, 142.

80. Dunham, "Early New York Collaborations," 142–143; Constance Valis Hill, "Collaborating with Balanchine on Cabin in the Sky," in *Kaiso! Writings by and about Katherine Dunham*, ed. VeVe Clark and Sara E. Johnson (Madison: University of Wisconsin Press, 2005), 239–240.

81. Burns Mantle, "Ethel Waters, Cabin in the Sky, Are a Hit at the Martin Beck," *Daily News*, October 26, 1940, 21B; Brooks Atkinson, "The Play," *The New York Times*, October 26, 1940, 19; Brooks Atkinson, "Cabin in the Sky," *The New York Times*, November 3, 1940, 137.

82. "Cabin in the Sky," *Variety*, February 10, 1943, 8; "Cabin in the Sky, a Musical Fantasy," *The New York Times*, May 28, 1943, 19.

83. Edward E. Gloss, "Name Band Smash Hit as Sissle Features Players Over Self," *Akron Beacon Journal*, October 26, 1936, 17.

84. Marc Connelly and Thomas Cripps, *The Green Pastures* (Madison: University of Wisconsin Press,1979), 106.

85. Martha Wolfenstein and Nathan Leites, "Movies: A Psychological Study," *The Library Quarterly* 20, no. 4 (October 1950): 30–32.

86. Brooks Atkinson, "Cabin in the Sky," *The New York Times*, November 3, 1940, 137.

87. "Cabin in the Sky, a Musical Fantasy, With Ethel Waters, at Loew's Criterion," *The New York Times*, May 28, 1943, 19.

88. Gavin, *Stormy Weather*, 125, 141.

89. Horne and Schickel, *Lena*, 153.

90. Wolfenstein and Leites, "Movies," 27.

91. Bosley Crowther, "Cleaving the Color Line," *The New York Times*, June 6, 1943, X3; Edwin Schallert, "Cabin in the Sky Rich in Melody, Humanness," *Los Angeles Times*, May 8, 1943, 17; Harold V. Cohen, "All-Colored Musical, Cabin in the Sky, Comes to Penn," *Pittsburgh Post-Gazette*, May 14, 1943, 10; "*Cabin in the Sky*," *Variety*, February 10, 1943, 8.

92. Rob Roy, "Critic Says Hollywood Caters to South in Pictures," *Chicago Defender*, June 26, 1943, 10; Moran Weston, "National Roundup," *The New York Age*, April 10, 1943, 6; "'Cabin' Picture Called Insult," *New York Amsterdam News*, June 12, 1943, 17.

93. Thomas Cripps, *Slow Fade to Black: The Negro in American Film, 1900–1942* (New York: Oxford University Press, 1993), 83–84; Hy Kraft, *On My Way to the Theater* (New York: Macmillan, 1971), 161.

94. Willard B. Gatewood, "The Formative Years of William Grant Still," in *William Grant Still: A Study in Contradictions*, ed. Catherine Parsons Smith (Berkeley: University of California Press, 2000), 21–35.

95. *Ibid.*; Daniel J. Leab, "Still, William Grant," in *Harlem Renaissance Lives*, ed. Henry Louis Gates, Jr., and Evelyn Brooks Higginbotham (New York: Oxford University Press, 2009), 471–473.

96. William Grant Still, "William Grant Still Quits 'Stormy Weather' Picture," *California Eagle*, February 17, 1943, 2B.

97. *Ibid.*

98. Cripps, *Slow Fade to Black*, 256; Donald Bogle, *Toms, Coons, Mulattoes, Mammies and Bucks: An Interpretive History of Blacks in American Films* (New York: Continuum, 1995), 47.

99. "To Remake Movie; 'Bo' Flops as Lover," *New York Amsterdam Star-News*, March 27, 1943, 1; "Admits Mistake in Casting 'Bo' As Lena's Romantic Lead," *The Pittsburgh Courier*, March 27, 1943, 1.

100. Harry Levette, "Harry Brand, Fox Publicity Director Denies Story 'Stormy Weather' Nixing Bill Robinson to be Re-Made," *California Eagle*, April 1, 1943, 2B; "'Bill, Lena OK In Roles,' Says Brand," *The Pittsburgh Courier*, April 10, 1943, 20.

101. Buckley, *The Hornes*, 174.

102. "Stormy Weather," *Variety*, June 2, 1943, 8.

103. "Colored Bing Crosby," *Brooklyn Citizen*, December 12, 1942, 10.

104. Harry Kramer, "Notes to You," *The New York Age*, October 19, 1940, 4.

105. M.J. Simpson, "Interview: Emmett Wallace," Cult Films and the people who make them, May 1, 2014, http://mjsimpson-films.blogspot.com/2014/05/interview-emmett-wallace.html.

106. Rex Reed, "A Life on Stage," *New York Daily News*, May 10, 1981, 13.

107. Shane Vogel, "Performing 'Stormy Weather': Ethel Waters, Lena Horne, and Katherine Dunham," *South Central Review* 25, no. 1 (Spring 2008): 106–107.

108. Dee Das, *Katherine Dunham*, 80; *Free to Dance*, episode 2, "Steps of the Gods," directed by Madison D. Lacy, aired on June, 2001 on PBS, www.youtube.com/watch?v=UcN0G7xItwo&list=PL6F003CE2A4B31581&index=4&t=0s.

109. "Stormy Weather," *Variety*, June 2, 1943, 8; John L. Scott, "Stormy Weather Joyous Gathering of Sepia Stars," *Los Angeles Times*, July 30, 1943, 11; "Stormy Weather, Negro Musical with Bill Robinson, at the Roxy," *The New York Times*, July 22, 1943, 15.

110. Herman Hill, "Coast Fans Applaud Lena Horne at Stormy Weather Opening," *The Pittsburgh Courier*, August 7, 1943, 20; Carrie Miller, "Backstage," *California Eagle*, August 19, 1943, 2B; Billy Rowe, "Says Hollywood Made A Promise It Hasn't Kept," *The Pittsburgh Courier*, March 6, 1943, 21; Thomas Cripps, *Making Movies Black: The Hollywood Message Movie from World War II to the Civil Rights Era* (New York: Oxford University Press, 1993), 85.

111. Clayton R. Koppes and Gregory D. Black, "Blacks, Loyalty, and Motion-Picture Propaganda in World War II," *The Journal of American History* 73, no. 2 (September 1986): 400.

112. "Hollywood Holding Up Pix Releases in Which Whites, Negroes Mix," *Variety*, June 30, 27.

113. Whitney Strub, "Black and White and Banned All Over: Censorship and Obscenity in Post-War Memphis," *Journal of Social History* 40, no. 3 (Spring 2007): 685–715.

114. Laurie B. Green, *Battling the Plantation Mentality: Memphis and the Black Freedom Struggle* (Chapel Hill: University of North Carolina Press, 2009), 151–155.

115. *Ibid.*; "More Negro Scenes Cut Out in Dixie," *Variety*, July 12, 1944, 1.

116. "More Negro Scenes," *Variety*, 1944, 1; "Brewster's Millions is Barred in Memphis," *The New York Times*, April 7, 1945, 10; Green, *Battling the Plantation*, 151–155; Cripps, *Slow Fade to Black*, 8.

117. W.R.W, "I Dood It," *Motion Picture Herald*, July 31, 1943, 1453.

118. Thomas M. Pryor, "Thousands Cheer, Lavish Metro Musical with an All-Star Cast," *The New York Times*, September 14, 1943, 27; Gavin, *Stormy Weather*, 125, 150.

119. James A. Byron, "Everything You Could Ask for in 'Broadway Rhythm,'" *Fort Worth Star-Telegram*, May 19, 1944, 14; Philip K. Scheuer, "Vaudeville Still Very Much Alive in M.G.M. Musical," *Los Angeles Times*, April 7, 1944, II-9; Bosley Crowther, "Word on Musicals," *The New York Times*, April 23, 1944, X3.

120. "More Negro Scenes," *Variety*, 1, 32.

121. Pope, "Lena Horne," *Lagniappe*, 3.

122. Horne and Schickel, *Lena*, 173; Buckley, *The Hornes*, 180.

123. Gavin, *Stormy Weather*, 163–164.

124. Horne and Schickel, *Lena*, 187–189.

125. *Ibid.*; "Disciplining of Lena Horne for Role Snub Denied," *Chicago Defender*, October 13, 1945, 5.

126. Barbara Saltzman, "Reassembled 'Ziegfeld Follies' Arrives on Laser," *Los Angeles Times*, August 5, 1994, F23.

127. "Ziegfeld Follies," *Variety*, August 15, 1945, 14.

128. Horne and Schickel, *Lena*, 196–197.

129. *Ibid.*; Edwin Schallbert, "Follies Splendiferous Show," *Los Angeles Times*, April 9, 1946, II-2; "Ziegfeld Film Censored," *The New York Times*, July 24, 1946, 30.

130. Buckley, *The Hornes*, 196–197.

131. Todd Decker, *Show Boat: Performing Race in an American Musical* (New York: Oxford University Press, 2013), 4, 15; Edna Ferber, *Show Boat* (New York: Grosset & Dunlap, 1926), 144–149.

132. Decker, *Show Boat: Performing Race in an American Musical*, 4.

133. Stephen Banfield, *Jerome Kern* (New Have: Yale University Press, 2006), 167.

134. Horne and Schickel, *Lena*, 189–190; "Show Boat Revival Booked at Ziegfeld; Sherwood Play Set," *Daily News*, August 22, 1945, 47M.

135. John Kobal, *People Will Talk* (London: Aurum Press, 1986), 389.

136. George Sidney, "More About Lena," *Los Angeles Times*, December 19, 1982, 115; Lee Server, *Ava Gardner: "Love Is Nothing"* (New York: St. Martin's Press, 2007).

137. Aline Mosby, "Lena Horne Quits Hollywood," *Greenville Daily Advocate,* March 30, 1950, 5; Michiko Kakutani, "Lena Horne: Aloofness Hid the Pain, Until Time Cooled Her Anger," *The New York Times*, May 3, 1981, 2-1.

138. Kakutani, "Lena Horne: Aloofness," 2-1.

139. Brooks Atkinson, "One Yes: One No: West Indian Musical," *The New York Times*, November 10, 1957, 143.

140. Horne and Schickel, *Lena*, 269–272.

141. *Ibid.*, 272–273; "Lena Hearing Slurs, Let Go with Shellfire," *Daily News*, February 17, 1960, 24; "Lena Horne Hurls Dishes, Lamp at Man in Restaurant," *The Colton Courier*, February 16, 1960, 1.

142. Horne and Schickel, *Lena*, 273–274; Gavin, *Stormy Weather*, 296; "Lena Horne Hurls Dishes," 1.

143. Ponchitta Pierce, "Lena at 51," *Ebony*, July 1968, 135; Kakutani, "Lena Horne: Aloofness," *The New York Times*, 2-1.

144. Gavin, *Stormy Weather*, 372–384.

145. Robert Windeler, "Lena Horne Plans Return to Screen," *The New York Times*, May 10, 1968, 55. Lewis B. Patten, *Death of a Gunfighter* (New York: Signet,1969), 18–110.

146. Robert Windeler, "In 'Patch' Lena's Just a Woman," *Wisconsin State Journal,* June 1, 1968, 2–11.

147. Howard Thompson, "'Death of a Gunfighter' Stars Widmark," *The New York Times*, May 10, 1969, 34. Joan Barthel, "Lena Horne: 'Now I Feel Good About Being Me,'" *The New York Times*, July 28, 1968, 81; "TV Special One of Many 'Firsts' For Lena Horne," *Sunday News* (Lancaster, PA), September 7, 1969, 1.

148. Kevin Thomas, "'Gunfighter' Begins Run," *Los Angeles Times*, June 11, 1969, IV-15; Marjory Adams, "Richard Widmark puts his stamp on 'Gunfighter,'" *The Boston Globe*, June 12, 1969, 37; Howard Thompson, "'Death of a Gunfighter' Stars Widmark," *The New York Times*, May 10, 1969, 34; Robert Taylor, "'Gunfighter' a Fine Western," *Oakland Tribune*, September 26, 1969, 50.

149. Bruce McCabe, "Someone cast a spell on film version of 'Wiz,'" *The Boston Globe*, October 28, 1978, 10; "The Wiz," *Variety,* December 31, 1977, https://variety.com/1977/film/reviews/the-wiz-1200424107/.

150. Charles Champlin, "The Wiz Moves to Film," *Los Angeles Times*, October 26, 1978, IV-1; Aaron Gold, *Chicago Tribune*, October 26, 1978, 2–9.

151. *Great Performances*, "Lena Horne: The Lady and Her Music," directed by Paddy Sampson, aired December 7, 1984 on PBS; Horne and Schickel, *Lena*, 284; Ida Peters, "That Glamorous Lady Lena," *Afro-American*," May 14, 1983, 11.

Chapter 5

1. Dorothy Dandridge and Earl Conrad, *Everything and Nothing: The Dorothy Dandridge Tragedy* (New York: HarperCollins, 2000), 218–219.

2. *Ibid.*, 204.

3. *Ibid.*, 15, 16.

4. "Ohio Deaths, 1908–1953," database with images, *FamilySearch* (https://familysearch.org/ark:/61903/1:1:XZTF-V86 : 8 December 2014), James Henry Dandridge in entry for Florence Dandridge, 24 February 1944; citing Cleveland, Cuyahoga Co., Ohio, reference fn 9978; FHL microfilm 2,024,192. Florence Dandridge's death certificate lists her father as born in England.

5. *Ibid.*; Donald Bogle, *Dorothy Dandridge: A Biography* (New York: Boulevard Books, 1997), 5–6.

6. Bogle, *Dorothy Dandridge*, 43–44.

7. Dandridge and Conrad, *Everything and Nothing*, 25.

8. *Ibid.*, 34.

9. *Ibid.*, 37–38.

10. Edwin Schallert, "'Sun Valley Serenade' Rates as Pleasing Henie Show," *Los Angeles Times*, August 30, 1941, II-7.

11. Bogle, *Dorothy Dandridge*, 167–168.

12. Earl Mills, *Dorothy Dandridge: An Intimate Biography* (Los Angeles: Holloway House, 1999), 79.

13. *Ibid.*

14. *Ibid.*, 90; Bogle, *Dorothy Dandridge*, 230.

15. Bogle, *Dorothy Dandridge*, 230, 232.

16. Hedda Hopper, "Otto Preminger Will Film Carmen Jones," *Los Angeles Times*, December 23, 1953, I-12; Hedda Hopper, "Lubin Plans Fifth in 'Francis' Series," *Los Angeles Times*, March 25, 1954, II-8.

17. Bogle, *Dorothy Dandridge*, 271–273; Dandridge and Conrad, *Everything and Nothing*, 167; Louie Robinson, "The Private World of Dorothy Dandridge," *Ebony*, June 1962, 119; "On the 'Bright Road' of 'Carmen' and 'Joe,'" *The New York Times*, October 24, 1954, X5.

18. Billy Rose, "Pitching Horseshoes," *The Kingston Daily Freeman*, January 27, 1954; "Pic Version of 'Carmen Jones' Rehearsals Set," *The Pittsburgh Courier*, May 8, 1954, 18.

19. Dandridge and Conrad, *Everything and Nothing*, 169–173.

20. Jeff Smith, "Black Faces, White Voices: The Politics of Dubbing in Carmen Jones," *The Velvet Light Trap* 51, no. 1 (Spring 2003): 31; Annegret

Fauser, "'Dixie *Carmen*': War, Race, and Identity in Oscar Hammerstein's *Carmen Jones* (1943)," *Journal of the Society for American Music* 4, no. 2: 134, 160.

21. Sam Zolotow, "Opening Tonight of 'Carmen Jones,'" *The New York Times*, December 2, 1943, 32; Lewis Nichols, "The Play," *The New York Times*, December 3, 1943, 6; Olin Downes, "Carmen Jones," *The New York Times*, December 19, 1943.

22. Smith, "Black Faces, White Voices," 31–33; Fauser, "'Dixie *Carmen*,'"134–160.

23. Oscar Hammerstein II, *Carmen Jones* (New York: Alfred A. Knopf, 1945), xviii.

24. Prosper Mérimée, *Carmen and Other Stories* (Oxford: Oxford University Press, 1989), 20–21.

25. Ian Hancock, "The 'Gypsy' Stereotype and the Sexualization of Romani Women," The Romani Archives and Documentation Center, April 2007, www.radoc.net/radoc.php?doc=art_d_identity_sexualization&lang=fr.

26. Mérimée, *Carmen and Other Stories*, 13–14.

27. "A New Beauty for Bizet," *Life*, November 1, 1954, 87; Philip K. Scheuer, "Carmen Jones Vital, High-Voltage Musical," *Los Angeles Times*, November 2, 1954, III-6; "The New Pictures," *Time*, November 1, 1954; "Carmen Jones," *Motion Picture Daily*, September 30, 1954, 10.

28. Edward Murrain, "Dandridge Dramatics Rescue Carmen Jones," *The New York Age*, October 16, 1954, 17; "Show Business," *California Eagle*, November 4, 1954, 9; Bosley Crowther, "Up-dated Translation of Bizet Work Bows," *The New York Times*, October 29, 1954, 27; Jane Corby, "Carmen Jones at the Rivoli Starring Dorothy Dandridge," *The Brooklyn Daily Eagle*, October 29, 1954, 9.

29. Bogle, *Dorothy Dandridge*, 317–339; Dandridge and Conrad, *Everything and Nothing*, 185.

30. Leah Rosenberg, "It's Enough to Make Any Woman Catch the Next Plane to Barbados: Constructing the Postwar West Indies as Paradise," *Third Text* 28, no. 4–5 (September 2014): 367; Peter Hulme, "Dominica and Tahiti: Tropical Islands Compared," in *Tropical Visions in an Age of Empire*, ed. Felix Driver and Luciana Martins (Chicago: University of Chicago Press, 2005), 89; Gordon K. Lewis, *The Growth of the Modern West Indies* (Miami: Ian Randle, 2004), 7.

31. M.L.E. Moreau de Saint-Méry, *A Civilization That Perished: The Last Years of Colonial Rule in Haiti*, trans. Ivor D. Spencer (Lanham, MD: University Press of America, 1985), 76–89.

32. *Ibid.*

33. *Ibid.*

34. Alec Waugh, *Island in the Sun*, (New York: Farrar, Straus and Cudahy, 1955), 117–118.

35. *Ibid.*

36. *Ibid.*, 8–9.

37. F. James Davis, *Who is Black? One Nation's Definition* (University Park: Pennsylvania State University Press, 1991), 106–107; Lewis, *The Growth of the Modern West Indies*, 5.

38. Waugh, *Island in the Sun*, 14.

39. *Ibid.*, 86–90.

40. *Ibid.*, 518–519.

41. *Ibid.*, 14.

42. *Ibid.*, 419.

43. Leonard Mosley, *Zanuck: The Rise and Fall of Hollywood's Last Tycoon* (Boston: Little, Brown, 1984), 288–289.

44. *Ibid.*

45. "Thinks New Movie Should Be Banned," *The Florence Morning News*, January 9, 1957, 4.

46. Edward Scobie, "Finds Island in the Sun Not Dimmed by Bias," *Chicago Defender*, February 9, 1957, 8.

47. Aline Mosby, "Belafonte Complaining: TV Sponsors, Movie Producers Shy Away," *The Daily Telegram*, July 23, 1957, 9.

48. Harry Belafonte and Michael Shnayerson, *My Song: A Memoir* (New York: Alfred A. Knopf, 2011), 166.

49. Hilda See, "The Dandridge Story: Mixed Romance on Screen," *Chicago Defender*, February 2, 1957, 14.

50. Louie Robinson, "Torrid New Love Story Stars Interracial Love Code Debate," *Jet*, December 13, 1956, 56–61.

51. Waugh, *Island in the Sun*, 535.

52. "Memphis Board Bans Island in the Sun," *The Montgomery Adviser*, July 5, 1957, 17; "KKK Parades to Protest Movie," *The Akron Beacon Journal*, August 16, 1957, 2; "Zanuck Would Pay Fines for Showing," *The New York Times*, May 11, 1957, 24.

53. "Island in the Sun," *Variety*, June 19, 1957, 6; "Hollywood's Summer Films Tackle Some Sweaty Topics with Varying Success," *Life*, July 22, 1957, 67; Crowther, "Barbados Is the 'Star' of Island in the Sun," *The New York Times*, June 13, 1957, 37.

54. Bosley Crowther, "Color or Class; Are Issues Evaded in Island in the Sun?, June 23, 1957, "Morbid Mess, says Sir Hugh of Island in the Sun," *The Daily Gleaner*, August 1, 1957, 1.

55. Leonard Mosley, "Island in the Sun: The messy stew of inter-colour relations," *The Sunday Gleaner*, August 11, 1957, 12.

56. *Inward Hunger: The Story of Eric Williams*, DVD, directed by Mariel Brown (Port of Spain, Trinidad and Tobago: Savant Ltd., 2011).

57. Bogle, *Dorothy Dandridge*, 341–356, 402.

58. Rebecca Prime, *Hollywood Exiles in Europe* (New Brunswick: Rutgers University Press, 2014), 126.

59. Robert Harms, "The Transatlantic Slave Trade in Cinema," in *Black & White in Color: African History on Screen*, ed. Richard Mendelsohn and Vivian Bickford-Smith (Athens: Ohio University Press, 2007), 62.

60. Eric Robert Taylor, *If We Must Die: Shipboard Insurrections in the Era of the Atlantic Slave Trade* (Baton Rouge: Louisiana State University Press, 2006), 3.

61. Lorenzo J. Greene, "Mutiny of the Slave Ships," *Phylon* 5, no. 4 (4th Quarter 1944): 346.

62. Bogle, *Dorothy Dandridge*, 346–380.

63. Davis, *Who Is Black?* 105–106.

64. Bogle, *Dorothy Dandridge*, 454–455; Christopher L. Miller, *The French Atlantic Triangle:*

Literature and Culture of the Slave Trade (Durham: Duke University Press, 2008), 224–225.

65. Geoffrey Warren, "Tamango Low Grade New Race Melodrama," *Los Angeles Times*, October 23, 1959, 23; Richard Nason, "Tamango From France," *The New York Times*, September 17, 1959, 48; Helen Bower, "Slavery's Beginning," *Detroit Free Press*, August 19, 1959, 33; "Tamango," *Variety*, February 12, 1958; Vincent Canby, "Tamango," *Motion Picture Daily*, August 31, 1959, 4; R.H. Gardner, ". . . A Book by Its Cover," *The Baltimore Sun*, September 28, 1959, 10.

66. Mae Tinee, "Five Films Top October List," *Chicago Tribune*, November 8, 1959, 7–12; William Leonard, "Tamango Is a Bloody, Brutal Film," *Chicago Tribune*, October 7, 1956, 56.

67. Vann Newkirk, "Washed Down in Blood: Murder on the Schooner Harry A. Berwind," *The North Carolina Historical Review* 91, no. 1 (January 2014): 29.

68. "No Sign of Blood," *The Wilmington Messenger*, October 14, 1905, 8. Newkirk, "Washed Down in Blood," 2–4.

69. *Ibid.*, 7–11; "A Strange Coincidence: Schooners Berwind and King Both at Baltimore," *The Wilmington Messenger*, March 31, 1906, 4.

70. "Mutiny Salvage Hers," *The Baltimore Sun*, January 9, 1906, 6.

71. Newkirk, "Washed Down in Blood," 13–26.

72. Dandridge and Conrad, *Everything and Nothing*, 199–200; Belafonte and Shnayerson, *My Song*, 184.

73. Stephen Watts, "Americans in Action on Britain's Film Front," *The New York Times*, July 19, 1959, X5.

74. Harold Sterin, "TV Keynotes: Acting Beats Singing," *The Morning Call*, February 19, 1962, 14.

75. Doris G. Worsham, "Lonette McKee Makes History as Julie," *The Cincinnati Enquirer*, October 3, 1982, F-21.

76. Ron Reeves, "Ron Around the Arts," *Santa Cruz Sentinel*, July 19, 1961, 14; E.B. Radcliffe, "Dayton Show Boat," *Cincinnati Enquirer*, June 14, 1962, 24; Barbara Bladen, "The Marquee," *The Times* (San Mateo), October 16, 1964, 31.

77. "Dorothy Dandridge Died of Pill Dosage, Coroner Now Says," *The New York Times*, November 18, 1965, 54; Bogle, *Dorothy Dandridge*, 552.

Chapter 6

1. John Istel, "Lonette McKee: Why the Caged Bird Sings," *American Theater*, February 1995, 40.

2. John Stark, "After Singing Her Own Blues, Lonette McKee Finds a Perch as Off Broadway's Billie Holiday," *People*, November 3, 1986, https://people.com/archive/after-singing-her-own-blues-lonette-mckee-finds-a-perch-as-off-broadways-billie-holiday-vol-26-no-18/; Lawrence DeVine, "Detroit's Own Soul Sister," *Detroit Free Press*, October 8, 1972, 30, 6-C; Stephen Holden, "Pop/Jazz; Making Cabaret Act Look Easy," *The New York Times*, October 23, 1987, C27.

3. Stark, "After Singing Her Own Blues"; Richard F. Shull, "The Soul Sisters Added to Winters Wacky World," *Times Colonist* (Victoria, BC), September 1, 1972, 7A.

4. Heather Ann Thompson, *Whose Detroit? Politics, Labor and Race in a Modern American City* (Ithaca: Cornell University Press, 2001), 12.

5. DeVine, "Detroit's Own Soul Sister," 6-C; Shull, "The Soul Sisters," 7A; Istel, "Lonette McKee," 40; Patrick Pacheo, "Life Upon the Wicked Stage," *Los Angeles Times*, September 25, 1994, 47.

6. Mildred Perkins, "Dramatic Career Is Sought By High School Cover Girl," *The Times Recorder* (Zanesville, Ohio), July 1, 1968, 8C; Martha Kinsella, "Jimi Hendrix' Detroit Concert," *Detroit Free Press*, December 6, 1968, 8D; Stark, "After Singing Her Own Blues"; Nan Robertson, "Voyage to Broadway By Show Boat Singer," *The New York Times*, May 12, 1983, C17.

7. Kathy McKee, "Kathy McKee: Biography," IMDb, accessed December 12, 2020, https://www.imdb.com/name/nm0571181/bio; Nancy Dillon, "Exclusive: Bill Cosby accused of raping ex-girlfriend of Sammy Davis, Jr.," *New York Daily News*, December 22, 2014, https://www.nydailynews.com/news/national/bill-cosby-accused-raping-ex-girlfriend-sammy-davis-jr-article-1.2052890.

8. Shirley Eder, "Sammy Gets Private Nurse, Jet," *The Philadelphia Inquirer*, September 16, 1970, 26; Gerald Fraser, "New Face: Lonette McKee Another Shade of Black," *The New York Times*, January 20, 1978, C11; Shull, "The 'Soul Sisters," 7A.

9. Shull, "The Soul Sisters," 7A.

10. *Ibid.*; DeVine, "Detroit's Own Soul Sister," 6-C; Pacheo, "Life Upon the Wicked Stage," 47.

11. Ed Guerrero, "The So-Called Fall of Blaxploitation," *Velvet Light Trap* 64, no. 1 (Fall 2009): 90; Mikel J. Koven, *Blaxploitation Films* (Harpenden Hertfordshire: Kamera, 2010) 9–16; David Walker, Andrew J. Rausch, and Chris Watson, *Reflections on Blaxploitation: Actors and Directors Speak* (Lanham, MD: The Scarecrow Press, 2009), vii–viii.

12. Howell Raines, "There Is a Lot to Like About Sounder," *The Atlanta Constitution*, October 25, 1972, 12B; William B. Collins, "Black Film Puzzle: Is Sounder the Answer?" *The Philadelphia Inquirer*, October 29, 1972, 1-G.

13. Donald Bogle, *Toms, Coons, Mulattoes, Mammies, and Bucks: An Interpretive History of Blacks in Film* (New York: Continuum, 1995), 242.

14. Vincent Canby, "Are Black Films Losing Their Blackness?" *The New York Times*, April 25, 1976, 79.

15. Fiona Lewis, "A Supreme Theme for a Ghetto Film," *Los Angeles Times*, November 30, 1975, 42; Howard Rosenman, "The Saga of Whitney Houston's Last Movie, *Sparkle*," *Daily Beast*, updated July 13, 2017, https://www.thedailybeast.com/the-saga-of-whitney-houstons-last-movie-sparkle.

16. Lewis, "A Supreme Theme," 42; Rosenman, "The Saga."

17. Pat McGilligan, "*Sparkle* adds up to a million-dollar miracle for film newcomers," *The Boston Globe*, August 10, 1975, A11.

18. Richard Eder, "Sparkle, a Sob Story with Its Moments of Force," *The New York Times*, April 8, 1976, 43; Kevin Thomas, "The Shimmer of Sparkle," *Los Angeles Times*, May 21, 1976, IV-18; Canby, "Are Black Films," 79; Pauline Kael, *5001 Nights at the Movies* (New York: Picador, 2011) 698.

19. Kael, *5001 Nights at the Movies*, 698; Canby, "Are Black Films," 79; Thomas, "The Shimmer of Sparkle," IV-18; Eder, "Sparkle, a Sob Story," 43; Joe Baltake, "Sparkle Doesn't Shine," *Philadelphia Daily News*, April 8, 1976, 60.

20. Armond White, "White on Black," *Film Comment* 20, no. 6 (November-December 1984): 15.

21. Chris Lee, "Smokey puts film under fire," *Los Angeles Times*, February 4, 2007, F14.

22. Mark Jenkins, "The Sapphires is a feel-good film that also tells of Australia's past injustices," *The Washington Post,* March 28, 2013, https://www.washingtonpost.com/entertainment/movies/the-sapphires-is-a-feel-good-film-that-also-tells-of-australias-past-injustices/2013/03/28/6b47f9aa-92aa-11e2-9173-7f87cda73b49_story.html?noredirect=on&utm_term=.2af1620d10b5.

23. "Detroit Actress Quits Big Role in Ali's Film," *Detroit Free Press*, October 27, 1976, 16-D; Keith Corson, *Trying to Get Over: African American Directors After Blaxploitation* (Austin: University of Texas, 2016), 8.

24. Ronald Harris, "The Man Who Makes Multimillionaires," *Ebony*, June 1979, 54; "Lonette McKee Knows the Way Up: $1.5 Million Deal," *Jet*, June 29, 1978, 58.

25. Christian Boone, "David McCoy Franklin: 1943–2008," *The Atlanta Journal and Constitution*, September 9, 2008, B1; Jim Galloway, "Political Insider: A Word from Shirley Franklin on the Death of her Ex-Husband," *The Atlanta Journal and Constitution*, September 8, 2008, accessed March 8, 2018, http://www.ajc.com/metro/content/shared-blogs/ajc/politicalinsider/entries/2008/09/08/a_word_from_shirley_franklin_o.html; E.R. Shipp, "Lonette McKee On Becoming Lady Day," *The New York Times*, February 22, 1987, A6; Stark, "After Singing Her Own Blues." David McCoy Franklin married Shirley Franklin in 1972. The couple had three children and divorced in 1986. That same year, McKee said she once lived with, and was the mistress of, a married man who had three children and "who insisted she take voice, dance, and acting lessons and be proud of being black…. He provided her with advice … as well as a maid, pool and a diamond ring." In 1987, McKee said that David Franklin told her to stop thinking of herself as mulatto and insisted that she take voice lessons.

26. "Black film maker series begins," *Daily News*, August 27, 1982, 15.

27. "We're still trying to get our projects made," *National Post* (Toronto), January 25, 2013, B6; Michael T. Martin, "I Do Exist: From 'Black Insurgent' to Negotiating the Hollywood Divide—a

Conversation with Julie Dash," *Cinema Journal* 49, no. 2 (Winter 2010): 1.

28. "We're still trying," B6; Martin, "I Do Exist," 1.

29. "Ask Mr. Entertainment," *Daily News*, July 3, 1983, 2; Roger Ebert, "She was dancing but not always singing," *National Post* (Toronto), November 10, 2000, B7.

30. Louella O. Parsons, "In Film Studios," *The Cincinnati Enquirer*, July 2, 1929, 14; Gene Voelker, "Show Boat Arrives at State Theatre," *The Daily Home News* (New Jersey), 14.

31. Laura A. Smith, "Giving Woman Her Say," *The Indianapolis Star*, September 7, 1929, 8.

32. Julia McCarthy, "Ghost Singer Tells Secret of Her Art," *Daily News*, December 26, 1938, 36.

33. Abe Greenberg, "Listening In," *Daily News*, August 12, 1933, 19; "Stars of Radioland," *The Journal Times* (Wisconsin), May 6, 1931; Mildred Bailey, "Mildred Bailey Tells Her Story," *Pittsburgh Press*, July 10, 1932; Hubbard Keavy, "Ghost Singer Puts Across Stars' Songs," *The Tampa Tribune*, March 11, 1934, 3–7; Jack Stone, "Three Magic Notes," *Pittsburgh Sun-Telegraph*, February 13, 1949, 10.

34. Guy Evans (Director), *Secret Voices of Hollywood*, DVD, BBC, 2013; Margalit Fox, "Marni Nixon, the Singing Voice Behind the Screen, Dies at 86," *The New York Times* (online), July 25, 2016; Susan King, "Vocalist Marni Nixon, Lip-Syncer Extraordinary," *Los Angeles Times*, November 17, 1990, F14; Roger Catlin, "Singer Marni Nixon to discuss singing—uncredited—for the stars," *Washington Post* (online), June 17, 2013.

35. *Secret Voices of Hollywood*, DVD, directed by Guy Evans (BBC, 2013).

36. *Ibid.*

37. Gayle Worland, "Film, stage star broke barriers," *Chicago Tribune*, January 4, 2004, 4–9; Claudia Luther, "Etta Moten Barnett, 102; Porgy and Bess Star Sang at the White House," *Los Angeles Times*, January 5, 2004, B9.

38. Pam Platt, "Life and Times of Etta Barnett," *Florida Today*, February 15, 1986, 1–2D.

39. John Howard Reid, *Hollywood Movie Musicals* (Morrisville, NC: Lulu Press), 2006, 68; Platt, "Life and Times," 1–2D.

40. "Sings for Brazilian Prexy," *Baltimore Afro-American*, June 20, 1936, 10.

41. Henry Louis Gates, Jr., *Thirteen Ways of Looking at a Black Man* (New York: Vintage Books, 1998), 180–203.

42. *Ibid.*, 180–203.

43. Philip Roth, "An Open Letter to Wikipedia," *The New Yorker*, September 6, 2012, https://www.newyorker.com/books/page-turner/an-open-letter-to-wikipedia.

44. Julie Dash, *Daughters of the Dust: The Making of an African American Woman's Film* (New York: New Press, 1992), 5.

45. Frank Rich, "The Stage: Show Boat, a Theatrical Treasure," *The New York Times*, April 25, 1983, C12; Trudy S. Moore, "Lonette McKee Stars in Broadway Hit Show Boat," *Jet*, October 31, 1994, 36.

46. Decker, *Show Boat: Performing Race in an American Musical*, 230.

47. Robertson, "Voyage to Broadway," C17; Stark, "After Singing Her Own Blues"; Shipp, "Lonette McKee on Becoming Lady Day," A6.

48. Diane Hubbard Burns, "Cotton Club film has author's blessing," *The Orlando Sentinel*, December 16, 1984, F6.

49. Michael Daly, "The Making of *The Cotton Club*," *New York Magazine*, May 7, 1984, 42–45; Jon Lewis, *Whom God Wishes to Destroy: Francis Coppola and the New Hollywood* (Durham: Duke University Press, 1995), 112–117.

50. Daly, "The Making of *The Cotton Club*," 43–60; Lewis, *Whom God Wishes to Destroy*, 112–117.

51. Daly, "The Making of *The Cotton Club*," 43, 46.

52. *Ibid.*, 43–47; Jeanie Kasindorf, "The 'Cotton Club' Murder," *New York Magazine*, July 24, 1989, 27.

53. Kasindorf, "The 'Cotton Club' Murder," 28–32.

54. *Ibid.*

55. Daly, "The Making of *The Cotton Club*," 43–46, 51; Lewis, *Whom God Wishes to* Destroy, 117–119.

56. Scott Yanow, *Jazz on Film* (San Francisco: Backbeat Books, 2004), 154.

57. Julie Salamon, "Gregory Hines Taps His Many Talents," *Wall Street Journal*, November 19, 1995, 1.

58. "Cotton Club Girls," *Ebony*, April 1949, 36–38; Jim Haskins, *The Cotton Club* (New York: New American Library, 1984), 33, 75.

59. "Cotton Club Girls," 34–35.

60. Desmond Ryan, "Cotton Club is part of the Hines family tradition," *The Philadelphia Inquirer*, December 20, 1984, 1C; Dinitia Smith, "Jelly on a Roll," *New York Magazine*, June 8, 1992, 47.

61. Smith, "Jelly on a Roll," 49.

62. Lewis, *Whom God Wishes to Destroy*, 133–135.

63. Sandra Salamans, "Cotton Club Is Neither a Smash nor a Disaster," *The New York Times*, December 20, 1984, C13; Lewis, *Whom God Wishes to Destroy*, 140.

64. "The Cotton Club: Uneven but still commercial Coppola spectacular," *Variety*, December 12, 1984, 16, 140; J. Hoberman, "Tall, Tan, and Not So Terrific," *Village Voice*, December 18, 1984, 77; Sheila Benson, "Cotton Club: Hot, Juicy, Concoction," *Los Angeles Times*, December 14, 1984, VI-1; Stephen Hunter, "The Cotton Club Sets Toes to Tapping," *The Baltimore Sun*, December 14, 1984, B1; Catharine Rambeau, "The Dancing is Elegant in The Cotton Club," *Detroit Free Press*, December 14, 1984, 1C; Vincent Canby, "Coppola's Cotton Club," *The New York Times*, December 14, 1984, C4; "The Cotton Club," *People's World*, December 22, 1984, 10.

65. "The Cotton Club: Uneven," 16, 140. Hoberman, "Tall, Tan, and Not So Terrific," 77.

66. "The Cotton Club," Box Office Mojo, accessed

December 13, 2020, https://www.boxofficemojo.com/release/rl307070465/weekend/.

67. Lewis, *Whom God Wishes to Destroy*, 141.

68. Anne Thompson, "Francis Ford Coppola: Why He Spent $500K to Restore His Most Troubled Film," *The Cotton Club*," *IndieWire*, September 1, 2017, https://www.indiewire.com/2017/09/francis-coppola-recut-the-cotton-club-telluride-1201872249/2/.

69. "The Cotton Club Encore Q&A," *The Cotton Club Encore*, directed by Francis Ford Coppola, DVD (Santa Monica, CA: Lionsgate Entertainment, 2019).

70. Robert Abele, "The Cotton Club changes door policy," *Los Angeles Times*, October 11, 2019, E5.

71. David Fear, "The Cotton Club: Francis Ford Coppola's Mangled Epic Gets an Encore," *Rolling Stone*, December 16, 2019, https://www.rollingstone.com/movies/movie-features/the-cotton-club-encore-review-francis-ford-coppola-896695/.

72. "Brewster's Millions Is Barred in Memphis," *The New York Times*, April 7, 1945, 10.

73. Holden, "Pop/Jazz," C27.

74. Geoffrey C. Ward and Ken Burns, *Jazz: A History of America's Music* (New York: Alfred A. Knopf, 2000), 206–207, 257, 358, 406.

75. Moore, "Lonette McKee Stars," 36; Stark, "After Singing Her Own Blues"; Shipp, "Lonette McKee on Becoming Lady Day," A6.

76. Shipp, "Lonette McKee on Becoming Lady Day," A6; Holden, "Pop/Jazz," C27.

77. Charisse Jones, "At Home with: Lonette McKee; A Life Between, On Stage and Off, *The New York Times*, December 29, 1994, C1.

78. Florence Fisher Parry, "On with the Show," *The Pittsburgh Press*, June 16, 1934, 4; Mollie Merrick, "Technique of Lew Cody," *The Spokesman-Review*, June 2, 1934, 5.

79. Kaleem Aftab, *Spike Lee: That's My Story and I'm Sticking to It* (New York: W.W. Norton, 2006), 168; *The Directors: Spike Lee*, DVD, directed by Robert J. Emery (New York: WinStar, 1997).

80. David K. Shipler, "A Gentle Young Man Who Would Be 16 Forever," *The New York Times*, November 10, 1991, BR11; "The Death of Yusef Hawkins, 20 Years Later," *The New York Times*, August 21, 2009.

81. David R. Roediger, *Working Toward Whiteness: How America's Immigrants Became White* (New York: Basic Books, 2005), 4–108; James Baldwin, "On Being White' ... and Other Lies," in *Black on White: Black Writers on What It Means to Be White*, ed. David R. Roediger (New York: Schocken Books, 1998), 28.

82. Ralph Richard Banks, *Is Marriage for White People* (New York: Dutton, 2011), 2–38; Kristen Bialik, "Key facts about race and marriage, 50 years after Loving v. Virginia," Pew Research Center, June 12, 2017, https://www.pewresearch.org/fact-tank/2017/06/12/key-facts-about-race-and-marriage-50-years-after-loving-v-virginia/; Tylisa C. Johnson, "The onus is not

on them: Breaking down stereotypes, misconceptions, and myths about black women," *The Philadelphia Inquirer*, February 19, 2019, https://www.inquirer.com/life/black-women-marriage-dating-patterns-free-library-20190219.html; "Race and attraction, 2009–2014, OKCupid, September 10, 2014, https://theblog.okcupid.com/race-and-attraction-2009-2014-107dcbb4f060.

83. Jill Scott, "Commentary: Jill Scott Talks Interracial Dating," *Essence*, March 26, 2010, https://www.essence.com/news/commentary-jill-scott-talks-interracial/.

84. Bebe Moore Campbell, "Black Men White, Women: A Sister Relinquishes Her Anger," in *Honey, Hush! An Anthology of African American Women's Humor*, ed. Daryl Cumber Dance (New York: W.W. Norton, 1998), 101.

85. Istel, "Lonette McKee," 40.

86. Todd Decker, *Show Boat: Performing Race in an American Musical* (New York: Oxford University Press, 2013), 227, 234.

87. Robertson, "Voyage to Broadway," C17; Jones, "At Home With: Lonette McKee," C1; Decker, *Show Boat*, 234; Istel, "Lonette McKee," 40.

88. Decker, *Show Boat*, 234, 236.

89. Kate Fillion, "Show Boat's Julie has no problem with the show," *Globe & Mail*, June 29, 1993, D1; Lonette McKee, "Dream Big," *The Huffington Post*, May 7, 2013, https://www.huffpost.com/entry/dream-big_b_3210649; Percy Howard, "An Interview with Lonette McKee, a conversation on artistry and life," A Necessary Angel, March 15, 2010, https://percy3.wordpress.com/2010/03/15/an-interview-with-lonette-mckee-a-conversation-of-artistry-and-life/.

90. Sarah L. Delany, A. Elizabeth Delany and Amy Hill Hearth, *Having Our Say: The Delany Sisters' First 100 Years* (New York: Dell 1997), 27–34.

91. Gregory T. Carter, "From Blaxploitation to Mixploitation: Male Leads and Changing Mixed Race Identities," in *Mixed Race Hollywood*, ed. Mary C. Beltrán and Camilla Fojas (New York: New York University Press, 2008), 206. Carter apparently coined the term "mixploitation" to describe a set of contemporary films that forefront mixed race movie actors.

92. James Mottram, "Jessica Alba: She wooed Hollywood with her sultry looks," *The Independent*, April 21, 2008, https://web.archive.org/web/20080421225750/http://www.independent.co.uk/arts-entertainment/film-and-tv/features/jessica-alba-she-wooed-hollywood-with-her-sultry-looks-ndash-but-now-shes-getting-serious-812464.html.

93. McKee, "Dream Big"; Howard, "An Interview with Lonette McKee."

Chapter 7

1. Jennifer Beals in Erica Marcus, "A Role She Can Relate To," *Newsday*, July 30, 2000, 3.

2. Joan Morgan, "Regarding Jennifer," *Vibe*, April

1995, 70; Cheryl Lavin, "Fast Track," *Chicago Tribune*, October 26, 1997, 10.

3. Chris Chase, "At the Movies; The camera that followed Eartha Kitt," *The New York Times*, May 13, 1983, C10.

4. Lynn Norment, "Who's Black and Who's Not," *Ebony*, March 1990, 136.

5. Robin Finn, "Such a Realistic Portrayal, the Guys Ask Him Out," *The New York Times*, May 28, 2003, B2.

6. "United States Census, 1940," database with images, FamilySearch (https://familysearch.org/ark:/61903/1:1:KWYM-QBZ: accessed 21 December 2016), Alford Beals in household of Charles Roberts, Ward 5, Chicago, Chicago City, Cook, Illinois, United States; citing enumeration district (ED) 103–309, sheet 6B, line 72, family 135, Sixteenth Census of the United States, 1940, NARA digital publication T627. Records of the Bureau of the Census, 1790–2007, RG 29. Washington, D.C.: National Archives and Records Administration, 2012, roll 930.

7. Luaine Lee, "Jennifer Beals: She's an actress who's not just a 'Flash Dance' in the pan," *The Town Talk*, October 23, 1997, C5.

8. "Brasil, Cartões de Imigração, 1900–1965," database with images, *FamilySearch* (https://familysearch.org/ark:/61903/1:1:V1S1-9SR: 1 December 2015), Alfred Leroy Beals, Immigration; citing 1961, Arquivo Nacional, Rio de Janeiro (National Archives, Rio de Janeiro); "Illinois, Cook County Deaths, 1878–1994," database *FamilySearch* (https://familysearch.org/ark:/61903/1:1:Q2MN-6NX7: 17 May 2016), Alfred L Beals, 06 Dec 1974; citing Chicago, Cook, Illinois, United States, source reference , record number , Cook County Courthouse, Chicago; FHL microfilm. 1961 Tourist Card and 1974 Death Certificate reflect Chatham addresses.

9. Wallace Best, "Turbull Park Homes Race Riots, 1953–1954," Encyclopedia of Chicago, accessed February 5, 2017, http://www.encyclopedia.chicagohistory.org/pages/232.html.

10. D. Bradford Hunt, "Chatham," Encyclopedia of Chicago, accessed February 5, 2017, http://www.encyclopedia.chicagohistory.org/pages/2461.html.

11. Jan Herman, "Ho-Hum, Jennifer Beals Has New Film and Hasn't Much to Say About It," *New York Daily News*, August 18, 1985, 73.

12. "Jennifer Beals on QTV," *Q with Jian Ghomeshi*, CBC, April 18, 2011, accessed on January 30, 2017. https://www.youtube.com/watch?v=AZx8vb4XBc0.

13. Dale Pollock, "Flashfight," *Los Angeles Times*, July 10, 1983, 18.

14. Michael P. Balzano, "Flashdance Message: A Renewal of Dreams," *The Courier-Journal* (Louisville, Kentucky), I-1; "Jennifer Beals biraciality," IMDb, accessed February 13, 2017, http://www.imdb.com/title/tt0085549/board/thread/155852501?p=1.

15. *Struggles in Steel: A Story of African American Steel Workers*, documentary video, directed by Tony Buba and Raymond Henderson (San Francisco: California Newsreel, 1996), https://digital-films-com.ezproxy.spl.org/p_ViewVideo.aspx?xtid=49765.

16. Kimberly Monteyne, *Hip Hop on Film: Performance Culture, Urban Space, and Genre Transformation in the 1980s* (Jackson: University of Mississippi, 2013), 179.

17. Laurent Bouzerau, "The History of Flashdance," *Special Collector's Edition Flashdance*, DVD, directed by Adrian Lyne (Los Angeles: Paramount Home Entertainment, 2007).

18. Gene Siskel, "Young Woman Comes of Age in a Refreshing Flashdance," *Chicago Tribune*, April 18, 1983, 46.

19. Peter Travers, "Flashdance Works as a Trashy, Zappy Bit of Entertainment Fluff," *The Journal News*, May 15, 1983, F6.

20. Tony Schwartz, "Hollywood's Hottest Stars," *New York Magazine*, July 30, 1984, 29.

21. Janet Maslin, "Under the 1983 Chic, Movies Still Leer at Women," *The New York Times*, May 22, 1983, H21; Betsy Light, "Film Fable a 'Flashdance' in the Pan," *The Indianapolis Star*, April 20, 1983, 24.

22. Richard Corliss, "Manufacturing a Multimedia Hit," *Time*, May 9, 1983, 82.

23. Michael London, "Beals Named as NAACP Image Awards Nominee," *The Los Angeles Times*, November 9, 1983, VI-1.

24. Michael Janusonis, "Jennifer Beals Puts Acting on the Back Burner," *Courier-Post*, September 8, 1985, 10B.

25. Marcus, "A Role She Can Relate To," 3.

26. Michael London, "Flashdance Star Taps Her Own Beat," *Los Angeles Times*, May 8, 1983, 21.

27. "Jennifer Beals: Sultry Student Strikes Stardom in Flashdance," *Jet*, June 6, 1983, 60–62.

28. *Ibid.*

29. "Flashdance's Beals Heads Back to Yale," *St. Louis Post-Dispatch*, August 7, 1983, 4.

30. Dale Hudson, "Vampires of Color and the Performance of Multicultural Whiteness," in *The Persistence of Whiteness*, ed. Daniel Bernardi (New York: Routledge, 2008), 138–142.

31. Mal Vincent, "Devil Co-Star Jennifer Beals is No Flashdance in a Pan," *The La Crosse Tribune* (Wisconsin), September 30, 1995, C2.

32. Lisa Liebman, "The Fascinating Old Hollywood Story That Inspired the Last Tycoon's Best Plotline," *Vanity Fair*, July 28, 2017, https://www.vanityfair.com/hollywood/2017/07/last-tycoon-jennifer-beals-merle-oberon.

33. Anne Stockwell, "Soul of the L Word," *The Advocate*, January 31, 2006, 46.

34. Johanna Neuman, "The Curious Case of Walter Mosley," *Moment Magazine*, September-October 2010, 26. Mosley takes the unpopular position that Jews are not white people.

35. Ed Guerrero, "Devil in a Blue Dress," *Cineaste*, April 1996, 38; Patrick Goldstein, "Easing into Old L.A.," *Los Angeles Times*, September 24, 1995, 79.

36. Werner Sollors, *Neither Black Nor White Yet Both: Thematic Explorations of Interracial Literature*

(New York: Oxford University Press, 1997), Chapter 10. See Sollors for a detailed discussion on the connection between miscegenation and incest in literature.

37. Jonathan Corncob, *Adventures of Jonathan Corncob, Loyal American Refugee* (London: printed for the author, 1787), 125–127.

38. Gary Thompson, "Actor's Career Took a Change of Direction," *Philadelphia Daily News*, September 29, 1995, 45.

39. Dinitia Smith, "Novelists Get Back at Hollywood, Mostly Gently," *The New York Times*, September 25, 1999, B9.

40. Walter Mosley, *Devil in a Blue Dress* (New York: Pocket Books, 199)1, 205.

41. Manhola Dargis, "Devil in a Blue Dress," *Sight and Sound*, January 1996, 38; Judith Egerton, "Devil in a Blue Dress," *The Courier-Journal*, September 30, 1995, B8; Janet Maslin, "A Black Gumshoe Who's Also Noir," *The New York Times*, September 29, 1995, C8.

42. Esther Breger, "The 'Hollywood Blackout' at the 1996 Academy Awards," *New Republic*, January 29, 2016, https://newrepublic.com/article/128584/hollywood-blackout-1996-academy-awards.

43. Pam Lambert, "What's Wrong with This Picture?" *People*, updated March 18, 1996, http://people.com/archive/cover-story-whats-wrong-with-this-picture-vol-45-no-11/.

44. Kent Anderson Leslie, *Woman of Color, Daughter of Privilege: Amanda America Dixon, 1849–1893* (Athens: University of Georgia Press, 1995), 2.

45. Leslie, *Woman of Color*, 1–57.

46. *Ibid.*, 57–64.

47. *Ibid.*, 64–75.

48. *Ibid.*, 76, 104.

49. *Ibid.*, 107–119; "Love and Mystery: A Peculiar Story of Colored People from the State of Georgia," *The Baltimore Sun*, April 26, 1893, 8. "Suing the Pullman Company," The *New York Times*, July 30, 1893, 2.

50. Leslie, *Woman of Color*, 117–119.

51. *Ibid.*, 119–120.

52. *Ibid.*, 120–123.

53. *Ibid.*, 129–133.

54. *Ibid.*, 38.

55. Andrea R. Vaucher, "Showtime's 'House' of a Different Color," *The Washington Post*, July 30, 2000, https://www.washingtonpost.com/archive/lifestyle/style/2000/07/30/showtimes-house-of-a-different-color/2f04816b-1bb1-454c-b03a-67894d37d9ca/?utm_term=.26939e90d135.

56. Leslie, *Woman of Color*, 115.

57. "Thomas Jefferson and Sally Hemings: A Brief Account," Thomas Jefferson, Foundation, Inc., accessed March 2, 2017, https://www.monticello.org/site/plantation-and-slavery/thomas-jefferson-and-sally-hemings-brief-account.

58. Kenneth Aslakson, "The 'Quadroon-Plaçage' Myth of Antebellum New Orleans: Anglo-American (Mis)interpretation of a French-Caribbean Phenomenon," *Journal of Social History* 45, no. 3 (Spring 2012): 710–713.

59. *Ibid.*, 709–734; Emily Clark, *The Strange History of the American Quadroon* (Chapel Hill: University of North Carolina, 2013), 97–102.

60. Aslakson, "The 'Quadroon-Plaçage' Myth," 714–721.

61. *Ibid.*, 717–719; Clark, *The Strange History*, 97–102.

62. Karl Bernhard, *Travels Through North America During the Years 1825 and 1826, Volume 2* (Philadelphia: Carey, Lea, and Carey, 1828), 61; "Quadroon Balls," in *The Companion to Southern Literature: Themes, Genres, Places, People, Movements, and Motifs*, ed. Joseph Flora and Lucinda Hardwick MacKethan (Baton Rouge: Louisiana State University, 2000), 700.

63. Aslakson, "The 'Quadroon-Plaçage' Myth," 91–92.

64. *Ibid.*, 719.

65. Liebman, "The Fascinating Old Hollywood Story"; "People in the News," *Hartford Courant*, April 26, 1983, A2.

Chapter 8

1. "Introducing Berry as Dandridge," *The Atlanta Constitution*, July 19, 1999, B3.

2. "Academy Awards Acceptance Speech Database," Academy of Motion Pictures Arts and Sciences, accessed December 22, 2020, http://aaspeechesdb.oscars.org/link/074-3/.

3. Melanie Minucci, "Halle Berry in Conversation with Elaine Welteroth at Cannes Lions 2017," Teen Vogue, June 27, 2017, video clip, https://www.teenvogue.com/story/halle-berry-in-conversation-with-elaine-welteroth-at-cannes-lions-2017.

4. Jill Gertson, "The Prom's Co-Queen Finally Gets Her Revenge," *The New York Times*, March 12, 1995, H15; Siobhan Synnot, "Halle's Blazing Comet," *The Scotsman*, November 24, 2002, http://www.scotsman.com/news/halle-s-blazing-comet-1-1379562; Tirdad Derakhshani, "Halle Berry Takes Steps to Shed Husband," *Philadelphia Inquirer*, April 24, 2004, C2.

5. "Strictly Business About Show Business," *Ebony*, February 1992, 40; Dana Kennedy, "Halle Berry, Bruised and Beautiful Is on a Mission," *The New York Times*, March 10, 2002, B1.

6. Michael Price, "Actress battles double stereotyping," *The Times* (Munster, Indiana), November 8, 1991, B6.

7. *Ibid.*

8. Bob Strauss, "Busy Halle Berry keeps her mind on her career," *The Tampa Tribune*, October 13, 1993, 5.

9. Gertson, "The Prom's Co-Queen," H15.

10. Valerie Gilbert, *Imitation of Dorothy Dandridge: Halle Berry and Mulatto Stardom*, MA Thesis, University of Washington, 2009.

11. *Biography,* "Halle Berry," aired February 21, 2008, on A&E (Santa Monica: Lionsgate Entertainment, 2010), DVD.

12. "Halle Berry on Playing Tortured Char-

acters," American Film Institute, November 19, 2010, video, https://www.youtube.com/watch?v=nb-RCQRveA4.

13. Donald Bogle, *Toms, Coons, Mulattoes, Mammies, and Bucks* (New York: Continuum, 1995), 167.

14. *Intimate Portrait*, "Halle Berry," aired 1998, on Lifetime (New York: Unapix Entertainment, 1998), VHS; Karen S. Schneider and Johnny Dodd, "Hurts So Bad: Halle Berry Planned Her Success Carefully, but She Did Not Foresee the End of Her Marriage," *People*, May 13, 1996, 102.

15. *Ibid.*

16. *Intimate Portrait*, Lifetime, VHS; "Strictly Business About Show Business," 40.

17. Tim Allis, "The Woman Who Would Be Queen," *People*, February 22, 1993.

18. Lisa Jones, "The Blacker the Berry," *Essence*, June 1994, 60.

19. *Intimate Portrait*, Lifetime, VHS; Karen S. Schneider and Johnny Dodd, "Hurts So Bad: Halle Berry Planned Her Success Carefully, but She Did Not Foresee the End of Her Marriage," *People*, May 13, 1996, 102; Liam Berry and Jess Cagle, "Halle Berry on Growing Up Biracial and Being Bullied at All-White School: 'We Got Called Oreos,'" People.com, August 7, 2017, http://people.com/movies/halle-berry-on-growing-up-biracial-and-being-bullied-at-all-white-school-we-got-called-oreos/.

20. *Intimate Portrait*, Lifetime, VHS.

21. "Ohio Beauty in Pageant 'Real Happy,'" *Daily Press*, July 3, 1960, 37; "Ohio Girl Is First Negro in Pageant," *The High Point Enterprise*, July 3, 1960, 17. "Powell's Captain to Wed Miss Huff," *The New York Times*, October 14, 1969, 20.

22. Jacqueline Trescott, "CBS' Jayne Kennedy: More than a beauty," *The Morning News* (Wilmington, DE), October 11, 1978, 41.

23. Roderick Mann, "Actress Has Soul in New 'Body,'" *Los Angeles Times*, February 16, 1982, VI-1.

24. Sal Manna, "Her Sports Connections Boost Jayne's TV Image," *Los Angeles Times,* April 15, 1984, 3; "CBS fires Jayne Kennedy," *Democrat and Chronicle*, July 3, 1980, 3D.

25. Manna, "Her Sports Connections," 3; Stuart D. Bykofsky, "TV Sports Pioneer Now a 'Legend,'" *Philadelphia Daily News*, March 30, 1983, 48.

26. Regina Brett, "Miss Ohio watches over Renaissance Ball pageant," *Daily Kent Stater*, November 19, 1985, 11.

27. Trescott, "CBS' Jayne Kennedy," 41; Gordon McKerral, "Jayne's poses don't spoil invitation," *Herald and Review* (Decatur), July 19, 1981, C3.

28. Alex Jackinson, *The Romance of Publishing: An Agent Recalls Thirty-Three Years With Authors and Editors* (Cranbury, NJ: Cornwall Books, 1987), 38–39; Walter Winchell, "Winchell …," *The Jackson Sun*, November 30, 1962, 18; Nancy Anderson, "Marriage Doesn't Attract Jeff Now," *Greeley Daily Tribune*, March 22, 1975, 14.

29. Jackinson, *The Romance of Publishing*, 38–39; Lucy Howard, "She's Ready for Her Close-Up," *Newsweek*, May 5, 1997, 8.

30. "Miss USA's bikini a national costume? Tell her rivals that," *The Palm Beach Post*, November 8, 1986, 3.

31. Kennedy, "Halle Berry, Bruised and Beautiful," B28.

32. Kaleem Aftab, *Spike Lee: That's My Story and I'm Sticking to It*, 2006, 160; Pandora, "Ep. 047 feat Spike Lee Pt.1," *Questlove Supreme*, podcast audio, August 30, 2017.

33. Kennedy, "Halle Berry, Bruised and Beautiful," B28.

34. David Bianculli, *The Platinum Age of Television* (New York: Anchor Books, 2017), 503.

35. Joseph Straubhaar, Robert LaRose, and Lucinda D. Davenport, *Media Now: Understanding Media, Culture & Technology* (Boston: Cengage Learning, 2016), 223.

36. David Zurawik, "CBS miniseries 'Queen' reigns with high ratings," *The Baltimore Sun*, February 18, 1993, 2E.

37. Maurice Weaver, "*Queen* takes another look at Haley's family roots," *Chicago Tribune*, February 14, 1993, 5.

38. Donna Gable, "For Berry, haunting parallels," *USA Today*, February 18, 1993, 3D; Drew Jubera, "Queen," *The Atlanta Journal and The Atlanta Constitution*, February 14, 1993, N1; Christopher John Farley, "Halle Berry's reign," *USA Today*, July 10, 1992, 1D.

39. Melinda Henneberger, "The Tangled Roots of Alex Haley," *The New York Times*, February 14, 1993, 2–1; R. Shohet, *Sunday Mail*, February 21, 1993.

40. Jess Cagle, "TV's Queen," February 12, 1993, *Entertainment Weekly*, http://ew.com/article/1993/02/12/tvs-queen/.

41. Henneberger, "The Tangled Roots," 2–1.

42. *Ibid.*

43. *Ibid.*

44. Kennedy, "Halle Berry, Bruised and Beautiful," B28.

45. Seth Margolis, *Losing Isaiah* (New York: Hyperion, 1993), 364.

46. John Shuppe, "Rodney King Beating 25 Years Ago Opened Era of Viral Cop Videos," *NBC News*, March 3, 2016, https://www.nbcnews.com/news/us-news/rodney-king-beating-25-years-ago-opened-era-viral-cop-n531091.

47. Martin Gottlieb, "Racial Split at the End, as at the Start: Reactions to the Simpson Verdict," *The New York Times*, October 4, 1995, A1.

48. "Position on Trans-Racial Adoptions," National Association of Black Social Workers (NABSW), November 21, 2013, http://nabsw.org/?page=PositionStatements; Jared Sexton, "More Serious Than Money: On Our Gang, Diff'rent Strokes, and Webster," in *African-Americans on Television: Race-ing for Ratings*, ed. David Leonard and Lisa Guerrero (Santa Barbara, CA: Praeger, 2013), 95.

49. Martha Brant, "Storming the Color Barrier-Race: Hollywood and the Hill Tackle Adoption," *Newsweek*, March 20, 1995, 29.

50. Don Lash, *When the Welfare People Come:*

Race and Class in the U.S. Child Protection System (Chicago: Haymarket Books, 2017), 40–41.

51. Dorothy Roberts, "Race and Class in the Child Welfare System," PBS, accessed December 22, 2020, https://www.pbs.org/wgbh/pages/frontline/shows/fostercare/caseworker/roberts.html.

52. Sally Kalson, "Wrapped Up in Racial Politics," *Pittsburgh Post-Gazette*, January 24, 1993, 4; "The Seesaw Battle Over Byron and Byrae," *Pittsburgh Post-Gazette*, January 18, 1996, A-4.

53. *Ibid.*, Matthew P. Smith, "Authorities take 'Baby Byron,'" *Pittsburgh Post-Gazette*, December 28, 1993, 1.

54. "The Seesaw Battle," A-4.

55. *Ibid.*

56. Sandra Patton, *BirthMarks: Transracial Adoption in Contemporary America* (New York: NYU Press, 2000), 133.

57. In the custody hearing, why, for example, wasn't more made of Margaret Lewin's stalking, and preying upon Selma to take her baby? Or why wasn't there more emphasis on the fact that the adoption was illegal, as is buying and selling babies?

58. Robert Welkos, "Marketing the Movie Through a Minefield," *Los Angeles Times*, March 17, 1995, F1.

59. Gertson, "The Prom's Co-Queen," H15; Marshall Fine, "Actress offers more than beauty," *The Times* (Shreveport, LA), March 16, 1995, 3D; Gene Wyatt, "Berry hasn't lost memories of heritage," *The Tennessean*, March 17, 1995, 6.

60. Wyatt, "Berry hasn't lost memories," 6.

61. Jill Gertson, "The Prom's Co-Queen," H15.

62. Carrie Rickey, "Losing Isaiah is an emotional rollercoaster," *The Central New Jersey Home News*, March 19, 1995, F6; Rosalie Efthim, "Losing Isaiah is not very realistic," *The Courier-News* (Bridgewater, New Jersey), March 24, 1995, 4.

63. Janet Maslin, "A Little Boy and a Plot Worthy of Solomon," *The New York Times*, March 17, 1995, C8.

64. Peter Travers, "Now Playing," *Rolling Stone*, April 6, 1995, 25; Frank Bruni, "Hearts in Conflict," *Detroit Free Press*, March 17, 1995, 1C; Jay Boyar, "Losing Isaiah works as a tear-jerker," *The Orlando Sentinel*, March 17, 1995, 22; Peter Rainier, "Lange, Berry Passionately Claim 'Isaiah,'" *Los Angeles Times*, March 17, 1995, F1.

65. Boyar, "Losing Isaiah works as a tear-jerker," 22.

66. Carrie Rickey, "Mother vs. mother in a battle for son," *The Philadelphia Inquirer*, March 17, 1995, 3.

67. Gary Dauphin, "Losing Isaiah," *Village Voice*, March 21, 1995, 57.

68. Laura B. Rudolph, "Halle Berry: Talks About the Pain of Divorce," *Ebony*, March 1997, 22–26.

69. *The Oprah Winfrey Show*, "Halle Berry discusses her suicide attempt," aired March 31, 1997, YouTube, November 25, 2015, video clip, https://www.youtube.com/watch?v=YX3B6Wh0KOo&t=292s.

70. Karen Schneider and Johnny Dodd, "Hurts So Bad," *People*, May 13, 1996, 102; "Justice Is Served," *People*, October 21, 1996, 64; *Intimate Portrait*, Lifetime, VHS.

71. Carla Hall, "A Best Friend's Wedding," *TV Guide*, February 21, 1998, 43.

72. "Troy Beyer: More Than Meets the Eye," *Ebony*, December, 1987, 102–108.

73. Esther B. Fein, "Robert Townsend Has Fun at Hollywood's Expense," *The New York Times*, April 19, 1987, H18.

74. Elaine Dutka, "Blowin' Up on the Big Screen," *Los Angeles Times*, April 23, 1996, F1.

75. *Ibid.*

76. Trinh Bui, "Actress' Acting Ability is Put to Test With change of Genre," *Daily Bruin*, April 2, 1997, http://dailybruin.com/1997/04/01/halle-berry-trades-tears-for-l/.

77. Esther Iverem, "Townsend's Black Gold," *The Washington Post*, March 29, C7.

78. Janet Maslin, "Trashy Chic Goes West and Finds Rodeo Drive," *The New York Times*, March 28, 1997, C21.

79. Richard Matthewa, "*BAPS,*" *Sight and Sound* 7, no. 8 (August 1997): 38–39; Jeannine Amber, "*B.A.P.S.,*" *The Village Voice*, April 8, 1997, 90; Jack Garner, "With a plain and predictable plot, you can play taps for *B.A.P.S.*," *Democrat and Chronicle*, March 31, 1997, 5C; Terry Lawson, "Contrived plot, weak jokes plague *B.A.P.S.*," *The Greenville News*, April 4, 1997, 8; Emanual Levy, "B.A.P.S.," *Variety*, April 5, 1997; Tonya Pendleton, "*B.A.P.S.* is S.T.U.P.I.D.," *Philadelphia Daily News*, March 28, 1997, 54; John Petrakis, "*B.A.P.S.* means Brainless And Probably Scriptless," *Chicago Tribune*, March 28, 1997, 7C; Leah Rozen, "*B.A.P.S.,*" *People*, April 14, 1997, 20; "Townsend's *B.A.P.S.* is another misfire," *The Courier-News*, March 27, 1997, D11.

80. Roger Ebert, "B.A.P.S.: A Royal Stinker," *Chicago Sun-Times*, March 28, 1997, https://www.rogerebert.com/reviews/baps-1997.

81. Bob Strauss, "Going on with Her Life," *Santa Cruz Sentinel*, April 1, 1997, A9.

82. Jay Bobbin, "Difficult Decision," *The Times* (Munster, Indiana), February 28, 1998, 5; Ellen Gray, "Class and Color Are Themes of Miniseries The Wedding," *The Greenville News*, February 21, 1998, 4B.

83. Cherene Sherrard-Johnson, *Dorothy West's Paradise: A Biography of Class and Color* (New Brunswick: Rutgers University Press, 2012), 5, 41, 71–72.

84. Dorothy West, *The Wedding* (New York: Anchor Books, 1996), 90, 93, 97.

85. *Ibid.*, 79–80.

86. David Blow, "With Raised Voice," *The Post-Star* (Glen Falls, New York), August 29, 1999, D1.

87. Steve Johnson, "HBO's 'Dandridge': Overearnest and overcautious," *Chicago Tribune*, August 20, 1999, 5-1; Chris Kaltenbach, "Bio doesn't do actress justice," *The Baltimore Sun*, August 21, 1999, E1; Mike Boone, "Dorothy Dandridge Adrift," *The Gazette* (Montreal, Quebec), August 22, 1999, D12;

David Bianculli, "Giving Dandridge Her Due," *Daily News*, August 20, 1999, 135; Eric Deggans, "Halle Berry rekindles a fame that flickered," *St. Petersburg Times*, August 20, 1999, 1D; Caryn James, "After a Climb to Stardom, a Tumble, Then Death," *The New York Times*, August 20, 1999, 26; Melanie McFarland, "Surrendering Dorothy," *The Seattle Times*, August 20, 1999, E1.

88. Mimi Avens, "Everybody Wanted to Play Dorothy Dandridge," *Los Angeles Times*, August 21, 1999, F20

89. "Who Should Play the Tragic Star?" *Ebony*, August 1997, 66–67; Avens, "Everybody Wanted to Play Dorothy Dandridge," F20; Howard, "She's Ready for Her Close-Up," 8; Janet Maslin, "Hollywood's Tryst with Dorothy Dandridge Inspires Real Love at Last," *The New York Times*, June 19, 1997, 15.

90. Avens, "Everybody Wanted to Play Dorothy Dandridge," F20.

91. Michael Ventre, "Berry Looks to Expand on Dandridge's Career," *Daily Variety*, February 11, 2000.

92. Allison Samuels, "A Legend Comes to Life," *Newsweek*, August 23, 1999, 64.

93. Bart Mills, "Halle's Comet," *Daily News*, August 15, 1999, 3.

94. Ventre, "Berry Looks to Expand on Dandridge's Career."

95. James, "After Climb to Stardom," 26.

96. Laura B. Randolph, "Halle Berry on How She Found Dorothy Dandridge's Spirit," *Ebony*, August, 1999, 91.

97. Kevin D. Thompson, "Berry bares all," *Palm Beach Post*, August 20, 1999, 1F.

98. *The Oprah Winfrey Show*, "Halle Berry discusses her suicide attempt," video clip.

99. Samuels, "A Legend Comes to Life," 64.

100. Deggans, "Halle Berry rekindles a fame," 1D.

101. Bianculli, "Giving Dandridge Her Due," 135.

102. Monte Morin, "Halle Berry Gets Probation, Fine," *Los Angeles Times*, May 11, 2000, B11; George Rush, "Halle Berry's Costly Car Trouble," *Daily News*, March 10, 2000, 18; Ann O'Neill, "The Ugly Truth About Ugly Words," *Los Angeles Times*, March 5, 2000, B9; Jim Calio, "Halle's Moment," *Good Housekeeping*, August 2002, 98; Janet Weeks, "Halle Berry: back on track," *TV Guide*, June 10–16, 2000.

103. Mark Dagostino and Paula Yoo, "Collision Course," *People*, April 17, 2000, 67.

104. *Ibid.*

105. Ann O'Neill, "Blair Berk makes stars' legal scrapes disappear," CNN, April 4, 2010, http://www.cnn.com/2010/CRIME/09/28/celebrity.lawyer.berk/index.html#.

106. O'Neill, "The Ugly Truth," B9.

107. Dagostino and Yoo, "Collision Course," 67–68; Monte Morin, "Halle Berry Gets Probation, Fine," *Los Angeles Times*, May 11, 2000, B11; "Woman Injured in Halle Berry Car Incident Sues," *Jet*, March 27, 2000, 65.

108. Francesca Chapman, "Hit-run crash knocked out Halle's sense of humor," *Philadelphia Daily News*, July 14, 2000, 38; Steve Johnson, "Despite Crystal's flashes, awards show drags," *Chicago Tribune*, March 27, B3; *The Chris Rock Show*, "Halle Berry 911," aired 2000, on HBO, YouTube, June 23, 2010, https://www.youtube.com/watch?v=-gFHRg-K2mhg; *The Tonight Show*, "Halle Berry Sets the Record Straight on Leno," aired July 26, 2000, on NBC, May 8, 2017, https://www.youtube.com/watch?v=oO6B3Sw_j10&t=358s.

109. "Question of Blame," *People*, May 29, 2000, 153.

110. Laura Randolph Lancaster, "Halle Berry on her public troubles, private joys & sudden desire for a baby," *Ebony*, August 2000, 148–154.

111. Francesca Chapman, "Halle Speaks," *Philadelphia Daily News*, June 6, 2000, 36.

112. Lancaster, "Halle Berry on her public troubles," 148–154.

113. Leslie Marshall, "Halle's journey," *Instyle*, July 2000, 221; Bill Hoffman, "Halle Recounts Her Brush with Suicide After Breakup," *New York Post*, June 16, 2000, 3.

114. Donna Freydkind, "To Halle and back," *The Globe and Mail*; July 15, 2000, R7; Alisha Davis and Dharma Betancourt, "Newsmakers," *Newsweek*, July 24, 2000, 64.

115. Weeks, "Halle Berry: back on track," 2000.

116. Freydkind, "To Halle and back," R7.

117. Marshall Fine, "A New Level of Comfort," *Los Angeles Times*, January 2, 2002, F1.

118. David S. Cohen, "From Script to Screen: Monster's Ball," *Script*, December 1, 2015, http://www.scriptmag.com/features/interviews-features/script-screen-monsters-ball.

119. Katherine Monk, "Canada will see more sex in Monster's Ball," *The Vancouver Sun*, February 1, 2002, F1.

120. Kam Williams, "This 'Ball's' a bust," *New Pittsburgh Courier*, February 13, 2002, B3.

121. Roger Ebert, "Monster's Ball," *Chicago Sun Times*, February 1, 2002, https://www.rogerebert.com/reviews/monsters-ball-2002.

122. Richard Corliss, "Monster's Ball," *Time*, January 14, 2002, 59; Stephen Hunter, "An Intricate Dance at the *Monster's Ball*," *The Washington Post*, February 8, 2002, C1; Robert Koehler, "Poetic, fragile Ball," *Variety*, November 19–25, 2001, 39, 44; Leah Rozen, "Monster's Ball," *People*, January 14, 2002, 29; "Billy Bob Thornton, Halle Berry, Heath Ledger and Marc Forster," *Monster's Ball: [press kit]*, 2001, 5.

123. Mark Caro, "A portrait of black and white," *Chicago Tribune*, February 1, 2002, 7A-1

124. Mark Caro, "Oscar makes history," *Chicago Tribune*, March 25, 2002, 5–1; Geoff Edgers, "Blacks' Oscars a symbolic step toward equality in Hollywood," *The Boston Globe*, March 26, 2002, D1; Stephen Rea, "Inspiring performances," *Democrat and Chronicle*, April 5, 2002, 1C, 6C. A.O. Scott, "Oscar's Step Toward Redemption," *The New York Times*, March 31, 2002, 2–11.

125. Rick Lyman, "Hollywood Questions the

Meaning of Its Historic Oscar Night," *New York Times*, March 26, 2002, A20.

126. Emanuel Levy, *Oscar Fever: The History and Politics of the Academy Awards* (New York: Continuum, 2001), 230.

127. Carrie Rickey, "Celebrity Buzz: Denzel's Oscar Is Overdue," *Philadelphia Inquirer*, March 24, 2002, A1, A22.

128. "Halle's Hollywood," *Vogue*, September 2010, 646.

129. Jordan Riefe, "Who Wouldn't Wanna Finance Halle Berry? Everyone, It Seems," *The Wrap*, December 14, 2010, https://thewrap.com/halle-berry-frankie-and-alice-23236/.

130. Maane Khatchatourian, "Why did Halle Berry's Frankie & Alice Languish on the Shelf?" *Variety*, April 2, 2014, https://variety.com/2014/film/news/why-did-halle-berrys-frankie-alice-languish-on-the-shelf-1201151777/.

131. Robert Abele, "Halle Berry is a bright spot," *Los Angeles Times*, April 4, 2014, D9; Neil Genzlinger, "Frankie & Alice," *The New York Times*, April 4, 2014, C8; Pete Hammond, "Frankie & Alice," *Backstage Magazine*, December 10, 2010, https://www.backstage.com/review/movie/frankie-and-alice/ond; David Hiltbrand, "Halle Berry in multiple roles," *The Philadelphia Inquirer*, April 4, 2014, W4; Roger Moore, "Berry's big role past its sell-by date," *Chicago Tribune*, April 4, 2014, 8; Michael O'Sullivan, "A lot of writers, little subtlety," *The Washington Post*, April 4, 2014, T35; Matt Pais, "The movie time forgot," *Chicago Tribune*, April 4, 2014, 24; Peter Travers, "Frankie and Alice," *Rolling Stone*, January 20, 2011, 72; Barbara Venechri, "Berry's fine performance can't rescue weak script," *Pittsburgh Post-Gazette*, April 5, 2014, B-7; D9.

132. Pete Hammond, "Oscar: Halle Berry's Last-Minute Entrance into Race with *Frankie & Alice*," *Deadline Hollywood*, October 25, 2010, https://deadline.com/2010/10/oscar-halle-berrys-last-minute-entrance-into-race-78627/.

133. "Halle Berry, Stellan Skarsgard, and Phylicia Rashad," *Frankie & Alice: [press kit]*, Lionsgate, 2014.

Bibliography

Archer-Straw, Petrine. *Negrophilia: Avant-Garde Paris and Black Culture in the 1920s*. London: Thames & Hudson, 2000.

Aslakson, Kenneth. "The 'Quadroon-Plaçage' Myth of Antebellum New Orleans: Anglo-American (Mis)interpretation of a French-Caribbean Phenomen." *Journal of Social History* 45, no. 3 (Spring 2012): 709–734.

Baker, Jean-Claude, and Chris Chase. *Josephine: Hungry Heart*. New York: Cooper Square Press, 2001.

Baker, Josephine, and Jo Bouillon. *Josephine.* Translated by Mariana Fitzpatrick. New York: Paragon House, 1988.

Belton, John. *American Cinema/American Culture*. New York: McGraw-Hill, 1994.

Bogle, Donald. *Bright Boulevards, Bold Dreams: The Story of Black Hollywood*. New York: One World, 2006.

Bogle, Donald. *Dorothy Dandridge: A Biography*. New York: Boulevard, 1998.

Bogle, Donald. *Toms, Coons, Mulattoes, Mammies, and Bucks*. New York: Continuum, 1995.

Bourne, Stephen. *Black in the British Frame: The Black Experience in British Film and Television*. London: Continuum, 2001.

Bourne, Stephen. *Nina Mae McKinney: The Black Garbo*. Duncan: BearManor Media, 2011.

Brown, Jayna. *Babylon Girls: Black Women Performers and the Shaping of the Modern*. Durham: Duke University Press, 2008.

Brown, Sterling. "Negro Character as Seen by White Authors." *The Journal of Negro Education* 2, no. 2 (April 1933): 179–203.

Buckley, Gail Lumet. *The Hornes: An American Family*. New York: Alfred A. Knopf, 1986.

Cameron, Kenneth M. *Africa on Film: Beyond Black and White*. New York: Continuum, 1994.

Crais, Clifton, and Pamela Scully. *Sara Baartman and the Hottentot Venus: A Ghost Story and a Biography*. Princeton: Princeton University Press, 2009.

Cripps, Thomas. *Making Movies Black: The Hollywood Message Movie from World War II to the Civil Rights Era*. New York: Oxford University Press, 1993.

Cripps, Thomas. *Slow Fade to Black: The Negro in American Film, 1900–1942*. New York: Oxford University Press, 1993.

Dandridge, Dorothy, and Earl Conrad. *Everything and Nothing: The Dorothy Dandridge Tragedy*. New York: HarperCollins, 2000.

Davis, F. James. *Who is Black? One Nation's Definition*. University Park: Pennsylvania State University Press, 1998.

Decker, Todd. *Show Boat: Performing Race in an American Musical*. New York: Oxford University Press, 2013.

Dixon, Thomas, Jr.. *The Clansman: An Historical Romance of the Ku Klux Klan*. Lexington: University Press of Kentucky, 1970.

Doherty, Thomas. *Pre-Code Hollywood: Sex, Immorality, and Insurrection in American Cinema 1930–1934*. New York: Columbia University Press, 1999.

Dyer, Richard. *Heavenly Bodies: Film Stars and Society*. New York: Routledge, 2008.

Elfenbein, Anna Shannon. *Women on the Color Line: Evolving Stereotypes and the Writings of George Washington Cable, Grace King, Kate Chopin*. Charlottesville: University Press of Virginia, 1989.

Ferber, Edna. *Show Boat*. New York: Grosset & Dunlap, 1926.

Fordin, Hugh. *MGM's Greatest Musicals: The Arthur Freed Unit*. New York: Da Capo, 1996.

Fry, Andy. "Du Jazz hot á 'La Créole': Josephine Baker Sings Offenbach." *Cambridge Opera Journal* 16, no. 1 (March 2004): 43–75.

Gaines, Jane. *Fire and Desire: Mixed Race Movies in the Silent Era*. Chicago: University of Chicago Press, 2001.

Gatewood, Willard B. *Aristocrats of Color: The Black Elite, 1880–1920*. Fayetteville: University of Arkansas Press, 2000.

Gavin, James. *Stormy Weather: The Life of Lena Horne*. New York: Simon & Schuster, 2009.

Gilbert, Valerie C. "Imitation of Dorothy Dandridge: Halle Berry and Mulatto Stardom." Master's thesis, University of Washington, Seattle, 2009.

Gledhill, Christine, ed. *Stardom: Industry of Desire*. New York: Routledge, 1991.

Green, Laurie. *Battling the Plantation Mentality: Memphis and the Black Freedom Struggle*. Chapel Hill: University of North Carolina Press, 2007.

Hammond, Bryan, and Patrick O'Connor. *Josephine Baker*. London: Jonathan Cape, 1988.

Harris, Michael D. *Colored Pictures: Race and Visual*

Representation. Chapel Hill: University of North Carolina Press, 2003.

Haskins, Jim. *The Cotton Club.* New York: New American Library, 1984.

Holiday, Billie, and William Dufty. *Lady Sings the Blues.* New York: Harlem Moon, 2006.

Horne, Lena, and Richard Schickel. *Lena.* Garden City: Doubleday & Company, 1965.

Huggins, Nathan Irvin. *Harlem Renaissance.* New York: Oxford University Press, 1973.

Hurst, Fannie. *Imitation of Life.* New York: Permabooks, 1959.

Janker, Kenneth Robert. *White: The Biography of Walter White, Mr. NAACP.* New York: The New Press, 2003.

Josephson, Barney, and Terry Trilling-Josephson. *Café Society: The Wrong Place for the Right People.* Urbana: University of Illinois Press, 2009.

Jules-Rosette, Bennetta. *Josephine Baker in Art and Life: The Icon and the Image.* Urbana: University of Illinois Press, 2007.

Lash, Don. *"When the Welfare People Come": Race and Class in the Child Welfare System.* Chicago: Haymarket Books, 2017.

Leab, Daniel T. "The Gamut from A to B: The Image of the Black in Pre-1915 Movies." *Political Science Quarterly* 88, no. 1 (March 1973): 53–70.

Leslie, Kent Anderson. *Woman of Color: Daughter of Privilege: Amanda America Dickson, 1849–1893.* Athens: University of Georgia Press, 1995.

Levy, Emanuel. *Oscar Fever: The History and Politics of the Academy Awards.* New York: Continuum, 2001.

Manatu, Norma. *African American Women and Sexuality in the Cinema.* Jefferson: McFarland, 2003.

Margolis, Seth J. *Losing Isaiah.* New York: Hyperion, 1993.

McManus, James. *Black Venus.* New York: St. Martin's Press, 2013.

Mérimée, Prosper. *Carmen and Other Stories.* Oxford: Oxford University Press, 1989.

Mills, Earl. *Dorothy Dandridge: An Intimate Biography.* Los Angeles: Holloway House, 1999.

Mizejewski, Linda. *Ziegfeld Girls: Image and Icon in Culture and Cinema.* Durham: Duke University Press, 1999.

Mosley, Walter. *Devil in a Blue Dress.* New York: Pocket Books, 1991.

Parakilas, James, "The Soldier and the Exotic: Operatic Variations on a Theme of Racial Encounter, Part I," *The Opera Quarterly* 10, no. 2 (Winter 1993): 33–56.

Patton, Sandra. *BirthMarks: Transracial Adoption in Contemporary America.* New York: New York University Press, 2000.

Peterson, Bernard L., Jr. *A Century of Musicals in Black and White: An Encyclopedia of Musical Stage Works by, about, or Involving African Americans.* Westport: Greenwood Press, 1993.

Pieterse, Jan Nederveen. *White on Black: Images of Africa and Blacks in Western Popular Culture.* New Haven: Yale University Press, 1992.

Roediger, David R. *Working Toward Whiteness: How America's Immigrants Became White.* New York: Basic Books, 2005.

Roediger, David R., ed. *Black on White: Black Writers on What It Means to Be White.* New York: Shocken, 1998.

Rose, Phyllis. *Jazz Cleopatra.* New York: Vintage Books, 1991.

Sampson, Henry T. *Blacks in Black and White: A Source Book on Black Films.* Metuchen: The Scarecrow Press, 1977.

Sampson, Henry T. *Blacks in Blackface: A Source Book on Early Black Musical Shows.* Metuchen: The Scarecrow Press, 1980.

Sharpley-Whiting, T. Denean. *Black Venus: Sexualized Savages, Primal Fears, and Primitive Narratives in French.* Durham: Duke University Press, 1999.

Smith, Jeff. "Black Faces: White Voices: The Politics of Dubbing in Carmen Jones." *The Velvet Light Trap* 51 (2003): 29–42.

Sollors, Werner. *Neither Black Nor White Yet Both: Thematic Explorations of Interracial Literature.* New York: Oxford University Press, 1997.

Stokes, Melvyn. *D. W. Griffth's The Birth of a Nation.* New York: Oxford University Press, 2007.

Stovall, Tyler Edward. *Paris Noir: African Americans in the City of Light.* Boston: Houghton Mifflin, 1996.

Sumner, Cid Ricketts. *Quality.* New York: Bantam Books, 1947.

Thompson, Shirley Elizabeth. *Exiles at Home: The Struggle to Become American in Creole New Orleans.* Cambridge: Harvard University Press, 2009.

Ward, Geoffrey C., and Ken Burns. *Jazz: A History of America's Music.* New York: Alfred A. Knopf, 2000.

Waugh, Alec. *Island in the Sun.* New York: Farrar, Straus and Cudahy, 1955.

Weisenfeld, Judith. *Hollywood Be Thy Name: African American Religion in American Film, 1929–1949.* Berkeley: University of California Press, 2007.

West, Dorothy. *The Wedding.* New York: Anchor Books, 1995.

Williamson, Joel. *New People: Miscegenation and Mulattoes in the United States.* Baton Rouge: Louisiana State University Press, 1995.

Wood, Ean. *The Josephine Baker Story.* London: Sanctuary Publishing, 2000.

Yanow, Scott. *Jazz on Film: The Complete Stories of the Musicians and Music Onscreen.* San Francisco: Backbeat Books, 2004.

Zanger, Jules. "The 'Tragic Octoroon' in Pre-Civil War Fiction." *American Quarterly* 18, no. 1 (Spring 1966): 63–70.

Screen Title Index

Silent Films

Short Films (Sound)

Feature Films

TV Movies

TV Series/Miniseries

Subject Index

Numbers in *bold italics* indicate pages with illustrations